BABAJI

THE LIGHTNING STANDING STILL

BY
YOGIRAJ GURUNATH SIDDHANATH

First Edition Published on Guru Purnima, July 15, 2011

by

Siddhanath Yoga Sangh
PO Box 277, Live Oak,
CA 95953

Siddhanath Forest Ashram
Sitamai Dara, Simhagad Road, Pune, India
Website: www.siddhanath.org
Email: info@siddhanath.org

Cover Design by Yogiraj Gurunath Siddhanath

Copyright © 2010 by
Sidhoji Rao Shitole (Yogiraj Gurunath Siddhanath)
Second Edition: January 5, 2012

Third Edition: October 25, 2025
Printed and Published in USA by
Alight Publications

ALL RIGHTS RESERVED UNDER INTERNATIONAL AND
PAN-AMERICAN COPYRIGHT CONVENTIONS.
NO PART OF THIS PUBLICATION MAY BE REPRODUCED, STORED IN A RETRIEVAL SYSTEM
OR DATABASE, OR TRANSMITTED IN ANY FORM OR BY ANY MEANS ELECTRONIC,
MECHANICAL, PHOTOCOPYING, RECORDING, OR OTHERWISE WITHOUT THE PRIOR
WRITTEN APPROVAL OF THE AUTHOR OR PUBLISHER.

Library of Congress Control Number: 2011932283

ISBN: 978-193 183324-0

Copyright Registration Number: TXu 1-725-064

DEDICATED TO

Babaji

THE HEART OF DIVINITY

THROBBING IN HUMANITY

ABOUT THE COVER

The Lightning Standing Still is one of the aspects of Babaji[1] as a Time-Reversed Phenomenon that happens faster than light. At this moment, time not only stands still, but is reversed back to the future. Anybody who has the ability to play with time is in total at-one-ment with God. He is everywhere and nowhere at the same time, and His mass is infinite.

But is the bolt of lightning that He holds in His hands also standing still?

No, and this is an important distinction.

This is the lightning moving at the speed of light, in the three-dimensional world of relativity. Therefore this light, called the Cosmic Kundalini[2] *Shakti*, is used in the work of the welfare of all humanities and their evolution.

---

1 'Revered father', in the *Nath* tradition, the name denoting Shiva Goraksha Babaji; 'The Youth of 16 Summers'; 'The Ever-Youthful Immortal Yogi'; also mentioned in *Paramhansa* Yogananda's book, *Autobiography of a Yogi*.

2 'Coiled serpent of the fire-*kund*', electro-magnetic pranic energy centralized in the spine; Kundalini is the lady of the cinders whom, when fanned by the alchemical fire of *Shiva–Shakti pranayam*, ignites and blazes up the chimney of the spine to unite with the immortal Lord Shiva in the crown *chakra* (*sahasrara*) to enlighten the yogi.

THE MEANING OF THE FIVE HIEROGLYPHS

1. The first blank page that follows depicts that from the nothing is the every thing created.
2. The dot on the second page represents the first stirrings of *Omkar* as light-sound.
3. The circle on the third page represents the undifferentiated fabric of radiant ether.
4. The dot in the circle on the fourth page represents the spirit of *Omkar* animating the universal mind of creation.
5. The line in the circle on the fifth page represents total interaction between spirit and matter to bring forth the three-dimensional creation.

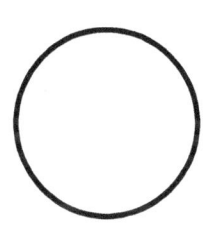

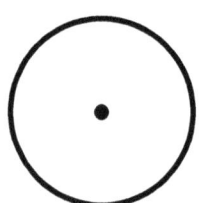

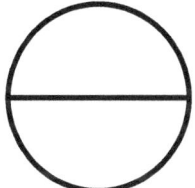

1
Boundless lay the Self in the Knowingness of Itself,
Spread beyond infinity, from eternity to eternity,
Was perfect absolute and calm; calm undisturbed,
For Creation was not yet conceived by the Creator.

2
Not this, nor that art thou, the essence of light and dark,
There was no darkness then, there even was no light
There was no action then to cause reaction, all was
Thy ineffable and endless consciousness of Bliss

3
For then in nothing was everything, in everything was nothing
These feeble words seek to express Thy majesty Oh All-In All
For even Absolute is limited to thee oh ineffable peace
That passeth all understanding.

4
Truth, the life of prana lay potential in Thee, Oh All-In All
Time was not, Space was not, Causation there was none.
Yet Oh Supreme, all were held in Thy bosom of duration
The Lord of light had not awakened but reposed in Thee.

5
If at one moment, time and place,
The sunburst of a countless suns occur.
That brilliance would scarce suffice to show Thy shadow
Oh Lord, what must be Thy Lightless Light!
Thou Alakh Niranjan[1] beyond cosmic day and night.

---

[1] A name for God. The Lightless Light which Lights that Light which Lights the Light of all our Souls.

6
The Eternal Spark had not impulsed to set causation in motion;
Then Maha Maya would birth all creation in relative sequence
And this Great illusion would go forth in Her celestial dance
Creating countless universes and galaxies to Thy glory.

7
Lo! Thou didst exhale Thy universal Self, Oh Calm
And Thy Infinite Mind did make the mighty Lord of Flame
Who exploding in His Light did Maya's Creation ignite
To set the wheel of causation and relativity in motion,
Creating the law of karma[2], dharma[3] & reincarnation[4].

8
The eternal Mother Adi-Shakti[5] then did make her galaxies
And other relative aspects of creation did begin,
Light-Sound sublime, created causation space and time
Originating in Thy transcendental matrix of light
Resounding in every atom of creation, Thy organ Omm!

9
Then Light and heat and moisture, they were born
Vast Nebulae did float the spaces infinite
To regulate themselves into galaxies of stellar night
Then by Myriad Permutation Combinations
Appeared the Suns and Stars in Thine immortal Song.

---

2 'Action', activity of any kind, including ritual acts; the law of cause and effect, of balance and justice, binding one to material condition; destiny; the condition of an individual birth.
3 'Bearer', law or lawfulness, also correct action, conduct and righteousness and virtue.
4 *'Punar Janma'*, the individual soul rotating in the repeated cycle of birth, death (the *kala chakra*) owing to bondage creating karma.
5 The primordial goddess energy.

10
Great masses of vibrating incandescent light
So large as to stagger human imagination
Mother really dost thou wear such jewels on Thy breast
And still find time to love us mortal children so far below?

11
These mighty vapors of jeweled-light they stud Thy brow
Of Thou Mother of Eternity Thy glory knows no night
These children galaxies of Thine, Stellar Solar systems hold;
By that force we mortals call Thy gravitational love,
In perfect harmony their cosmic dance unfolds.

12
Came then the Sons of light, of Shakti[6] they were born,
Blazing in their power and truth they worked
Through froth and foam and worlds and stars
Cooling the hot, heating the cold, moistening the dry
And perfecting in their harmony all undue disharmony.

13
The Cyclic Motion of Creation then began,
It was causation's dance in relative Oceans
The day came on and gave birth into the night
The breeze raced over vast tracts of solid lands
and liquids filled the hollows of the earth.

---

6 'Power', the kinetic aspect of the potential Shiva (God-realization), the power to transform and evolve aspirants to this enlightened state.

14

Oh Mother nurturer, by whose womb we mortals were born,
Our endless salutations to Thee.
Oh Thou Divine spouse of the great preserver, Vishnu[7].
Our Universe of Endless stars lives its life in Thee
Only so long as Thou dost wish it to be.

15

Earth Bhumi[8] Ma, Thy other name was Vasundhara
Who came to be so that she may mother the mortal Man.
Then did begin the evolution of the future Man
That spark of life first entered the mineral rock,
His first primeval home, for the spark was of Vasundhara

16

The Earth was born from the watery space,
Which was born of the Solar essence,
Whose original source was the fabric of radiant ether,
Known as Padma-Matrika[9], meaning the Lotus Mother,
Who was essentially of Brahma[10], the Creator.

---

7 'Pervader', the preserver; worshipped by *Vaishnavas* and who has had nine incarnations, including Rama and Krishna, with the tenth incarnation (avatara) Kalki coming at the start of the Aquarian age.

8 Mother Earth.

9 The cosmic womb; the universal lotus mother from which the later word, matrix evolved. Padma Matrika was also later called the transcendental matrix, which contains the farther-most limits of the mind and matter of the universe.

10 'He who has grown expansive', the creator of the universe, the first principle (tattva) to emerge out of the ultimate reality (Brahman). Brahma. The Creator, also called Vidhata, the God of the destinies of all nations and humanities.

17
The group Soul spark grew from the mineral rock,
Into the plant, wherein it did flourish.
Dying out from the plant the Spark of life
Was born into the fish and then the mammals.
Migrating from the lower form to a more expressive one.

18
I died out from the rock to live in the plant.
I died out from the plant to live in the fish and reptile.
Then live in animal form and lastly enter the house of man,
Wherein did I become the lesser by dying?
For dying was only another form of life.

19
And all along Evolution's path did I travel,
My outer coats are more expressive than the former,
But essentially I was the same.
And finally awaited me the temple of Man
But it was only a man of clay, until I entered my ray.

20
I entered into man as ray of thinking light,
I was that consciousness of Supreme delight.
I gave the house of flesh to know I was the child of light.
The Ego it was formed by me for future generations to be
The delusive "I" of the mind, the segregator of all Mankind.

21
I came into the physical house of man,
To rule over that Tabernacle[11] of the body,
But was deluded by the Satanic[12] desires of the Flesh
Into thinking I was a body and not the knowing light.
This Heresy of separateness covered my sight.

22
Forgetting I was potentially Divine,
Illusive Maya's veil covered my Soul spark
Separating me from my True identity
To tempt me by the sensual life
And haunt me in the darkness of body flesh.

23
Then man looked up to the portending stars
to question whether they his life did make.
The stars replied "Nothing can Thy Immortal Essence take."
Then girding up His Loins, the human did begin
His upward evolution striving to be the Divine within.

24
Thou nature's eve, Thou didst hide my thinking Self
From my Father the Spirit Self within.
Evolution began to unite the thinking Self that was me
To me Father Divinity and a free Soul to be;
Then the Self began its rounds of cyclic evolution.

---

11 A tent and portable dwelling place for the divine.
12 Of the quality of Satan; he slips you into devious ways of illusion.

25
It persevered until the mind-Self
Defeated the passional ego-Self
To become one with the higher mind intelligence
Then unite with Atma, the inner knower,
Who one was with the Universal Knower

26
The Father Spirit, the Mother Intelligence
And Mind-Child had become one.
Lo! The deluded Mind-Child
Had regained His lost birthright and
Entered into the Father-Mother bosom of Light.

27
The fallen state regained: Lo!
Behold the lesser ones to come.
The lower animals had to struggle up.
Oh Sons of light help them! Guide them!
The plants, the rocks must be evolved too.

28
For in all is the essential spark of Atman[13].
The Cosmic Divine Self must
Help the individual human Self.
This is the Divine decree promulgated by Babaji
Who is called Mahabinishkaran, the Great Sacrifice.

---

13 'Self', the true Self, the individual spirit or soul, which is eternal and superconscious; our true nature or identity; sometimes a distinction is made between the atman as the individual self and the *parama-atman* as the transcendental Self; see also purusha, Brahman.

29
The molecules in each mineral substance did contain
Vast quantities of atoms, each representing
A miniature Solar System revolving and evolving
Powered by the compassion of Babaji, out revered Father
Who is the ineffable Cosmic essence of the Self Atma.

30
His Spirit is the essence of All, both big and small,
Hot and cold, light and dark, doth contain
That one essential spark, The electrons in its essence
Positrons that were composed of mesons whose energy
Lifetrons[14] traveled through the breath of man.

31
But finer than the lifetrons of prana was the
Essence of God-thought,
One with the all-pervading Spirit, the Atman.
There was no segregation in this Spirit of God-thought,
For from this was the dream fabric of Creation composed.
This was the vastest infinity of manifest Divinity.

32
From the essential substance of God thought
the Sun and the Moon and the Stars were built,
Stella and Solar Systems also had their sway
Because God thought was in them to stay.
All was God thought, God thought was One thought,
The divine thought of the universal oneness of Eternity.

---

14 A subatomic particle composed of pranic lifeforce energy.

33
For being the subtlest of the all from it was made the all;
It was the smallest of the small
Far beyond human imagination.
Would it then be correct to call that God-thought non-Being?
And thereby express its absolute entirety over Creation in Being?

34
The All-being was the God-thought which was
Babaji the essential Self, of every atom of creation.
The Self that all pervading consciousness
Of stillness through eternity composed of nothing
Yet of which all else is sure composed,
It stands supreme beyond all dreams eternally reposed.

35
Spirit is the God-thought, there is nothing it is not.
The All is One, the One is all, the All-in All Paramartha[15]
Oh, Absolute Majesty of sublimest existence,
Oh ineffable peace beyond human understanding,
Our ceaseless salutation to Thee
Who ever was, even is now and shall forever be.

---

[15] Science of the study of the true self (Atma Vidya).

CONTENTS

About the Cover

Autobiography of the Self

Sri Shiva Goraksha Rahasya

Preface

Who Is Babaji?

Chapter 1	Knowing the Being..	1
Chapter 2	Babaji is None Other than Goraksha Nath	11
Chapter 3	Sages Who Are Not the Babaji...............................	17
Chapter 4	The Goraksha Mystery	25
Chapter 5	Meeting The Immortal Babaji	29
Chapter 6	My Childhood Bond With Babaji..........................	53
Chapter 7	Babaji - Ancient Origins..	59
Chapter 8	On Being A Disciple Of Babaji	83
Chapter 9	The Rudraprayag Experience	95
Chapter 10	Babaji And Mataji	103
Chapter 11	The Avadhoot Avatara Doctrine	109
Chapter 12	The Initiation Of Avataras By Babaji	129
Chapter 13	The Immortal Naths	155
Chapter 14	The Ancient Of Days	177

Chapter 15	Kalki Avatara and Babaji Mahavatara	195
Chapter 16	The Original Kriya Yoga	219
Chapter 17	Goraksha Shataka	247
Chapter 18	The Ancestry Of Kriya Yoga	271
Chapter 19	The Sages Of All Ages	277
Chapter 20	The Divine Alchemist	289
Chapter 21	The Manus And Manavantars	327
Chapter 22	The Great Indian Calendar	349

Appendix	363
Glossary	387
Index	439

FACT BECOMES HISTORY,
HISTORY BECOMES LEGEND,
LEGEND BECOMES MYTH,
AND MYTH EXPERIENCED BECOMES FACT.
THIS IS THE TRUTH OF THE TURNING WHEEL OF TIME
CALLED THE KAAL CHAKRA

YOGIRAJ SIDDHANATH

SRI SHIVA GORAKSHA RAHASYA[1]

Sati Parvati uvaca:

भगवन्! देवदेवेश रहस्य गोरक्षाय मे।
ब्रूहियेन भक्तिं कुर्यात् साधको गोरक्ष शिवम् ॥१॥

Bhagavan! devadevesha, rahasya Gorakshaya mey |
Bruhiyena bhakthim kuryaath, Saadhako Goraksha shivam ||1||

Sati Parvati said:

O Lord of Lords, tell me the *Goraksha Rahasyam* (the hidden knowledge of Goraksha worship) knowing which one may worship Shiva-Goraksha Nath.

Sri Shiva uvaca:

शृणु देवि परं गोप्यं कथयामि सुशोभनं।
रहस्यं सिद्धिदं साक्षाद् गोरक्षस्य महात्मनः ॥२॥

Srhunu dhevi param gopyam, Kathayaami sushobanam|
Rahasyam siddhidham saakshaadh, Gorakshasya mahathmanah ||2||

---

[1] The Shiva Goraksha Rahasya is a *Shiv-Parvati Samvad*, a dialogue between Shiva and Parvati. Its origins are lost in the night of prehistory, however it is recorded for eternity in the Akashic Records of the misty past, and can be accessed in its pure spiritual essence in the super conscious state of samadhi. It expounds the innermost mystery of who Goraksha Nath actually is. He is not only the essence of the Supreme Lord Shiva, but is the Lord God Shiva Himself, directly manifest as Reality in Relativity.

Sri Shiva said:

Listen, O Devi[1], I disclose to you the hidden knowledge about Goraksha Nath[2]. This great secret is most hidden and is a bestower of *siddhis*[3] (spiritual powers).

गुरू गोरक्षनाथस्य साधने ये निरूपिताः।
उपाया निष्फलाः सर्वे विना ध्यानेन सर्वथा ।।३।।

Guru Gorakshanathasya, Saadhane ye nirupithah |
Upaayaa nishfalaah sarve, Vina dhyaanen sarvathaa ||3||

All means to worship Guru[4] Gorakshanath fail to bring about the desired results unless one practices dhyana (meditative) yoga.

यो ध्यानं साधनं हित्वा उपायं चान्यथा श्रयेत् ।
न सः सिद्धिमवाप्नोति नरो वर्ष शतैरपि ।।४।।

Yo dhyaanam saadhanam hithva, Upaayam chaanyatha shrayeth |
Na sah siddhimavapnothi, Naro varsha shathairapi ||4||

He who intends to attain (results) without dhyana yoga sadhana cannot succeed in hundreds of years.

---

1 'Shining one', the feminine aspect of deva; a goddess or feminine angelic being such as Parvati, Lakshmi, or Saraswati.
2 'Lord Goraksha', Babaji; also called Shiva Goraksha Babaji, a renownly well documented Maha avatar of Indian Yogic tradition, responsble for hastening the spiritual evolution of humanity. The personal aspect of Lord Shiva. see also Mahavtar.
3 'Accomplishment/perfection', spiritual perfection, the attainment of flawless identity with the ultimate reality (atman or brahman); paranormal ability, of which the Yoga tradition knows many kinds.
4 'One with gravity', a teacher who cultivates the spiritual knowledge of a disciple.

स्वयं ज्योतिः स्वरूपोऽयं शून्याकारो निरंजनः ।
दशदिक्षु सदा व्याप्तः गोरक्षः प्रथितः प्रभूः ॥५॥

Svayam jyothisvaroopoyam, Shoonyakaaro niranjanah |
Dhasadhikshu sadha vyapthah, Goraksha prathithah prabhuh ||5||

Guru Goraksha Nath is *jyoti-swaroop* (whose form is of the nature of Lightless Light) *shoonyakara* (formless) and *niranjana* (absolutely pure). He pervades all the ten directions and is famous as jati (the all perfected) Goraksha Nath.

अहमेवास्मि गोरक्षो मद्रुपस्तन्निभोऽधत ।
योगमार्ग प्रचारार्थं मया रूपमिदं धृतम् ॥६॥

Ahamevaasmi Gorakshanathsho, Madhroopasthannibhodhatha |
Yogamaarga prachaararth, Mayaa rupamidham dhrtham ||6||

I, myself, am Goraksha Nath. He is my embodiment. I assumed His form to promote and expand yoga *marga* (the path of yoga).

यस्य शून्यमयी माता यस्य चाविगतः पिता।
निरंजनो महायोगी गोरक्षः सर्वदा गुरुः! ॥७॥

Yasya shoonyamayi maathaa, Yasya chaavigathah pithaa |
Niranjano mahayogi, Goraksha sarvadha guruh! ||7||

He is born of *shoonya* (absolute reality) and *avigath* (the ever present) is his father. He is mahayogi and *niranjana*[5].

---

5 A term used by Nath Yogis for the highest state of consciousness (samadhi).

रूद्राक्षमालाधरः शान्तः कुण्डल प्रभयान्वितः ।
भुजंग मेखलादिव्य जती गोरक्ष शोभनः ॥८॥

Rudrakshamaalaadharah shaanthah, Kundala prabhayaanvithah |
Bhujanga mekhalaadhivya, Jathee Goraksha shobhanah ||8||

He looks so graceful wearing a necklace of rudraksha[6], *kundals*[7] and a divine girdle of serpents.

गजासुर-विमर्दी च भूत बेताल शोभितः।
श्मशानारण्यवाशी कर्परालङ्कृतः शिवः ॥६॥

Gajaasura-vimardhi cha, Bhuth bethaal shobhithah |
Shmashanaranyavaasi, Karparaaladkrthah shivah ||9||

Guru Goraksha Nath who destroyed Gajasura (the demon), lives in cremation grounds with *vaitalas* (Bhairava) and *bhutas* (spirits) and keeps roaming the jungles, carrying a *khappar* (skull bowl).

ज्ञानवन्तः दयावन्तः मम प्रिय स्वरूपजः ।
उत्पत्ति स्थिति संहाराय गोरक्षाय नमो ऽऽदेशम् ॥१०॥

Jnaanavanthah dhayaavanthah, Mama priya svarupajah |
Uthpathi sthithi samhaaraay, Gorakshaaya Namo Aadhesham ||10||

He is all-knowing and compassionate. He supervises the origin, sustenance and dissolution of the world. He is my own beloved image. I bow down to him.

---

6 The seed of a tree, sacred to Shiva (sacred bead).
7 Earring worn by men.

यतीन्द्रं योगीन्द्रं सकल वसुधाया हितकरं ।
सदा सेव्यं भव्यं कलिमल-दहं साधु सुखदम् ।।
परंपारं ज्योतिर्जं निभृतहरं कारणं परम् ।
भजेत् तत्रूपं श्रुति कीर्तितं नतपदं गोरख प्रियम् ।।११।।

Yatheendhram yogeendhram, Sakala vasudhaayaa hithakaram |
Sadha sevyam bhavyam, Kalimala-daham saadhu sukhadham ||
Parampaeram jyothirjam, Nibhrthaharam kaaranam param |
Bhajeth thathrupam shruthi kirthitham, Nathapadham Gorakshan-
atha priyam ||11||

We worship him who is the lord of the *yatis* (female yogis) and yogis, most benevolent to this earth, worthy of adoration by the great. He is the destroyer of *kalimal* (negativity) and provide joys to the sadhus.

He is the embodiment of *param jyoti* (supreme light), the cause of the world, the liberator from birth and death whose praises have been sung in the *srutis* (scriptures).

सुरेशं योगीशं निखिलजनत्रयतापहरं ।
दयालुं गोपालं निजजनसदा पालने तत्परम् ।।
स्वभक्तेभ्यो योगं वितरति सदाकष्टहरणाय ।
भजे तं तत्रूपं श्रुतिकथितंनतपदं गोरख प्रियम ।।१२।।

Suresham yogisham, Nikhilajanathrayathapaharam |
Dhayaalam gopaalam, Nijajanasadha paalane thathparam ||
Svabhakthebhyo yogam, Vitharathi sadakashtaharanaaya |
Bhaje tham thathrupam shruthikathitham, Nathapadham Gorak-
shanatha priyam ||12||

Lord of the gods and lord of the yogis Guru Goraksha Nath removes all three kinds of suffering - body, mind, and soul. He is full of compassion, tending cows and always providing for His devotees. He dispenses *yogavidhi* (the way of yoga) to His bhaktas to remove their miseries, we worship him whom the *srutis* praise.

ब्रह्मा विष्णुश्च रुद्रश्च मरीच्याद्या महर्षयः ।
गोरक्षं प्रणमन्ति तं सदा सम्पन्न मानसम् ॥१३॥

Brahma vishnushcha rudrashcha, Marichyaadyaa maharshayah |
Goraksham pranamanthi tham, Sadhaa sampanna maanasam ||13||

The sublime-minded Goraksha Nath is worshipped by Brahma, Vishnu, Rudra, and the rishis such as Marich (the first of the Rishis - informing spirits - of the Great Bear constellation).

महायोगी कृपासिन्धु नानाभरणैः भूषितम् ।
धर्मार्थं काममोक्षाणां दातारं तं नमाम्यहम् ॥१४॥

Mahayogi krupaasindhu, Naanaabharanaih bhushitham |
Dharmartha kaamamokshaanaam, Daathaaram tham namaamyaham ||14||

He is mahayogi, ocean of compassion, and is decked with diverse embellishment. He is the bestower of dharma (religion), *artha* (prosperity), *kama* (passion) and moksha (freedom from all relativity). I bow down to him.

शृणुदेवि प्रवक्ष्यामि गोरक्ष मंत्रमुत्तमम् ।
येन मंत्र प्रभावेन जतीजाप शुभोभवेत् ॥१५॥

Shrnudhevi pravakhsyaami, Goraksha manthramutthamam |
Yen manthra prabhaavena, Jathijaapa shubhobhaveth ||15||

Listen, O Devi, I tell you the mantra[8] of Gorakshanath. The worship of *jati* Gorakshanath will bear fruit by virtue of the recitation of this mantra.

---

8 From the root *man* 'to think', a sacred sound or phrase, such as *om*, *hum*, or *om namah shivaya*, that has a transformative effect on the mind of the individual reciting it; to be ultimately effective, a mantra needs to be given in an initiation by a Master.

अनेन मंत्रजापेन गोरक्ष दर्शनं लभेत् ।
अतिगुह्यतरं देवी देवनामपि दुर्लभम् ।।१६।।

Anena manthrajaapena, Goraksha darshanam labheth |
Athiguhyatharam dhevi, Dhevanamapi dhurlabham ||16||

The chanting of this mantra ensures the *darshan* of Goraksha Nath. This *rahasyam* is most hidden and is concealed even from gods and goddesses.

गोपनीय प्रयत्नेन स्वयोनिरिव पार्वती ।
मारणं मोहनं वश्यं स्तम्भनोच्चाटनादिकम् ।।१७।।

Gopaniya prayathnena, Svayoniriva paarvathi |
Maranam mohanam vashyam, Stambhanocchhaatanadhikam ||17||

पाठमात्रेण संसिध्दयेत् गोरक्ष स्तोत्रमुत्तमम् ।।१८।।

Patamaathrena samsiddhayeth, Goraksha sthothramutthamam ||18||

O Parvati, keep it hidden. The chanting of the Goraksha Rahasyam bestows success in attaining *maran* (destruction of lust, anger), *mohan* (attaining the attention of the isht, personal deity) *vasikaran* (enhancing the mind), *stambhan* (weaning the senses away from low enjoyments) and *uccatan* (craving for moksha) ||17|| ||18||

The Mantra (Gayatri[9])

ॐ ह्रीं श्रीं गों गोरक्षनाथाय विद्महे
शुन्य पुत्राय धीमहि। तन्नो गोरक्ष निरन्जनः प्रचोदयात ।

Om hreem shreem gom, Gorakshanathaya vidhmahey
Shoonya puthraaya dheemahi thanno, Goraksha niranjanah prachodhayath |

Mantra

ॐ ह्रीं श्रीं गों हुं फट् स्वाहा ।
ॐ ह्रीं श्रीं गों गोरक्ष हुं फट् स्वाहा ।
ॐ ह्रीं श्रीं गों गोरक्ष निरंजनात्मने हुं फट् स्वाहा ।

Om hreem shreem gom, Hoom phat svaha
Om hreem shreem gom, Goraksha hoom phat svaha
Om hreem shreem gom Goraksha, Niranjanathmane hoom phat svaha

(or)

ॐ शिव गोरक्ष योगी

Om Shiva Goraksha Yogi

Note : it is not essential or even desirable to know the meaning of the *bijas* (letters) contained in the mantra given above. The knowledge of their meaning is impossible to attain. This is enough to chant them devoutly.

---

[9] A Vedic mantra recited to enlighten the intellect and give liberation (moksha) chanted at the junctions of sunrise and sunset (*sandhikal*).

एवं ध्यात्वा जपित्वा च साधकाः शुध्द-मानसाः ।
साधयेत् सर्व कार्याणि नात्र कार्यविचारणा ।।१९।।

Evam dhyathva japithva cha, Saadhakhah shuddha-maanasah |
Sadhayeth sarva kaaryaani, Nathra karyavicharana ||19||

Those who meditate and chant this mantra with pure mind and sincere devotion attain what they desire. This is beyond doubt.

यो धारयेन्नरो नित्यं मंन्त्रराजं विशेषतः ।
सा योगसिध्दमाप्नोति गोरक्षस्य प्रसादतः ।।२०।।

Yo dhaarayennaro nithyam, Manthraajam visheshatah |
Sa yogasiddhimapnoti, Gorakshasya prasaadhathah ||20||

Those who adopt this mantra after receiving initiation in the recitation from a satguru[10] attain yoga *siddhi* (perfection in yoga).

नमस्ते रूद्र रूपाय सादेशं शत्रुमर्दिनां ।
नमः जती महायोगी सादेशं आत्मदर्शनम् ।।२१।।

Namasthe rudra rupaaya, Sadhesham sathrumardhinaam |
Namah jathi mahayogi, Sadhesham aathmadharshanam ||21||

I bow down to Rudra-incarnate Goraksha Nath, the vanquisher of all enemies. I bow down to the *mahajati* (the great all-perfected being) and mahayogi. I bow down to the one who is *atmadarsani* (he who reveals his Divinity in the souls of all human beings).

---

10 'one with gravity', a Master who brings to light the Spiritual knowledge inherent in man; an enlightened aspect of the Divine.

नमस्ते विघ्नहर्ताय काम क्रोधादि नाशिने ।
जाग्रतं हि महायोगी जप-सिद्धि कूरूष्व मे ॥२२॥

Namasthe vighnaharthaaya, Kaama krodhaadhi naashine |
Jaagratham hi mahayogi, Japa-siddhi kurushva mey ||22||

I bow down to the *vighnaharta* (remover of obstacles), to the one who destroys *kama* (lust) and *krodha* (anger). O Mahayogi, awaken my japa[11] and make it accomplished.

ॐ कार सृष्टिरूपाय ह्रींकार प्रतिपालने ।
श्रींकार वरदायकाय गोंकार योग रूपिणे ॥२३॥

Omkaar srushtirupaaya, Hrimkaar prathipaalane |
Shreemkaar vardhaayakaaya, Gomkar yoga rupine ||23||

(O Goraksha Nath), You are the whole creation in the form of *omkar* (the birthing hum of creation); in the form of *hrimkar* (the protectie sound vibration), You foster the world; in the form of *srimkar*, You are a bestower of boons, and in the form of *gomkar*, You are yoga embodiment (controller of all senses).

गोरक्ष गोरक्षाय बीज रूपं नमोस्तुते ।
विदमहे चाभायदाय नित्यादेश मंत्र-रूपिणे ॥२४॥

Goraksha Gorakshaya, Bija rupam namosthuthe
Vidhmahe chabhayadaaya, Nithyaadesha manthra rupine ||24||

As Goraksha you protect the cow, the bull, the earth, speech, *yajna*[12] and you are the seed (origin) of the whole world. I bow down to You. As *vidmahe* you offer *abhaya* (assurance of protection from fear).

---

11 'recitation', the repeated recitation of mantras to focus and clarify one's mind for meditation.
12 'sacrifice', ritual fire sacrifice involving the chanting of mantras and shlokas. Yoga also knows of an inner sacrifice of kindling the internal flame of kundalini.

शुंश-शान्ति-रूपाय शून्य-पुत्राय आदेशं ।
धीमहितु ज्ञान रूपाय तन्नो रूपाय नाथस्य ।।२५।।

Shunsha – shaanthi – rupaya, Shunya-putraaya Adhesham |
Dheemahi thu jnana rupaya, Tanno rupaaya nathasya ||25|

As *shunsha* (of peaceful nothing) you bestow peace. O Born of *Shunya* (absolute entity), I bow to You. As *dhimahi* (meditate on) you are knowledge and as *tanno* (in that), You are the *nath* (Lord).

निरंजनो, निराकार गोरक्ष निरंजनात्मने ।
हुं हुं हुंकार रूपाय जंजं जती गोरक्षस्य ।।२६।।

Niranjano, niraakaar, Goraksha niranjanathmane |
Hoom hoom hoomkaar rupaya, Jamjam jathi Gorakshasya ||26||

As *hoom hoom*, You are a roar, as *jan jan*, You are in the form of *jati* Goraksha. You are niranjana, *nirakara* (formless) and *niranjana atmasvarupa* (pure self-image).

भ्रां भ्रीं भ्रूं भैरवनाथाय मोक्ष-मुक्तिदायकम् ।
धां धीं धूं धर्म नाथाय महानाथो नमो नमः ।।२७।।

Bhraam bhreem bhroom, Bhairavanathayaay moksha mukthidaayakam|
Dhaam dheem dhoom dharm nathaya, Mahanatho namo namah ||27||

In the from of *bhram bhrim bhrum*, You are Bhairava (a fierce aspect of Shiva which destroys negativity) Nath. In the form of *dham dhim dhum*, You are lord of dharma, Dharmanath. O Mahanath, you are the bestower of moksha. I bow down to You again and again.

सां सीं सूं सर्वांगनाथाय महासिद्धं नमो ऽद्देशम् ।
कां कीं, कूं कलेश्वराय महाकाल कालरूपाय ॥२८॥

Saam seem soom sarvamganathaya, Mahasiddham namoadhesam |
Kaam keem koom kaleshvaraaya, Mahaakaal kaalarupaaya ||28||

In the form of *saam seem soom*, You are Sarvanga Nath and in the form of *kaam keem koom*, You are Kalesvar (Lord of time). As *kala* (time) you are *mahakala*[13]. O Mahasiddha, I bow down to You.

लां लीं लूं च लाल ग्वालाय महायोगी योग लिलाय ।
वां वीं वूं विघ्ननाशाय विमलनाथो नमो नमः ॥२९॥

Laam leem loom cha laal gvaalaaya, Mahayogi yoga lilaaya |
Vaam veem voom vighnanaashaaya, Vimalanatho namo namah ||29||

In the form of *laam leem loom*, you are Lalagvala Nath and as mahayogi, you perform *lila* (the play of the divine mother as Maya); as *vaam veem voom*, You are the destroyer of difficulties. O Vimal Nath, I bow down to you.

गों गीं गूं गुरू गोरक्षाय सर्वत्र रोग नाशाय ।
जूं सः मृत्युंजयाय च महाकाल नमो नमः ॥३०॥

Gom geem goom guru Gorakshaya, Sarvathra roga naashaaya |
Jhoom sah mrithyunjayaay cha, Mahaakaal namo namah ||30||

In the form of *gom geem goom*, you are Goraksha Nath who is the remover of all maladies. In the form of *jhoom sah*, You are *mrityunjaya* (vanquisher of death) and mahakala. I bow down to you.

---

[13] 'The Great Beyond Time', epithet of Lord Shiva in whose presence, causation/light, space and time stands still and subdued and this is the end of relativity and the beginning of supreme consciousness.

खड्दर्शन गोरक्षाय खां खीं खूं खेचरी तथा ।
रां रीं रूं रहस्य नाथ मंत्र सिद्धि कुरूष्व मे ॥३१॥

Khaddharshan Gorakshaya khaam, Kheem khoom khechari thatha |
Raam reem room rahasya nath, Manthra siddhi kurushva mey ||31||

In the form of *khaam kheem khoom,* you are *khechari* (mover in the sky or one who assumes the mudra - aspect of the Ultimate Being). You are *khaddarsani* (who has seen or realized all six chakras[14] through kundalini yoga). Bestow on me, in the form of *raam reem room*, the siddhi (accomplishment) of this mantra.

इदं गोरक्ष रहस्य मंत्रो जागरति तव हेतवे
अभक्ते नैव दातव्यं गोपितं रक्ष पार्वती ॥३२॥

Idham Goraksha rahasya, Manthro jaagarathi thava heythavey |
Abhakthe naiva daathavyam, Gopitham raksha parvathi ||32||

This is the Goraksha Rahasyam mantra with which accomplishment may be attained. O Parvati, keep it hidden from those who do not have faith and devotion.

पाठ मात्रेण मन्त्राणामुच्यते सर्व किल्विषैः ॥३३॥

Paat maathrena mantharanaa, Muchyathe sarva kilvishaih ||33||

He who chants the mantra of Goraksha Rahasyam is freed from responsibility of the gravest sins committed by him.

---

14 'pranic wheel', the psycho-energetic centers of the subtle body (sukshma-sharir). Classically seven of such centers are given: muladhara chakra at the perineum, svadhishthana chakra at the base of the spine, manipura chakra at the navel, anahata chakra at the heart, vishuddhi chakra at the throat, ajna chakra in the middle of the head, and sahasrara chakra at the top of the head.

रहस्यं ध्यानमुत्तमम् गुह्याद् गुह्यतरं महत् ।
तस्मात् सर्व प्रयत्नेन सर्वकाम-फल-प्रदम् ।।३४।।

Rahasyam dhyana mutthamam, Guhyad guhyatharam mahath |
Tasmaath sarva prayathnena, Sarvakaama-phala-pradham ||34||

I have made all efforts to reveal to you the most hidden Goraksha Rahasyam, which bestows (on one) all desired rewards.

नाथरहस्य प्रसादेन त्वं सर्वमान्यो भविष्यसि ।
सर्व रूपमयो नाथः नाथमयं जगत् ।।३५।।

Natharahasya prasaadena thvam, Sarvamaanyo bhavishyasi |
Sarv rupamayo nathah Nathamayam jagath ||35||

Being a recipient of Guru Goraksha Nath's grace you would be respected by all. Sri Guru Goraksha is every form in this world and the whole world is in Him.

विश्वरूपं परमयोगी अतोहं आदेशं कुरु ।।३६।।

Vishvarupam param yogi, Athoham adhesham kuru ||36||

I bow down to the Paramyogi Visvarupa Gorakshanathji.

This completes the Sri Shiva Goraksha Rahasyam

PREFACE

Shiva Goraksha Babaji is a direct manifestation of Supreme Shiva Himself and is beyond mortal birth and death. Still alive, His deathless presence hallows the Himalayan ranges even till today. Well-authenticated references about Him occur throughout Indian scriptural writings – from the Vedic and Puranic Ages to the modern times. This is the true Babaji whom I have personally experienced and mentioned in my books and verbal discourses.

Legends are rife about Him throughout the length and breadth of India. Also known as Mahavatar Babaji, this Being is the radiant head, the fragrant heart, and the undying soul of eternal knowledge. He is called the Ancient of Days, and the Great Banyan Tree, from which all avatars, prophets, and divine incarnations have sprung. Even the devas[1] and celestial beings have worshipped Him ceaselessly, beseeching Him to redeem the world of its bondage and suffering. It is He who has enlightened the modern age with the soul-liberating science of Kriya Yoga through His disciple Yogavatar Lahiri Mahasaya.

---

1 'Shining one', a male deity, such as Shiva, Vishnu, or Brahma—either in the sense of the ultimate reality (*Mahadeva*), or a high angelic being.

WHO IS BABAJI?

In my communications and dialogues with seekers all over the world, I have become aware of how much confusion exists as to who the mighty being called 'Babaji' is. Therefore, to clear all doubts and put to rest this perplexity with finality, I have in this book, based on my experience and subsequent realization, revealed who is the true Babaji.

Throughout my childhood, adolescence and later years, I have felt and seen His guiding presence, as if preparing me for the experience at Badrinath in the Himalayas in 1967, when I was a youth of barely twenty-three.

Babaji enlightened the modern world with the original Kriya Yoga[1], through His disciple Yogavatar Lahiri Mahasaya, whom He initiated into this soul-saving science in 1861. When Paramhansa[2] Yogananda published his all-time classic *Autobiography of a Yogi* in 1946, Mahavatar Babaji became known for the first time to the public at large.

It is to this *parampara* or grand lineage that I belong, and through which I am privileged to impart the sacred science of Kriya Yoga

---

1 '*Yoga* of doing', the 'lightning path' which brings you to the path of non-doing (*akarma*); given by Babaji Goraksha Nath for the dissolution of karma and acceleration of human evolution to divinity.

2 'Supreme swan', (also Paramahamsa) the 4th level of initiation of a yogi; an honorific title given to great adepts, such as Ramakrishna and Yogananda.

to humanity. All the yogas, such as Raja Yoga, Kriya Yoga, Bhakti Yoga, Jnana Yoga, Karma Yoga, Hatha Yoga, Laya Yoga, Tantra Yoga and Hamsa Yoga emanate, for the grace and salvation of humankind, from the same source—the Visible-Invisible Savior of All Beings called Babaji.

The future accomplishment of Earth Peace Through Self Peace shall, more than the United Nations Organizations, be brought about by the United Minds Organization—through the practice of the peerless science of Kriya Yoga, which is a non-denominational and nonsectarian pathway to world peace and self-realization.

The stream of humanity and its evolution may be channelized and directed to the practice of the correct Kriya Yoga and to knowing that Shiva Goraksha Babaji and Babaji of *Autobiography of a Yogi* are one and the same Being. This purpose may be served through the reader's understanding of this book. The central themes and spiritual purpose of my writing this book are given below.

1. To unveil before the world, the great mystery that Shiva Goraksha Babaji is the Babaji of *Autobiography of a Yogi*. All other writings of people, persons, places and things are subservient and should only be used to serve the accomplishment of this purpose. This book is not about Lahiri Mahasaya, Sri Yukteshwar, or Paramhansa Yogananda. So, when I write a chapter about Yogananda, that chapter is only a facility to use that reference to prove that Babaji and Shiva Goraksha Babaji (Goraksha Nath or Gorakh Nath) are one.

2. The second critical factor and linchpin to expound upon and clarify to a misguided public, is that the yogic treatise *Goraksha Shataka*[3] and the original Kriya Yoga given by Mahavatar Babaji to Lahiri Mahasaya are also one and the same. My purpose is to prove that the original source of Babaji's Kriya Yoga is the *Goraksha*

---

[3] *Goraksha Shataka* is the first part of *Goraksha Paddhati* written by Shiva Goraksha Babaji. *Goraksha Paddhati* is a system of *yogic* techniques for self-realization.

Shataka and *Manu Smriti*[4]. This, not only clarifies that the *Goraksha Shataka* and Kriya Yoga are one, but further goes to illuminate that Babaji and Goraksha Nath are one and the same Being.

In medieval times, the immortal Babaji manifested as the eternal Goraksha Nath. In modern times, the immortal Goraksha Nath has manifested as the eternal Babaji. Therefore, both of them are one and the same Being, who revealed Himself to me as Shiva Goraksha Babaji.

Many people speak of Babaji and Goraksha Nath, and great confusion prevails among them because some speak of Him in His terrestrial dimension, others in His celestial dimension, and yet others talk of Him in His cosmic dimension. Some writers speak of Him in His 'conscious' state, others in His 'super-conscious' state, while yet others endeavor to speak of His 'supreme-conscious' state. So, while the Being we are talking about is not different, each author speaks of Him only in reference to the limit of his understanding, and the fact is that nobody can truly comprehend Him. So, it is only by His grace that this, that, or any other book can be written.

I have tried to clarify this as best as possible in the section titled 'Babaji's Dream Bodies' in chapter 19 ('The Sage of All Ages'). We all know Babaji in His limited form on Earth, but it is impossible to comprehend His eternal Being, which is beyond relativity and creation. This book will mainly deal with the terrestrial, celestial and divine aspects of Babaji, in relativity and in creation.

---

4 *Manu Smriti* (also known as *Manav Dharma Shastra*) was written by Manu, who is considered mankind's first law-giver. Encoded in this treatise are the ethical and spiritual laws of humanity and its evolution.

Examining some untruths

I have come across many a book published about the cults, creeds and religions of various sects belonging to Kabir[5], Guru Nanak[6], Alam Prabhu[7] and Balak Nath[8]. The devotees and followers of these saints and spiritual teachers, in order to prove their master the best and more superior to the rest, have made almost all of them engage in either a physical or a philosophical combat with the greatest of all sages—Shiva Goraksha Babaji. It was their belief that unless their own master or satguru had defeated Goraksha Nath in a philosophical debate or a combat of *siddhis*[9], he would not be recognized and find an elevated position in society as a great saint or an avatar[10]. Goraksha Nath, so to say, became the ultimate benchmark for testing, without which no saint could be accepted as a saint by the masses.

This somehow created a psychological schism in the minds of bigoted followers, and they contrived false stories in which Goraksha Nath was worsted in philosophical debates or a combat of siddhis, even though there was a gap of two or three hundred years between their masters incarnations and Goraksha Nath. Having scant regard for the time and periods in which their master lived, they were so keen to prove that their masters were the greatest, that they went to any lengths and interpolated false information in their religious scriptures and texts.

---

5 Kabir was a medieval saint of India who received *Kriya Yoga* from Babaji. He also received the *mantra* of 'Rama' from his guru Ramananda.

6 Guru Nanak was another great medieval saint and founder of the Sikh religion. He has sung praises to Babaji Goraksha Nath in the *Japji Gutka*, a Sikh scripture.

7 Alam Prabhu was a saint who existed 150 years after Babaji Goraksha Nath. Babaji appeared in his vision one night and blessed him. The story of the physical meeting of these masters is not a historical fact.

8 Baba Balak Nath and the thousands of *yogis* who followed the Nath tradition during the Middle Ages were all disciples of Babaji Goraksha Nath.

9 'Accomplishment/perfection', spiritual perfection, the attainment of flawless identity with the ultimate reality (*Atman* or *Brahman*); paranormal ability, of which the *yoga* tradition knows many kinds.

10 'Descent', the descent of the divine into a terrestrial light-body for spiritual work and the salvation of the world; identified outwardly by specific signs, such as the tendency of the *avatar* to cast no shadow.

The fact of the matter is that even the historical Shiva Goraksha Babaji of medieval times lived around 150 to 200 years before the time of Alam Prabhu, Balak Nath and Guru Nanak. As a matter of fact, it was Goraksha Nath, the Sage of All Ages, who inspired and influenced Lord Bharthari Nath, Kabir and Guru Nanak in all their poetry and writings. These great beings of lofty, avataric stature had no hand whatsoever in the concoction of false stories depicting that they defeated their greatest benefactor and master, Goraksha Nath. They were certainly in no need of such bravado.

So, a person who reads a book that projects a jaundiced view, or a slant towards a cult, must beware of being misled by untruths about this great master of all masters whose presence hallows the Himalayan mountains even today. He upholds the spiritual edifice of the land of Bharatvarsha[11], called India. Kabir sang the *purusharth*[12] and masculinity of the philosophy of Goraksha Nath, and the great woman saint Meera sang the devotional heart of Goraksha Nath. Yet, both these great saints were unable to completely expound upon the philosophy and truth of Shiva Goraksha Babaji. But, if Goraksha Nath were to move and shift a little, the whole edifice of India's philosophy and yoga would, to give an analogy, register a 6.6 shift on the seismic scale. The blessings of this Sage of All Ages, who has said nothing in His defense, have continued to uphold the truth in all the religions and philosophies and yogas of the world.

Seeking Babaji

You Are Babaji To The Extent You Know Babaji and very few people really know Babaji. This is not to discourage any humble seeker from taking the path, but just to check the arrogant seeker seeing Babaji and imagining he knows everything about everything, and everything special about Babaji. The danger lies in the delusion that we have met Babaji, and nobody but the person claiming to

---

11 Present-day India—the land whose people are wedded to the divine light.
12 'Human purpose'—the effort to know the true self within the mind of our bodies.

have seen Babaji can testify to it. He has to be true to his own self; to what extent he had a vision of Babaji or saw Babaji. Whether he experienced Babaji through the chirping of a bird, or as a light breeze; saw Him in a dream or in a *drishtanta*[13], saw Him in a *sakshatkar*[14], i.e. actually experienced Him as *Sat*, known His *Chit* and felt Him as Ananda[15], or experienced Him in the highest state of Brahma-Nirvana[16] which is called the 'Isness of the Zero not Zero'[17]. How many of us have experienced and been one with Him as the Non-Being Essentiality[18]?

While experiencing the various states of spiritual awareness, one has to be true to oneself. I am not sitting here in judgment of what is true and what is not. On my part, all that I know is that I am being inspired to serve, and to guide. My pen just writes because He wants it to write. Perhaps the purpose of this book is to tame our egos and enable each of us to develop a humbler sense of proportion as to where we stand, and where the great Being Babaji stands. Remember, that the great sages, alive through the ages, can see through the hearts and minds of humanity. They know exactly where each individual stands in the hierarchy of his personal evolution and the depth of his devotion to God.

---

13 Spiritual vision.

14 A true vision of the Divine Lord.

15 *Sat-Chit-Ananda* —Existence-Consciousness-Bliss.

16 Merging in the transcendental core beyond the universe, and being everywhere and nowhere at the same time. Highest state of enlightenment.

17 Yogiraj Siddhanath has coined this term. The zero represents the nothing of creation. The Zero not Zero represents the 'everything' of creation and the Isness pervades them and goes beyond both states.

18 A phrase coined by Yogiraj Siddhanath; this word represents a paradox because *Para Brahma* is so beyond mortal conception that He is a Non-Being as far as we are concerned; and yet He is the essential component of the very fabric of our soul-essence and creation.

A shadow of Yogiraj Siddhanath's actual experiential
vision of Shiva Goraksha Babaji

CHAPTER 1

KNOWING THE BEING
The Cosmic Lightning Holder

Beyond the ken of mortals is the great Spiritual King of our world, who rises from the still waters of our innermost Consciousness – the mighty *Lakulish*[1] of our lilac lagoons. Himself the unfathomable Consciousness, He holds in His hand the Lightning of Immortality – the Cosmic Kundalini Shakti that is the very mystery of life and death. The Holder, the Wielder and the Moulder of this Lightning is the one and only Babaji. In the aspect of Holder, He is Shiva – the Lightless Light beyond light. In the aspect of Wielder, He is *Ardhnarishwar*[2] where He can either maintain His state of lightless light, or become the light in creation. In the aspect of Moulder, He is transformed into His Shakti, Mataji – the moulding light of creation.

In order to form the connection between the descent of Spirit into Matter, we must first understand that as Spirit descends, it creates Matter in its various forms and yet remains pristine and unchanged. How it can be in the Matter of creation and yet not be involved in it, is the mystery of all mysteries and may only be understood if the Supreme Consciousness wants it to be so. So humbly taking it from there, I have evolved a simple formula as a working hypothesis to delve into the mysteries of the unfathomable Truth. This formula

---

[1] The 'staff-holder', 'He who holds the lightning-staff of evolution', a representation of Lord Shiva or Babaji-Gorakhnath; also deified as the ancient founder of the Shiva Pashupat sect of yogis.
[2] Shiva and Shakti depicted as half-man, half-woman in one body, showing to us that the balance of the universe is rooted in reciprocity.

states that, *"Consciousness is infinitely greater than yet coequal to energy which is equal to mass multiplied by the square of the velocity of light."*

$$C \infty \geq E = mc^2$$

In its present state, this equation has been experienced by many enlightened souls and advanced Yogis. This formula of existence has certainly been validated by their personal experience. However, even though it matters not to the Spirit, for the sake of the intellect of humanity, the challenge is to prove the above formula as a measured test in the laboratory. Whether it is proven or not in the future doesn't really contribute to the evolution of our consciousness, because both humanity and its intellect are transient in the constancy of the Eternal Consciousness. Rather than attempt to prove the existence of reality with the intellect, it is far more purposeful to become one with Reality by experiencing it, as the Yogis did. So Nothing matters; only God spirits! This means that, "Consciousness creates the Universe and yet remains the same." I speak for you here the great spiritual formula of high math, voiced by the Sages of the Ancient of Days:

Om purnamada purnamidam
Purnat purna mudachyatae
Purnasya purna madaya
Purna meva vashisyathae

From the complete, if the complete is taken away, the complete still remains complete. This is what makes the enlightened Yogi exclaim, **"Oh Lord, the Universe, a bubble in my consciousness; my consciousness, a nothing in thy Nothingness!"**

To further expound the meaning of *The Cosmic Lightning Holder*, Babaji is the innermost quintessential Spirit of our souls and is thus understood by the personal aspect of our spiritual selves. The Formless Spirit of Babaji, beyond creation, is represented by the still waters of our consciousness. In creation, the spiritual form of Babaji is represented by Lakulish – The Lightning Staff Holder, arising from the lilac lagoons that represent the sacred shores of our individual souls.

The lightning represents His dynamic aspect in creation as Mataji, and the lilac waters represent His potential spirit beyond creation, as Shiva. We humans fail to delve into the still waters of our own consciousness, because they are muddied by the bedlam of misery created by our own thoughts. We cover the eyes of our souls with the hands of our minds, and then cry that we cannot see! All we need to do is remove the hands of the mind from the eyes of our soul with the persistent practice of Kriya Yoga, and behold the Divine In-dweller Shiva Goraksha Babaji – the Heart of Divinity throbbing in humanity.

'The Lightning Standing Still' is one of the aspects of Babaji where He plays the Time-Reversed Phenomena – faster than light. When the speed of light is reached, time stands still. But when surpassed, it has no space in time, hence, time ticks back towards the future. Because the future lies behind you in the great storehouse of *sanchit karma*[3], it comes from over and behind as time moves forward. However, as you travel along the forward road, you are treading your past and working out your karma as you go along. So, the future lies behind you and the past is before you, as you walk forward to work out your past karma. Therefore, it is said that when you finish your karma, your purity enables you to travel back to the future unimpeded by karma. So your future life depends upon the actions of your past. Your actions that you do now are by total free will, but once your free will is hardened in the mold of time, then you must bear the consequences, good or bad, of the deeds you have determined by your own free will. The best way to get out of

---

[3] Those past karmas collectively stored in the unconscious mind of the individual

this catch-22 is to practice Kriya Yoga and live in the Eternal Now, which is a name for Babaji.

This is the great enigma of the space-time continuum. You lengthen time to shorten the distance; you shorten time to lengthen the distance. Time becomes space as distance, and space becomes time as duration. Time is eternity, and distance is infinity. When eternity meets infinity, time becomes space, and space becomes time. This is said to be the 'Eternal Now'! That is why meeting Babaji is always in the 'Present'; there is no past, no future; everything is in the present.

The Being that has the ability to play with time and space is in total At-One-Ment with God.

He is everywhere and nowhere at the same time, and His mass is infinite. I have penned a few lines to show how important it was for me to know, and to become one with Time.

> *Oh Time, could you with me conspire*
> *To relive my past life film entire*
> *Fashioning my future picture show*
> *In tune with God's own mystic flow*
> Yogiraj Siddhanath

So, is the lightning that He holds in His hands also standing still? No. This is the lightning moving at the speed of light in our three-dimensional world of relativity and, therefore, this light, also called the Cosmic Kundalini Shakti, is used for the evolution and welfare of all humanity. It is said that Shiva Goraksha Babaji burst forth from the heart of His own supreme consciousness, called Shiva, for the celebration of Creation. In a flash, He unites with the Womb of Creation, which is His own beloved Shakti energy, permeates it with His Divine Consciousness and yet remains unchanged, immutable and free.

This is one of His important dynamic aspects as Mataji, whom Yogananda refers to as Babaji's sister, and whom I refer to as Babaji's feminine, constructive, light energy. Although the Lightning Holder, the Wielder and the Moulder are a flow guided by the Continuum-Consciousness called Babaji, they are the same and yet they are apart, because the Lightning Holder is the Lightning Standing Still, who is the Spirit of Babaji beyond creation. The Wielder is also Babaji, who is a channel leading into creation and the Lightning itself. Traveling at the speed of 300,000 kilometers per second, is Babaji in creation called Mataji. Now in Hindu philosophy, she is called the Padma Matri or Mata, meaning – the Universal Lotus Mother, later referred to as the transcendental matrix.

Babaji holds the very mystery of life and death. He directs the entire evolution and dissolution of the world, not only of humanity but also of devas, nature spirits, and all creatures of our world. He is called *Vaidhatra* (The Cosmic Lightning Holder) of the destiny of all nations and beings, from the celestial to the terrestrial. Vaidhatra derives from *vidyut*, which means cosmic electricity. Vaidhatra also means 'First from the Creator' who is known as *Vidhata*[4] which, in turn, refers to Brahma, the Creator. The divine Babaji was the first to be manifested from *Nilalohita Shiva* (the Blue Void of Consciousness) through the divine mind of Brahma. He is the 'Time-reversed White Hole' from which creation came into manifestation.

Let there be no shadow of doubt that Babaji is the Cosmic Lightning Holder, far more vast and expansive than Indra and Saint George, who are also lightning holders; however, they are only an aspect of Babaji. Babaji is also the Lightning of Cosmic Kundalini that in turn becomes the Universal Lightning, then Celestial Lightning and, then, the individual Lightning of Human Kundalini; which is the birthright of every person to use for his own evolution. Such is the decree ordained by Babaji, the sage of all ages. Babaji as the lightening standing still is faster than light. He is **THE TIME REVERSED BLACK HOLE** from which creation came into manifestation.

---

[4] A name for Brahma, who holds the destinies of humanities, the nations and creation.

To put it in the phraseology of quantum physics, I would say that Babaji is the rarest of the rare stars of lightless light found in the naked singularity of certain super-massive black holes – because light is swallowed up by a black hole, along with time and space. So, the star of lightless light cannot emit light as we know it, because it is swallowed up by the intense gravity of the black hole. This particularly rare star has to be of a superior radiance of sorts. I choose to call the star 'The Lightless Light'. This dazzling star of very special black holes has been discovered and known by quantum physicists throughout the world. Those who think of Babaji with feeble hearts and dull minds shall know Him to that extent and those who absorb him in samadhi[5] will know Him in a much vaster Truth and extent.

Cosmic Kundalini Holder

As steward of the cosmos through the ages, it is Shiva Goraksha Babaji who undertakes the task of guarding the seeds of creation through the birth, destruction, and rebirth of each of the created universes. Each universe comes into being with a tremendous explosion of light and sound known as the 'Big Bang', where, within a billionth of a second, matter explodes and expands in all directions at an inconceivable velocity to form the phenomena called Creation. This is called the *Omkar* or the 'sound of instant creation'.

After a duration of time, known in the ancient Indian astronomical system as *Mahakalpa*, the universe folds in upon itself with a tremendous gravitational force withdrawing all light, time, space, and matter – the wholeness of the created universe contracts into one tiny point of light, the size of a *bindu*, a single spark of Divine Light in the

---

5 'putting together', the ecstatic or unitive state in which the meditator becomes one with the object of meditation; the eighth and final limb (anga) of Patanjali's eightfold path; there are many types of samadhi, the most significant distinction being between samprajnata (super-conscious) and asamprajnata (supra-conscious) ecstasy; only the latter leads to the dissolution of the karmic factors deep within the mind; beyond both types of ecstasy is enlightenment, which is also sometimes called sahaja samadhi or the condition of 'natural' or 'spontaneous' ecstasy, where there is perfect continuity of supra-conscious throughout waking, dreaming and sleeping.

womb of the Great Void. To western scientists, this event is known as the 'Big Crunch', but, in ancient India, the rishis and sages knew it as the process of *pratiprasava*, that is the 'drawing in of all the elements of nature and creation' to a single focal point of *nagna satya*, the naked truth, which outlasts all manifested creation and which, in contemporary quantum physics, is called the 'naked singularity'.

This Cosmic Lightning descends to become Universal Lightning, then Celestial Lightning and then the Terrestrial Lightning of human kundalini.

The Human Kundalini

Kundalini, which literally means a 'coiled spiral', is the electromagnetic pranic energy that lies dormant in human beings. The word itself stems from an earlier root – *kunda* – that means the 'fire pit'. Kundalini lies coiled three-and-a-half times around the base of the spine like a cobra. When it is awakened, it can propel a yogi from the static state to kinetic activation in a split second. The kundalini is actually intensified spiritual prana. If pranic energy is compared to an atomic bomb, the charge of the kundalini energy benefits the guided yogi like a benevolent hydrogen bomb. The kundalini *shakti* or force is activated and awakened during the Kriya Yoga pranayama which I call the kundalini 'breath'. It is hidden and latent within the nervous system of all human beings.

The kundalini has seven layers of consciousness. If all the seven layers of kundalini consciousness are awakened, then the soul finally departs from its abode on earth. No one can awaken even the sixth layer of kundalini and live for a very long time. Such a person must dissolve in Cosmic Consciousness. So, we are now talking of not only the human kundalini but also the cosmic kundalini.

The Cosmic Kundalini

The cosmic kundalini is a totally different noumenon from the phenomenon of human kundalini. She is the Serpent of the Fathomless Deep, *Aja Ek Pad* – the 'Unborn Standing on One Foot'; the *Ahirbudnya* – the 'Serpent of the Fathomless Deep'. She is called Shakti when united with Shiva. She is the 'Mother of the Great Deep'; *Amba*[6], also known as *Bal Tripura Sundari*. The naked singularity, is Shiva fused with His Shakti, whom no one can fathom; whom no one can know intellectually in their ultimate seven-fold form. I am referring here to the cosmic kundalini of Shiva Goraksha Babaji.

A yogi practicing the Kundalini Kriya Yoga of Babaji, with sincerity, is sooner or later bound to awaken this divine force. When he gets absorbed in this yogic practice, the kundalini opens up the treasures of the yogi's body, mind, and soul, and he is endowed with divine experiences such as: knowing all past life experiences, reading the future, and seeing the aura[7].

Fusing the Cosmic and Human Kundalini

An aspirant has to bridge the gap between the cosmic and his own kundalini. If, for example, the cosmic kundalini travels at 300,000 km/sec and the individual's kundalini travels at 30m/sec, then one has to bridge this gap. For this, one needs a transformer; a spiritual stepdown system. This transformer is the Satguru – one who has realized the Truth. Only he can help speed up the aspirant's kundalini, lessen the speed of the cosmic kundalini, and then help both the kundalinis fuse together to give the individual's soul an evolutionary boost. Thus, his soul-awareness takes a quantum leap, which

---

6 'Great Deep', appellation for an aspect of the Divine Mother. The waters of the unfathomable deep. Also known as the goddess Bal Tripura Sundari.

7 The astral/celestial radiance round the body of a meditating yogi and a saint, the nimbus/halo predominantly emits from around the head area.

could be too over-powering and difficult to handle for the aspirant, unless guided by the Satguru.

As one keeps attending more and more of the Satguru's satsangs or gatherings, one will see the kundalini at work. Experiencing the radiance of the Satguru's aura, witnessing the changing dimensions and observing the stillness within, are the powers bestowed by the kundalini.

CHAPTER 2

BABAJI IS NONE OTHER THAN GORAKSHA NATH

He is called the Nameless One and yet He goes by many names, the foremost among these being Babaji. He is the Ancient of Days, Forefather of all Adepts, King of Kings of the divine dynasties called The Earliest and The Last. He is the Mahavatar, the Fountainhead of all Knowledge and Evolution of Humanity made known to today's world first by the Yogavatar Lahiri Mahasaya, then by Gyanavatar[1] Sri Yukteshwar, and then by Paramhansa Yogananda, who spread the soul-liberating science of Kriya Yoga from India to the western world.

The existence of Babaji was first made publicly known in Paramhansa Yogananda's *Autobiography of a Yogi*[2]. This treatise revealed that He was the immortal yogi alive throughout the ages for the welfare and spiritual evolution of humanity. Babaji, we are told, is the name given to this Being by Yogananda's Paramguru, the Yogavatar Lahiri Mahasaya, who was initiated by Babaji into Kriya Yoga. It is through Yogavatar Lahiri Mahasaya that the knowledge of Babaji's evolutionary Lightning Path of Kriya Yoga has now spread across the world. Although it is through this legacy that several details of the Mahavatar have been revealed to us, it has been done with a degree of conscious discretion. The great spiritual masters of those

---
1 Divine incarnation of wisdom.
2 A spiritual classic written by *Paramhansa* Yogananda in the 20th century.

times were very careful to reveal only certain details of the Being called Babaji. The mysteries of Babaji were kept shrouded due to the inadequate state of spiritual development of the people at that time. Certain details of Babaji's life and legacy were considered not fit for disclosure to the people at large, as they were not yet ready to receive Him.

The time has now come to unveil the truth of as much of this Being as is comprehensible to mortals, the Deathless Mahavatar, who has come to guard and guide and to bless our humanity and the world.

Yogananda, in his *Autobiography of a Yogi*, says:

> *I give in these pages on Babaji merely a hint of His life—only a few facts which He deems fit and helpful to be publicly imparted.*

Knowing in advance that a time would come when sincere seekers, with minds ripened and ready to receive the truth of Babaji, would thirst for the knowledge of this mighty Being, Yogananda left behind a host of clues about His identity that were to be revealed later. Perhaps the greatest indication of this is given to us in his autobiography where he tells us that Babaji is but one of the many names of the Mahavatar; that He is called variously by a host of names that are *Shaivite* in origin. About Babaji, he says:

> *He has adopted the simple name Babaji (Revered Father); other titles of respect given to Him by Lahiri Mahasaya's disciples are Mahamuni Babaji Maharaj (Supreme Ecstatic Master), Mahayogi (The Great Yogi), and Trambak Baba or Shiva Baba (Titles of avatars of Shiva).*

This is no slip of Yogananda's pen, but a clear indication of who is he referring to as Babaji. From these names, even the lay reader can easily conclude that Lahiri Mahasaya and his disciples understood Babaji to be an avatara and aspect of Shiva. This aspect of Shiva isn't described as any ordinary avatara, but as an exalted and immortal manifestation of Shiva, for Babaji is none other than the immortal Shiva Himself, known famously throughout India as Shiva Goraksha, the Sage of All Ages and founder of the Nath tradition. In esoteric circles, and to the Himalayan yogis, He is known as Shiva Goraksha Babaji. To the common man, He is simply known as Goraksha Nath or Gorakh Nath.

The identity of Babaji as Goraksha Nath is further reaffirmed when we consider the details of Yogananda's life. In *Mejda* ('Older middle brother' in Bangla[3]), the book authored by Yogananda's younger brother Gora, who was named after the sage Goraksha Nath, we are given a description of the events from Yogananda's childhood.

Mejda (Yogananda) was born in Gorakhpur. A saint of the highest stature, it was not by mere accident that he was born in this city. I see his deep connection with Goraksha Nath, whom he later called Babaji in his celebrated *Autobiography of a Yogi*. This is the holy center for devotees of Goraksha Nath, as this region was hallowed by the presence of Shiva Goraksha Babaji in the Middle Ages. This temple is His cardinal temple in India from where divine dispensations, missions, and blessings are given to seekers. It was here that Yogananda was born, magnetically pulled to the location of Goraksha Nath's holiest of temples by the force of his sheer love and reverence for the Being.

Yogananda's parents were ardent worshippers of Goraksha Nath and regularly visited the temple for guidance and blessings. At the tender age of four, Yogananda experienced the power and grace of Shiva Goraksha Babaji and was filled with the ecstasy of expanded consciousness in this holy temple. The experience was recorded in *Mejda* as follows:

---

3 The language spoken in the Indian state of Bengal.

> *"Customarily, our parents took Mejda with them to the temple of Gorakh Nath to worship every Sunday and on holy days. However, on one Sunday they didn't go to the temple because a religious festival was being held at our house...As the guests were departing, Mother realized that she had not seen Mejda for several hours. The house and neighborhood were searched, but he couldn't be found. Knowing well her son's nature, and at last taking this into account, Mother said to Father, 'Since we go to the temple of Gorakh Nath every Sunday for worship, but we have not gone today, perhaps Mukunda [Yogananda's birth name] is there.'*
>
> *"Father and some of the guests went directly to the temple. As Mother had surmised, there was Mejda, sitting like a little sage absorbed in meditation. While the family was enjoying the festivity, he had quietly slipped out of the house to make his customary Sunday visit to the temple—more than a kilometer away; a great distance for such a young child.*
>
> *"....Dawn was approaching.... Mejda at long last opened his eyes, and was at first surprised to see so many people gathered around him. Then he realized where he was and why everyone was so anxious about him. With a sweet little smile he gazed at Father, and then bowed his head in recognition of the trouble he had caused. Father addressed him in a grave voice: 'Come home now. It is late. We were so worried about you'".*

Goraksha Nath, the Being who blessed Yogananda at this early age, is the very Being who would later guide and bless his journey and mission of spreading Kriya Yoga in the West. It is also this very Being who would later become famously known as the great Mahavatar Babaji, in Paramhansa Yogananda's autobiography.

CHAPTER 3

SAGES WHO ARE NOT THE BABAJI

In my dealings with sincere seekers all over the world, I have become aware that much confusion prevails as to who actually is the Being called Babaji. As mentioned earlier, Babaji simply means 'Revered Father', an appellation by which many wise men are known in India. Therefore, to clear all doubts and put an end to this perplexity, I find it necessary to explain who is not, or cannot be, the real Shiva Goraksha Babaji.

Babaji Haidakhan I

This Babaji appeared in 1861 and lived amidst the Kumaon mountains in a place called Haidakhan. He was popularly known as Haidakhan Baba. Many people believed that he was Ashwatthama[1], son of rishi[2] Dronacharya[3]. After the great battle of *Mahabharata*[4], he became *chiranjeeva*, an immortal, and still lives in his astral or physical body. Some devotees believe him to be a partial manifestation of

---

1 One of the eight *chiranjeevs* (immortals); he was present during the time of the great Mahabharata war, about 3102 BCE, and is still said to be present in the Himalayas.

2 A sage or a seer, the Lord of Irradiant Splendor; the Sages of the Fire Mist; a category of Vedic sage; an honorific title of certain venerated masters and cosmic beings.

3 A *Deva Rishi*, who existed during the period of the Mahabarata, guru of the Kauravas and Pandavas, and father of Ashwatthama.

4 'Great Bharata', one of the two of India's ancient and famous epics during the time of Lord Krishna that tells the story of the great war between the Pandavas and the Kauravas, and serves as a repository for many spiritual and moral teachings.

Shiva[5]. In 1924, he disappeared into the Himalayas and is now believed to be roaming there, incognito, as Ashwatthama. This is not Mahavatar Shiva Goraksha Babaji, whom I am referring to and who is a complete manifestation of Shiva. Nor is he the Babaji referred to in Yogananda's autobiography. Swami Rama has equated the spiritual status of Haidakhan Baba to that of Sombari Baba and his own master, Bengali Baba, thus providing further proof that he is not Shiva Goraksha Babaji who is *anupadaka*—undying and eternal—a direct manifestation of Shiva.

Babaji Haidakhan II

A few years after the disappearance of Haidakhan Baba I, a young boy from Nepal came to the Kumaon region to the ashram[6] of the former Haidakhan Baba and claimed that he was the Baba in this new, youthful body and he now also went by the name of Haidakhan Baba. Both the Babas took the name of the place where they were staying (Haidakhan), which is a common practice in India. About Haidakhan Baba I, there is some ambiguity about his disappearance. Some say that he took mahasamadhi (voluntary withdrawal of the life-force from the body through yogic means) in the remote Himalayan ranges, while others say he changed his *chola*[7], meaning that his soul exited his old body and entered a new body—that of this young Nepali boy. This young *siddha*[8] performed many miracles during his mission. He was greatly praised and worshipped as the true, immortal Babaji, but in the year 1984, he gave up his

---

5 'The Benevolent One', the Consciousness of the universe. The great destroyer of delusion and spiritual regenerator of mankind. He is the divine potential aspect of His own kinetic *shakti* (energy); also called *Mahadeva* or 'Great God'.

6 'Where work or effort is made', a hermitage; also any one of the four stages of life—(i) student life or *brahmacharya*; (ii) becoming a householder or *grihastha*, (iii) having completed the householder stage moving into the forest to dwell there (*Vanaprastha*), and finally (iv) becoming a complete renunciate (*Sannyasin*).

7 Refers to the physical, apparent body of a yogi, which he can change into at his own will, when his former body garment becomes decrepit and old. This may be done by the process of entering another's body or by the process of *Kayakalpa* (Body rejuvenation). Or he may choose to maintain the body in perfect health by the *sanjeevini* (rejuvenating) process of Kundalini Kriya Yoga.

8 'Accomplished', a perfected master or adept; a *mahasiddha* or 'great adept'; denoting one of the Nine Immortal *Naths*.

mortal body. Though he may be a partial avatara, or an aspect of the Immortal Babaji, a shadow of a doubt was cast when he left for his Heavenly abode. Haidakhan Baba has historical evidence to his earthy existence but he died a mortal death; hence he is clearly not *the* Immortal Mahavatar Babaji.

Gorakha Narayana

Also known as Gorakh Baba, this sage lives in the region of the Kumaon Himalayas. He is at times called Sri Babaji, as popularized in the book *Sri Babaji,* where it is written that Gorakh Narayana also goes by the title Shiva Goraksha Babaji. This yogi, Gorakh Narayana, may go by the name Shiva Goraksha Babaji, but let me state explicitly that he is *not* the legendary Mahavatar Shiva Goraksha Babaji to whom I am referring to in this book. Nor is he the Babaji of Yogananda's *Autobiography of a Yogi*. Gorakh Narayana explains that in a former life, he was Kripacharya who lived during the period of the *Mahabharata* war. The Shiva Goraksha Babaji I am referring to is a direct manifestation of Lord Shiva Himself. During the time of the *Mahabharata* war, Babaji, the Cosmic Mahavatar, had blessed the birth of the six divine sons of Kunti[9]. He was far beyond being enmeshed in a war. On the contrary, He was the Silent Watcher, the Divine Presence and Witness to the *Mahabharata* war. Clearly, He was not Kripacharya who was involved in the great battle between the Pandava and the Kaurava clans.

In the manner of the yogis living in the Himalayas, Gorakh Narayana resides at an ashram where pilgrims and wayfarers may easily contact him to seek his blessings and guidance. The Babaji I am referring to, Shiva Goraksha Babaji, is a Divine Being, and may only be contacted by His own choosing. Even in His terrestrial form, He manifests as and when the need arises, for the sole purpose of providing guidance or as an evolutionary boost to humanity or, in rare cases, to particular individuals. These interactions are very personal, extremely powerful, and phenomenally arcane.

---

9 Mother of the Pandavas.

Babaji Nagaraj

We are making dedicated efforts to establish the historical existence of a certain sage from South India called Babaji Nagaraj. We have researched his name in the Sarfoji Saraswati[10] Mahal Library in the town of Thanjavur in Tamil Nadu. It is thought that this sage was born there. Enquiry and research has also been conducted in various parts of Tamil Nadu, such as Cittargiri[11] but, so far, we have yet to discover any historical evidence with regards to the existence of such a being, other than a modern temple founded and dedicated to his name, in the last years of the twentieth century. But this temple seems to have been on the private property of the person who wrote about Babaji Nagaraj and his book on Kriya Yoga.

It is strange that Babaji Nagaraj was given the name of the original Babaji, only after the mahasamadhi of Paramhansa Yogananda and not while he was alive. If that had been done, it would have been good because Yogananda could have endorsed and blessed the claim that the Babaji of his *Autobiography* and the South Indian Babaji are one and the same person. But this did not happen. What's more, the people of Tamil Nadu also do not know anything of Babaji Nagaraj, while they know plenty about the other Tamil siddhas such as Tirumular, Bogar Nath, Sambandhar, Karur Siddha and Ramlinga Swami. The Kriya Yoga of Babaji Nagaraj also does not seem to match the original Kriya Yoga. However, all yogas are good—whether ancient or invented anew. I make the distinction here only so that people can practice the yoga they intend to practice, and not something else. Insofar as the historical evidence of a personality called Babaji Nagaraj goes, we have to date found no reference or evidence to any saint by that name in the context of any of the Tamil siddhas (known as *cittars* in South India).

---

10 The goddess of learning; she is the informing spirit of the mystic word of learning called *Vach*; hence the name Vach Saraswati.

11 A place in southern India also known as the hill of the *siddhas*.

Statues of the 18 Siddhas at a temple in the town of Cittargiri.
Shiva Goraksha Babaji, leader of the Siddhas,
is at the centre with flowers placed at the base of the pedestal.

Going in search of Babaji Nagaraj, we approached the small town of Cittargiri, a town aptly named for its legacy of the tradition of the eighteen South Indian *cittars*. There we saw statues of the *cittars* but did not find any mention of Babaji Nagaraj. However, in the midst of the eighteen statues there was one at the feet of which we found flowers, thus distinguishing him as the leader and guru. This figure was of Shiva Goraksha Babaji who, as we were told by the temple priest, brought yogic knowledge from the North of India to the South, along with rishis Agastya and Sunder Nath from the Himalayas.

There is an account in Nepal, according to which Shiva Goraksha Babaji once manifested as the spiritual king of the *Nagas*[12]. He is depicted in one of the relics in a samadhi posture, sitting upon a yogic throne made by nine *nagas*. *Naga* means 'cobra of wisdom' and *raja* means 'king'. Thus in certain parts of India and Nepal,

---
12 Serpent beings who are harbingers of changing weather phenomena.

Shiva Goraksha Babaji is also known as the 'Subduer or King of the Cobras of Wisdom'. The temple of the eighteen *cittars* in Cittargiri seems to concur with the possibility that the name 'Nagaraj' may have emerged as Shiva Goraksha Babaji's fame in Nepal spread to South India. So, Nagaraj is merely an epithet for Shiva Goraksha Babaji.

Other than this, there is a second century alchemist by the name of Nagarjuna, a disciple of Shiva Goraksha Babaji, who also hailed from North India. It may be that Nagarjuna's fame reached South India and he was later called 'Nagaraj'.

It is also important to note that if there was such a person named Babaji Nagaraj who was born in Tamil Nadu and lived his life there, his birth is claimed to have been a mortal, human birth and, therefore, he cannot be the Mahavatar, the Immortal Babaji, spoken of in *Autobiography of a Yogi,* and of whom I speak here.

The true Shiv Goraksha Babaji - sitting on the throne of Nagas

CHAPTER 4

THE GORAKSHA MYSTERY

Lord Krishna[1] once asked the revered Garga Rishi, "Which God is Babaji Goraksha Nath? By what mantra may He be invoked and worshipped? And, what type of meditation should be done to invoke the presence of this Being? Please tell me."

Responding to Lord Krishna, Garga Rishi narrated this interesting story:

"In the most ancient of days, all the devas (gods) and rishis (sages) asked Shiva, the Lord God, 'Please tell us about the nature of Goraksha Nath.' They further pleaded, 'Oh Shiva, please tell us how this great, omniscient ascetic Goraksha Nath was born?' Lord Shiva replied, 'The formless Lord Goraksha Nath is *Jyoti-swaroop* (embodiment of light), the void is His mother, and Consciousness His father. Goraksha Nath was born *Aja* (from Himself). Know Goraksha Nath to be Myself. To spread the true Yoga, to end the suffering of humanity, I have incarnated as Goraksha Nath. Any mantra chanted of Goraksha Nath gives one the powers of the soul.' The devas and rishis then asked, 'Oh Lord Shiva, how do we perform the puja[2] of Goraksha Nath and what is the mantra we should recite with it, please tell us all this?' Lord Shiva said, 'Oh devas, now lis-

---
1 An incarnation (avatar) of the God Vishnu, the Purna Avatar whose teachings can be found in the Bhagavad-Gita and the Bhagavata-Purana.
2 'worship', prescribed rituals usually accompanied by the recitation of mantras or shlokas, an important aspect of many forms of yoga, notably Karma and Bhakti Yoga.

ten to the prayer and rituals that should be performed for Goraksha Nath. Visualize his image in your heart, for this type of meditation will give you the siddhis and all spiritual powers for self-realization."

Lord Krishna worshipping Shiva Goraksha Babaji

Then Lord Krishna said, "Oh rishi Garga, the best amongst sages, all glory be to you. What you have narrated about Goraksha Nath has deeply intrigued me and I am very interested to know the process of His meditation." Rishi Garga then told Krishna, "Oh Radhika Nath (Beloved of Radha), listen to the secret mantra and meditation of Goraksha Nath which I shall now tell you."

And so, he goes on to tell Sri Krishna the secret process of the worship and meditation of Shiva Goraksha Babaji.

The Mystery Unveiled

Rishi Garga's narration definitely gives us a clue that, during those times, the Aja (unborn) Krishna/Narayana had drawn upon Himself the veil of his own maya (illusion), and He was asking these questions not only to unveil the mystery of His higher Self and Spirit called 'Shiva Goraksha Babaji' - but also to guide others to worship their own, impersonal, supreme Spirit - the Atman. We must understand that the higher Self of Kalki Maitreya[1] is Krishna, whose higher Self is Shiva Goraksha Babaji. This is insofar as the whole scheme of our human evolution is concerned. So close is the connection between Krishna and Babaji that, sometimes, Lord Krishna is called 'Shambhu Chaitanya' who is Babaji Himself.

This explains the statement of Lahiri Mahasaya: "That who is Krishna is the ancient Babaji Himself."

Babaji is to Krishna, as Shiva is to Vishnu. In the Shiva Mahapurana, Lord Shiva says, "Know Vishnu and Myself to be One." Those who know this are enlightened.

---

[1] The coming avatar of Lord Vishnu, 10th in order.

CHAPTER 5

MEETING THE IMMORTAL BABAJI
The Cosmic Rebirth

The eternal Babaji in His infinite compassion has left behind on this terrestrial plane an infinitesimal portion of His immortal essence. He shall be ever-present to the faithful few, the keepers of the flame, who dare to ignite the message of Kriya Yoga for the self-realization of humanity.

I feel honored to be following the hallowed footsteps of the great yogis and sages who have gone before me in robes of light, gone into the lofty Himalayas in search of the ultimate reality.

On my sojourn to visit this ineffable presence called Babaji, my mind appeared to lose its boundaries and I was unable to tell when my body became my mind and when my mind flowed into my consciousness. The shreds of karma, which composed my body, mind and soul, melted into an awareness, which gave me the import of a realization that at the level of consciousness, matter and mind lie subservient to that consciousness, the true gnosis[1].

This brings to my mind a poem I composed, excerpted from my poetry book *Dewdrops from the Soul*:

---
1 A knowing of reality, without the intervention of mind.

To fill waters from wisdom's spring
Our minds we must to stillness bring
Then our crystal bowl of tranquil mind
Fills with gnosis of supernal kind

Then tamed and tuned to nature's flow
Mind melts into the opal glow
Which radiates from the soul within
Where wisdom's mystic fire is king!

from the poem *Mind Transformation*
by Yogiraj Siddhanath

It was the year 1967, when I began my quest and journey to meet this Great Being. He is the Nameless One, yet people call Him by many names. He is the Visible–Invisible Savior of Mankind; such enigmatic titles seem to baffle the rational mind today. And so I set off on this sacred pilgrimage to the holy of holies.

As I walked into the rarely-accessed reaches of the Himalayas, the very vastness made my mind lose its boundaries, to give way to a knowingness of Babaji's Presence, which seemed to say to me, 'I am everywhere, I am nowhere, and I am now here'. The evening sunset cast its lengthening shadows, the Earth washed by the amber gold of the Sun.

The sunset shades of melting hue
White-maned clouds rolled home
The violet canopies heavenly vault
Melts in the self-same dome

Yogiraj Siddhanath

As the sky darkened, the stars appeared, and the yogis on the mountain-sides lit their evening fires. The stars in the night sky told many a story of the sages of yore. As I lay down to rest on my half-torn sleeping bag, I looked up at the night sky, which is so clear in the Himalayas. There I could see the *Sapta Rishis*[2] the Seven Sages (The stars comprising the Great Bear) so ancient that I wondered who wrote their biographies. Musing to myself, I thought of the antiquity of India's spiritual heritage, where a biography was written about each of the seven stars of the Great Bear (Also known as the Big Dipper). You know, at night, when the sky looms low, God appears to be nearer to our souls, and as I scanned the sky, my eyes fell upon the penultimate star of the Great Bear. This was the primeval sage, Vashishta, who had by him a small star called Arundhati, his faithful wife. And when all the other wives of the Seven Primeval Sages left them, this celestial couple held together in faithfulness. Therefore in India, after every wedding, the married couple has a view of these two, to remind them of the lifelong faithfulness they should have to one another. These subtle observances show that the antiquity of Indian culture originated in the night of prehistory. As I marveled at the depth and insight of the glorious land of India, I soon found myself snoring under the canopy of stars. But wait a minute! Was it me snoring or some wild animal of the bush grunting and groveling for food?

I soon found that although my body was asleep and snoring, my mind was wide awake. This is called a samadhi of sorts, and this was not the first time I had an experience of my body sleeping and my mind being awake. Whatever my state, sleeping or waking, I was still searching for and yearning for the Visible-Invisible Savior.

The location where I was then sleeping was at Rudraprayag. *Prayag* means the holy confluence of two rivers, and the junction of Mandakini and Alaknanda is one such confluence, which is symbolized as flowing from the hoary dreadlocks of Lord Shiva, personified by the mighty Himalayas themselves. This pilgrimage is renowned for the knowledge of music, which Lord Shiva gave to *Deva Rishi*[3] Narada,[4] the celestial sage. Remember, we have now

---

2 'Seven Sages'; they are the informing spirits of the *Sapta Rishi* constellation, also known as Ursa Major.
3 Third in the hierarchical order of *rishis* or sages.
4 A *Deva Rishi* and devotee of Shiva who taught him divine music at Rudraprayag. He is the author of the *Bhakti-Sutras* as given by Lord Shiva.

entered the region of Garhwal, meaning 'land of the gods'. Many yogis and sages have meditated and done *tapas*[5] in these hallowed regions and have been successful in attaining enlightenment.

The Majestic Kedar Nath Mountain

People are intrigued to know how the desire arose in me to meet Babaji. The answer is that the desire is already stored and compressed in the memory banks of the yogi that is born, and when the time is ripe, the desire fructifies into action. But let me clarify that the desire is only realized by the grace of the Divine Guru. And so I carried on my journey, trekking my way to Badrinath, partly by foot and partly hitchhiking. As I gazed upon the lofty Himalayan ranges rising peak after peak, my heart also rose high and soared to salute them.

As a child I was told that the antiquity of the Nath yogis was as old as the Himalayas themselves and that they were the true guardians of

---

5 'Glow' or 'heat', austerity or endurance of extremes, an element of all yogic approaches, since they all involve renunciation and transcendence; in yogic meditation, the act of stewing in one's own pranic energies thereby channeling and storing them.

the Himalayan ranges. Not only this, but so ancient were they, that their physical bodies became petrified rock mountains in time; and for me represented the very mountain I beheld. The great mountain of Kedarnath was the form of Lord Shiva meditating as a diving yogi. So also was the case with the mountain of Tunganath, which means 'strong-armed Shiva'. Then along my sojourn, as I visited Kalpanath, I beheld the dreadlocks of Shiva spread all over the mountain and ravines, a yogi in deep meditation. So each of the lofty Himalayan mountains were a sacred pilgrimage and the symbol of a divine yogi in meditation, frozen in time. Then, there was the Madh Maheshwar representing the mid-belly of Shiva, and Rudra Nath representing His face. These five pilgrimages form what is called the *Panch Kedar*, and also represent the five monumental Nath yogis who were a direct emanation of Lord Shiva Himself. The whole ambience was a deep meditation of which I myself became a part.

The rich aroma of the pine cones was all about me and fallen berries were unwittingly crushed underfoot. A fresh mountain breeze blew through me, bringing its inspiring message that the soul is immortal and the body but a boat to ferry us across the ocean of illusion to self-realization, that we are not a corruptible body but a divine soul.

Excerpt from 'Déjà vu'

In wooded valleys berries crushed
The flavor of the mystic musk
Within me did old memories rise
Devotions to the sunset skies

Forest aroma deep 'n damp
Wild smell of the wooded pines
Oh! The déjà vu of jungle times
Of long past meditations lives

Where in sylvan bowers I sat
Not in this world nor in that
Just in the joy of selfing mirth
The odor of the fragrant earth!

My mind a laughing gurgling stream
Running the bedrocks mossy green
Becomes a calm meandering dream
Flowing into myself serene

With body dead, consciousness live
Expanding in eternal skies
Beyond maya's conditioned dream
The self merging in Self supreme

Yogiraj Siddhanath

The ancient land of India was originally called Bharat, named after the ancient king and grandson of the great *Brahma Rishi*[6] Vishwamitra. Vishwamitra, along with Vashishta, were two of the seven *Sapta Rishis*. The name Bharat has a very mystic meaning. It is the 'land whose people are wedded to the light of the soul', or simply wedded to radiance.

And so I carried on walking and bathing until I reached the pilgrimage of Badrinath, the sacred playground of Shiva and Parvati. It is said in ancient folklore, that the sage Narayana fell in love with the pilgrimage of Badrinath, and wanted to use the place as his own. But since Shiva ignored his request, the sage Narayana took the form of a child lost in the Himalayas. Upon seeing this orphan child, the mother in Parvati awoke and nurtured the child. Then Shiva had compassion and blessed Narayana to stay at Badrinath and use it for his *lila* and meditation. The Lord Narayana and Nara are established in meditation for the welfare of the world. They are Krishna and Arjuna[7] respectively. But esoterically, the divine cosmic being

---

6 A rishi who has reached the final stage of emancipation; a fully enlightened being.
7 One of the five Pandava princes who fought in the *Mahabharata* War; disciple of the *Purnavatar* Krishna whose teachings can be found in the *Bhagavad Gita*.

Krishna Narayana is meditating for the evolution and welfare for Nara, representing the whole of humanity.

Badrinath Temple, dedicated to Lord Narayana, is at a height of 11,398 feet, tucked away in winter amidst the Himalayan snows. The temple stands at the foot of the majestic Neelkantha (meaning 'blue-throated God') Mountain, dedicated to Lord Shiva, which soars to 3,900 feet or more. Its snow-capped peak is usually covered by clouds. Flanked by the two mountains, Sonar Suli and Narayana, on a clear day the Neelakantha peak looks like a snow diamond. When I am there on a clear day, it appears as though Neelakantha as Babaji, Narayana as Krishna, and Nara as Arjuna are standing before me in all their majesty to bless the world.

Here is an excerpt from *Wings to Freedom*:

I tarried at Badrinath a few days to acclimatize. During my stay I used to visit the temple to meditate. In India, as a mark of respect, we circumambulate all the temples except that of Lord Shiva. Such an act is called *pradakshina*. During one of these rounds, I saw a most awe-inspiring painting of the monumental Siddha with his matted dreadlocks covered with snow. Each rudraksha bead of his mala had a hint of snow. Yes, this was he whose photo I had in my underground meditation room in Sinhagad in Pune! This was none other than the majestic Raja Sundar Nath.

I stood in awe, lost in admiration of this divine yogi of the Goraksha Nath lineage. He was recently, in 1924, the *Mahant* (Head) of the Goraksha Nath temple at Gorakhpur, which is of the Dharma Nath sub-sect of Goraksha Nath yogis. Sundar Nath is the same yogi who entered the body of a South Indian cowherd and became the Siddha Tirumular who wrote *Tirumantiram,* the famous treatise on yoga. He is still alive in his *Sanjeevan* body at Alkapuri on the Indo-China border.

The Nath, established in *Svaroop Samadhi*[8], is truly among those

---
8 Also called samadhi with form and *Sanjeevan Samadhi.*

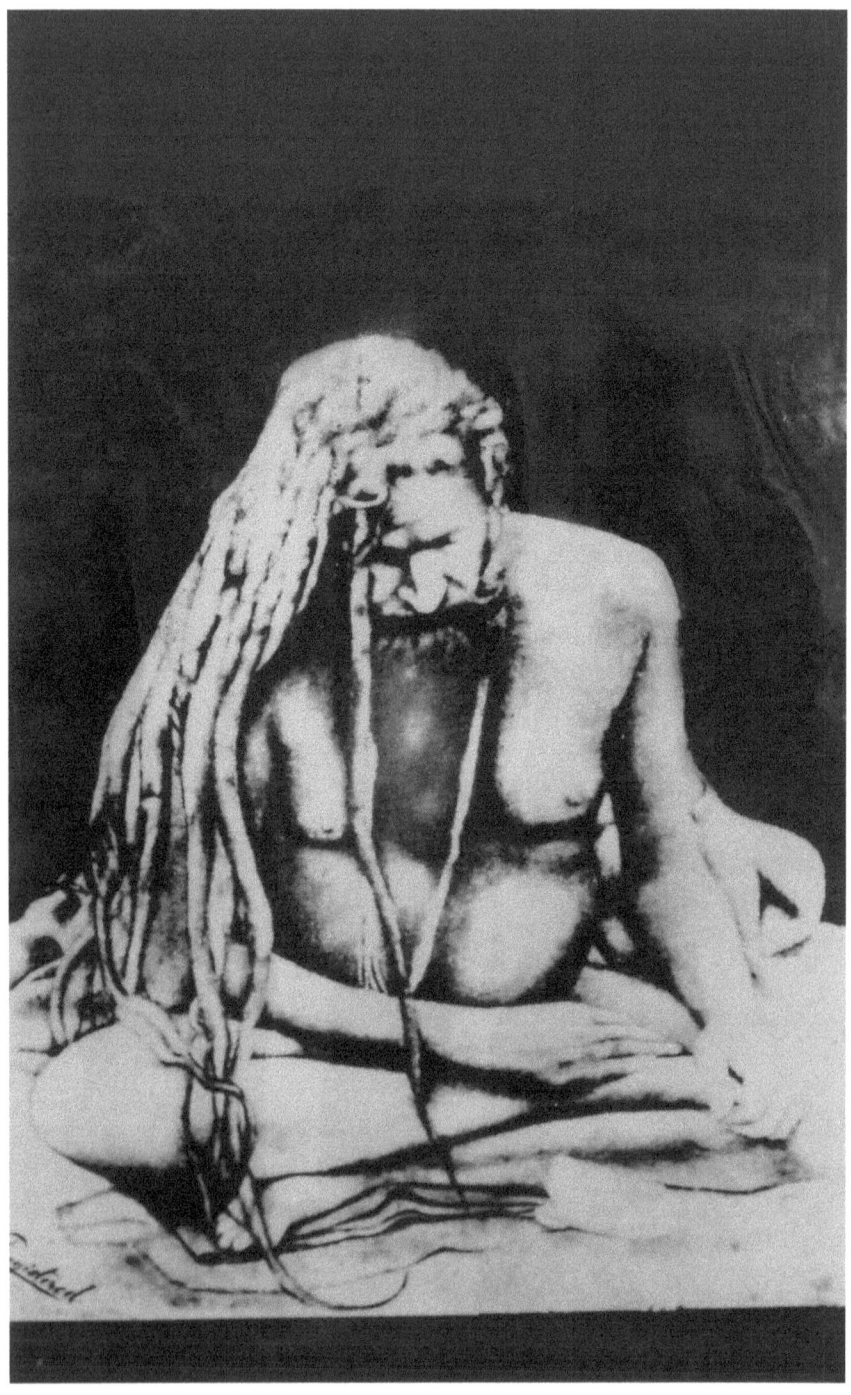

The legendary yogi Raja Sundar Nath, presently immersed in samadhi at Alkapuri, by the Indo-China border

who saved India's spiritual heritage from the fate that befell ancient Egypt, Babylon, China, Tibet, and the Mayan civilization of South America. India is as spiritually alive today as it was 10,000 years ago. It is the spiritual dynamo of the world today, destined to lead the material world to its haven of spiritual truth in the coming new age. Many of these ancient spiritual cultures have long since been dead. Not only this, but from time immemorial such Siddha Nath yogis have been the guardian wall of our humanity and guardians of the Himalayan peaks, according to popular belief. The classic pose of this yogi depicting India's past and present glory threw me into a blissful trance. Here is an ethos where a yogi sacrifices his all in his quest for God, not caring where his next meal is coming from, putting his life on the line. His passion for God consumes his entire life and transforms him into the Divine Superman like Goraksha Nath and other sages who have gone before him in robes of light. He pursues the divine with single-minded purpose. Travelling on foot from Kedarnath to Badrinath, often going hungry, this pilgrim and ascetic gives his all to seek his beloved Lord. The yogi possesses nothing yet owns the world.

Then, I proceeded to walk towards *Charan Paduka* (meaning 'holy sandals'), another holy stop where Rama, the seventh avatara of Vishnu, had rested during his sojourn in the Himalayas. The cave which I was headed to was the *Jhilmilee Gufa*[9], located near the Neelakanteswar (meaning "blue-throated god") mountain. The path that I took was a beaten trail often used by the yogis of those regions. As the climb toward the mystic abode of Babaji became steeper, my awareness became deeper and entered a new dimension, which made me more aware of my consciousness and less of my mind. I seemed to enter another-worldly Utopia[10]; a kind of Shangri-la if you may call it, the original of which is pronounced Shamballah or Sambalpur. Now, the borders between the mind and consciousness disappeared as I trod into an other-worldly dimension. But as

---

9 The name of one of Babaji's caves, tucked away in the Himalayas.
10 A spiritual land, which we in India call Shamballah, also called Shangri-la in which an egalitarian and a happy society live in peaceful co-existence. Shamballah is the land from where the Kalki Avatara is expected to come as the second advent of Christ.

I walked forward, a strong urge made me look back, and lo and behold, I saw a young girl of about twelve to fourteen years of age. She was wearing a *ghagara-chunari* (a colorful skirt, shirt and shawl). This was an unearthly-looking girl with a divine radiance in and about her. She seemed to be from this world, and yet not of it. She stood with such confidence that the world seemed to belong to her, with the vast Himalayan mountains as a backdrop. As I looked at her, I felt as if I were a child of two and I asked her the question, 'Don't you feel afraid here all alone in the Himalayan mountains?'

She smiled at me and again I felt I had become a two-year-old child. I then wondered if I was asking the proper question to the proper person, and my mind opened up to a vision that she was an aspect of divine mother in her *kanya* (girl who has yet to attain puberty) form. Her dark piercing eyes, her cheeks rosy as the Himachal apples and her dark black hair flowing over her shoulders gave me to know that she was indeed the Divine Mother. But I could not bring myself to believe this. Anyway, I continued to speak and asked her, 'Do you know the way to Babaji's cave?' As though she had not heard, she responded indirectly saying, 'Everything will be alright with you. Be happy, like me. See, I am happy'. So I thought to myself that if she's not bothering to answer my question why should I bother to ask her about the road? I flung my cares to the breeze and said to myself, 'Let me go where the breeze takes me'. Well if nothing really matters, why not go where the breeze takes you. So I went in the direction the breeze was taking me. I must be out of my mind. I had no context of the relation between my body, mind and consciousness. I was certainly not in a state of devotion, emotion or any other rational state. As I have tried to explain, when the mind loses its boundaries it also loses the limitation between the past and present lives and the barriers between the body, the mind and the soul. This is why Babaji is 'The Eternal Now'. When one is blessed by his presence, past, present and future time melts into Now.

After I took a few steps I looked around and the Himalayan maiden had vanished from my sight. I felt that I had missed an opportunity to touch Her blessed feet and get Her blessings for my onward journey to meet Babaji. This certainly rang a bell in my mind that Babaji was always accompanied by Mataji, like Shiva and Shakti. And this was like a precursor and a good omen indicating that I would meet the incomprehensible Babaji in the near future. I had been without food for almost three days. However, my whole system and body chemistry was fine-tuned to higher dimensions. I remember that after this incident, another young girl came and gave me chewing gum from between the bark of a tree. And as I chewed this latex-like substance, my breath, which was heavy, became light, the tiredness in my limbs vanished and I was fresh again. This second young girl was an assistant to the Divine girl-goddess I had met before her, which truly helped me realize the significance of the first interaction.

It was only after the Divine Mother disappeared that it dawned on me that She was an aspect of the Goddess Mataji who was guiding my footsteps to the cave of Babaji. I felt very exhilarated and remorseful at the same time for not having had more of Her blessings. However, I carried on my ascent to the cave of Babaji, I knew not where.

My footsteps took on a certain momentum as I walked with a rhythmic gait. I became stronger in my conviction that Babaji is the veritable Lord Shiva Himself. With beads of perspiration on my forehead trickling down over my eyes, I felt overheated in the cold surrounding snow. I was physically exhausted, but my spirit was enthused and fired by an incomprehensible delight. I saw the whole Himalayan range from the lower mountains near the cave. The view of the mountains was breathtaking and the great panorama of the chain of mountains made me feel that I was observing the laughter of Shiva. Each peak was like His white teeth glistening in the oblique rays of the Sun.

This was not an ordinary journey, I was jolted into realizing. This was a pilgrimage to the holy of holies, where all the souls of the world unite to meet in God's love. Did this mean that I was called off-season to some conclave where the other masters were not present?

Exhausted, I lay supine for a breather on the gentle slopes below the cave, and imagined myself gliding off the slope into eternal space above the snow-capped mountains beyond the clouds. At the same time, the Sun went behind the clouds and it became chilly and dark, with my astral body floating well beyond my physical body lying on the grassy slopes. After sometime, with my eyes closed, I beheld another light and I could not make out what it was.

'Ah! The Sun has come back,' I thought to myself.

To my thoughts a voice responded, 'Indeed, if you think it is the Sun, it is'.

I saw a great shimmering light filling the whole area of my consciousness, as well as outer space. I saw the lightless light, the spiritual aura. The spiritual feel of the whole scene was of another world.

It may be Babaji. It may not be Babaji. Who it is, I cannot say.

I felt it was not proper for me to be supine on my back, so I willed my lifeless body with great effort to turn on my stomach. I then did the *Shastanga namaskara* (prostration on the ground and joining both hands in salutation). I was lost to myself, in Him and did not know what to make of the whole situation.

Lost in wonder and in awe, I asked Him, 'Who are you?' I asked the Nameless Being, this Great Presence. And from this question an ode sprung forth like a fountain.

Who art thou? I know thee not
And yet I am of thee
I cannot comprehend thee, Lord
Thou Emperor of Divinity

I sit and melt in silence
Of thy love, O infinite
Make me thy truth
Make me thy love
Eternal Lord of Light

Yogiraj Siddhanath

He said, 'Whoever thou thinkest me to be, that I am for thee'. My innermost intuitions told Me that though my ego was limited to certain deities like Shiva, Ganapati, Christ[11] and Buddha[12], He was beyond the Christ, the Ganapati and the Buddha because He was, and is, the *Non-Being Essentiality*. In our limited understanding and rational thinking, we fail to realize that because He is so vast, He is nothing. Nevertheless He is the source of everything. Even if we were to take everything away from this Great Sacrifice called Babaji, He would still remain complete.

> *Om purnamadaha purnamidam*
> *Purnat purna mudachyatae*
> *Purnasya purnamadaya*
> *Purnameva vashisyatae*

'

The ultimate formula of high math was given in this beautiful Sanskrit verse. This is not a figment of imagination, but stands true, the bona fide test of true mathematics. 'If from the complete, the complete is taken out, the complete still remains complete.'

This is what He was! I could not capacitate His voltage. So I

---

11 The seventh degree initiate; the world teacher; an *avatar* such as Kalki, Maitreya, Matsyendra Nath, Avalokiteshwara, Vithoba (the man crucified in space).

12 Term designating Gautama, the founder of Buddhism, who lived in the 6th century BCE.

saw Him from my past life associations with Him, and my lips took the proper shape and my voice said, 'Shiva Goraksha Babaji'. No sooner had I said this, than His voice rang out in the firmament of my heart and in the surrounding mountains, '*Tathastu, Tathastu!*' (So be it!)

The connection with Shiva Goraksha Nath was the memory in my super-conscious mind. He wanted to pull my desire out of my own memory bank so that the word would come from me and not from Him, as to who He was, who this Eternal Now was. He would not comment. As Shiva Goraksha Babaji has gone beyond the 'Rings-Pass-Not' with no possibility of His return to our world cycle, His being with us on the planet is a stupendous mystery. The Rings-Pass-Not is the incomprehensible spiritual attainment of celestial beings, who have broken the light barrier and gone beyond the relative rings of time and space to live in the Eternal Now, never to return to this terrestrial sphere, for their work is way beyond our creation. Babaji remaining behind in an infinitesimal body is the greatest enigma in the history of humankind.

Babaji's blessings to make me utter the words from my mouth as to who He was, was definitely a past life connection where He wanted to pull out from my memory bank my karmic past lives with His non-karmic Presence. There He waited for an answer from me.

I said, 'Who art Thou? I know Thee not and yet I am of Thee'.
He said, 'Who you think Me to be, that I am to thee! I Am That I Am!'

He was non-being, egoless, the formless, eternal unborn Self who has no identity, not as far as any human understanding is concerned.

As I lay down on the slope of a mountain outside the cave, I found a strange wave running from the top of my head to my toes. It was a cold and warm sort of current, you know. It was a cold wave coming up from the bottom of my feet to the top of my head, and a warm wave washing my body from the top of my head to my toes.

Then the process reversed itself. It was as though I was doing the *sushumna* Kriya Yoga breathing and being cleansed.

I thought after meditating ten to twelve hours daily, a person's *nadis*[13] would be cleansed and he would be pure to receive Him. In my own voice He replied, 'This is true, but you have to go to a higher level of samadhi, which you have not achieved as yet. You will be given this divine state of realization due to past good *samskaras*[14] and karma. This preparation is therefore necessary for brain and body'.

As I moved out of my body after the experience of hot and cold, as I was totally oblivious to time, I had no idea how long the process lasted. There was no time or space continuum. I was just absorbed by this other-worldly bliss and light of Babaji's grace. I do not know where my eyes were or what is meant by 'eyes'. I moved out of my physical body and expanded into the emotional body. Then after some time the emotional body expanded into the mental body. Then the mental body expanded into soul consciousness. My crystal soul dissolved and expanded into awareness, which was boundless. It seemed like I was undergoing a gentle series of transformative implosions to expand the essence of my being!

The happening was the ascent of consciousness from grosser sheaths of matter to the finer ones, where the involuted consciousness decided to evolve from the physical body composed of the Earth element to the etheric, then to the emotional body, composed of the emotions and feelings. Of course the feelings and emotions should be sufficiently purified, and desires must be fulfilled in that body for one's consciousness to withdraw from the emotional body into the mental sheath, composed of all its thought forms and mental

---

13 'Conduit', one of 72,000 subtle-astral channels along or through which the life-force (prana) circulates; the three most prominent being the *ida nadi, pingala nadi,* and *sushumna nadi.*

14 'Activator', the subconscious impression left behind by each act of volition, which, in turn, leads to renewed psychomental activity; the countless *samskaras* hidden in the depth of the mind are ultimately eliminated only in *Asamprajnata Samadhi* .

processes.

This yoga took place within me through a series of gentle implosions. And it is very vividly etched in my consciousness that each time I transited, say from the physical to the emotional body, my awareness expanded, and then as I moved out from my astral/emotional to my mental/thought-body, my consciousness expanded. When I went from my mental body to my intuitive body of bliss, my consciousness was expanded to such a great extent that I was able to participate in the dynamics of existence and feel myself in the birds, the trees, the clouds, the sky. The Earth, the planets, the stars and the galaxies were me and were breathing my breath and prana. The Sun's rays were me. There was this vast unity in diversity. It was only then that I was able to capacitate the messages given me by the Nameless Being whom the world knows as Babaji, whom I, due to my past associations with Him, know as Shiva Goraksha Babaji.

All was within me and I was within the all. My true self, the conscious seer had retraced itself from the grosser sheaths of matter to the subtlest robe of light. This salvaging of a crystal consciousness from the trammels of the senses was in that moment of time happening by the Grace of Babaji, and now, although I perceived divinity in nature, it was still through divine mind, a state of *Savikalpa Samadhi*[15]. And then, as I have mentioned before, due to the very Presence of Babaji, who was the *Non Being Essentiality*, I myself transcended the subtle film of the body of radiant light, the *Anandamayee Kosh*[16], which became a shining star involuting upon itself. I left my star-gate as my spirit expanded and lost itself in the ineffable ecstasy of the *Non Being Essentiality*, where in the Everything was the Nothing and the Nothing was the Everything, All was the absolute and blissful consciousness of bliss; calm, undisturbed, the supreme state of the *Nirvikalpa Samadhi*, also

---

15 State of ecstasy with attributes of human perception.
16 The intuitional body of bliss; the highest of the five 'envelopes' (*Koshas*) covering the self.

called the *Asamprajnata Samadhi*[17] in yogic parlance.

Later, as this soul returned after the experience of both His form and formless Self, I felt, 'Oh Babaji! The universe, a bubble in my consciousness, my consciousness a nothing in Thy Nothingness! Such is Thine ineffable majesty, no mortals, no angels, can describe. Oh Thou highest of the high, of the Angelic hierarchy of the Heavenly Host. Thou art all the heavenly host at once and yet beyond them. Only the Supreme Lord God may comprehend Thee, Shiva Goraksha Babaji, Thou about whom naught may be said!'

His message was not in words. It was in photons of light. His message came to me in shafts of light, in photons, sparks, whatever you call it. I do not know, I do not know the words, but it came to me so fast that volumes were encapsulated in those shafts, in those photons of light, the message to humanity. The message of my serving humanity, becoming the servant of humanity, which is the most honored thing that could happen to me. My self-imposed karma encoded in my genes and replicated in my DNA, was being released to match this experience and support it, but the divine experience far surpassed my good karma. It was pure blessings of the Great One.

It is important to know that I was receiving this information in my super-consciousness, without the participation of my mind. I can say my analytical mind lay subservient to my super-conscious *avastha* (state of being). A great lesson was learned that the analytical mind was an inferior instrument for education and should only be used in daily life for absorbing practical knowledge. The true means for acquiring divine knowledge is by vigilant consciousness, which absorbs true wisdom and gnosis.

And when I come to describing His form, I would say that no words would do justice to even get near the shadow or imagination of His appearance. But I am making a humble effort

---

17 The yogic ecstasy of expanded consciousness, equivalent to the *Vedantic* ecstasy of *Nirvikalpa Samadhi*.

to present before you what I absorbed of Him with my mindless mind. And out of the lightless light He came, manifesting Himself as *the lightning standing still!* His hair touched His heels and was ablaze with the radiant fire of heaven. His countenance shone with an unbearable dazzling splendor, which no mortal or celestial eyes could perceive without shutting. This experience made me express the following words:

> *If at one moment time and place*
> *The sunburst of a countless suns occurred*
> *This would scarce suffice to show Thy shadow*
> *Oh Lord what must be Thy light*
>
> Yogiraj Siddhanath

His eyes were the fathomless Ocean of Compassion, which after seeing, no being could help but drown in. But it was not possible to see His eyes with our eyes. We could only partake of them and be them. Here too the radiance of the light that emanated from those eyes, gave the message of His ever being in far country in the boundless land and yet simultaneously present within us. His eyes had a quality of being so far away and yet so close that they felt as though they were our eyes looking at Him; they sang the poetry of creation from dawn to dusk. Yet I saw in a fraction of a second that they contained the nothingness of eternity far beyond the hue and cry of humanity. He is the Silent Watcher who broods over His infant humanity. I could never, in all my life, come to terms with the paradox of His eyes reciting the poetry in creation and yet containing the nothingness of infinity beyond creation.

Even with closed eyes, His smile appeared grave, and the gravity of His lips appeared to smile. We could see both these indications in His smile and yet His facial expression was beyond both the gravity of His smile and the smile of His gravity. The word gravity comes from the word 'guru' which means, 'the weighty one', and when the weight reaches a critical mass, it transforms the fabric of space-time into the soul star, the gravity of which causes one's soul-star[18] to

---

18 The *Kutastha Chaitanya* seen in the third eye; one's individual star-gate, penetrating which, one enters from *Savikalpa Samadhi* to the *Nirvikalpa Samadhi* state.

involute upon itself, and passing through itself, enter the liberated Cosmic Consciousness.

'Can we but measure in our minds or gauge Him by our depth of heart? In Him the Lord's own Presence manifests beyond all human thought'. You see, here I have tried to describe the joyful gravity on the face of the King of Kings. It is gravity that breaks down causation, space and time and takes the divine yogi beyond the Rings-Pass-Not of all relative bondage and limitations. So the smile of gravity on His face showed to me that He was the supreme Satguru who broke down the mayic fabric of space and time to take divine beings through the Rings-Pass-Not to the land of no return. Gravity is the factor that takes one through the star-gate. The gravity of His smile held the promise of liberating all souls through their own star-gate of the third eye.

His body, if we may call it so, appeared wet, as though He had had a bath in the Alaknanda River, and yet was dry. Medium height and slender stature, both of which were lost in the splendor of His aura, He wore a black buck skin with a *kamandalu* (water vessel) in His hand. I perceived that His feet were not touching the ground, but were a few inches above it. As my consciousness flowed into His infinite Consciousness, I felt the oneness of all Creation in Him. And yet, beyond Creation His Consciousness was the Fathomless Deep. As I lost myself to myself in Him, the deathless fragrance of His body told me the tale of His immortality.

Even in samadhi, I was thunderstruck, dumbfounded by His spiritual majesty. His Consciousness expanded beyond the seven infinities, and my consciousness expanded to merge in an infinitesimal part of His; I was lost and died unto eternity.

Babaji Goraksha, the greatest Raja yogi who ever walked the Earth, in His compassion for humanity created the science of Hatha Yoga as a stepping-stone, making thereby an easier approach to Raja Yoga. Let not people of feeble minds interpret and limit Shiva

Goraksha Nath as a Hatha yogi alone.

My journeys entailed many a solitary expedition to places and caves graced by the most magnificent presences. Travelling and meditating alone had its rewards of a ceaseless river of peace flowing through me, and clarifying my mind to visualize and experience higher realms of consciousness, which I would not have been able to avail of myself with more people around. Even at that time, I was not ready, not capacitated, but due to His grace, I was able to get this experience. This mighty Being called the Nameless One, the Lightning Standing Still, was the head, the heart, the seed, and the soul of undying Knowledge, spread from eternity to eternity, beyond infinity. He could not be understood, only experienced.

Babaji plays with causation, space and time as a child plays with soap bubbles. If He were to smile in His innocence, He could shatter the world. Babaji as I saw Him, truly was, is and ever shall be, the Lightning Standing Still.

It is difficult to relate the inner experience. It seemed like a vast expansion of inner space, in a different dimension. To me it was like a limitless nothingness, so blinding and bright that it appeared dark, like a massive, benevolent black hole, the likes of *Mahankala Shiva*. It was so intense that it became very, very soft, but I felt I was merging into this Divine Being Shiva Goraksha Nath. As you know, absolute light is total darkness that is the nature of light. I know that it is difficult to comprehend this kind of celestial light.

That's why we have known that describing it is a futile task, which doesn't even do a shadow of justice to the experience. So when I flash into light, it is as if there is an explosion of a countless supernovae in front of my eyes. He just let my awareness, my state of being, play its role and confirm that it was true. This light is always there when a person is totally dissolved into the Eternal Now, called God. Babaji is not even an *avatar*, not even a divine being. He is beyond that, a total Isness of the

Zero not Zero, Non-Being, the Formless One, and more. The more I talk about Him, the more of a mess I get into, as the King is beyond all words.

The Shiva Goraksha Babaji whose experience I had, is the veritable Lord Shiva Himself. He is the Consciousness of the Universe. He must not be confused with Babaji Nagaraj, a South Indian saint, or the various yogis going around today with the name of Babaji.

Due to my past *samskaras* I experienced Him as Shiva Goraksha Babaji. However, each time I go deeper into my consciousness, the truth is that I experience Him more as the 'Non Being Essentiality', fathomless and incomprehensible. As a result of this life-transforming experience, I was blessed and empowered by the Great One, and at His behest, my service to humanity crystallized gradually into my mission, which may be stated in three parts.

1. The first is that it is meditated to the furthering of human awareness by my initiating people into Mahavatar Babaji's Kriya Yoga, through *Shaktipat*[19].

2. The second part is dedicated to serving humanity as my larger self by giving my unified consciousness experience as *Shivapat*[20]. By this experience, people can realize the unity of human consciousness, to live in peaceful coexistence.

3. The third part, is devoted to making people's lives a celebration, by teaching them healing enlightenment techniques through *pranapat*[21] (breathing through their breath). All these ways and means lead us to Earth Peace Through Self Peace.

---

19 'Descent of *Shakti*', one of the three blessings *Satgurunath* bestows upon his disciples for their spiritual progress; the awakening of the dormant *kundalini* energy of a disciple.

20 'Shiva's grace', the *satguru*, as consciousness, 'awares' himself into the mind-disciple, transforming that mind into his own consciousness to the degree of the disciple's receptivity to his consciousness.

21 A term coined by Yogiraj Siddhanath to denote the grace of a *satguru*, when he breathes through the breath of the disciple.

The receiving of these techniques and the Declaration of Human Rights, after the experience with Shiva Goraksha Babaji, left me in a daze. After entering my body gradually, I was no longer in that higher state of *Nirvikalpa Samadhi*. As I came back to my own original state and *sadhana*, the voiceless voice seemed to say to me, 'Make your own equation, work out your own karma, and be your own enlightenment!'

CHAPTER 6

MY CHILDHOOD BOND WITH BABAJI

The revelation of the identity of Babaji I am giving here is not a matter of mere speculation, but one brought about by my personal experience and subsequent realization of this supernal Being. It is by His grace alone that I offer this information so that those sincere seekers thirsty for spiritual progress may know more about the truth of His invisible, yet ever manifest Presence. Those who yearn with the eyes of spirit shall see; those who don't shall never see. The Lord of the world is humble and never forces Himself on others but waits for them to take the first step and then showers them with His grace.

I have been aware from childhood that I was born with the blessings of Shiva Goraksha Babaji. It was not until after my deep and subtle connection with Babaji, that I discovered that the sanctum sanctorum of our family temple in Gwalior was dedicated solely to this immortal Being. My grandfather had built this temple after he had been blessed with a son, i.e., my father. The sanctum of this temple had been built in honor of Shiva Goraksha Babaji, and the temple itself in the name of his disciple, king Guga Nath. Our family satguru Guga Nath Chauhan addressed Shiva Goraksha Babaji as 'Guru Maharaja'—the same deathless Babaji, who is still alive through Ages in the vastness of the Himalayan ranges.

My mother told me that just before my birth, she was given *vibhuti,* the sacred ash from a fire ceremony held at our ancestral temple in Gwalior. She kept this sacred ash safely in her trinket box and since she could not eat much food during her pregnancy, she would fortify her diet by drinking the sacred ash that she diluted with water. Every Monday, she would go to the temple at the Gwalior palace and partake in the ceremonies there. She believed my birth was blessed and ordained by Babaji. For years, she had studied astrology and used to tell me that I would be a yogi. She often reminded me that as I was born on the 10th of May in 1944, my stars were positioned in a manner that I was bound to meditate and lead a spiritual life of a householder yogi, like the great kriya master, Gyanavatar Sri Yukteshwar with whom I share my birthday. She had also predicted my going to far-off lands to teach this timeless science of Kriya Yoga.

Many saints and astrologers had also predicted my birth. They had announced that a boy would be born into a royal family and that he would become a yogi. They often visited my grandfather and spent long hours holding discourses with him on matters of philosophy, yoga and astrology. They told him that his grandson, though born into royal luxury, would ultimately forsake material riches and follow the path of renunciation. They had also predicted that only later in life, would his work be appreciated as a contribution to yoga and to the welfare of human kind. They prophesied that he would spread *Sanatana Dharma* (Eternal Truth) in its true essence, without the religious and ritualistic ceremonies, for the benefit of humanity.

Later during school and college days, my meditations became deeper and through them, I heard whispers of my soul telling me that my future lay neither in academics nor in the world of material rewards; it lay in gaining yogic awareness. All along, I felt and saw Babaji's guiding presence, as if preparing me for the experience I had when I turned twenty-three in 1967 at Badrinath - Lord Vishnu's shrine in the Himalayas. Gradually, I began renouncing the affluent lifestyle into which I had been born. I have since been leading an utterly simple life. The result of this natural weaning away from material wants has been a deep, inner peace of mind. This inner tranquility is the result of Babaji's presence within me.

In this way, my life's work of imparting Babaji's evolutionary science of Kriya Yoga to truth-seekers across the world was foreshadowed by the events of my early life. I was guided and blessed throughout my youth by this immortal Sage, until my meetings with Him in the Himalayas, where I was transformed by His Divine Presence.

The Ocean of Endless Compassion

Despite having met Babaji, and the many blessings He has bestowed upon me, I am dumbstruck when asked to paint an accurate portrait of Him. I find it difficult to find any one or more words that can do adequate justice to 'Who' or 'What' He is.

Suffice to say that He is the Being about Whom naught can be said. How can words, limited by thought, describe a limitless Being? How can a drop of water describe the ocean? He is, after all, the 'Ocean of Endless Compassion', the very 'Isness' of Being, spoken of in parables and mysteries by saints and sages of yore. And still, like a sculptor with faulty tools, I must endeavor, through insufficient words, to give an account of this lofty Being born before the beginning of time. A poetic tribute to Babaji:

From *Reality*

That all pervading Consciousness
Of stillness through eternity
Must of necessity proclaim
Its ultimate reality

Composed of nothing, yet of which
All else is sure composed
He stands supreme beyond all dreams
Eternally reposed

Whose one dream atom
Doth our universe contain
Its myriad worlds and planets
He doth orderly maintain

To this everlasting truth of love
This infinite divinity
Countless creations homage pay
Throughout His own eternity

        Yogiraj Siddhanath

Babaji is the dynamic energy of our three-dimensional world and the Consciousness of the Absolute, with His center everywhere and circumference nowhere.

His Divine Play of Consciousness, known only to Him, is paradoxical in the sense that both His dynamic and potential energies are simultaneously enacted as well as embodied. He *is* the Lightning, and yet He holds it in His hand. This is the greatest anomaly known to humankind, praised by ancient sages as the Divine *Lila*[1] of Shiva and Shakti.

Now there, and gone within a flash, yet never having changed His place, Babaji is everywhere and nowhere at the same time. He is veritably 'The Lightning Standing Still'.

Babaji remains in the universe for the whole lifespan of its creation, sacrificing Himself to assist in the evolution of all sentient and non-sentient beings. He is the cause of the ceaseless process of the involution of spirit into matter, and the evolution of spirit from matter. This sacrifice is far beyond the comprehension of not only mortal man, but even that of celestial beings and the gods. He is, therefore, also called *Mahabinishkaran*[2] or 'The Great Sacrifice'.

---

1 The play of the Divine Mother as *Maya*.
2 'The Great Sacrifice', the author refers to Shiva Goraksha Babaji, the highest Be-ness of Divinity, who explodes Himself to enter the atoms of all sentient and non-

In His unfathomable compassion, Babaji has left behind a finite portion of His infinite Consciousness to evolve humanity into the likeness of divinity. In countless explosions of supernovae, He has infused every atom of creation with His spirit of livingness, wisdom and truth to redeem not only humankind, but also all life and matter, to its pristine state of Consciousness. This spark of Babaji's Divine Isness is the soul-seed of spiritual knowledge that, through individual effort, may be cultivated and expressed as Divine Consciousness.

Not only is He the seed of Divine Consciousness but, Babaji, the Heart of Divinity throbbing in Humanity, has imparted to humankind the science of Kriya Yoga. This is the process through which wayward man, lost in materialism, may reclaim his birthright as an immortal soul and return to his home of infinite being, knowledge and bliss. It is through the persistent practice of Kriya Yoga that one may flower into the likeness of his own divinity. This has been the salvation of mankind time and time again, age after age.

---

sentient beings and evolves humanity and creation to divinity. As the ceaseless sacrifice continues, this divinity gives completely of itself and yet remains complete. This Divine enigma is beyond the scope of our humanity and gods to understand.

CHAPTER 7

BABAJI - ANCIENT ORIGINS

Shiva Goraksha Babaji is the name that was enlightened to me during my vision in the Himalayas of the great Sage of All Ages. At other places, He goes by various names such as Babaji, Goraksha Nath, Gorakh Nath, Korrakh Nath, Tryambak Baba, Mahashiva Baba, the King, The Great Sacrifice, and so on and so forth. I have also added to Him certain names which arose from within me, such as The Lightning Standing Still, The Sage of All Ages, The *N*on Being Essentiality, and finally, His name is synonymous with Lord Shiva Himself called, 'The Everywhere And The Nowhere'.

This is the celestial hierarchy of the nine Lords of divine light called the Nav Naths. The first is Shiva Goraksha Babaji as Lord Shiva (the Consciousness of the Universe). Then Udai Nath, who is Parvati, the feminine energy of the universe. The third is Kartikeya-Alakh Nath (the centripetal-inflowing evolutionary vortex of creation), and the fourth is Matsyendra Nath[1] (he who throws the cosmic veil of maya, then liberates all souls from this great illusion). The fifth is Shel Nath (who signifies Vishnu, pervader and preserver of creation by infusing in it His Consciousness), and the sixth is Chowrangee Nath (the holder of the nectar of the Moon which gives immortality). Next comes Satya Nath (as Brahma, the creator of the mind of the universe), and then

---

[1] 'Fish Lord' an early *Nath* and *Mahasiddha*, who founded the *Yogini-Kaula* school of *tantra* and who implored Shiva to give him a disciple more advanced than himself; the guru of Goraksha Nath on the earthly plane yet His disciple in the celestial plane.

Achalachambu Nath (who signifies time as Adishesha, the serpent of infinity; there are seven infinities in a day of God's creation), and Kanthad Nath (who signifies Ganesh, the outflowing centrifugal force in Brahma's creation). These are the Sages of the Fire Mist and belong to the seventh, eighth and ninth degrees of initiation.

The Gaatha
In Glory of Shiva Goraksha Babaji

Deathless splendor fearless bold
Goraksha the living lightning holds
Savior of gods and humankind
Liberates them from the karmic grind

The son of Shiva and Parvati
Goraksha in Ganesha Goshti
Being Shiva Himself in formless form
Taught Ganesha the samadhi of divinity

From your sacred fire did You take
The potent ashes of your dhuni[2]
And give it to Vishnu and Brahma
Creation to again remake

You battled the Goddess of Hingalaaja
And freed her from mayic mirage
To Datta[3] you gave his mantra as draum
Enlightened him to its origin from Om

---

2 A sacred fire lit by the Nath yogis to demarcate their power centers of meditation (*Dhuna*).
3 A short epithet for the yogi Dattatreya.

Hanumana and Bhima at territory war
You pacified both and settled the score
First testing Arjuna by killing the boar
Then gifting him with the Gandiva bow

To Mary the gift of Christ You bestowed
In Gabriel's apparel You were clothed
It is written in the books of Dabisthana[4]
To the Prophet You gave knowledge of dhyana

Shiva born the disciple of Macchendra Yogi
Took the name of Goraksha Mahayogi
Steered Macchendra off the mayic tryst
Illumined and melted his karmic mist

Desires for golden palace by Bharthari
You fulfilled in the incarnation of Lahiri
Chowrangee disciple of Goraksha Ishwara
Reincarnated as Yogi Yukteshwar

The glories of Krishna did Meera sing
But her life and living to Goraksha bring
He did Alam Prabhu's ignorance efface
And showed to him Goraksha's God-own face

Kabir was born as Yogi Sri Chandra
Then Lahiri the conqueror of Indra,
Vikramaditya was your disciple true
Born as Siddha Nath, Kriya work to do

---

[4] An ancient book on mysticism written by a Kashmiri scholar Moshan Fani.

Irradiant Lord beyond death and grave
To Ramananda the joy of Rama you gave
To Kabir the Kriya Yoga of prana
To Nanak you gave the true Sat-nam[5]

The king of mystics was Gyan Nath
Initiated by brother Nivritti Nath
Who in turn was blessed by Gahni Nath
Your kundalini disciples on yogic path

In Gorakpur was Yogananda born
He was chosen for the yogic norm
Sent by Sri Yukteshwar to the west
To spread Kriya Yoga and to do his best

Yogiraj Siddhanath

Ancient Origins (Texts, Mythology and Legend)

The different ancient texts have referred to Goraksha Nath variously as Lord Shiva, The *Trimurti*, or even beyond the relative aspects of The *Trimurti*. According to this reference, that He is equivalent to or even beyond the manifested forms of The *Trimurti*, namely Brahma, Vishnu, and Shiva, is asserted in the Shastras (science), which states, "Guru Gorakh Nath is the supreme manifestation of Divinity. The shastras tell stories in which the great trinity (Brahma, Vishnu and Maheshwar) seek His grace in times of difficulty."

The *Trimurti* have descended from the Supreme and have sacrificed Themselves to operate in the universe of relativity. They are the universe but choose to enact the drama of creation, preservation and destruction for the salvation and evolution of humankind and all kind.

Shiva, Vishnu and Brahma are hierarchical offices occupied by ever enlightened Presences descended from the Divine

---

5   The true name, usually referred to as Omkar.

Consciousness to rule and to run smoothly the inner government of our universe. These Presences therefore limit themselves to the laws of nature and the three gunas[6] in order to operate those laws of nature. They are hence incarnate divinities who are assisting in the process and growth of all sentient and non-sentient beings. The ancient texts say that Shiva Goraksha Babaji is beyond the consciousness of the *Trimurti*. This means that Babaji has transcended the three gunas of *satva*, *raja* and *tama* corresponding to electrons, protons and neutrons respectively, of which the world of relativity is made. Hence in the continuum-consciousness sense, He is beyond the self imposed limited consciousness of Brahma, Vishnu and Shiva who have accommodated themselves in order to operate these laws and rule the inner government of our world for the progress of humanity.

There are allusions in Vedas[7] and Puranas[8] to the great protective aspect of the personality of Babaji Goraksha Nath. The Lalitpur Purana and Brahmanda Purana both describe Him as the Divine 'Yogiraj[9]' living in perfect bliss in the world of the great winds called 'Mahadyuti' with celestial yogis around Him. In the forty-second chapter of the *Kedar Khanda*, part of the *Skanda Purana*, Lord Shiva tells His spouse Parvati that Goraksha Nath lives in 'Gorakshya Ashram', which is recognized as the holiest of the places. In the seventh chapter of the Shiva Purana there are verses in which Brahma calls Gorakh Nath the incarnation of Lord Shiva. The *Goraksha Gita* presents an episode where Indrayani, the queen of the gods, requests Brihaspati, the guru of the gods, to go to Gorakh Nath and beseech Him to help bring her husband Indra back on the throne of the heavens. Accordingly, these ancient references prove without any shadow of doubt the antiquity of Goraksha Nath, and his oneness with Lord Shiva himself – all Goraksha Nath.

---

6 'quality', refers to any of the three primary constituents of nature (*prakriti*): *tamas* (the principle of intertia), *rajas* (the dynamic principle), and *sattva* (the principle of lucidity).

7 'Knowledge', the body of sacred wisdom found in the four Vedic hymnodes that form the source of Hinduism: Rig-Veda, Yajur-Veda, Sama-Veda, and Atharva-Veda; also the collective name for these hymnodies.

8 'Ancient', often referring to the ancient spiritual literature of India dealing with royal genealogy, cosmology, philosophy, and ritual; there are eighteen major and many minor works of this nature.

9 'King of Yogis', a title of exaltation and praise granted to a spiritual Master.

In the Trivandram edition of Gorakshanath's composition *Maharth Manjari*, He introduces Himself in the following manner: "The perfect Mahadeva (great god, an epithet for Shiva) is my father and the great Matsyendra Nath my teacher (in actual fact, Shiva Goraksha Babaji was and is still the divine Guru of even Matsyendra Nath). Those who know about me call me Gorakh Nath and those who know me call me Maheshworananda (The Blissful Supreme; Shiva)." The ancient text *Goraksha Stotra* contains verses in which Lord Krishna and Rukmini sing His praises, thus further establishing His antiquity and His purported immortality. The ancient text S*hree Nath Tirthawali* refers to Gorakpur as the principal pilgrimage location in the east. On the northern point of this sanctified region rests the shrine of Babaji Goraksha Nath. According to this text, in the 'Treta yug' (considered by Sanatana Dharma to be a prehistoric time period), Guru Gorakh Nath was beseeched to come and bless Lord Rama, the seventh Avatara of Vishnu, during his coronation. The Supreme Guru was however deeply absorbed in samadhi. Hence His disciples, as a mark of honor to Lord Rama, brought prasad[10] from Shiva Goraksha Babaji as His holy blessings.

According to *Shiva Mahapurana*, Shiva said that he was inexorably connected to Vishnu; "All of you except Pashupat don't realize that both of us (Lord Shiva and Vishnu) are inseparable and there is no difference between us. Pashupat is aware of this and hence he has been accorded the highest honour." Having said this, Lord Shiva revealed His universal form of Sada-Shiva to the Ganas/followers. The Ganas were bewildered upon seeing the whole universe existing within SadaShiva. He then transformed his appearance into that of Lord Vishnu. The Ganas also viewed the forms of deities like Indra, Surya and Lord Brahma, etc. in Him. They were now convinced that both Lord Shiva and Lord Vishnu were the same. I give this example because in the Nath tradition, Vishnu's avatara was Matsyendra Nath and Shiva's Mahavatar was Goraksha Nath. Matsyendra Nath invoked Lord Shiva to give him a disciple superior to himself in order to help him with his divine mission. Lord Shiva compassionately agreed to do so, and incarnated

---

10 Food consecrated by the Guru or a deity.

as his great disciple Shiva Goraksha Babaji, who not only helped in the divine mission of evolving the world disciple/humanity, but also brought back to Divine Consiousness, His earthly guru Matsenyndra Nath from his illusionary work in the kingdom of women, governed by the queen Tilotama who was an avatara of Lakshimi herself. This shows us the divine play (*lila*) between these two lofty beings, who came as two different individuals, and yet, at the deeper level were two facets of the same Divine Being.

Shiva Goraksha Babaji, Master of Parashurama, The Teacher of Kalki Avatara

According to the Nath tradition, there is a spiritual journey undertaken every twelve years during the Simhasta-kumbha[11] spiritual gathering. This is called the Navnath Jhundi Yatra[12], meaning the spiritual journey undertaken by the nine-nath tradition of yogis, with the prime purpose of washing away of the sins of the world. Navnath Jhundi began nine lakh and one hundred and three years back (one lakh is 100,000) along with the first journey on foot by nine Naths and eighty-four Siddhas, because Parashurama kept his axe down on the ground after testing the divine incarnation of Lord Rama and went off to the forests to meditate. He started suffering from the guilt of making the earth devoid of Kshatriyas time and again. He wondered how to make amends for the huge number of human lives he had taken.

It was not correct to take human lives even after being gifted by God with the four arts. Only Lord Shiva had the right and responsibility to destroy life. So, in order to achive mental peace, Parashurama started travelling and seeking the blessings of sages, ascetics and saints. All the sages and saints suggested to him to go to Guru Goraksha Nath. He was the only one who could provide a

---
[11] The collective consciousness of our humanity, which is striving to disengage itself from the trammels of the senses and the mire of materialism and ultimately find its inner light assisted by the great masters of Shamballa.
[12] The great Leo-Aquarius fair that occurs every twelve years in India, which over 40 million pilgrims attend, undoubtedly.

Nine Naths and Eight-four Mahasiddhas

solution.

Lord Parashurama set out on his search for Shiva Goraksha. He reached Kaligarh Mountain and found Him in samadhi on the Anupan Rock. He bowed down at the feet of Goraksha Nath and expressed all his grief and pain. Goraksha Nath ordered Parashurama to extend his hands and put Patra Devta[13] in his hands. Patra Devta remained there for moments. Parashurama could not even sense when Patra Devta came in his hand. Then Guru Goraksha Nath told him to go and meditate in a place where no one had ever meditated before and seek a land that he had not gifted to anyone.

Parashurama came back to Shiva Goraksha Babaji and said that he was unable to find a place where no one has meditated before. Then, Babaji asked him to go towards the south, and he would get land there. He should keep walking without looking back. Parashurama went on walking and reached the seashore. He then started thinking

---

13 Literally 'divine vessel'; here, it signifies the ability to receive and contain divine knowledge and truth

that Shiva Goraksha had asked him not to turn around, but there was the sea ahead. He thought that perhaps Shiva Goraksha Babaji had asked him to make amends by drowning in the sea. As he started walking towards the sea, the water started retreating backwards. It retreated twenty-four miles, and land appreared where no one had ever meditated before. Parashurma then established the Patra Devta there and began a rigorous meditation. Babaji was satisfied with that meditation and appeared from the Patra Devta physically. The mist that loomed there disappeared. Parashurama saw and was blessed by Shiva Goraksha Nath.

Since then, Shiva Goraksha was also called Manju Nath. The Mahaguru emerged from the light and blessed Parashurama by telling him that his genocide had been atoned for by his meditation. Parashurama reverently bowed to Goraksha Nath. At that time the Kumbh festival was happening at Tryambakeshwar (Nasik). Nine Naths and eighty-four Siddhas reached Anupan Rock in the Kumbh seeking Shiva-Goraksha's blessings. There they did not find the Mahaguru. Then they came to know by their yogic powers that Guru Goraksha Nath was present at Parashurama's meditation site in order to bless him. The nine Naths and the eighty-four Siddhas set forth to seek Shiva Goraksha's site. They reached via Tryambakeshwar to the place where Shiva Goraksha Babaji had descended to appear as Manju Nath.

Today, Mangalore is the place that exists in the name of Manju Nath. After reaching there, everybody was blessed by the Mahaguru and bowed at His feet. Shiva Goraksha addressed Parashurama and told him that though his killings had been atoned for, the earth would get rid of the sin of all those killings only if he touched the feet of the nine Naths and the eighty-four Siddhas. Then Shiva Goraksha Babaji addressed the nine Naths and eighty-four Siddhas and told them that the Treta Yuga was at its end and after it the Dwapara and Kali Yugas will come respectively with more sin spreading all across the world, and made them vow to come to that place walking at the end of every Simhasta/kumbha (the great spiritual fair), so that the world can get rid of the sins that have happened in the last twelve years and life can foster happiness. Shiva Goraksha Babaji also said that He Himself would be present with them. Since then, the "Jhundi" or group of nine Naths and the eighty-four Siddhas have been undergoing this journey every twelve years from the Simhasta Kumbha Fair, with the aspiration of ridding the earth of its sins. This journey is called the "Jhundi Yatra" undertaken every Simhasta.

In a later episode, Shiva Goraksha Babaji called Guru Matsyendra Nath back from his tapa and made Gopichandji immortal, Guru Matsyendra Nath blessed the Siddhas by showing and teaching them His Divine powers to work in all the seven heavens. By Divine siddhis, he was present in three places at the same time. Establishing a kingdom in Singaldweep, meditating along with the nine Naths and eighty-four Siddhas and keeping His body well protected in the cave, He showed his glory by parkaya-pravesha ('external body entry'), where He entered and resurrected the dead body of King Satyavana, keeping to his promise. Because of Matsyendra Nath's supreme authority, the Siddhas beseeched Him to be their Master and lead them at the Simhasta Jhundi Yatra. Guru Goraksha Nath specially requested Him to lead the journey and told Him that not just Singaldweep[14], but He should also reign over the minds and bodies of the nine Naths and eighty-four Siddhas, leading the journey as a king. Matsyendra Nath agreed to the appeal and led the procession from the front as a king with Patra Devta in His hands. The honour of king started in Jhundi ever since then. This honour is conferred upon the kings/leaders of the twelve Paths turn by turn.

---

14 Another name for Sri Lanka.

The Jhundi Yatra undertaken by the Nath yogis to rid the earth of sin

Shiva Goraksha, Vishnu and Creation

Gorakhnathis believe their sect existed before the world was created. When Vishnu emerged from the lotus at the creation, Gorakh Nath was in Patala, the underworld abode of the Nagas or dragons. This means that the formless presence of Shiva Goraksha lay in the latency of infinity, inactive but aware. The Nagas and serpents of wisdom represented symbolically the various cycles of time and infinity that were also in Patala. The world Patala here represents the unformed and unmanifested state from which creation was to spring in the future. Vishnu was terrified at the waste of waters and went to Goraksha Nath for help and was given a handful of ashes from His eternal fire. The eternal fire here means the Lightless Light, which is father Shiva Goraksha, which lights that light (which is mother Mataji) which lights the light of all our souls. All souls collectively are Vishnu or Vasudeva, the son. This eternal fire, the ashes of which He gave to Vishnu, held within it the potential seeds of creation and humanity. The ashes here represent the unmanifested masculine seeds of the universe and humanity. By sprinkling the ashes on the secondary feminine principle of water, the union of both male ash and female waters brought forth a dynamic process of creation. After the creation, Brahma, Vishnu, and Shiva, again manifested in relativity and became the first disciples of Goraksha Nath, who in truth is incomprehensible and therefore can rightly be called The Non Being Essentiality or Mahankala, The Great Beyond Time.

There are many fascinating legends about Him which run the length and breadth of Bharat (India). Bengal literature describes Him as the purest and strongest of yogis. Goddess Durga[15] was humbled by Goraksha Nath's purity and strength. Medieval saints such as Kabir composed songs to Him, and one tradition says they held a religious discourse together. He is said to have had a discourse with Guru Nanak, a Hindu saint who later came to be worshipped by the new religion called Sikhism. Nath literature says that traditions throughout India saw Shiva Goraksha Babaji as the supreme Guru. Because of this mass of accumulated legends it is impossible to construct a historical account of the life and teachings of this "Timeless Being."

Different legends account for His direct manifestation. In Bengal, He came from the matted hair of Mahadeva (Shiva). His place of manifestation is the subject of different controversial legends. One account gives Punjab, another Kathiawar, while Nepalese tradition says He lived in Nepal in a town called Gorakha, in the cave of an ancient deity called Gorakha, which must have been His own Self in a former world cycle. His accounts are lost in the records of prehistory and one thing is certain, whether you believe it or not, without Him, no other religion or cult or figure assumes any gravity, because watermark of the ideal and classical saint of eternity, and, it is He who is called The Ancient of Days. No saint in India can be gauged or measured by spiritual standards unless they included in their lives a meeting with the immortal Goraksha Nath. Additionally, in order to prove their saints and avatars as the greatest, they bent to the extent of concocting false stories and making their own

---

15 The white evolutionary energy; name for the goddess mother.

masters defeat Goraksha Nath in a philosophical debate or a show of spiritual miracles. But Goraksha Nath, being the eternal truth was unmoved and remained as the silent support of not only the saints and prophets of India, but for the whole world at large.

The name Gurkha is derived from Goraksha Nath. He was the original inhabitant of Gorakhpur in Uttar Pradesh. A preponderance of tradition and the importance attached by Gorakhnathis to Tilla in Jhelum in Punjab makes Punjab the likely home of Goraksha Nath. In His life, Goraksha Nath travelled throughout India and is associated with: Afghanistan, Baluchistan, Punjab, North-West India, Sind, Uttar Pradesh, Nepal, Assam, Bengal, the state of Maharashtra in Deccan India, which was in ancient times called Pratishthaan, as well as South India and Sri Lanka. His great influence was also spread throughout other great religions of the world where He walked through the pages of all the major scriptures.

Shiva Goraksha Saves Matsyendra Vishnu from the Kingdom of Women

The doctrine of yoga and tantra[16] was given for the salvation of the world by Shiva to Matsyendra Nath, then known as Lokeshwar. The unique story is as follows. When his parents were travelling in a boat, a great storm occurred and the little boat capsized, as per the chain of events which the great Nath Avatara pulled upon himself (pulling on himself the veil of maya to be swallowed by the whale of maya).

At that time it so happened that, by the sea, Shiva was teaching the secrets of yoga to Parvati. She fell asleep but Matsyendra Nath heard everything from within the stomach of the fish. In a rock carving of the legend at Srishailya, he is shown with his head out of the mouth of the fish, listening to the secret doctrine. From then

---

16 'Warp', the tradition of tantrism and practice of *tantric* rights by which the laws of nature are manipulated and overcome; the esoteric and arcane practices of *sadhus* in India by which the *sadhak* may attain spiritual powers (*siddhis*) by means of *tantric* practice and *tapa*.

Lokeshwar was called Matsyendra Nath, 'Lord of the Fish'. But, he was discovered and at Srishailya an adjacent carving shows Shiva pointing to a fish to show Parvati where the true seeker of knowledge was hidden and that She should also be alert like him. Parvati became aware of what had happened and took immediate steps to do what She had to do. She had to get this divine knowledge of yoga and tantra out to the world for its evolution. Therefore, She directed an energy charge to Lokeshwar in the form of a curse, which has proven to be a soul-saving blessing, even to this day. The science of yoga and tantra given by Matsyendra Nath is such a blessing.

As per Parvati's curse, Matsyendra Nath, the great Yogavatar in full knowledge of the drama he had to play, went into the land of women called the Kadali-vana to play the drama divine and save all humankind. It is a unique matter to note how for lack of a better word, we use curses and blessings in the rotation of the wheel of evolution. It is interesting to note that Matsyendra Nath cooperated with the electrical essence of Parvati to involute himself into the world of illusion and maya. He also cooperated with the magnetic essence of Shiva as Goraksha Nath to evolute himself out of *maya* into the Spirit. So Parvati cursed him and Shiva blessed him. He did the work of the great sacrifice and moved on to higher planes of divine work.

Since the universal work of the procreation and evolution through yoga had to go on as decreed in the divine kalchakra, the wheel of time, Parvati set in motion a karmic law which not only involved Matsyendra Nath's going to Kadali-vana, but also his spreading the magical knowledge of tantra and mystic knowledge of yoga. Let me make the inner purpose of Indian terminology very clear regarding the words 'curse' and 'blessing'. In ancient language, the wheel of time and evolution was not only set in motion by blessings and curses, but at a deeper level the curse was an excuse to trigger off a series of karmic evolutions. Similarly, blessings were also bestowed as a means to give joy and confidence to the evolving soul. So it was a way of saying that Parvati 'cursed' Matsyendra Nath to be born on Earth and teach the evolutionary science of tantra (*kaula gyana*[17]) and yoga. She further cursed Matsyendra Nath so that he would forget all yoga in Kadali-vana. Then, knowledge of tantra was heightened and the knowledge of how to procreate spiritual children was spread amongst the people of the Earth. This was the 'involution of spirit into matter', the work which maya always does. The first part of the mission of Matsyendra Nath was complete, which was telling the world how to improve those genes and DNA that beget spiritual children.

It was time now for Shiva Goraksha Babaji to somehow get the message through to His terrestrial master; that the second part of his mission, which was that the spiritual evolution through yoga now had to begin. It was now time for Matsyendra Nath to become aware himself of his next mission, which involved saving and helping humanity in the ascent of its spirit into consciousness.

So Babaji Goraksha Nath set up a small musical team with dancing women and people playing musical instruments, while He took upon Himself the role of the drummer. This musical troupe headed towards the land of Kadali-vana. Babaji Goraksha Nath was fully aware that the city He was going to was ruled by the Queen Tilotama, who was an incarnation of Goddess Lakshmi, and that Matsyendra Nath was an incarnation of Vishnu Himself. When Babaji and His musical troupe approached the city, they told the women guards posted at Queen Tilotama's palace that they had come to entertain the royal couple with song and music. Although no men were allowed inside the city, the appeal of Goraksha Nath was so overwhelming that the women relented and opened the gates for them to enter.

As they walked through the beautiful gardens towards the palace, they came across the most enchanting flowers, which made one swoon with their fragrance. The birds could all appropriately be called the birds of paradise. The troupe eventually presented themselves before the royal couple and commenced to dance and sing. Babaji Goraksha Nath produced from His drum, the soul-awakening vibration. This

---

17 Also *Kaula marga*, the *Kaul Tantra* originated by Matsyendra Nath as disclosed in the *Kaula-Jnana-Nirnaya* involving the divinization of the body through stimulating the flow of 'the nectar of immortality' (*amrit*).

"Jaag Macchendra Gorakh Aaya"

sound vibration was heard as '*Jaag Macchendra Gorakh Aaya*', which literally means: 'Awake Matsyendra, Goraksha's here'. This sound fell upon the ears of Matsyendra Nath. He then moved from the tantric dimension of his mission to the yogic consciousness of his future mission. We could also say that he moved from his self-taken state of the tantric *Savikalpa Samadhi* to the yogic *Nirvikalpa Samadhi*. And then these two lofty beings moved out into their vaster mission to teach the divine evolutionary science of yoga for the salvation of the world.

Shiva Goraksha Babaji Is Mahavatar Babaji

The connection between Shiva Goraksha Babaji and *Mahavatar* Babaji has been established in several sources. In folklore and medieval texts it is mentioned that Goraksha Nath initiated Kabir and taught him the ways of the Nath yogis. Paramhansa Yogananda also writes in his autobiography about the connection between Mahavatar Babaji and Kabir. There he related that Babaji Himself had mentioned to Yogavatar Lahiri Mahasaya that He initiated Kabir into Kriya Yoga. Babaji also initiated Yogavatar Lahiri Mahasaya, and Lahiri Mahasaya categorically stated that he was Kabir in his former life. It therefore follows that Mahavatar Babaji and Babaji Goraksha Nath are one and the same person, thus establishing the direct connection between the two.

In my own autobiography, *Wings to Freedom: Mystic Revelations from Babaji and the Himalayan Yogis*, I have also connected Kabir directly with King Bharthari Nath of the Middle Ages, as well as with Yogavatar Lahiri Mahasaya:

> *"And later on, as I meditated that night by the Shipra river haunted with the romantic tales of the legendary Nath yogis, before my mind's eye again came this majestic Yogi king, Bharthari, who transformed himself into the smiling Lahiri Mahasaya, the Kriya Yoga master. With him also I had the vision of master Kabir. And both in unison said, 'Alakh Gorakhia Babaji. Alakh Gorakhia Babaji'. On reflection, I realized as an afterthought, in deep meditations that Bharthari had been taken for his mission and penances by Goraksha Nath when his queen Maharani Pingala died, and he had left with a heavy heart".*

Goraksha Nath saw to it that the desire for a grand palace and the householder wife Pingala were preserved in Bharthari Nath's causal body, so that in a later incarnation, Babaji could pull this lofty soul down and get him married to Queen Pingala, reincarnated as the divine Kashi Moni. Then, after he became a householder yogi as Lahiri Mahasaya, Babaji fulfilled the purposefully kept desire of seeing the grandest palace a mortal could ever imagine. If Babaji had not kept this desire preserved in the mind of King Bharthari, nobody could ever make such a lofty soul as Yogavatar Lahiri Mahasaya incarnate into the haunts of mortal man. No power in the world could keep Lahiri Mahasaya away from his Guru Goraksha Nath Babaji, the Mahavatar. So blessed be Babaji Goraksha and blessed be King Bharthari Nath who incarnated as the householder Yogavatar Lahiri Mahasaya, for the salvation of the world.

This vision of mine goes to show that such great divine masters as King Bharthari reincarnated as Kabir, who reincarnated as Yogavatar Lahiri Mahasaya, are at the highest divine level of avatara consciousness. That is, the nirvanic consciousness of Yogavatar Lahiri Mahasaya and Kabir are also One. These bodies are a mere choosing of a garment for the particular divine missions on this terrestrial world.

Yogananda also writes in *Autobiography of a Yogi* that "other titles of respect given [Mahavatar Babaji] by Lahiri Mahasaya's disciples are Mahamuni Babaji Maharaj (supreme ecstatic saint), Maha Yogi (greatest of yogis), Trambak Baba and Shiva Baba (titles of avatars of Shiva). Does it matter that we know not the patronymic of an earth-released master? Lahiri Mahasaya wrote in his diary, "The old father, Babaji, is Lord Krishna". Krishna was born to Devaki fully enlightened, and also cast his *mayavi swaroop* (illusionary body) with impunity, as only a full *avatar* can don and discard a body of divine light at will (see Chapter 11, 'The *Avadhoot Avatar* Doctrine' for full details). In the esoteric doctrines Krishna is also addressed as Shambhu Chaitanya, meaning Shiva the Irradiant Lord.

Although Shiva Goraksha Babaji is timeless and deathless, He chooses to manifest Himself time and again to balance the gunas on Earth and bless humanity through His avataric work. In one of

Shiva Goraksha Babaji venerated in Divine form

His manifestations, He appeared sometime between the eighth and eleventh centuries. Babaji was also known to be present at the time of Adi Shankara in the eighth century, and an infinitesimal portion of His Being continues to be present to some high initiates, even to this day.

In my work and teaching, I have made this humble effort and endeavor to contribute to the yogic treasury of knowledge some truths and facts regarding the origin and essence of this Divine Being called Shiva Goraksha Babaji. He is called the Nameless One. I have also called Him the Non Being Essentiality in reference to the paradox of the simultaneity of His form and formless Self. He is also called The Lightning Standing Still, and The Great Sacrifice, referring to His promise to stay ever present in the material sphere of creation and guide humanity towards God-Consciousness, rather than to permanently merge into His own inconceivable spiritual Consciousness. Just as Shiva goes by many names, so also, Shiva Goraksha Babaji goes by many names that elucidate the depth and truth of His Being.

Though people know Him by many names, yet He is called the Nameless One. He broods over the infant humanities from eternity to eternity. Heaven and Earth shall pass away, but He shall be with us to stay. The limited vision of sages, siddhas, philosophers and yogis cannot pierce His transcendental star. His spiritual stature is indescribable. He is the collective Elohim of the angelic hierarchy of the heavenly host, the spiritual essence of the nine Celestial Nath Lords combined. He is the Great Sacrifice, who in countless supernovae explosions, infused every atom of creation with His spirit of livingness, wisdom and truth to redeem not only humankind but all life and matter to their pristine state of consciousness. He is the cause of the inconceivable process of the involution of spirit into matter and the evolution of matter into spirit, the original 'Integral Yoga' known to the Nath yogis from ancient times.

Shiva Goraksha Babaji is regarded as a manifestation of Lord Shiva Himself. He has bestowed upon humanity the practices to evolve human consciousness, in particular, the Divine alchemy of Shiva–Shakti (Kriya Yoga), which exercises a double action to hasten the evolution of the self-soul. This expands consciousness and burns away past evil karma. Babaji, known by various names in other traditions and mythologies, is the fountainhead of the spiritual evolution of humanity and the founder of the Nath *Sampradaya* (tradition). He reveals Himself when the time is right for a particular individual; usually He remains invisible, guiding humanity through His disciples. He has revived the ancient science of divine knowingness in modern times.

His timeless presence continues to manifest through the inspiration and work of all seekers of the truth. There is a great mystery and a sacrifice to the ninth level of divine Awareness which is self-born. This is the state of Brahma Nirvana from which the ineffable Shiva Goraksha Babaji descends to redeem humanity, yet maintains His state. How this is possible is known only to Him. He is the collective consciousness of the seven primordial Sages of the Fire Mist, already present at the beginning of Time. He is the Lightless Light of the highest Elohim; and yet in His unfathomable compassion has left behind a finite portion of His Infinite consciousness to evolve humanity into the likeness of divinity. This finite and immortal portion of His Being manifests amongst the haunts of men from time to time as the need arises. Throughout eternity, this Eternal Now watches over the evolution of humanity until it is liberated. Truly, He is called the Visible-Invisible Savior of humanity – The Great Sacrifice!

Babaji, the Divine Being, is the personal aspect and Universal Isness of the Absolute Consciousness, Shiva. The Divine Babaji, who is your potential true Self, may be realized through persevering Kriya Yoga practice. He is not born but comes into manifestation at the beginning of the creation of our three dimensional world. Although present in the midst of the world of causation, space and time, the Divine Being Shiva Goraksha Babaji is not subject to the karmic law of cause and effect. He is not bound by any third-dimensional laws that govern the mortal body and mind.

The Three Mysteries

There are three Mysterious Presences beyond human comprehension:

The Presence About Whom Naught Maybe Said

This is the Presence that we refer to as the ineffable Being, the Sage of All Ages, Shiva Goraksha Babaji, working in our existential creation. We all have a faint glimmer of Babaji's manifestations in creation and relativity, but nobody can pierce His transcendental star and go into His beyond-relativity state. It is absolutely unfathomable, infinite and inconceivable.

The Presence About Whom We Know Nothing

This is the great ineffable Being beyond all existence, to whom countless creations are but a dream atom, and their googols of time cycles are but the wink of an eye. This is the Param Shiva, the *Mahankala*, the Great Beyond Time, who by His doing Nothing, brings into manifestation infinite eternities.

The Presence About Whom Nobody Knows Nothing!

This is the ineffable Presence about whom even The Presence About Whom We Know Nothing Knows Nothing! (Dear reader, the above statement is but a figure of speech, to awe the mind into silence.) Nobody knows Nothing that is to be Known or Unknown. He is beyond the comprehension of even the highest of Gods and non-Gods, all that is and is not. This is the Great Incomprehensible Isness of the Zero not Zero, the Non Being Essentiality. No words can ever do justice for the Incomprehensible beyond comprehension.

CHAPTER 8

ON BEING A DISCIPLE OF BABAJI

Ye sons of light delusion flight
Be constant in your day and night

As per my experience and incernment[1], Babaji in His aspect as Lord of the World has taken no new disciples. The last two disciples He did take were Yogavatar Lahiri Mahasaya and Gyanavatar Sri Yukteshwar. They had transformed their bodies into light. Only someone whose body is free from the ravages of time, in a perpetual state of *Nirvikalpa Samadhi*, is fit for such a direct relationship.

It is one thing to have an experience of Babaji, but to be a DIRECT DISCIPLE of Babaji is quite a different echelon of realization. Many people have claimed to have experiences of the ineffable Babaji, however, this is totally different from being a direct disciple of Babaji, where both the Supreme Guru and the disciple are in a state of Continuum-Consciousness. This is an extremely rare happening, where the Mahavatar Guru and the avataric disciple are in rapport with one another and in an expanded ecstasy of desireless consciousness (samadhi).

If, for example, a high initiate who is below the level of an avatara, were to interact with such a lofty essence as that of Babaji, in spite of his intense meditations and lower samadhis, he would still be unable to capacitate the incoming surge of Babaji's

---

[1] A word coined by me corresponding to *Sat-Sad Vivekh Buddhi*; it is the distinction of inner knowingness between apparent and Real. Esoterically, it is the capacity to realize the difference between *Pratibha* (buddhic light) and *Purush* (atmic light).

supernal splendor and would most likely explode his physical and celestial bodies in that splendor. But such a fortunate blessing is not permitted by the great grandmaster Babaji, because He deems it premature for any high disciple or *avadhoot* or even *bodhisattva* to explode into His blissful essence before their time is right.

The spiritual interaction between a human being and such a lofty phenomenon would completely shatter the so-called disciple's body. If Babaji were to, in His compassion, connect with the half-awakened kundalini of the general masses of people, that would, in all its love, be more harmful than beneficial for the gradually evolving humanities. Therefore, it is always necessary for the spiritual essence and the consciousness of Babaji to be filtered down through the avatara, then the *avadhoot*, then the siddha, then the Paramhansa and then the hamsa;[2] and then His spiritual essence and blessings can be absorbed by humanity at large and people can avail of the optimal blessings of this great Being called The Nameless One. This demonstrates the descent of grace from the highest pinnacle of God's power, wisdom and love to humanity's power, wisdom and love, which is no wisdom at all.

The nervous system, brain cells and astral chakras of a normal mortal being are not designed to capacitate the spiritual influx of such a Cosmic Being as Mahavatar Babaji. Only an avatara is qualified to be a disciple of a Mahavatar. Any lesser being would merely be floating in the figment of its own imagination. In reality, if cosmic lightning struck a mortal being, no matter however gently, with the utmost love, that mortal frame would vanish into nothing, unless one is an avataric consciousness, like the Buddha, Christ, Krishna, Adi Shankaracharya, Bharthari Nath, Chowrangee Nath, Yogavatar Lahiri Mahasaya and Gyanavatar Sri Yukteshwar, who can capacitate the voltage of the incoming Christos[3] called Babaji.

---

2 'Swan', the soul, the individuated consciousness (*jiva*); also refers to the life-breath (prana) as it moves within the body; the lateral ventricles in the human brain in the shape of a swan in flight, with its wings thrust toward the forehead and its posterior ventricle as its head pointed to the back, like a swan flying back to the future, faster than light; see *jiva-atman*.
3 The divine higher-self called Archangel Michael, Narayan 'the Lord of Irradiant

Anyone claiming such a relationship would have to demonstrate the states of Yogavatar Lahiri Mahasaya or Gyanavatar Sri Yukteshwar, such as the following.

- *Shambhave Mudra*: unblinking outward gaze with inward mind, transformed into Cosmic Consciousness.

- Perpetual state of *Nirvikalpa Samadhi*: permanent expanded ecstasy of desireless consciousness, also called the *Nirbija Samadhi*, only experienced by beings of avataric stature.

- Resurrection: self-resurrection like Yogavatar Lahiri Mahasaya, Gyanavatar Sri Yukteshwar and Premavatar Christ; avatara means 'a divine descending savior'. These three Beings are divine descending saviors of Yoga, Wisdom and Love, respectively.

When a person says he has a direct experience of Babaji, it is his word against the belief of the people. There is no way to prove or disprove such an assertion. Only that person in his heart knows what he is saying, and Babaji metes out the final karmic justice.

Many people have had visions, visitations, blessings and guidance from this lofty Being. This is possible and this may be true. But so much is the spiritual difference between Babaji and mortal humans that even a minimal spiritually-charged experience of such magnitude would leave the yogi in a daze for many months to come. Nevertheless, a minimal blessing would grace all the souls who have and have not seen Babaji to march along the path of spiritual progress towards their final beatitude: Babaji Himself.

It is sad but true that human nature has a tendency to 'jump the fence', and wants to do the Ph.D. course before finishing kindergarten. To have a vision is okay, but to perpetually bathe in the cosmic aura of the Being About Whom Naught May Be Said, is quite a different

---

Splendor', and Amitabh the Buddha. The Christos has crossed the eighth degree of the great initiations. Above them there is only one, 'The Eternal Now,' Shiva Goraksha Babaji.

ball game. Although He is the divinity of the consciousness of the life of our breath, closer to us than our very selves, let us truthfully introspect and be honest with ourselves as to where we stand in relation to Babaji. Our existence is His proof—He is totally in us but how much of us have we realized in Him? That is the question. To elucidate this point further, what exactly is meant by He being in us and we not being in Him? By this is meant that Babaji's essential spirit is the essence of our souls and He is in there to abide as the moving spirit of all sentient and non-sentient beings in creation. But this essential spirit of Babaji who is in us is covered by different layers of our intellect, our mind, and various strata of our emotions.

We identify ourselves with the not-self of our body, emotions and mind, and not with the true spirit of our beings, which is the spirit of Babaji trying to move humanity towards the eternal spirit, which we may call God, for lack of a better word. Now, as we, by the practice of Kriya Yoga and other spiritual pathways, purify the grosser sheaths of our physical, emotional and mental bodies, after long years and lifetimes of practice, we begin to perceive the dim light of our souls whose spirit I have said to be Babaji. As we travel more and more along the spinal path, refining and cleaning the lamp-glass of our body, mind and soul, the flame of our soul, which is the temple of Babaji, shines forth from within, and we begin to partake more and more of the spirit in Babaji and identify less and less with our body-minds and souls. This is what I meant by asking the question: 'Babaji is the spirit of the innermost core of our beings, but how much of us is in Babaji?'

So by the rich spiritual legacy of yoga and meditation given to us by our founding fathers, we may identify more and more with our true selves, the spirit which is Babaji, and less and less with our idle worshipping ways of admiring our physical contours, emotional passions and mental idiosyncrasies. By the practice of Kriya Yoga, as we let go of our material desires and inhibitions, we live more and more in the spirit of Babaji, since Babaji is so close, He is the very essence of our true beings, and yet we have to make great efforts to see and meet Him. He is called The Near and The Far, and therefore

I encourage all of you to question, 'Babaji is within us, but how much of us is in Babaji?'

Babaji's entourage includes very high initiates of the eighth degree, known as the Sages of the Fire Mist (The *Agni Svatta Rishis*). Those are His disciples, if we can call them so; thirty-three in graded order, clothed in their glorious bodies, great beyond man's reckoning, their celestial forms came to Earth 18.5 million years ago to infuse the spirit of the divine into the human phenomenon and form the first spiritual hierarchy for this present White Boar[4] world cycle. If the ancient scriptures of India are read carefully, the name, identity and the time of coming of all these great beings is given. These beings are great Presences beyond the scope of birth and death. When we say of them, 'He is dead!' But, behold, He is alive! And He appears somewhere else. It's magical. These glorious beings never die for they were never born!

Here we must make a special mention of some lofty Sages of the Fire Mist who stand at the dizzying heights equal to the planetary and Solar Gods in the spiritual hierarchy. They include Sanat Kumar, who represents Kartikeya, the son of Shiva, and is equivalent to the Archangel Michael, the angel of the face of God. The second Sage of the Fire Mist is Sanak, who is Ganapati, the Lord of Hosts and the Enunciator of all auspicious events, who, in western terminology, is known as the Archangel Gabriel, the Enunciator. Then we have Sanandana, then Sanat-Sujata, then Panchashika, then Kapil and Ribu. These seven Sages of the Fire Mist correspond with the seven cosmic, not planetary, Archangels in the Christian world (the exact correspondences of these divine ones are not available at present). Next come the high initiates and the great cosmic life-force energy *kundalini* personified as the virgin light Uma Nath, also known as Mataji.

The great *Yogeshwari* Uma Nath, the consort of Shiva, is also called Mataji. She is one with Babaji, as well as expressing His

---

4 The name of our present *kalpa* (in Sanskrit, the *Shweta Varaha Kalpa*). We are at present, halfway through this grand world cycle of the White Boar. The duration of the complete cycle is 4,320,000,000 years.

dynamic aspect of Cosmic Kundalini. She is also working at the eighth level with the Sages of the Fire Mist, assisting the evolution of human consciousness to attain the final realization.

We then have Shankaracharya who was directed by Shiva Goraksha Babaji to infuse the highest science of non-dual truth (*Advaita*) and spiritual evolution to thirsty humanity. The second of the lofty beings is the great Dattatreya, who also gave to this Earth the philosophy of *Advaita* and the mystic science of Tantra Yoga. Working in the cosmic aura of Babaji, the King of Kings, the Lord Vaivaswat Manu is the king of the inner hierarchy. The Kalki avatara (Maitreya Buddha) is the world teacher, also called the Second Coming of the Christ, preparing to establish righteousness on this planet. Yogavatar Lahiri Mahasaya, working with Babaji in the cosmic-causal spheres beyond our comprehension, will succeed the world teacher. Gyanavatar Sri Yukteshwar has been given the responsibility for evolving higher souls in the realms of *Hiranyaloka*[5]. He will succeed Vaivaswat Manu as the next Manu Savarni. They shall all be ruling in the realms of the spiritual hierarchy of the inner government of the world.

Then we come to some of the *chiranjeevs*, the immortals—Lord Hanuman, Ashvatthama, Karna, Arjuna, Nagarjuna, Aaryasangh, Count St. Germain, Parashurama, Bali, Kripacharya, Dronacharya. Lord Surya Kashyab (our Sun) is one of the most glorious and venerated Sages of the Fire Mist, who works alongside Shiva Goraksha Babaji. So high is His spiritual stature that there are very few words to say.

It must be remembered that when one claims to be a disciple of Babaji in the spiritual sense, his kundalini energy must be ceaselessly connected with the Cosmic Kundalini of Babaji. This means that the light essence of his dynamic energy should be at a perpetual critical state of the speed of light, which makes the avatar's mass infinite, his celestial body ageless, and his awareness in the now! Only when

---

[5] 'Golden world', the highest astral heaven of luminosity to which some yogis ascend, to practice higher forms of yoga under the guidance of divine teachers (*divya* gurus) such as Gyanavatar Sri Yukteswar.

such a rapport is established can the disciple feel himself as one with Babaji, whose center is everywhere and circumference nowhere. This is what it means to be a direct disciple.

After the last cases of Yogavatar Lahiri Mahasaya and Gyanavatar Sri Yukteshwar, I see no less a person being able to maintain a Guru-disciple relationship with this Cosmic Being. No doubt, they can be blessed or have visions, which are based on the famous painting of Babaji inspired by Yogananda's experience, and hence those visions fall under the category of *Savikalpa darshan*. However to have the core experience of Babaji, a divine being must go beyond the *Dharmamegha Samadhi*, the great 'Rings-Pass-Not'.

Overenthusiastic practitioners and swamis must guard against hallucinations or mistaking a three-dimensional vision as a certificate for being a direct disciple of Babaji; a sense of proportion is needed. There are many diseased and feeble neophyte devotees and swamis who, by the mere vision of Babaji, have been cured of their ailments. This does not qualify them to be disciples of this Cosmic Avatara. Of course, let me add that there are other 'babajis' about whom people have written. Some are mortal, some are true historical beings, and some are totally fictitious. These babajis go by various names. About these babajis and their disciples and followers, I have nothing to say, since any elderly person can call himself 'babaji' (revered father), and claim to have had a direct vision and even build a temple in his name.

Now I would caution the western world about recognizing the true Babaji, and not be led into believing a figment of their imagination. To be on solid ground, look for authentic historical evidences of temples, books and other literature, which are ancient documents written about this wondrous Being. Because other wondrous beings, like the Lord Krishna and the Lord Christ, also appeared to people on Earth and told them where they were born, and where they were crucified. The vestiges and traces of their historical episodes are still on Earth today.

Shiva Goraksha Babaji

Who art thou? I know thee not
And yet I am of thee
I cannot comprehend thee Lord,
Thou emperor of divinity

I sit and melt in silence
Of thy love, Oh infinite
Make me thy truth, make me thy love
Eternal Lord of light

Countless creations do you make
Goraksha Nath Divine
A thought projected by you
Makes causation, space and time

There never was a sage nor saint
Who was not born of Thee
Thou art the essence of their souls
Divine Paramatma[6] Free

We jivatmas also Lord
Have our birth and being in thee
Then thou must also be in us
Supremest monarchy

How shall I love thee Babaji?
Words are so dry and dumb
I can't express thy majesty
My intellect runs numb

---

6 'Supreme Self', the transcendental Self, which is singular, as opposed to the individuated self (*jiva-atman*) that exists in countless numbers in the form of living beings.

My heart it bursts, oh all in all
To love thee endlessly
But Lord I cannot bring to words
I'm tongue-tied hopelessly

Give me the strength to shout thy love
Across the seven seas
Deluging this world with light
For infinite eternities

In solitudes of my mind
My devotion it doth burst to hear
Thy song immortal song of love
Thou everlasting seer

As long as darkness covers me
And ignorance doth do us part
So long in agony I'll be
Striving to be with thee, my heart

Through pain and hunger I shall strive
To touch thy feet oh Lord
It matters not if bones or body
Perish in this battle fort

I'm burning in my love for thee
Eternal infinite
I cannot rest in peace now
Till I do become thy light

In silent supplications
I do burn and yearn to be in thee
Hear thou my soul cry
Break my bonds
Babaji set me free!

Set me free to be in thee
Let there be none of me
Then me in thee
Thy love in me
I shall become of thee

                                        Yogiraj Siddhanath

CHAPTER 9

THE RUDRAPRAYAG EXPERIENCE

The autumn air was crisp and the leaves on the trees were taking on a yellow and orange hue as I made my way in the interior of the Himalayas towards the pilgrimage of Rudraprayag. Rudra is an epithet for Shiva, and *prayag* means, 'the confluence of any two sacred rivers'. In this context they are called the Mandakini and Alaknanda, symbolized as flowing from Shiva's dread-locks represented as the ridged canyons and ravines of the Himalayan mountains. As I approached this sacred town on both sides there were shanty tea-stalls and small shops displaying Indian sweets. I stopped by the side, ordered a cup of tea and a *samosa* made of fried dough and stuffed with spiced potatoes—not very hygienic but very tasty. I then relaxed, and my mind went into meditation on Shiva Goraksha Babaji, the Visible–Invisible Savior of Humanity.

'One never knows,' I thought to myself, 'Nothing is impossible for such divine beings, accommodating themselves to the limited understanding of us mortals. They could appear right here in the middle of the market if they chose to do so'. But I knew that they would never make such appearances for a trifle, unless it would assist people to evolve spiritually; also all the people present would have to be karmically fit to receive such a spiritual surge. The musings of my mind went on as I sipped the blessedly hot cup of tea. I had heard stories of sages and great masters, the great divine beings who came and bathed at the

The Rudraprayag Experience

confluence; these stories came from the superconscious spheres of my mind, from yogis, from *sadhus* and sages about the wonders of the places in the Himalayas—Panch Kashi, Panch Kedar and Panch Prayag are sacred to pilgrims and yogis.

I then got up and carried on with my journey. When I entered the main Rudraprayag temple, I was welcomed by the priest and told that this was the sacred place where Lord Shiva Himself taught Deva Rishi Narada symphonies and the intricacies of the music of the Gandharvas[1]. Narada was himself a chief of these heavenly musicians, and it is said that it was here that he was also taught the Shiva Bhakti Sutras[2] (Shiva's devotional verses), which later became popular as the *Narada Bhakti Sutras*.

The various confluences and pilgrimages which are nestled in the Himalayan ranges have many wonderful stories associated with them; they are rich with anecdotes of Shiva–Parvati and all the Himalayan residents. As dusk descended on the little town, I took my asana[3] and made my way to the confluence of the two rivers. I laid the *asana* down, and found the whole evening had a strange and mystic aura about it. My heart was full of the yearning for the great Being about whose spiritual stature I had no comprehension. My mind automatically began to steady itself and become more and more tranquil as the evening melted into the velvety silence of the night. On the one hand, I could hear the thunderous roar of the Alaknanda, and on the other, the silent swish of the Mandakini's waters. The chirping of the mountain birds rose to a crescendo and then gradually subsided as evening transformed itself into night. And slowly the sound of the roaring Alaknanda became distant, soft and disappeared as my mind entered a deep reverie, and was partially losing itself to another dimension which was not of mind but was of a true state of myself.

---

1 Heavenly songsters and *devas*.
2 'Aphorism of Devotion', a work on devotional yoga authored by Sage Narada.
3 The 'seat' upon which a yogi sits during meditation; also a physical posture of meditation; also the third limb (*anga*) of Patanjali's eightfold path (Ashtanga Yoga); originally, this meant only a meditation posture, but subsequently, in Hatha Yoga, this aspect of the yogic path was developed further; see also *anga, mudra*.

I was partially the conscious seer that represented my true self and partially my mind, which represented my not-self; this gave me the insight that the mind was in a sense the great deceiver in time with its multifaceted temptations and distractions. As I gradually began to leave behind my mind and its fabric of material thoughts (no matter how pure they were), I was simultaneously awakened into a partial state of the divine consciousness. As the night wore on, I remained in that partial state of the half-mind of consciousness.

So engrossed was the mind and so fascinated was the mind by my consciousness that it began, so to say, falling in love with my consciousness. In gravitating towards it, the mind withdrew, loosening its grip from the trammels of the senses. As the prana began to recede in the spine-consciousness by the practice of Kriya Yoga it gradually relieved my captive body-consciousness held in bondage by that very prana. But a slight body-consciousness still persisted and I knew it would disappear in due time.

The dynamic I was experiencing between my body-mind and consciousness was unique, beyond any description. I have done my best to describe it above and know that this cannot do justice to the true experience. I have written about this same experience in my autobiography *Wings to Freedom*, but because the mind cannot always reproduce the total experience at one time, my memory recalls different fragments of the same experience each time I write about it. I have written twice about my experience at Rudraprayag in a totally different manner, but let me assure you that the essential awakening was and will remain the same till today. As I meditated, my consciousness expanded, and suddenly the river was flowing through my stomach and up my spine; my awareness grew into the night, and as I waited in an indescribable state, I entered a steady gaze called *Shambhave*.

And so I kept going deeper, the inner yearning for Babaji was becoming so strong that my consciousness appeared to elongate and expand into another dimension. And then, from the far end, all along the length of the river, which now became the Ganga, came a dazzling light, like a whirling aurora borealis of many hues and colors. There were lilacs and indigoes and blues and the centre of this whirling depth of light was white. All of a sudden, I lost body awareness; my innermost being became my outermost core and my outermost core became my innermost being. My consciousness was unable to grasp the magnitude of this ineffable experience. My 'I' was drowning in a dimension which was so vast that it appeared to be as Nothing! This great Nothingness engulfed me, but in spite of all this, I had a very unique experience that I was partaking of my innermost essence. It was as though the Great Presence called Babaji was giving an experience to Himself in me. I was awed by the majesty of this experience. How could such a great awakening happen to me? In spite of this, the paradox was that the experience appeared to be given by the Self to the self. You see, the divine infinite consciousness was connecting and awakening its finite human consciousness. By this time, the half-consciousness, half-mind state had totally disappeared while I, the Conscious seer, entered the dimensionless dimension of Babaji and totally partook of His ineffable truth. As I am writing now, I am not sure that I should venture to write this experience, because as expressed before, I know that words are totally inadequate and the mind is unable to express even an iota of the no-mind state.

It must have been a state of *Nirvikalpa Samadhi*. Even though the *Nirvikalpa Samadhi* was given to me by His grace, the grace is not something that you get idly. The divine masters or *avatars* do not simply come, bestow grace, and give you samadhi. They give it to you because you loved and practiced yoga in your past lives. It is a well-deserved spiritual harvest that you reap. Put your shoulder to the wheel of *sadhana*, practice and love. I believe that to each one is meted out his exact and proper due. Otherwise everyone would say, 'Shiva is going to give me samadhi in any case, so what are these yogis doing in the Himalayas meditating?' Why strive? Why make the necessary sacrifice? It is simply a wrong mindset and philosophy to be lazy. You have to be assiduous and practice, be pure, go in the direction of your spiritual practice of Shiva-Shakti, do Babaji Kriya Yoga and the fruit will be yours in this life or the next.

The whole ambience was in radiance of His Lightless Light deep in splendor, and yet I knew I was sitting near the flowing Ganga[4]. I was reveling in a state of my own. I did not lose my identity but I was more than my own. I was His Consciousness and identity, twinkling in the stars, roaring in the powerful river of the Alaknanda, flowing gently in the feminine nature of the Mandakini. It was like a union of Shiva and Shakti. Suddenly there was an inconceivable flash that came from the aurora borealis of Babaji's light. It was the mother of all light. So His Lightless Light which lights that light which lights the light of all our souls, was this indescribable light, a great Nothingness of such truth that it was immaterial. As the light actualized into a *'Non Being Essentiality'*, the essence of a nothing, its majesty ignited all existence. *The whole of nature and creation stood in awe with folded hands and bowed head.*

Suddenly I saw Babaji's form bathing at the confluence of the Alaknanda and Mandakini rivers. I had no idea of time and location, or my whereabouts. Babaji's body of Lightless Light was bathing in the river and gentle moonlight. He then walked out of the river and came towards me. He had prepared my mind to be in the unperturbed and non-active state, or else I might have gotten very excited or dumbfounded by the gravity of this tremendous awakening. I was looking at Him from within my eyes to without, or was I looking at Him from outside within me; it was both and thus I knew I was in a high state of *Shambhave Mudra*. All I knew when I looked into His eyes was that it was like looking into the fathomless deep.

He beckoned to me to follow Him as He walked up the hillside. How long the walk lasted, or to which secluded spot He took me I haven't the faintest idea. He then told me to sit down. There were trees all around and some seeds of trees were lying there as well as some onions. He told me to take an onion and peel it. I did as told and did not ask any questions, for I was so overwhelmed by His Presence

---

4 At every pilgrimage confluence, various rivers join together and compose the making of the great river Ganga (or Ganges). When she reaches the sacred pilgrimage of Rishikesh then all the names of the other rivers drop off and she is singularly called the sacred Ganga.

The Rudraprayag Experience

even though I was in a state of trance, or *unmani avastha*[5]. As I peeled the onions, layer after layer, I felt as though I was peeling the layers of ignorance from my mind, which had covered the splendor of my soul. There were no words here, no talk, what an experience of a lifetime this was. As I peeled layer after layer, I felt the obstacles of ignorance, ego, desire, hate and lust-for-life melt away and free my inner spirit consciousness. This would in future enable me to unite with the All Pervading Consciousness. This brings to my mind what Babaji is. Shiva Goraksha Babaji is so one with God that their descriptions and revelations are the same:

> *The All-Being was the God-thought which was*
> *Babaji, the essential Self of every atom of creation*
> *That all-pervading consciousness of stillness through eternity*
> *Composed of nothing yet of which all else is sure composed*
> *It stands supreme beyond all dreams eternally reposed*
>
> *Spirit is the god-thought, there is nothing it is not*
> *The all is one, the one is all, the all-in-all Paramartha*
> *Oh, absolute majesty of sublimest existence*
> *Oh ineffable peace beyond human understanding*
> *Our ceaseless salutation to thee*
> *Who ever was, even is now and shall forever be.*
>
> from *Autobiography of the Self*
> (see front matter of this book)

However, after I had almost finished peeling the onion, He told me to carry on removing its layers of skin until completion. A thought entered my mind as to why He had not called me 'son'. But then I reflected that I might not be His son but His grandson. However, this was an idle drifter of a thought and was soon consumed by my still consciousness. He asked me, after I had reached the core of the onion, 'What is in it?' And I replied 'Nothing'. He told me to pick up the nearby seed and open it; in that too, I found a hollow space and then He told me the highest philosophy and truth that I had never heard before. He said, 'My son, the

---

[5] A clear-mind; ecstasy of thoughtless awareness.

secret of secrets is this: that from the Nothingness is the everything created'. His words gave me the realization that when the Universe in its coats of illusion (that is maya) is removed, pure Consciousness is revealed, which to the material world, is nothing. It is totally immaterial. And from that Nothing does the whole of creation arise. He laughed! I do not know what happened after, for when He laughed I passed out and was not aware of myself. Later, when I regained normal consciousness, I realized with gratitude the knowledge given to me.

This truth has never been uttered before; anything close to this was uttered in the *Chandogya Upanishad*[6] where the father tells his son that just as there is a subtle essence in the seed from which the whole banyan tree is created, in the same sense is the world created from subtle matter. But here the point of great import is that Babaji does not use the words 'subtle essence of matter'. He told me that 'From the Nothingness is everything created'. Even the *samkhya*[7] philosophy does not go to this extent, but Babaji goes even beyond s*amkhyan* logic of the law of conservation of mass into energy. To my way of thinking, to create something from nothing is impossible for mortals to do or to achieve. Only God can create the whole universe from nothing. THAT IS WHY GOD IS GOD.

---

6 One of the oldest scriptures written before the 7th century BCE; its contents elaborate on the nature of Om and prana.

7 'Number', one of the main philosophies of yoga, which is concerned with the classification of the principles (tattvas) of existence and their proper discernment in order to distinguish between spirit (purusha) and the various aspects of nature (prakriti); this influential system grew out of the ancient (Pre-Buddhist) Samkhya Yoga tradition and was codified in the *Samkhya Karika* of Ishvara Krishna, 3500 BCE.

CHAPTER 10

BABAJI AND MATAJI
One at the Celestial Level

On a quiet evening, while I was sitting at the temple of Jageshwar[1] in the Kumaon region, I looked at all the vast temples around me and went into a nostalgic euphoria—before my mind's eye were pictures of long-gone sages from another era. I could not bring myself to understand why these sacred temples were so desolate and deserted when I went there. And then as my body stilled, I settled into myself, my consciousness changed. My mind gave way to my consciousness, and even the fleeting pictures of the long-past events melted into the quiet pool of my consciousness. I seemed to be entering an other-worldly dimension, but I was the same. The temples and trees were the same. Even the ground I sat on was very real and solid. Unlike the stark and masculine nature of the Garhwal terrain, the sylvan surroundings of the Kumaon mountains were more feminine in nature, and the green coniferous and deodar trees melted into a green pool of peace before my mind's eye and disappeared into my consciousness. The slanting rays of the setting Sun made the temples cast their lengthening shadows upon me, and a gentle breeze blew by, which carried with it an aroma of the wild forest, so fresh and alive.

I sat within myself, quiet, non-wanting and content. And then from behind the quiet evening sunlight appeared the figure of a very unassuming and simple youth. It was not clear to me whether He appeared from the outside surroundings or from the quietness

---

1 A holy pilgrimage of Ardhnarishwar in the Kumaon region.

within, but His manifestation seemed to coincide with both. I knew it, but I didn't know that this was He, whom in mystic circles, they call The Nameless One, and yet this Being went by so many names, which each yogi or swami used to suit their individual temperaments and beliefs. However, as this young Being, who could be aged anywhere from sixteen to twenty, came and sat before me, about fifteen to twenty feet away, He was a dream so real that even reality seemed to be a dream compared to Him. And even in my still-mind (*unmani*) state, I marveled at His enigmatic majesty. He was desireless and immaculate, and I had no desire. What did He come for? To reveal something? To tell me a story? And as I gazed at His form, He smiled at me, and then I had a very unique darshan and insight of His nature-not-nature. Half His body took on a feminine form, and His features, the contours of His features, including His breast, transformed so that half of His body was totally of the Divine Mother, the other half of His body had the masculine structure of a youth of 16 summers—Immortal were they in their companionship. For He had given me a vision that Babaji Himself was Mataji. They were not different. Babaji was Shiva, and His Shakti was Mataji, who emanated from Him as the dynamic creative force and liberating force in creation. So Babaji and His Shakti, I was given to know, were not separate[2].

This was a great lesson I had to learn, as I always thought that Babaji and Mataji were different. This may also be true in a lower sense of relativity, but as a yogi advances in his spiritual insight, the difference of gender disappears, not only at the soul level, but also at the physical level. I came to know this truth that Mataji and Babaji form what we call in Indian spiritual language, a complete Truth called *Ardhnarishwar*[3], which means Shiva and Shakti are one. This Ardhnarishwar was the divine androgynous being, with Shiva Goraksha Babaji representing the consciousness and Mataji

---

[2] As He left, He showed His form again, with the *kundals* (earrings) in His ears, the likes of which Shiva wears. This left no shadow of doubt in my mind that Shiva Goraksha Babaji of the *Nath* tradition and the Babaji mentioned in *Paramhansa* Yoganandaji's autobiography are one and the same.

[3] Half-Shiva and half-Shakti, akin to the later Greek god, Hermaphrodite, half-male, half-female respectively.

representing the Shakti energy, the Cosmic Kundalini, which works for the evolution of humankind in this world of relativity. After I came down from this samadhi revelry, I turned around and went into the main Jageshwar temple and was dumbfounded to find out from the priest that this was the only temple in the world where the *shivalinga* is half Shiva and half Shakti.

This is the only temple in the world where the divine androgynous being Ardhnarishwar is worshipped as Shiva-Shakti in the same *shivalinga*. People have an expression saying, 'My mind was blown away'. Not only was my mind blown away by this stupendous concurrence, but my samadhi also got blown away. I write this because of a lack of a better way of expression. This experience was too good for words. I came out of the temple and sat on the rocks of the afternoon winter Sun, and said truly, 'Babaji is beyond light, beyond the Rings-Pass-Not of relativity. He is the Lightless Light, which makes Him faster than light; and He is a time-reversed phenomenon, standing absolutely still at the hub, while Mataji-Shakti's light and kundalini swirls around Him, managing the whole of creation. Because He is still, She is moving, and because He is Nothing and incomprehensible, She is Everything and comprehensible to the whole world as the primal light of creation. Babaji is the Noumenon beyond creation, because of whom exists Mataji, the Phenomenon of creation'.

After this, as I came into myself, the Sun had set, and the stars were already twinkling and beginning to appear in the evening sky. I could already see the evening star representing Mataji called Venus, which is known as *Sitara* in India, or *Tara*, meaning the female goddess star. Exhilarated, I walked back from the temple to my camp and resting place. I know the Kumaon region is infested with panthers, leopards and other wild animals, but I had no fear for my safety. Once Babaji appears to any of His devotees, fear automatically vanishes from their heart, and they send out friendly vibrations of love and courage to the world. That night my body slept in peace, but my mind expanded into my consciousness, far and wide, a waking sleep, a Noumenon in the phenomenon.

I have also explained before that Mataji is not only Babaji's emanating power of feminine energy, who superintends the process of the evolution of humanity through kundalini, but She also plays the role of the World Mother and is the divine receptacle, whether it be an immaculate conception or otherwise. Whenever Mataji further projects Herself into the terrestrial regions of relativity, She permeates from the eighth dimension to the seventh dimension of an avataric degree as the World Mother. It is whispered in the mystic circles of the knowers of reality that no spiritual being can take a higher body than the seventh-level avataric body and still exist on our planet. This is because any higher awareness is unable to function in a terrestrial world of relativity since they are beyond the space-time continuum and their mass is infinite. Mataji holds in Her womb, the transiting embodiment of all avatars and divine beings who are born on this Earth. First She was Renuka, the mother of Lord Parashurama, then Kaushalya, the mother of Lord Ram, then Devaki, the mother of Lord Krishna. Then She took birth as Maya, the mother of Buddha. And then She came to Earth as Mary, the mother of Jesus. Kunti was no less a Divine Mother, who had all the Pandavas by Immaculate Conception. Then was Sumitra, the mother of Kalki. Anandamayi Ma was also an important aspect of Mataji. So Mataji is truly the Regina Mundi, Jagadamba, the World Mother.

Elsewhere, I have also emphasized the fact that when Babaji is the Lightning Holder, Mataji is the evolutionary Lightning who assists in the evolution of human races. I have also depicted Her as the World Mother who is the divine receptacle to hold and give birth to all the avatars.

Mataji has often been depicted as the sister of Babaji. It is not the physical relation that matters so much as Her divine work. She can come in as any relation to Babaji, according to the nature of the work. I have depicted Her as the Shakti (divine energy) of Babaji. The important factor to understand is that Mataji is the integral divine energy of Babaji and may come into play as His divine *lila* as the need or occasion arises.

Babaji and Mataji gave vision at Jageshwar as Ardhnarishwar.

CHAPTER 11

THE AVADHOOT AVATARA DOCTRINE

In today's spiritual culture, the word avatara is very loosely used without knowledge as to its true significance and what it really means. Anyone who can whip up a temporary hysteria is classified as an "avatara" by the masses who themselves haven't the slightest clue of what "avatara" means. In order to give people an understanding, it has become necessary to guide them and give a clear vision as to what an avatara actually is, the different types of avataras, and what their work is.

The Divine Work and Advent of the Avatara

The word avatara is composed of two words, ava meaning to descend and tara meaning to save by bridging the gulf between humanity and Divinity. The Divine Consciousness descends to incarnate in the haunts of mortal beings to save their souls by ferrying them across the delusive ocean of samsara (the material world), into the haven of Self-Realization. This is the classic Indian thought coupled with the idea that the avatara deals with the spiritual evolution of human consciousness. Like the Biblical Noah, who in his ark played savior to all species of life at the physical level, saving them from the floods, the avatara is a savior to all life at the spiritual level. He saves all souls from the quagmire of materialism.

The Avadhoot Avatara Doctrine

The avatara is the descent of Divinity into flesh. It is aja (unborn) so that it can never die. Normally, in spiritual evolution a *Paramahansanath Yogi* evolves to a *Siddhanath Yogi* who then further progresses to the evolutionary stature of an *Avadhootnath Yogi*. He is then the beacon of spiritual light to the world, unfettered and free. He is the "enlightened swan" flying high and soaring beyond the limited comprehension of mortal man. Being supremely free, he has no karma to fulfill and attains to the final *Niranjana Nirvana*[1]. Having merged into the Supreme Divinity, he returns to the world no more. But if he does return under very rare circumstances, fully robed with the Light and Love of God, he comes for a world liberating mission. Then and only then may he be said to be the *Avatarnath Yogi*.

The classical and well-known avataras are Rama, Krishna, and Buddha. The work of the avatara is to protect the righteous, to destroy all negativity and darkness, and to establish the dharma of right living. They come from age to age. Gyanavatar Sri Yukteswar, in his book *The Holy Science,* has clearly given the length and duration of the four human yugas or ages, as being different from the four celestial ages. The first two ages are Satya Yuga (golden age of 4800 years), followed by the Treta Yuga (the silver age of 3600 years). Then comes the Dwapara Yuga (copper age of 2400 years.) Finally comes the dark age of Kali Yuga (iron age of 1200 years). The coming of these lofty Beings of Truth, and the periods in which they incarnate, has also been mentioned in the *Bhagavad Gita*. The avatara incarnates at the most needed hour of humanity.

In the case of Shiva Goraksha Babaji, He is a *Swayambhu*[2], also called a Mahavatar. This shall be explained later.

---

[1] The final salvation; a state of God Realization

[2] 'great unborn', the self-manifestation and personal aspect of Lord Shiva. The cosmic being Babaji-Gorakshanath will not incarnate from age to age, but is perpetually present until the world cycle (mahakalpa) is over. He broods over humanity, his children, from eternity to eternity and is thus known as "the Great acrifice." His work is far beyond the comprehension of mortals.

The Divine Signs of a True Avatara

1. The body of an avatara is composed by Kriya Shakti of pure spiritual light and is not subject to disease, decay or death. This body of light is beyond the ravages of time. On occasion, the avatara casts no shadow.

2. The footprints of an avatara are not impressed on the seashore or the sands of causation and time, because he has no karma (deed), only akarma[3] (divine work).

3. The birth of an avatara is not bound by karma, but he chooses it by divine will, whatever the manner of birth may be. Whether it is through the womb of a mother, by immaculate conception, or birth in a lotus, it is the divine will of the avatara, free from karma. A divine avatara has the capacity to pull over himself the veil of cosmic illusion and incarnate into the world of mortal beings. It is a divine descent, being in the world of matter and maya, and yet not of it.

4. Resurrection. The avatar's body is composed of divine, undecayable light. It has the capacity to die and then transform the atomic cells into a transfigured body of light, resurrecting itself to show the glory of the Lord Most High on the earth of mortal man. Resurrection is the special feature of the avatara alone. People who claim to be avataras, but who are incapable of resurrecting their bodies after death, are spiritually evolved beings of a lesser stature; they cannot be classified or called avataras. They may be saints, yogis, Hamsas and Paramhamsas.

---

3 'actionless action', karmaless action.

The Different Types Of Avataras

The Mahavatar (Swyambhu). This is specifically the great unborn, Self-manifestation of Shiva and has a much loftier work than the avatara. The Cosmic Avataras of Shiva. Also called the manifestations of Lord Shiva, the Shiva Kumars. Standing at the eigth level of Cosmic Consciousness, they are usually invisible and unknown. However, they incarnate specifically for the yogic and spiritual evolution of human consciousness. They are not limited to the yuga cycle as are the avataras of Vishnu, but manifest when the need of spiritual evolution arises. They are also called the Agnishvatta Rishis (the Sages of the Fire Mist).

Avataras of Vishnu. These are the classic Avataras at the seventh level of Cosmic Consciousness who come for the salvation of mankind from age to age according to the yuga cycle. They are in order, Matsya (fish), Kacchha (tortoise), Varaha (boar), Narsimha (man-lion), Vaman (dwarf), Parshu Rama (ancient man), Rama (perfect man), Krishna (divine man), Buddha (enlightened man) and Kalki (divine savior). These incarnations not only signify the physical evolution, but evolve the consciousness of all humanity as well. The last three are Purna Avataras.

Purna Avataras (complete descent of Divinity in human body). The Purna Avatara is that consciousness of Divinity which descends in the haunts of human beings to establish righteousness and spiritually evolve human consciousness. This God-made-flesh comes to Earth every yuga. Krishna, the Buddha, and the Kalki are ideal examples of the Purna Avatara. The last is yet to incarnate in the world at the junction of the Leo-Aquarius age, which is in the year 2499, that is 487 years after 2012. These beings are at the eigth level of Cosmic Consciousness. We must also understand that from 2499 to 2700, the divine race called the sixth root race will be established on the western coast of America, mainly in California. The same sixth root race is all of us present now, who form the sixth sub race, and as we evolve with the practice of Kriya Yoga, we shall be a part of the making of the sixth root race, to work under the guidance and blessings of the Kalki avatara, and his successor the World Teacher Yogavatar Lahiri Mahasaya. Then comes the Vaishvaswat Manu and his great succesor will be Gyanavatar Yukteswar as the World King of the inner government.

In my observation, a similar evolutionary process of the ten avataras is replayed at a lower human scale in the womb of a mother. Here the embryo first appears as the fish avatara, then the tortoise, the boar-faced, then man-lion, then the miniscule dwarf, then the human achetype (Parshuram), then the human form receiving sensations (Ram), then emotions (Krishna), then the developed embryo receiving ideations from the mother (Buddha). Finally, the fetus is fully evolved, ready to be born into a whole new consciousness, which represents the Kalki Avatara.

Aunsh Avataras. This is the partial avatara who manifests for the evolution of all human souls. The partial avatara, like the full avatara, has already attained to *Nirvana Moksha*, the seventh level of Cosmic Consciousness. The difference between the two is that the partial avatara, when descended on earth, manifests only a part of his Divinity commensurate with his work. The nature of his work on earth needs him to manifest only so much of his Divine Consciousness as can complete his mission. The full avatara has no such limitations.

I am bringing to light that the Avataras of Vishnu are considered to be his direct emanation through one of the seven primeval flames, called the Seven Rishis of the ancient of days, the archangels of the heavenly host and collectively the sacred Elohim of eternal living fire. Lord Krishna, for example, was a direct emanation of Sanatana Rsi Naryana. He is, however, the descent of Deity in form (*mayavi rupa*[4]) of individuality. His appearance to man on earth is objective but in sober fact is not so. His illusive form has no past or future, nor does he have reincarnations due to karma, which has no hold on him.

---

4 Illusive form.

The consciousness of all avataras is fully enlightened, far beyond the comprehension of humans, totally and wholly merged into the Absolute. Pulling the veil of the cosmic illusion, it creates for itself what is called a *mayavi roop*, meaning an illusionary idea body composed of the three gunas of *sattva* (luminosity), *rajas* (activity), and *tamas* (inertia). Then the Divine materializes the radiant astral body, which ultimately forms a physical body that can appear and disappear at will. The divine body of congealed light casts no shadow and no footprints. It is the divine light in a material world.

The work and mission of the avatara has been explained above and the details of the Kalki, our coming Messiah, will be given now.

The Being called Babaji Goraksha Nath will not incarnate from age to age, but is perpetually present until the world cycle is over. He broods over humanity, His children, from eternity to eternity. His work is far beyond the comprehension of mortals. He stands at the ninth level of Cosmic Consciousness.

The Mahavatar Babaji and His Assistants

The doctrine of the avatara unfolds as we study the ancient scriptures of India. The *Kalki Purana*[5], the *Bhavishya Purana*[6] and the *Chandogya Upanishad* give us fascinating insights into the nature of this Divine Shiva Kumar, loftier in spiritual stature than even the Purna Avatara.

He goes by many names and one of which is The Eternal Now," meaning that for Him there is no past-present-future in this world of relativity. For Him, everything is in the Now! as his awareness comprehends relativity in the present moment. This also shows that He is beyond the limitation of causation, space and time as there is no such barrier in the Eternal Now. But out of His unfathomable compassion for humanity, an infinitesimal portion of His Being is

---
5 An ancient treatise about the coming of the Kalki Avatara/Maitreya who shall restore spirituality on this earth, and reinstate the Solar Dynasty.
6 An ancient text prophesying future events.

ever present to serve humanity as His larger Self. Sacrificing the inconceivable bliss of God-Being for the countless suffering souls on earth, He is rightly called The Great Sacrifice. Not only this, but He is also the Ceaseless Sacrifice beyond human comprehension.

In the spiritual inner government of the World, He has with him three mighty Rudra Kumars to help Him with His work of evolving planets and humanities. Then assisting the Rudra Kumars are the thirty great Beings of Avataric stature. Their glorius bodies are created by Kriya Shakti and they were the ones who form the first spiritual hierarchy, eighteen-and-a-half million years ago, which in their consciousness is very recent.

Some of the lofty *Rudras* (aspects of Shiva), of His hierarchy are Sanatana, Sanandana, Sanaka-Sujata, Lord Dakshinamurti[7], Lord Dattatreya, Adi-Shankaracharya, Buddha, Christ, Hermes, Patanjali[8], Lord Kalki Maitreya and Lord Vaivashvat Manu.

In the next echelon we have the Chiranjeevs ("Immortals"), Lord Parshurama, Lord Hanuman, Ashvathama, Bali, Vikramaditya / Morya[9] (Gyanavatar Yukteshwar), Devapi (Yogavatar Lahiri Mahasaya), Arjuna, Aaryasangh/Jwala Kula ("family flame") and Count St.Germain.

The partial celestial manifestation of Shiva Goraksha Babaji appeared on earth eighteen-and a half-million years ago at the begining of the *Vaivashvat Manvantar*, the duration of the reign of the seventh spiritual king, Vaivashvat Manu. There are fourteen such Manus in one kalpa[10] or day of Brahma. We are currently in the middle of the Shweta Varaha Kalpa (World Cycle of the White Boar). He is now the Silent Watcher who directs all avataras and prophets in their evolutionary work and mission. The deeper nature of His

---

[7] A name for Lord Shiva, facing the South. It is said that this Sage was a youth and taught his disciples in silence.
[8] The Master of Yoga who authored the Yoga-Sutras.
[9] Chandra Gupta Morya/El Morya; the first emperor of India destined to be the future World King of the inner government of the world, the Manu Saverni of the sixth root race.
[10] The lifespan assigned to our planetary system.

own work is beyond our comprehension. This deathless Presence of eternity, keeps in his aura, even the coming of the Kalki Avatara and all of the manifestations Divine. It is not given to us to know what arrangement for a spiritual impetus to humanity shall be given at the beginning of the new millennium, but it is said that a tremendous Being, a manifestation of Shiva Babaji Himself shall incarnate at the end of the millennium in one or many souls and do as great a work on the spheres of the inner consciousness of humanity as the Kalki Avatara will do on the outer consciousness of humanity.

A galvanic spiritual impetus shall come from this manifestation of Shiva. This evolutionary surge given by this lofty Being called the Mahavatar is to avoid the dire consequences of wiping out humanity from the face of the earth while spiritually enabling it to take the paradigm shift so glibly talked about by parrots of the parlour. Of course, the great Babaji, The Presence, will ever be a silent witness to this divine drama.

The Avadhoot/Avatara Doctrine

The difference between an avatara and an *avadhoot* is that the avatara is the involution of the Divine into the human and the *avadhoot* is the evolution of the human into the Divine. The *avadhoot* literally means "cast-off." He has shaken off all worldly ties and concerns; the highest renunciate ever-absorbed in Supreme Consciousness. He is a yogi who has crossed the sixth degree of initiation, meaning that even the last vestiges of his karma of stored impressions have been worked out. He, the Conscious Seer, in *nirbija samadhi*[11], is totally free from the seed of the mind and matter of the universe. The cycle of birth and death ceases for him and karmic desire cannot pull him down to reincarnate on earth unless he chooses to do so. However, when he does reincarnate, it is as a savior, a partial avatara.

One of the prevailing views about a soul who has evolved to the stature of an *avadhoot* through a series of incarnations and accu-

---

11 Consciousness without seed; the highest form of samadhi before the final dissolution of dharma megha samadhi.

mulated merit, is that his meditations and good karma cannot make him a *Nirvani*[12], but can lead him to a divine Sat-Guru. Then by the Guru's grace, he will be initiated into the mysteries of *Niranjana Nirvana* and attain to divine union. The other view is that from our works alone we obtain *moksha*, and if we take no pains there will be no gains. Grace from the Deity (Maha Guru) does not come to the lazy. In order to procure the grace of the Guru, the disciple must make the initial effort. Therefore, it is maintained that the Buddha, though an avatara in one sense, is a true *Param-mukta Avadhoot*. Owing to his personal merit and endeavor, he attained nirvana[13] and is more cherished than an avatara.

My personal view is that both individual effort in yoga and devotion bring about the grace of the Guru, which is necessary to achieve the blessed state of *Nirvana Moksha*. The grace of God and Guru, like the sun, shines equally on all beings because in the eyes of the Divine, all are equal, and the God-essence is no respecter of personal egos. Grace is planted as conscience in the minds of each of us and it is we who bring about the grace and disgrace of God in our lives, by either hiding in the dark room of karmic negativity or exposing our selves to sunshine of divine grace through good deeds. We are responsible for the grace of God in our lives and disgrace of ourselves by our own deeds. Only past life effort of good works makes it appear as grace in this life because we have no memory recall of the past. The truth is that a particular Soul that appears to be graced by the Divine has already made the effort in a past or present life.

Incarnations and Rebirths

There is a very subtle difference between a partial avatara and an *avadhoot*. In fact, in terms of self-realization they have both attained *moksha*. The difference is that the *avadhoot* does not enter his entire causal and spiritual consciousness into *Nirvana Moksha*. He makes his spiritual self (*atma*) experience the wisdom of nirvana

---

12 Fully enlightened being.
13 Cessation of all desire. synonymous with enlightenment.

The Avadhoot Avatara Doctrine

while keeping his causal body intact to reincarnate as a saviour of humanity with this same causal body. From this later evolved the *Bodhisattva*[14] doctrine of Indian Buddhism[15]. On the other hand, the partial avatara merges his all into *Nirvana Moksha*. His causal body and *atma* are both transformed and resolved into *Brahma Nirvana* (*Nirvana Moksha*). To sum it up, we can say that an *avadhoot* who enters *Nirvana Moksha* never returns and if he does, he comes as a partial avatara.

For the sixth degree initiates, the next question is this: if an *avadhoot* purifies his causal body to the extent of having no residual karma in it, then the causal body, as per the *Advaita Vedanta*[16] philosophy, shall resolve in pure consciousness. Hence, in order to incarnate on the terrestrial plane, he involutes to pull around himself a vesture composed of sub-atomic particles of light, creating this veil of maya by his own yogic power (kriya shakti). This is the *mayavi* or illusionary body of light that he can use to incarnate when needed.

The other option he has is to keep that slender film of causal body of good karma to enable him to reincarnate for the salvation of humanity. The fifth degree process of *Jivan Mukta*[17] is that he is one level lower than the *avadhoot* and has not dissolved his pure body film.

Rebirths may be classified into three categories:

1. Divine incarnations (avatar naths)
2. Adepts who forego Nirvana to help humanity (avadhootnaths)
3. Natural rebirths as per law of karma (ordinary people)

---

14 'enlightened being', the Chiranjiv immortals and avadhoots who's bodhi-chitta (buddhi) are purfied to such a degree of compassion that they spurn Nirvana (moksha) to serve humanity.

15 After Gautama Buddha, a Hindu prince who attained enlightenment and his followers who were called Buddhist. Buddha was not a Buddhist but followed the traditional Hindu/Indian lifestyle.

16 Culmination of vedas in monism.

17 An adept who, while still embodied, has attained liberation (moksha) from his material condtion (samsara).

In very exceptional rebirths, the high initiate *avadhoot*, before disappearing in *Nirvana Moksha*, can, for reasons best known to him, cause his body of causal light to remain behind. Not being an avatara, he is a knower (an enlightened being). The *avadhoot* has achieved *Nirvana Moksha*, but chooses not to enter that final state, remaining instead on our planet for the salvation of humankind.

A lower degree of incarnation that of a Siddha (*aulia*), is able to transfer the memory of his past life to his body with traces of it to be worked out. These traces may be a result of having taken on the karma of some of his disciples.

In the third degree, a practicing Hamsa Yogi, who has passed on from this life to the next, would, commensurate with his karma, choose a suitable body and circumstances in that incarnation to progress in his spiritual evolution, but in most cases, would lose all memory of his previous incarnation.

The most intriguing mystery of the *avadhoot* lies in the fact that how and when his consciousness is in nirvana, his causal body associates with the astral desire body of one of his worthy disciples, teaching it to safely channelize the kundalini energy to the state of a successful *nirvikalpa samadhi*.

A Unique Feature of the Non-Dual Phenomena

We now go on to the most marvelous evolutionary occurrence in spiritual history: a non-dual *advaita*[18] process, the most incomprehensible and awesome miracle between spirit and matter.

When the *kama sharir* or astral desire body of a high initiate is left behind, it purifies itself by contact with its Divine Rishi, one of the nine flames of the Cosmic Naths. This sage helps the astral body assimilate more of the intuitional nature and purity of mind. The astral desire body is then too pure to be dissolved in the astral

---

18 'nonduality', the truth and teaching that there is only One Reality called Atman or Brahman, especially as found in the Upanishads.

plane, its intermediate state between two incarnations. It lives on to evolve towards purity and finds its own degree of salvation in a wisdom body, which then is assimilated in that celestial body. It then becomes itself the luminous star of the soul. This star introverts upon itself, turning itself inside out, to involute through its own Divine mind star-gate to vanishing point, and evolute to become infinite divine consciousness. How does it do that? The answer is by the Rishi Guru's grace, which is reciprocating the mind-star's right endeavor. In scientific parlance, the gurutva akarshan (intense gravitational attraction) of the Rishi Guru pushes the mind-star out of four-dimensional existence into a Self-Realized Consciousness.

Lord Maitreya will inhabit the causal mind-star of Purna Avatara Krishna to re-incarnate as the Kalki Avatara and complete his mission as the next savior of all sentient and non-sentient beings. The causal mind-star shall thereafter gravitate through its own star-gate and finally merge into infinite Consciousness. Presently, the Kalki-Maitreya is established in the Supreme Conscious ecstasy of Yoga with his Cosmic Nath Guru, the Brahma-Rishi Parashara, abiding in the bosom of duration until the commencement of the Leo-Aquarius age when he shall descend in flame and fire to establish righteousness amongst the people of the Earth.

This is the story of the evolution of the astral desire body into the Soul Consciousness, a very rare happening because it defies both the *samkhya* philosophy and the economy of nature.

Normally all bodies, physical, astral and causal, composed of the sub-atomic particles of *tama*, *raja* and *sattva* gunas resolve back into the transcendental matrix of the matter and mind of the universe. They do not transform to Divine Consciousness, as is the rare case of this non-dual *advaita* phenomena given above. This is one of the inexplicable mysteries of the Avadhoot-Avatara doctrine. So, what I'm saying is that in the case of the *avadhoot* or avatara, such a quantum leap of evolution is possible even for their cast-off astral bodies, once they associate with their Divine Being, the Cosmic Naths.

The Avadhoot and Avatara Personalities

Gajanan Maharaja from the village of Shaegaon (India) was a nineteenth century *avadhoot* who helped a lesser *mast* initiate to such a degree that he himself appeared to be the *mast*, but in fact was assisting his disciple to work out his karma by actually wearing the astral body of the disciple. Besides this, he had also worked with many normally evolving students as well. The enlightened *avadhoot* takes it upon himself to empower his student from a *mast*-intoxicated state of a *savikalpa samadhi* to a *nirvikalpa samadhi*. Holding back one's own entry into *Brahma Nirvana* for the sake of younger souls to come is surely a divine way of serving humanity as one's larger Self.

Sai Nath of Shirdi in Maharastra (India) is one of the greatest enigmas in the spiritual hierarchy of Nath Yogis. He behaved exactly like an *avadhoot* but in the reality showed all the signs of an avatara. His raising the dead, casting no shadow from his body on occasions, and himself appearing in resurrected rainbow body of light, leads me to realize the avataric stature of this Nath Yogi. At the same time, his losing body consciousness and falling down, behaving like a *mast* and losing control of his body, makes one think he is an *avadhoot* deeply involved in assisting many divinely intoxicated yogis and Sufis to evolve along the spiritual path. Since this great being also helped in the spiritual evolution and karmic dissolution of normal initiates and people, Sai Nath is truly the most mystic of the modern-era of avataras. The avatara takes on the furthering of human awareness in deeper dimensions of Consciousness.

Gyan Nath (Jnaneswar) "The Avatara of Wisdom" was born in the village of Alandi (Maharashtra, India) in the thirteen century. He is called the king of mystics by the high initiates of the secret circles of the Nath Mandala[19]. His Maha Guru was Babaji Goraksha Nath himself, who initiated the young Gyan Nath into the mysteries of Nath Yoga and the ultimate realization of *nirvikalpa* and *sanje-*

---
19 The electromagnetic spiritual field of the Nath Yogis.

evan samadhi[20]. Having successfully accomplished the Nath yogic practices, he however found them too demanding for the normal people and householders. As a result, he advocated the simple devotional pathway to God. From this evolved the bhakti[21] tradition of the *Varkaris*[22]. His miracles were not intended to aggrandize his spiritual stature, but to instill faith in the Divine into the hearts and minds of the then skeptical masses. However, his mahasamadhi also known as the *sanjeevan samadhi* (*saroub samadhi*), meaning the preservation of his rainbow-body of light in life and death, clearly points to his Nath knowledge. This more than shows us his avataric stature and mission that not only is his Consciousness immortal, but the body and mind too; a distinct feature of immortality of the Siddha-Nath yogic tradition.

Mahavatar Babaji, "the Lord of Irradiant Splendor," is also called *Sanata Kumar*, meaning "the eternal virgin youth." He came to be by direct manifestation from Nilalohita Shiva (blue void of absolute Consciousness) infused in Brahma who is *viraj-vaak* (light-sound). Holding in his hands the evolutionary lightning of life and death, Babaji is called "*Vaidhatra*" meaning "the Cosmic Lightning Holder of Divine Destiny." This word (*vaidhatra*) also means, "first from the Creator." Accompanying Shiva Goraksha Babaji are thirty-three lofty beings, the Shiva-Kumars, the immortal virgin youths. Babaji is *Jaggan Nath* (Lord of the Universe), the head of the spiritual hierarchy of the Sages of the Fire Mist with their rainbow bodies of light, all in graded order, to assist him in his divine evolutionary work. The *kumars* are the true progenitors of spirit in humanity and because of these incomprehensible beings, the holders of the sacred flame, the spiritual evolution of humanity was and is continuously made possible. In ancient texts, they incensed the devas (the celestial beings) for imparting the secrets of the Divine to mortal men. Wonderful accounts about this wondrous Being and his Divine as-

---

20 Immortal state of samadhi.
21 'devotion' or 'love', the love of the bhakta toward the Divine or the Guru as a manifestation of the Divine.
22 A sect of Bhagvat devotees who worship Lord Krishna in the form of Lord Vitthal or Lord Pandurang.

sistants are given in the *Markandeya Purana*[23], and the *Samkhya Karika* of Ishvar Krishna.

Meeting with An Avadhoot

Talking of *avadhoots*, I have an interesting story to relate. I was, during my younger days, very fond of an Indian sweet called *jalebi*[24], and visited a simple roadside sweet shop (*dhaba*[25]), where we dipped the freshly made hot *jalebis* in milk and ate them. A smiling mendicant used to visit the shop and his nonchalant appearance intrigued me. This carefree wanderer, with his eyes gazing out into the unknown, pretended to relish with us the sweets. He, however, was not aware of what he ate. Nor did he appear to possess his body, which hung loosely about his person. Many a person came to the sweet shop and the young ladies who visited the place would be teased by this stranger. Many passed him off as a mad man.

Then one day I saw him lying on the footpath near the shop. He had apparently been beaten up by some ladies and their men for teasing. I went close to him and a strange sight met my eyes. He was lying on the floor smiling, his head bleeding, and a far away voice from within his body asked, "Are you happy, have you had enough now or do you want some more?" I opened my eyes wider and immediately felt attracted to this being, so that night I searched out his hut. When I peeped into the hut, I was agog to behold a blue halo of light surrounding this being who, during the day, played out his drama of teasing girls. His body was breathless and as rigid as a rock lost in the splendor of samadhi. With the wings of light, he had fled to his divine abode of Cosmic Consciousness (*Paramartha Satya*). His higher, real Self was in nirvana, while the apparent body he had acquired was to assist some of his pupils in working out their karma. To show such love for a pupil is very mysterious, an aspect of the Master-pupil relationship only understood between the two.

---

23 The Purana written by the rishi Markandeya.
24 A round and round and round sweet. Then stop. At the stop, the maximum syrup is attained. Shape of the coiled kundalini, lying in three-and-a-half coils.
25 A place of roadside fast-food in India.

He alone can explain why an a*vadhoot* would do as he would do. So I closed my eyes and slid into my dhyana meditation. Truly Oh Lord! Thy ways are and ever shall be incomprehensible to man.

Meeting with an Avatara - Anandamayi Ma

She was the bliss-permeated Mother. I had the good fortune to meet her on many occasions, and had many sweet memories in the aura of this Divine Being. One rainy afternoon, I left home in haste. I was homesick and I wanted to be absorbed in her presence. On reaching her ashram in Pune, I found the door to her room closed. I did not want to disturb her but stood in the rain, my eyes transfixed on the door as if I would stare it open. It did open, but only after I had practiced rain yoga for twenty minutes or so, a mild tapa to wash away some negative karma before meeting with the Divine, I thought to myself.

She smiled and called me indoors saying I was a stubborn child, and so I was. Before I sat, I proceeded to touch her feet (which she normally does not permit), but as I touched her feet, I was shocked to find my hands go through her bones and flesh to touch the floor. My body was electrified at that. I remembered that an avatara is an illusion of light in the illusion of the world. It can at will, to increase a person's faith, make one experience his or her body of light. No flesh, no shadow, no karma. How can a nobody have any karma? An avataric Being is karma-less, when it does work in maya, it leaves no *samskaras*. It's like writing on water. When the unliberated student does his daily chores or work, he creates karma. It's like writing on the sand. Uplifted and wonder-struck by this experience, I settled in a trance-like state and saw her radiance flooding the whole ashram and countryside. As my body elongated, my Consciousness left it to expand and merge in her wondrous aura. I was blessed, and when I opened my eyes, the surroundings were still radiant with her presence. An hour later she said, "You are your own Guru, go and spread the word of the Lord in far lands," and went into samadhi again.

In all my travels and spiritual experiences, in all my meditations and direct experiences, the realization that has dawned on me is that Anandamayi Ma is the only woman avatara of the century. She is often loosely and wrongly equated with popular modern women saints, yoga teachers, or others of similar names. We are blessed to have such divine avataras with us, without whom pure spirituality would have vanished from the face of this Earth long ago.

The False Avataras

A certain thing needs to be cleared about what is called the false masters and avataras. This, dear souls, is intended for nobody in particular, but just offers basic guidelines to the excitable sort of psychology which tends to take wings at the slightest provocation of anybody behaving in an other-than-ordinary manner. The human mind is gullible, volatile, and easily impressed by the true as well as the false teachers and masters roaming around amongst us. As no proof is required by the people, pseudo-masters claim to be the Maitreya, Buddha, the Kalki avatara, and the second advent of Christ. Be alert. For you are only deceiving yourself by these paranoid schizophrenics who no doubt are good souls, but are totally out of touch with Reality. Neither do they possess the powers nor the truth which can enable them to fulfill the World Prophecy.

I do admit that the common person caught in the material quagmire of stress and emotional suffering may find it a great solace to believe in a man of peace, and make that solace his sufficient criteria to accept even an ordinary teacher as a divine Master like the Maitreya or the Krishna or Kalki. The common human being, coming in contact with such egotistic and self-opinionated beings may well be deceived into thinking these self-styled Masters to be the Kalki Avatara or the Maitreya. Let us beware, and immediately withdraw our minds from these false flights of fancy, because if these pseudo-buddhas and christs do not satisfy our innermost aspirations and do not give us the experience of healing kundalini transmission or show the light to self-realization, and finally share the experience of samadhi, the ecstasy of expanded consciousness, then at the end of the day we shall be deeply disappointed and find ourselves in a state of depression and delusion. Therefore, it would be wise to avoid such megalomaniacs who masquerade as world teachers and divine beings. We must have the courage to tell them gracefully, or write to them making them aware of who they really are. This would greatly help their spiritual progress.

It is not good to stand in judgment over other beings. But when those other beings are misleading the masses, we must take it upon ourselves to firstly guide the masses in the proper direction, and secondly, to respectfully tell those self-opinionated pseudo-saviors that they must do some more humble introspection and put themselves in their proper places in society. Thereby they will do a great good to society. They may serve humanity from the humble place that they are at, and not look up to the stars and claim they are the avataras, and the next moment fall into the ditch below them. May all people on Earth be blessed with a proper sense of proportion as to who they are, where they come from, and where they are going. May God bless us all.

CHAPTER 12

THE INITIATION OF AVATARAS BY BABAJI

Mythology is not fiction; it is folklore tradition. It is a series of unwritten facts and culture which are passed down to use from timeless heritage.

Shiva Goraksha Babaji walks through the pages of spiritual history. He is called the Supreme Initiator, the great banyan tree from which branched out all the great avataras and divine beings. In former world cycles, He initiated the Sages of the Fire Mist, the Seven Rishis of the Great Bear, and the celestial beings: Kubera, Indra, Varuna[1], Surya and Yama[2]. Divine beings such as Parashara, Rama, Krishna, Enoch, Hermes and Apollo were also initiated by Babaji in previous world cycles.

He first took the form of Rudra of the Ancient of Days. He then manifested in 6000 BCE as Kalagni Nath. Subsequently, He came in 5000 BCE in the holy city of Kashi (Benares[3]) as Dakshinmurti, during which time He initiated Himself. In 3000 BCE, 100 years after the Great Bhishma Pitamah left his body, Shiva Goraksha Babaji initiated Melkizedek, who is to be the future Manu King Savarni of the 6th root civilization. In 1400 BCE, He initiated Moses through the burning bush as the great Yah-veh (Jehovah). In the year 70 BCE, He manifested Himself as Goraksha Nath, at the time of king Bharthari

---

1 The deity presiding over the element of water and the oceans.
2 The name of the gatekeeper of the netherworld; 'The First Mortal'.
3 The sacred city of the pilgrimage to Kashi Vishwanath (Lord Shiva).

Nath and his younger brother Vikramaditya and initiated them both. Then continuing His divine play, He came to King Shalivahan[4] and blessed his elder son Chowrangee Nath whom He initiated into yoga. Babaji is also mentioned in *Autobiography of a Yogi* as having initiated the first, or *Adi*, Shankaracharya.

Blessing and Initiation of Lord Rama (7000 BCE)

Lord Rama, the seventh avatara of Vishnu, had an eventful worldly manifestation. When, following a 14-year exile, he returned to the kingdom of Ayodhya there was great rejoicing and celebration. Preparations for his coronation were made with great pomp and splendor. The divine Shiva Goraksha Babaji was in deep samadhi during this period and it was through this samadhi that He sent His heartfelt blessings to Lord Rama, also initiating in the latter's mind a sense of spiritual expansion and a desire for the creation of a sound administration for his subjects in Ayodhya. As the Great Guru Goraksha Nath was unable to attend Lord Rama's coronation, He sent a small band of His disciples with *prasad* as a token of His blessings.

Blessing and Initiation of Lord Krishna (3102 BCE)

In ancient times, when Lord Krishna was once out on a journey, he happened to come to the ashram of the great rishi, Garga. In his satsang with the great sage, the topic of the immortal Being called Goraksha Nath came up. Krishna, very interested in knowing more about this mysterious and immortal Being called Shiva Goraksha, asked the great rishi, 'Who is this god called Goraksha Nath? By what mantras and means may he be appropriated, and what type of meditation is to be done?'

---

4 Also known as the Satavahan king, variously pronounced as Solomon, or Suleiman by other traditions.

Thus having obtained the knowledge of Shiva Goraksha Babaji, he was said to have performed intense meditation and penance for sixty thousand divine years (not the same duration as Earth years), both in the Himalayas and at the pilgrimage of Jaggan Nath Puri. Shiva Goraksha Babaji then appeared to Lord Krishna and gave him initiation into the highest mysteries of the Self and the Divine. As Babaji's Consciousness has within it the trinity, one of His forms is Lord Krishna, who in occult circles is called Shambhu Chaitanya (Shiva of Irradiant Consciousness). This explains Yogavatar Lahiri Mahasaya's statement: 'That who is Krishna is the ancient Babaji Himself'.

Babaji is to Krishna, as Shiva is to Vishnu. In the *Shiva Mahapurana*, Lord Shiva says, 'Know Vishnu and Myself to be One'. Those who know this are enlightened. Both Shiva-Goraksha and Vishnu-Krishna know that at the level of divine consciousness their essence is one, but in relativity, their functions are different. Krishna is the sustainer of souls in creation and Shiva Goraksha is the dissolver of the human phenomenon to take all souls to the Absolute Reality.

Blessing and Initiation of Moses (1400 BCE)

Shiva Goraksha blessed and initiated Moses at Mt. Sinai through the burning bush as the great Yah-veh (Jehovah). Jehovah said unto Moses, 'Take off thy shoes, for the ground on which thou standest is holy ground'. We must understand that Babaji appeared to Moses as Yah-veh (Meaning, *Mahankala*, The Great Time). He also appeared to Bharthari Nath and Yogavatar Lahiri Mahasya as *Mahankala*. Babaji went on to initiate Moses into the mysteries of the self and gave him the Ten Commandments, which initiated him and blessed him to be the future law-giver and succeed the Lord Vaivaswat Manu (Noah/Melchizedek) as Manu Savarni of the sixth root race.

He further initiated Moses into the truth that 'Thou shall not have any idol before Me,' which means that no man should worship or dote upon the idol of his physical body, but instead, through meditation shift his identity from his apparent body to his true consciousness. The delusion lies in thinking of oneself as the corruptible body and not the divine soul. Idol worship is the admiration and veneration of one's physical body, which Moses told his people to stop, and worship instead the divine consciousness within.

This is the most grossly misunderstood concept in the Ten Commandments, where people think that idol worship is only of physical statues; but people fail to understand that they are falling into a greater trap of worshiping their life-forms of flesh. To get souls out of this heresy of mistaken identity, was the task that Moses was not able to fully complete. Hence, he had to reincarnate as Maurya[5], Vikramaditya and then Gyanavatar Sri Yukteshwar to set the score straight and put people on the right track to enlightenment. Here they will realize that they are divine souls and not corruptible bodies to be idol worshiped. The new commandment is:

Humanity our Uniting Religion
Breath our Uniting Prayer and
Consciousness our Uniting God
                              Yogiraj Siddhanath

Blessings and Initiations of Bhog Nath (Lao-Tzu) (500 BCE)

Bhog Nath was initiated by Babaji through one of his powerful emanations called Kalagni Nath at Benares, a pilgrimage in Northern India. Both Kalagni Nath and Bhog Nath belonged to the ancient Nav Nath tradition. Bhog Nath was also called Bogar Nath when he travelled to South India, and was later called Bo Yang when he

---

5 400 BCE first emperor of India, who also incarnated as the legendary king, Vikramaditya, 57 BC. Then as king Arthur in 600 CE and then the righteous king, Shivaji, then as Gyanavatar Sri Yukteshwar. It is this being who is destined to be the future Manu Savarni of our sixth root race.

travelled to China at the behest of Shiva Goraksha Babaji.

Shiva Goraksha Babaji being the immortal alchemist that He was, taught the sacred science of immortality through the transformation of mercury into the philosopher's stone. Special alchemical mercury tablets were also made, the use of which was taught to Bhog Nath to attain an immortal body. Of course, along with this came a vast and in-depth knowledge of herbs and *kayakalpa* in-depth techniques, which Babaji initiated him into. Bhog Nath, or Bo Yang as he was called in China, established the Taoist movement and gave the sacred Kundalini Yoga as a gift to the people, which went by the name of Yin-Yang Yoga. Yin stands for Shakti, the divine female principle, while Yang is Shiva, the divine male principal.

The sacred science of India's priceless yoga was taught to thousands of people in China and Bo Yang later became known as the celebrated Lao Tzu. He went on to teach them the Indian science of pranayama balance, known in China as Tai-Chi. This was accomplished by breathing to unite the male and female principles at the crown *chakra* and enter the yogic state of golden samadhi. Last but not least, the greatest mystery of the Nath tradition of India, was taught to Chinese disciples. It came under the category of Tantra Yoga as the transformation of sacred to spiritual energy. But alas, the later disciples in China were unable to comprehend the spiritual import of this technique of Tantra Yoga, and it fell into disrepute being used for commercial and sexual purposes. However, in India, the science is still maintained in its pristine purity and not given out easily to inquisitive tourists from the West or the East.

Bhog Nath also visited South America, as is confirmed by accounts left by the Incas; they say he gave the laws to the Muycas of present day Chile. He looked every bit an Indian *rishi* with a white beard, wearing white robes. They say he regulated their calendar and established their festivals; that is why we heard accounts of a Lord Ganesha *murthi* (statue) being found somewhere in South America and then vanishing. The immortal Bhog Nath also vanished from their culture in time.

There were other great teachers who had come from other dimensions according to the numerous legends of the Mayans, the Incas and the Aztecs. Bhog Nath gave to them the knowledge that one world cycle ended in 2012, which was mistaken as the end of the world. Instead, this misconstrued information really meant that 2012 would be the end of a cycle and the dawning of a new era. I have explained this in the chapter on the 'Great Indian Calendar', which I have put before the reader later in this book.

Blessing and Initiation of Alexander the Great (400 BCE)

Although the great Kalagni Nath lived in 6000 BCE, being one of the immortals and a powerful emanation of Shiva Goraksha Babaji, he continued his life drama along the corridors of time until a great being called Alexander was born. This being was destined to conquer a large portion of the Earth, but in him a strong flame to know the divine burnt brightly. As Alexander grew up, he was healthy, strong and very active but also had the capacity to go into deep states of reverie. In his states of inwardness, he envisioned himself to be a great king and a conqueror of the world; he may have thought this to be his imagination, but in reality, it was a state of precognition of his future. As days went by, his dreams began to take shape. Being the king of Macedonia, he amassed a well-trained cavalry and steady infantry.

He then set out on his exploits and conquests, sweeping across Europe in magnificent fury and conquering nation after nation. He was a military genius indeed, but also a soul upon whom fortune smiled to put the stamp of victory on his head. At last he came to the land of sages and yogis, where the military genius of Alexander met more than his match in the spiritual genius of the great yogi Kalagni Nath (variously mispronounced as Kalanos, Kalinath, Kalangi Nath). Kalagni Nath means 'The Lord of the Consuming Fire of Time'.

Of course, Alexander had this idea that he was the son of Zeus, and with this in mind he sent a messenger to call the great yogi. Kalagni Nath sent back the message with the reply, 'Tell your master, that another son of the divine awaits him, and it would be more appropriate that Alexander should come to him'. Sure enough, Alexander appeared before the great yogi and pleaded for him to come to Greece; the master then agreed. He initiated Alexander into the great yoga of renunciation. Later on, the great yogi departed the world by *yogic siddhi*. He entered the flames of his own funeral pyre before the entire Macedonian army to show that the soul was immortal and the body but a perishable garment.

When Alexander was on his deathbed, the immortal master resurrected himself and was present by his side in Macedonia. There he convinced Alexander to keep his hands outside his grave when he died, teaching the world the greatest lesson of renunciation, that man comes into this world empty-handed and empty-handed does depart. A human being should establish himself in immortal consciousness and not the evanescent tinsel wealth of this world.

Yogavatar Bharthari Nath (80 BCE – 57 BCE)

The last Chandravat Raja[6] of the Parmars[7] was Bharthari Nath, the king of Ujjain. He abdicated the throne after the death of his Queen, Pingala, and took the renunciate's vow of *sanyas*[8] to become an immortal and a disciple of Goraksha Nath. He undertook *tapa* and meditation in the Himalayan regions keeping his awareness and celestial body intact until the time came for him to reincarnate in a physical body about 1000 years later in the year 1010 CE. Immediately after his induction, his younger brother Vikramaditya succeeded him to rule Ujjain from 57 BCE. It was Bharthari Nath who directed Vikramaditya to renovate and rebuild

---

6 A clan of the ancient Moon dynasty.
7 A Rajput clan descended from the fire gods, Agnivamshas.
8 'Casting off', the state of renunciation, which is the fourth and final stage of life (see *ashram*) and consisting primarily in an inner turning away from what is understood to be finite and secondarily in an external letting go of finite things.

the sacred city of Hardwar[9].

The information about the reincarnations of Bharthari Nath is clearly the outcome of my personal meditation and experience; people are free to interpret this as per their own understanding.

The reincarnations of Bharthari Nath are very illustrious, and unravel some of the mysteries of this great being who is to be our future world teacher. Below is a picture of Bharthari Nath being initiated by his great Guru Shiva Goraksha Babaji. In his former lives, during the period when the great events of the *Mahabharata* era were played out, he was (as envisioned by me) the great king Devapi, who renounced his throne and was succeeded by his younger brother Shantanu, the father of the great Bhishma *Pitamaha* (or Great Father), who is well known in the epic of the *Mahabharata*. King Devapi went into intense *tapa* and yogic meditation being prepared, so to say, to be the successor to the world teacher, Lord Maitreya, the Kalki Avatara to be. After this he reincarnated as a partial avatara of Vishnu and went by the name of Aryadev Chanakya, who enthroned Chandragupta Maurya as the king of Magadha and played a part in the establishing of Maurya as the first emperor of the Indian Empire.

Babaji initiating Bharthari Nath

---
9 The entrance to the abode of Lord Shiva a place of pilgrimage at the foothills of the Himalayas.

Maurya himself is destined to be the spiritual king of the future and it is very interesting to note that life after life, the world teacher and the world king usually make their avataric descent together or a few years apart. Next came the avataric descent of the king Bharthari Nath, the to-be world teacher, accompanied by his younger brother Vikramaditya, to be the future world king in the spiritual hierarchy of the inner government of the world. King Bharthari's was a checkered life of romance, spirituality and renunciation, in which he showed to the world that every actor must play his part on the stage of life and yet not lose his true identity of soul individuality to the actor personality.

Then we go on to the next incarnation of the great poet-saint Kabir, whom Yogavatar Lahiri Mahasaya mentioned as himself in a former incarnation. Kabir's life was a deep spiritual journey of trying to unite the various religions and ideologies of differing societies and people. He was initiated by the great Shiva Goraksha Babaji into Kriya Yoga and the devotional path to God. And as we travel along the passage of time, this lofty soul descends once again as the great avatar Jnaneshwar, whose message of yoga and devotion spread across the length and breadth of the land of Maharashtra. He practiced the divine science of Kriya Yoga and his Bhakti movement and philosophy was *Sphurti Vada*. It is interesting to note that his sister Mukta Bai was a reincarnation of Queen Pingala, the wife of King Bharthari. So this makes King Bharthari and Pingala, who were husband and wife in a past incarnation, a brother and sister as Jnaneshwar and Mukta Bai in the subsequent incarnation.

My actually seeing Bharthari Nath at Ujjain and my later vision of him at the Shipra River, where he transformed into Kabir and then into the smiling Yogavatar Lahiri Mahasaya, corroborates the above fact. There is a good two to three hundred year gap between the incarnations of Bharthari, Kabir and Yogavatar Lahiri Mahasaya, all of whom had a mission to fulfill. My ancestral family temple of Lord Rama is near the great *Mahankala* Temple of Lord Shiva in Ujjain. Both temples are in the vicinity of where I had the experience of seeing Lord Bharthari Nath and Yogavatar Lahiri Mahasaya in visions.

There are two masterly works of literature written by Bharthari Nath—*Shrinagar Shatak* and *Vairagya Shatak*[10]. The *Shrinagar Shatak* talks about royal life, the ways of beauty and maya, while *Vairagya Shatak* is a composition about non-attachment and abandonment, the life and path of a yogi, the path of sacrifice and renunciation.

In this context we can note the absolute oneness of Babaji Goraksha Nath and Babaji Mahavatar:

Babaji Goraksha Nath	Babaji *Mahavatar*
Initiated Bharthari Nath at Ujjain 10 CE	Initiated Yogavatar Lahiri Mahasaya at Ranikhet 1861 CE.
Babaji Goraksha Nath was respectfully ushered by king Vikramaditya and enthroned on a golden throne	Babaji Mahavatar was also respectfully ushered by a seraphic disciple and was also enthroned on a golden throne
King Bharthari then saw the Enthroned Babaji Goraksha Nath holding the sceptre of life and death in His hands giving His disciple a vision of himself as *Kaal* the Great Time	Yogavatar Lahiri Mahasaya also saw the enthroned Mahavatar Babaji holding a sceptre of life and death in His hands giving His disciple a vision of Himself as *Kaal* the Great Time

This leaves no shadow of doubt that not only are Babaji Goraksha Nath and Babaji Mahavatar one and the same, but also that king Bharthari Nath and Yogavatar Lahiri Mahasaya are also one and the same.

---

10 The treatise on renunciation by king Bharthari Nath.

Gyan Avatar Adi Shankaracharya (788 – 822 CE)

Adi or the first Shankaracharya is widely regarded as India's greatest philosopher. He was a rare combination—a saint and a scholar. He was born in the village of Kaladi, Kerala in South India. It is said that this great incarnation of wisdom could read by the age of two and had mastered the *Vedas* by the age of eight. He is largely known as one of the fathers of *Advaita Vedanta*[11], the core philosophy that complements the actuality of yoga as expounded in Patanjali's *Yoga Sutras*. Many scholars and men of reason attempt to divide the philosophy of *Advaita Vedanta* and the practice of yoga, not knowing that Adi Shankaracharya was a yogi himself and an avatar. He is said to have authored an important commentary on the *Yoga Sutras* called the *Vivarana*. Shankaracharya organized and founded the four *Maths* (monastic schools) in India's four directions: Jyotirmath in the North, Sringeri in the South, Puri in the East, and Dwarka in the West.

Matsyendra Nath doing *parkaya pravesh*, which he taught to Adi Shankar

---

11 '*Veda's* end', the teachings forming the doctrinal conclusion of the revealed literature (*shruti*) of *Sanatana Dharma*.

Babaji initiated this great monist in Kashi (Benares) and empowered his mission of spiritual reformation. This fact was first made known to the public in the pages of Paramhansa Yogananda's *Autobiography of a Yogi,* where it is mentioned that Babaji recounts His meeting with the great monist to Yogavatar Lahiri Mahasaya and Swami Kebalananda.

To this I have added my findings that in the story of Adi Shankaracharya, when he was challenged to defeat Mandana Mishra's wife in debate, he was asked to describe the experience of married life. As a monk he would have been unable to do so; however, he used his powers to enter the body of a dead king, experience married life with his queen, and was able to win the debate. It is well documented in Shankayacharya's annals that he entered the body of the king by the process of *parkaya-pravesh*[12] taught to him by his Nath gurus and mentors, Matsyendra Nath and Gorakhsha Nath (see *Shankara Digvijaya* by Madhav Vidyaranya). This reveals, beyond a shadow of a doubt that the Babaji in the book *Autobiography of a Yogi,* who was the Kriya guru of Shankaracharya, and Babaji Goraksha Nath who Shankaracharya himself mentions as His guru, are one and the same. The Lord of our world is ego-less, hence He veils Himself from public recognition of which He certainly is in no need of.

Yogavatar Kabir (1440 – 1518 CE)

Born near Kashi (Benares), of Hindu parents and brought up by Muslim weavers, Kabir was a man of wide religious culture and enthusiasm, whose legacy and memory live supremely through his mystic poetry and song. A simple man who made his living at the loom, Kabir dedicated himself to bringing to all the love of a God beyond the various creed and caste distinctions that prevailed in his time. His philosophical affinities lay chiefly with the mystical thought of the celebrated Hindu ascetic Ramananda, of whom he was a disciple, though Kabir also had leanings toward Persian mysticism. Often he would say of himself, 'I am the child

---

12 The entry of a yogi into another body whether alive or dead.

of Rama and Allah'[13]. Of God, he proclaimed: 'He is neither in Kailash[14] nor in Kaaba'[15] and said God was more accessible to the washerwoman and the carpenter than to the self-righteous holy man.

Though involved at the physical level in the culture and politics of the times, the core of his spiritual ancestry lay at a much deeper level, in the *Saivism*[16] of the Nath yogis and in his Maha-Guru Babaji Goraksha Nath. Babaji imparted to the great saint and poet the sacred mysteries of the science of Kriya Yoga, the knowledge of the six chakras, *Shabda* (*shabad*) *Yoga*[17], and the *Omkar* meditation as the *Anahata Nada*[18] or the 'unstruck sound', often referred to in his poetry. Kabir praises Babaji in his work, 'The Guru neither eats nor drinks, neither lives nor dies: Neither has He form, line, color, nor vesture. He who has neither caste nor clan nor anything else—how may I describe His glory? He has neither form nor formlessness, He has no name, He has neither color nor colorlessness, He has no dwelling place'.

A testament to the power of his practice of Kriya is made known through his healings when he was nearly sixty years of age. He was brought before the Emperor Sikandar Lodi and charged with claiming the possession of divine powers, a heresy to Muslim law. Lodi, a ruler of considerable culture, tolerance and diplomacy, however decided to banish Kabir rather than have him executed citing his Hindu birth and Muslim upbringing.

True to his spiritual ancestry stemming from Babaji Goraksha Nath, Kabir relinquished his body in Maghar near Gorakhpur, his Guru's city. After his death, Hindus and Muslims disputed the possession of his body in order to perform the funeral rites obligatory to their respective customs. The Hindus wanted a

---

13 A name for God.
14 The sacred mountain where the spirit of Lord Shiva is said to dwell.
15 The sacred place of worship for Islam.
16 The religious path followed by worshippers of Lord Shiva.
17 Mantra Yoga.
18 The unstruck sound, usually heard in the heart/*anahata chakra*.

cremation, the Muslims a burial. As they argued, Kabir appeared before them and commanded them to lift the shroud that veiled his lifeless body. When the shroud was removed, it was discovered that the great master had, through the power of Kriya, transformed his lifeless body into a bed of roses to be divided equally among the two groups and resurrected his true self, his soul-consciousness, appearing to his disciples as a living saint. This miracle was performed to bring about harmony between Hindus and Muslims, the cause to which Kabir had dedicated his life.

It is documented in Kabir's own works that Shiva Goraksha Babaji enlightened him by Kriya Yoga. It is also documented in the book *Puran Purusha* that Yogavatar Lahiri Mahasaya stated he was Kabir in his former life. This leaves no shadow of doubt that Kabir and Lahiri Mahasaya were one and the same being and that their common spiritual master was Shiva Goraksha Babaji.

Kabir, the medieval saint, often praises Shiva Goraksha Babaji, Gopichand and Bharthari Nath, the latter whom I have already established was his own former incarnation. He feels indebted to them for initiating him into the knowledge of Kundalini Kriya Yoga. Alakh Niranjan[19] is the spiritual name for Shiva Goraksha Babaji (refer *Shiva Goraksha Rahasaya*). Whenever Kabir uses that word in prose or poetry, he is praising or glorifying Alakh Niranjan as Goraksha Nath, as God unmanifest. This is a great clue to the high esteem or reverence in which he held Shiva Goraksha Babaji.

In one of his famous songs Kabir has praised the wisdom of Babaji Goraksha Nath and connected Him deeply with Lord Rama as he sung his favorite song, '*Rama guna beladiyan Gorakh Nath hi jaane*', which traces the creeper of Rama's spiritual qualities to its ultimate revelation, that is Goraksha Nath. So in my opinoin it is saying that he who wants to know the essence of Rama must follow and know Shiva Goraksha Babaji, for He as Shiva is the source and

---

19 'The Lightless Light which lights that light which lights the light in all our souls'; a name for God and a greeting, voiced by Nath yogis.

ishta-devata[20] of the Raghuvanshi spirituality. For example, when Lord Rama went to battle against Ravana, he prayed to Lord Shiva for victory offering 108 lotuses, the last of which was hidden by Parvati as a test.

Without hesitation, the lotus-eyed Rama put the arrow to his eye to complete the prayer of offering 108 lotuses. This shows that Lord Shiva was the highest spiritual God for Rama, for whom he was prepared to lay his life on the line without a moment's hesitation. This assumes great importance in the face of great opposition of the Kabir-*panthis*[21] against Goraksha Nath. Kabir himself was a complete devotee of his beloved Rama and yet accepted Babaji Goraksha Nath as the supreme authority, not only knowing Rama, but being the essence of Rama. Therefore, this establishes Goraksha as the guru preceptor of Kabir in the form of Rama.

Blessings and Initiations of Guru Nanak / Janak (1470 CE)

In the Middle Ages a child was born to Hindu parents in the North Indian state of Punjab. In those days, the timeless Shiva Goraksha Babaji roamed the length and breadth of the land. His name was remembered with the Gods and the highest avataras of those times. Later, Guru Nanak's *Japji* prayer book makes it a point to mention Goraksha's name with the likes of Shiva and Parvati, showing the high esteem in which he was held in Nanak's time, being worshipped with the Gods.

Guru Nanak's parents were totally devoted to Shiva and as the child Nanak grew up, research appears to have been undertaken which led his parents to believe that he was a reincarnation of the great king Janak, the father of Sita. Therefore, it is most probable that his name would be Janak, rather than Nanak. Nanak does not appear to have been a popular name in the Punjab; the

---

20 Personal beloved deity.
21 Those who follow the tradition or path laid down by Kabir.

name only became popular after his name was mispronounced as such. Therefore, it makes more sense to say that his name was Janak and his sister's name Janaki, which was the name of Sita.

As Janak grew up, he led a pious life preparing himself to meet his great Guru, Shiva Goraksha Babaji. He married a beautiful girl called Sulakshana. The great Shiva Goraksha Babaji then appeared to Guru Janak and taught him the deepest mysteries of *Omkar Kriya*[22] meditation, *Surat Nam Yoga* and *Shabad Yoga*. Careful research of ancient books and the local *gurudwaras* give a sufficient clue as to the monumental influence which the Nath tradition had on both Kabir and Guru Janak, as well as all of the medieval saints of India.

Guru Janak and Sulakshana upon meeting the great Shiva Goraksha, beseeched Him to bless them with a spiritual child and the great Guru Goraksha Nath told them that He Himself would be born into their family. The signs of His birth would be that the child would have large *kundalas*/earrings infused into the lobes of His ears, like Shiva Goraksha had Himself. As the Timeless Shiva Goraksha Babaji had said, so it happened. Unto Guru Janak and Sulakshana was born the most radiant child avatara with the *kundalas* in His ears like a little Sun God. These earrings were a sure sign that a strong emanation of Shiva Goraksha Babaji was born as Yogi Sri Chandra into the household of Guru Nanak and Sulakshana, whom I prefer to call Guru Janak and Sulakshana.

Yogi Sri Chandra, Janak's son, was the founder of the *Udaseena Sampradaya* to whom the Golden Temple of Amritsar then belonged. It was later handed over to the Sikh gurus, who worshipped Yogi Sri Chandra as the greatest satguru that ever lived. Even to this day, in all true-to-tradition *Udaseena akhadas* and their *gurudwaras*[23], the *dhunas* (sacred firepits) are lit in honor of Shiva Goraksha Babaji. No true *aarti* is complete in such places of Sri Chandra without the final *aarti* being done to Shiva Goraksha. Shiva Goraksha, being

---

22 This is a special technique in Kriya Yoga with which all *Kriya* meditations begin. It consists of listening and experiencing the triple divine quality of light sound creation.
23 A school of discipline in the Nath yogic tradition.

Shiva Himself and Yogi Sri Chandra being Shiva Goraksha's avatar, are one. And in truth, no conflict exists in this fact. Only the ignorant divide and quarrel with their own minds; as a result of which, many *akhadas* have excluded Shiva Goraksha's *aarti* and broken the age old tradition.

Yogavatar Lahiri Mahasaya (1828 – 1895 CE)

The nineteenth century disciple of Babaji was the Yogavatar Lahiri Mahasaya, whose miraculous life is detailed in Yogananda's *Autobiography of a Yogi*. Lahiri Mahasaya stated he was given the task of reviving Kriya Yoga, the science of God-realization for modern man, irrespective of cast or creed, or ascetic and householder walks of life. He was born on September 30, 1828 into a pious Brahman family in the village of Ghurni in the Nadia district of Bengal. His mother, who passed away during his childhood, was an ardent devotee of Lord Shiva. From an early age he was often observed sitting in yoga posture under the sand, his body completely hidden except for his head. In 1846 Shyama Charan Lahiri, his full name, was married to Kashi Moni who bore him two daughters and two sons. In 1851 he took the post of accountant in the Military Engineering department of the British Government.

By his thirty-third year, Lahiri Mahasaya met his great guru Babaji near Ranikhet in the Himalayas. There Babaji struck Lahiri Mahasaya gently on the forehead sending a current through his brain, and releasing the seed-memories of his previous life and *yogic sadhana* at that location, and his past lives with his beloved guru. The meeting is narrated in *Autobiography of a Yogi*:

'Though you lost sight of Me never did I lose sight of you,' Babaji said to him. 'I pursued you over the luminescent astral sea where the glorious angels sail. Through gloom, storm, upheaval, and light I followed you, like a mother bird guarding her young. As you lived out your human term of womb life, and emerged a babe, My eye was ever on you. When you covered your tiny form in the lotus posture under the Ghurni sands in childhood, I was invisibly

Yogavatar Lahiri Mahasaya was the Yogi Saint Kabir in one of his former lives and in a life before that, he was king Bharthari Nath, disciple of Babaji Goraksha Nath.

present. Patiently month after month, year after year, I have watched over you, waiting for this perfect day. Now you are with me!'[24]

In 1861 unbeknownst to the general public, a great spiritual renaissance began in Kashi, Benares as devotees, like bees to a flower, sought the spiritual nectar of this polestar of Kriya, Yogavatar Lahiri Mahasaya. Yogananda writes, 'As the Ganges came from heaven to Earth, in the *Purana* story, offering a divine draught to the parched devotee Bhagirath, so in 1861 the celestial river of Kriya Yoga began to flow from the secret fastness of the Himalayas into the dusty haunts of men'. As instructed by Babaji, Yogavatar Lahiri Mahasaya imparted the divine science of Kriya Yoga to ascetics and householders alike, answering the challenge of balancing family duties with yogic meditation.

Gyanavatar Sri Yukteshwar (1855 – 1936 CE)

Gyanavatar Sri Yukteshwar Giri was born in Serampore on May 10, 1855 the son of a prosperous businessman who was to leave to his son the family mansion that later became his hermitage. His family name was Priya Nath Karar. While still very young, he took the responsibility of head of the household, but his wife died giving birth to a daughter, who also died in her youth after marriage. In his twenty-ninth year he received initiation into Kriya Yoga from Yogavatar Lahiri Mahasaya. He took to *sanyas* at Bodhagaya sometime after 1906, under the blessing of *Srimat* Swami Krishna Dayal Giri who conferred on him the title of Swami with the spiritual name Yukteshwar Giri. He attained mahasamadhi in March of 1936.

In his life, Gyanavatar Yukteshwar Giri acquired proficiency in music, astronomy, anatomy and physiology, naturopathy, homeopathy, and gained a profound knowledge of mathematics. Truly he was known as the Gyanavatar, 'Incarnation of Wisdom'. He did not reject western science. On the contrary, as with everything, he found unity: 'All of creation is governed by laws,' he explained. 'Those that manifest themselves in the external world, discovered by the scientists, are called natural laws, but there are

---

24 *Autobiography of a Yogi* p. 308.

The Initiation Of Avataras By Babaji

Gyanavatar Yukteshwar blessed with darshan of Babaji on three occasions

more subtle laws that rule the kingdom of the conscious that can be experienced only through the practice of Yoga. The occult spiritual planes have their laws and natural principles of operation. It is not the physical scientist but the completely self-realized master who understands the true nature of the matter'.[25]

One of Gyanavtar Sri Yukteshwar's passions was astrology. He was deeply interested in unraveling the mystery of how man, being the most perfect within creation, could be influenced by the stars that were but masses of material, and he endeavored to work out a system that could counteract the stars' influences. When Yogavatar Lahiri Mahasaya gave him the technique of Kriya Yoga, he found that through this he was able to control the influence of the stars on himself and on the cosmos.

He was blessed with the *darshan* (vision) of Mahavatar Babaji on three occasions, once at a Kumbha *mela* (fair) at Prayag, where Babaji addressed him as Priyanath Swami and directed him to write a book synthesizing eastern and western religious philosophy, which became the famed work *Kaivalya Darshanam* known in the west as *The Holy Science*. He was further directed to spread Kriya Yoga to western countries: 'I saw that you are interested in the West as well as in the East,' said Babaji to the Gyanavatar. 'East and West must establish a golden middle path of activity and spirituality combined... India has much to learn from the West in material development; in return, India can teach the universal methods by which the West will be able to base its religious beliefs on the unshakable foundations of yogic science'.[26]

In accordance with Hindu tradition, Gyanavtar Sri Yukteshwar was a complete yogi; he led a married life and then lived as a renunciate. He had all the qualities of a yogi in accordance with the *Vedas,* though he went unnoticed in the streets and made no fanfare of his remarkable wisdom and power. He was human even to the small details that characterize the common man, he even had

---

25 *Karar Ashram Diamond Jubilee* p. 11.
26 *Autobiography of a Yogi* p. 335.

the reputation of thoroughly bargaining to the last rupee. Three months after passing away, he appeared to Paramhansa Yogananda in Mumbai with an entirely new body, identical to the body which Paramhansa Yogananda himself had buried under the sands of Puri. During this miraculous experience Gyanavtar Sri Yukteshwar revealed to his disciple fantastic details of the astral spheres where a new mission awaited him in *Hiranyaloka*, where he was to evolve highly advanced souls to the yet higher causal heavens.

Paramhansa Yogananda (1893 – 1952 CE)

Although Paramhansa Yogananda was not initiated by Babaji, I have taken the liberty of mentioning his name in this chapter because he was blessed by Babaji to first introduce the spiritual knowledge of India, and the divine science of Kriya Yoga to Western seekers. His *Autobiography of a Yogi* has inspired millions around the world to take up the path of self-realization for Earth peace.

From his birth on January 5, 1893, Paramhansa Yogananda was blessed by the guiding presence of Babaji Goraksha Nath. It is not by any coincidence that Paramhansa Yogananda was born in Gorakhpur and lived there during the first eight years of his childhood. He was guided by the divine hand of Babaji. This spiritual presence was to guide and bless the whole of his life from his birth to the event of his miraculous passing (mahasamadhi). His parents were Goraksha Nath devotees. They visited the temple every Sunday to receive the blessings of Babaji Goraksha Nath and even named one of their sons Gora after the divine Goraksha Nath. Paramhansa Yogananda himself had been named Mukunda. Later, when his younger brother went with him to visit Gyanavatar Sri Yukteshwar, he revealed to the boys that his name was given to him after the family deity, Goraksha Nath.

From a young age Yogananda demonstrated the spiritual qualities of not only a Paramhansa, but of a perfected siddha. The child, Mukunda, on one occasion slipped away from his home during a religious festivity. After a lengthy search he was found more than

Paramhansa Yogananda in samadhi.
He was blessed by Babaji to spread *Kriya Yoga* in the West.

a kilometer away at the Goraksha Nath temple in yogic posture, entranced in a divine state. People gathered around him and patiently waited for the young child to come back to his normal state. What more of a proof do you want that the parents of Yogananda were Gorakhnathis? He performed many miracles including the stopping of the rain in Chittagong.

Before his historic voyage to America, Yogananda prayed ardently for an experience of divine consultation: '...I began to pray, with an adamant determination to continue, even to die praying, until I heard the voice of God...'. At that moment there was a knock at his door. Upon answering, Yogananda beheld the majestic form of Babaji Goraksha Nath. He blessed Yogananda and revealed to him many things. Babaji said to him, 'You are the one I have chosen to spread the message of Kriya Yoga in the west. Kriya Yoga, the science of God-realization, will ultimately spread in all lands, and aid in harmonizing the nations through man's personal, transcendental perception of the Infinite Father'.[27] Babaji blessed the family of Paramhansa Yogananda, and the great mystery is that they were ardent devotees of Goraksha Nath and went to the Goraksha Nath temple. This gives us a clear indication that Babaji of *Autobiography of a Yogi* and the legendary Goraksha Nath, the manifestation of Shiva, are one and the same Being.

Only a perfected master can choose the time and event of his death. Paramhansa Yogananda demonstrated this unique yogic ability of mahasamadhi. On March 7, 1952, at a banquet held in honor of Indian Ambassador Binay R. Sen at the Biltmore Hotel in Los Angeles, Yogananda finished his speech with a few lines from his poem, *My India*. Then, his eyes lifted, he turned slightly to his right and sank gracefully to the floor. The miracle of his mahasamadhi continued to unfold even after death as the master, by yogic will, preserved the cells of his physical body, the account of which is given below by the mortuary director, Harry T. Rowe, of

---

27 Stone, Joshua David (1995), *The Ascended Masters Light The Way*, Light Technology Chapter 37 of *Autobiography of a Yogi*.

Forest Lawn Cemetery[28]:

"The absence of any visual signs of decay in the dead body of *Paramhansa* Yogananda offers the most extraordinary case in our experience.... No physical disintegration was visible in his body even 20 days after death...no indication of mold was visible on his skin, and no visible desiccation (drying up) took place in the bodily tissues. This state of perfect preservation of a body is, so far as we know from our mortuary annals, an unparalleled one.... At the time of receiving Yogananda's body, the Mortuary personnel expected to observe, through the glass lid of the casket, the usual progressive signs of bodily decay. Our astonishment increased as day followed day without bringing any visible change in the body under observations. Yogananda's body was apparently in a phenomenal state of immutability...no odor of decay emanated from his body at any time....

"The physical appearance of Yogananda on March 27th, just before the bronze cover of the casket was put into position, was the same as it had been on March 7th. He looked on March 27th as fresh and as unravaged by decay as he had looked on the night of his death. On March 27th there was no reason to say that his body had suffered any visible physical disintegration at all. For these reasons we state again that the case of *Paramhansa* Yogananda is unique in our experience."

Mortuary Director Forest Park
Los Angeles, CA

---

28 Yogananda, *Paramhansa* (1946), *Autobiography of a Yogi*, Fifth edition 2005, pp. 478, Yogoda Satsang Society: Kolkata

CHAPTER 13

THE IMMORTAL NATHS

They are "the Ancient of Days," composed of the divine essence of the "Being About Whom Naught May Be Said." These immortal Divinities are ever watchful over the welfare and evolution of the destinies of nations and their humanities. Since they are *aja* (unborn) they can never die although their essences do incarnate for the salvation and evolution of humanity. I have detailed below an order of the celestial hierarchy of the heavenly host.

Lord Shiva

Parvati **Alakh (Kartik)**

Maha-Maya **Vishnu**

Chandrasoma **Brahma**

Adi-Shesha **Ganesha**

Celestial hierarchy above corresponds to the Nine Naths below:

Shiva Goraksha Babaji

Udai Nath Kartikeya

Matsyendra Nath Rama (Shel Nath)

Chowrangee Nath Satya Nath

Achalachambu Nath Kanthad Nath

The Immortal Naths

The Nine Naths are followers of Adi Nath Shiva and the Nath lineage represents one of the oldest yogic order ascetics whose origins are lost in the night of history. As I have mentioned, these Nath Siddhas are living in many secluded parts of India, mainly in the Himalayas They guide the eighty-four Siddhas who form the Guardian Wall of Humanity. These great Naths in everlasting meditation are infused in the Himalayan ranges, including the highest mountain called Gauri Shankar. Despite the objections of surveyor Sir George Everest, British cartographers named it Mt. Everest.

Although the Nine Naths are Immortal, for the inspiration of humanity and for future generations to come, there are nine sacred shrines (samadhis) in the Himalayas associated with the Nath tradition. They are Amarnath, Kedarnath, Badrinath, Pashu-Patinath, Kailasnath, Tunganath, Rudranath, Vishwanath (Kashi), and Jaggannath.

It is interesting to note that all of the Nine Naths have evolved beyond the sixth level of consciousness, called *avadhoots*. Some of them, with tremendous yoga and tapa, have evolved to the *avasta* (state) of an Avatara Nath Yogi, beyond the seventh level of universal consciousness. Their consciousness is of such an advanced state that it is extremely difficult to comprehend their spiritual stature.

Nath yogis have also gone on to the eighth level of divine consciousness. They are known as Rishis, the custodians of our human evolution. These Sages of the Fire Mist are great beyond man's reckoning. Gautama Buddha, the fully enlightened, ascended to this eighth level. Lord Narayana as Krishna, descended from it to be amongst mortals and hence was a Purna Avatara, the descent of Divinity in flesh. In the case of Matsyendra Nath and Jalandara Nath, they ascended to achieve the state that Buddha had already attained and Krishna already was.

Still higher, there is a great mystery and sacrifice involved in the ninth level of Divine awareness. Such cosmic avataric descents are Self-taken and are one of a kind in human history, that is, each would be unique. These levels of spiritual consciousness are way beyond the understanding of human beings, devas or gods. The stupendous magnitude of their work is incomprehensible. They also go by the name of the Sages of the Fire Mist.

I have not written about all the primeval Nine Naths mentioned above. Instead, I have given accounts of later Nath yogis, with some of whom I've had personal experiences. I have explained the journey of the soul and the various levels of consciousness, from the first to the ninth degree in my book *Wings to Freedom*, in the chapter "*The Way of the White Swan*."

Adinath (Lord Shiva)

This means the "First Lord" who is Shiva himself, the unborn undying deathless "Lord of Liberating Yoga." He is the Eternal Now as Adi Nath, whose Self-taken work for the world cycle is to reabsorb an erring humanity into its original state of consciousness, by awakening them to and teaching them the Yoga of Self-realization. Both the Kaula tradition of Matsyendra Nath and the Nath tradition of Goraksha Nath acknowledge Him as their primal Lord and Master. Identified with Lord Shiva, he is held to be the original giver of divine yogic wisdom in a long line of masters and teachers of the Yogacharya[1] schools. The title Adi Nath is also given to Rishub Nath, the first of the twenty-four enlightened teachers called the "bridge builders" (*tirthankars*) of the Jain[2] tradition, which is an integral part of the social and spiritual order of India.

Adi Nath was the primal yogi and a direct manifestation of Shiva and it is from him that the yogis trace their lineage. He came much before the time of Mina Nath and is lost in the hoary antiquity of the misty past. His positive Shakti energies are Uma Nath, Udai Nath, Parvati Nath, Jagad Amba, Gauri and Bhavani. Some of His dark fiercer Shakti energies are personified in Durga, Shyama, Chandi, Bhairavi, Chinna-masta and Kali Nath. To balance the world, speed

---
1 An adept of Yoga capable of teaching others.
2 Spiritual values followed by Mahavir which later became a religion Jainism.

up evolution of souls and to accomplish what needs to be done, he may exercise any of his divine consort's Shakti energies. To try and comprehend more would be futile in words. It would be more fruitful if we practiced the ways to enlightenment and realized our true selves.

Udai Nath (Parvati)

She is the manifestation of Parvati, the consort of Adi Nath Shiva. Udai Nath heralds the dawn of the age and time of spirituality. At one end, she helps the practitioner of yoga burn the seeds of all past negative karmas. On the other end, she supplies the light of inspiration to progress along the yogic path. All throughout the passage of time she was the semi-divine goddess who played the role of world mother.

There are two aspects to her nature, one bright part, the other dark. In Shakti, the two aspects of Shiva are manifest. In her milder personification she is known as Uma, Gauri, Parvati, Jagadamba and Bhavani. In her dark and fierce character she is Durga, Shyama, Chandi Kali and Bhairavi.

Uma is the gracious consort of Adi Nath Shiva and the daughter of Prajapati Daksha[3]. She, out of total love for Shiva, assumed a body so that she could be united with him in due form. This incident is related in the account of the sacrifice of Daksha as to how Shiva was insulted by not being invited to the sacrifice and later being ridiculed. This led to the violation and mortification of Uma, who then became Sati, sacrificed for the sake of her Lord. Then Shiva, grief-stricken, carried her over his shoulders telling Vishnu to dismember her. As he walked along, various parts of her sacred body fell at various sites, which now make the fifty-two holy Shakti Pithas (sacred places of worship). After this, she was reborn in the family of the sage Himavat and is thus called Parvati (daughter of the Himalayan

---

3 An ancient sage known as the first and the last. He is also the father of Parvati. When Shiva was not invited to his fire ceremony, he upset the cosmic law and the result was a war in which his Yadnya was foiled and his head cut off. This refers to a mystic type of initiation.

Mountains).

Shiva and Parvati are described as living together on the sacred Kailash Mountain. They are ever immersed in the samadhi of love, at times engaged in deep philosophical discourse to show the path of salvation to humanity lost in the theories of a material world. From these discourses, many a treatise on yoga and tantra have been gifted to the world. These priceless treasures are their blessings to humanity and have been the cause of the liberation and bliss for countless yogis, saints, and common souls the world over. Parvati, of a darker complexion, spiritually sought a more perfect attunement with her Lord in samadhi to match and completely merge into her Lord's being and becoming. So she took to severe penance (*tapasya*), the result of which was that she was transformed in body, mind, and spirit to a light golden colour, assuming the form and name of Gauri (fair). She is also called Jagad Amba, the "fathomless deep of the universe."

Parvati Nath - divine consort of Shiva

When we go on to the more formidable aspects of Shakti, let us not for a moment forget, the spirit of love and of the evolutionary push for the souls' salvation, which the Divine Mother has for us in her heart. Durga "the Unconquerable" is Adi Nath Shiva's consort in the aspect of warrior. She derives her name from the demon she slew. She is often depicted with eight arms (*Asta Bhuja*) or ten arms (*Dasha Bhuja*) during the festival of the nine nights of prayers (*Navaratri*).

Then we have the four-armed Kali[4] with sword and a garland of heads around her neck, her red tongue protruding, thirsty for the blood of the demonical forces and demons. She is ever ready to destroy their outer body garments in her fierce compassion to liberate their souls to a higher form of life and awareness. The darker the negativity and evil on this earth, the fiercer and more aggressive her form becomes to overcome the evil and create a balance of the gunas. She is then Kala Bhairavi and Chinnamastu, where she cuts off her head and the triple sprouts of blood are drunk by her assistant yoginis[5] and her own severed head. The Mother will go to the farthest extremes to liberate her children's souls from ignorance and hell damnation. She shows here that sacrifice is the ultimate solution to spiritual evolution and the attainment of *Brahma Nirvana*.

Kalagni Nath (400 BCE)

This Nath appeared during the reign of King Mahandatta. Nobody knows of his spiritual appearance or his Mahanirvan. Some people link this mysterious being with the Great Time itself who presides over the world cycles and therefore intimately connects him with Kal Bhairava, an aspect of Shiva, and with Goraksha Nath as well. This great Nath yogi is from the ancient of days as he lives on from age to age. No definite time frame is given for his work or mission. He predated the Buddha and his two Indian teachers, Aradhya Kalam and Udraka Ramputra. He in all probability taught them the great Nath yogic tradition of India, which was later passed on to

---

4 A Goddess embodying the fierce (dissolving) aspect of the Divine.
5 A female practitioner of Yoga.

Gautama the Buddha. The various names by which this mysterious being is mentioned are Kalagni Nath, Kalagi Nath, Kali Nath and Kalonos.

Kalagni Nath belonged to the Nav-Nath (Nine Nath) tradition and appeared in Varanasi (Benares), India, around 600 BCE. He initiated the Siddha Bhoga Nath of Benares into the Divine Nath Yoga as well as taught him the science of immortality called Sanjeevani Vidya[6], where the aging process of the body is arrested and the yogi can live for an indefinite period of time. This ancient Nath science of Yoga called *Sanjeevani Samadhi* (*Svaroop Samadhi*) was taken by Bhoga Nath from Banares to the south of India and came to be known as *Saroub Samadhi* in Tamil. In south India Bhoga Nath is popularly known as Bogarnatha. He further travelled to China where he was known as Bo Yang or Lao-Tze, and revolutionized China with his yogic teachings of body immortality and Tao Te Ching[7]. He taught Golden Immortality and Yin Yang Yoga, where Yin, the Kundalini energy, rises, piercing the six chakras, and uniting with Yang, her Lord Shiva, in *sahasrara*[8].

Kalagni Nath, a master of *Kaya Kalpa*[9] and *Sanjeevani Samadhi* lived during the time of Alexander the Great, when the conqueror entered the borders of India. His soldiers were exhausted after defeating the king, Porus. Alexander's army was ready to beat a retreat when he happened to meet this great yogi, Kalagni Nath, whom the Greeks called Kalanos. The great conqueror sent his soldiers to summon the yogi, whom he found to be most enigmatic and intriguing. The soldiers said to Kali Nath, "The son of Zeus calleth Thee." The yogi replied, "Tell Alexander that there waiteth for him another son of Zeus and if he had need of me, he should come himself." Alexander came to meet Kali Nath and offered him anything he wished. The yogi smiled and asked him to step aside for he was blocking the

---

6 The yogic process of bringing others back to life, ressurecting their physical body, for specific spiritual work.

7 A treatise written by Lao-Tzu, specifically to do with the taming of the bull of one's own passions and the practice of Indian yoga, such as the pranic Kriya Yoga.

8 Thousand petaled lotus; crown chakra.

9 An ancient yogic/ayurvedic process form of rejuvenation.

sunlight, something Alexander could not give him. Alexander was humbled by this yogi. He owned nothing, and yet made him feel so inadequate, that he requested him to come to Greece. Several years later, the yogi lit his own funeral pyre in front of the Macedonian Army and entered the flames. As he went in, he told Alexander he would meet him in Babylon. Then, sitting in lotus posture, he calmly let the flames consume what was to him his illusionary body.

Later on, as Alexander lay dying on his bed in Persia, the Great Sage of the Ancient of Days kept his word and appeared by the bedside of the emperor. He told the monarch to instruct his servants to keep his empty hands out of his bier after he died. This was to teach the world a lesson that, be it the emperor of the world, or be it an ordinary man, both come into the world with nothing and depart with nothing. Only Divine-realization is everlasting as Kalagni Nath proved to Alexander in life and in death with his own immortality and his Divinity.

Raja Bhartari Nath (80 BCE – 57 BCE)

The king Bhartari Nath was the legendary disciple of Shiva Goraksha Babaji. He was the last Chandravat kings of the Parmar dynasty, which then ruled the holy city of Ujjain. After the death of his queen Pingala, he took to sanyasa, was initiated by Goraksha Nath, became an immortal and is living in the celestial realms even till today. It is by the power of his tapa and yoga that he maintains his celestial body, but physically he takes many bodies to play the drama divine to assist his supreme guru Goraksha Nath in the evolution of human kind. He lived in tapa and meditation in the Himalayan regions keeping his awareness and celestial body intact till the time came for him to reincarnate in a physical body about a thousand years later in the year 80 BCE. Immediately after his induction, his younger brother Vikramaditya succeeded him to rule Ujjain from 57 BCE. Vikramaditya succeeded Bhartari Nath as the king of Ujjain. He was told by his elder brother Bhartari Nath to renovate and rebuild much of the old city of Haradwar.

There is the famous story of how the King Bhartari Nath, wanting to test his queen's love for him, sent a false message of his death to her. Although her Asso Pat plant revealed to her that the King was alive, she decided to prove her fidelity to him by dying on the funeral fire. The King later arrived at the palace only to see the funeral pyre. He was completely ravaged by her passing away and inconsolable. Shiva Goraksha Babaji, who always lived in the Present, had no past, present or future. He is rightly called The Eternal Now and He could see the whole sequence of events of this great soul. Thus, He decided to orchestrate the life of King Bhartari Nath and his queen in such a way that they could reincarnate again and fulfil the mission of teaching to the world the evolutionary science of Kriya Yoga. Babaji advised the king not to cry for losing anything in the evanescent world even if it his own wife. To make His statement valid, He sprinkled the funeral pyre with water from His kamandalu (yogic water container) whereupon twenty-five queen Pingalas appeared on the scene. Shiva Goraksha Babaji told the king Bhartari to chose the true queen, which the king could not do since they were all identical. This is the game of maya, He said, grieve not for that which is evanescent. Then, sprinkling water again on the twenty-five Pingalas, He made them disappear and only one was left. But by now, the great Avatara king Bhartari was totally in renunciation mode and both left one another to go on their spiritual journey, only to meet again in the future life of the nineteenth century where Bhartari Nath was born as Yogavatara Lahiri Mahasaya who married the Queen Pingala who was born as the Divine Kashimoni.

The Queen Pingala and the King Bhartari had both parted in that terrestrial life as fully realized souls, but nevertheless, the Mahaguru Goraksha Nath kept embedded in the mind of both the king and the queen a latent desire for remarriage and the other desire that he kept as a latent seed in the mind of the great yogi Bhartari Nath to see a golden palace, feel it, roam in it and fulfil his last desire in which he was not interested himself but which was kept in his mind by his Mahaguru Babaji. The purpose of keeping these two desires: of seeing a golden palace, and completing reunion with his wife, was actually for a deeper purpose and mission - which was to spread the liberating science of Kriya Yoga to the world.

Matsyendra Nath 7th century CE

There is a legend of the Naths that, one day as the great yogi sat fishing in his boat in the Bay of Bengal, he hooked a huge fish that pulled so hard on his fishing line that his boat capsized and the whale swallowed him whole. This is similar to the Biblical story of Jonah in the stomach of a whale. In this story, Matsyendra Nath was protected by his good karma. At that time, the Lord Shiva had created a beautiful setting under the ocean. He was expounding to his spouse, Parvati, the sacred doctrine of yoga and tantra, which he had never given to anyone else. The large fish happened to go to this very site.

So it came to pass that the Nath was able to hear the secret discourse which Shiva gave to Parvati, without being noticed. After some time Parvati fell asleep, and when Shiva asked, "Are you listening?" A prompt "Yes!" came from the belly of the fish. Using his Shiva Netra (third-eye), Shiva gazed into the belly of the fish, where he saw Mina Nath (another of Matsyendra Nath's many names). He was overjoyed at the discovery and said, "Now I know who my real disciple is." Turning to his sleepy spouse He said, "I will now first initiate Matsyendra Nath," who gratefully took the initiation and then for the next twelve years, all the while remaining in the belly of the fish, dedicated himself to the tantra yogic practices given to him by the Lord Shiva himself. At the end of the twelve years, another fisherman caught the monster, and upon opening it, Matsyendra Nath appeared as a fully realized Master.

Matsyendra Nath is responsible for the transmigration of all evolving souls. In his hands are the keys to the gates of salvation (*moksha*). He gives liberation to the deserving and bondage to fools. He is the immortal Master of Hatha and Tantra Yoga. His deva celestial form is called Avalokiteshwara, which means, "The Lord Who Looks Down from On High." In Tibet, he is the Bodhisattva Avalokiteshwara who gave to humanity the liberating mantra, "Om mani padme hum." In Nepal, he is venerated as the guardian deity of Kathmandu in the form of Shveta Matsyendra (White Fish Lord). In India, he is the Nath Matsyendra, celebrated in song and legend as the saviour and spiritual redeemer of all the Nath Yogis. In Maharashtra, India he is worshipped as Vithoba (Panduranga) with fish earrings. He has a shivalinga on his head. This is the mystic connection between Vithoba Krishna and Shiva Goraksha. In his *Tantra Aloka*[10], the great Abhinav Gupta[11] salutes Matsyendra Nath as his Guru. The book called *Kaulu-Jnana-Nirnaya*, meaning "ascertainment of Kaula Knowledge," was authored by Matsyendra Nath around the tenth century and is one of the oldest available sources of information about Kaulism.

According to a legendary account in this book, he is said to have recovered the canon of the Kaulas called Kulagama from a large fish that had swallowed it. He is specifically associated with the Kaula sect of the siddha movement, within which he founded the Yogini-Kaula branch. This tantric sect derives its name from the word *Kula*, which is the ultimate reality in its dynamic feminine aspect called Kundalini Shakti. The word *Kula* has various meanings. One is meaning "flock" or "multitude", but more significantly it means "family of respect." It is thus called the *Kula Kundalini*[12] because it is both the source of many multi universes as well as the final home and security for yogis who awaken and abide in her secrets. The Lord Shiva in tantrism is called Akula[13], that which transcends all dualities and differences. Therefore the concept of Kaula stands for the *avasta* (state) of enlightenment, gained through the union of Shiva and Shakti. Kaula also refers to a practitioner of this particular path.

---

10 Abhinav Gupta's magnum opus, which discusses in great depth the metaphysics and spiritual practice of Tantrism from the viewpoint of Kashmir Shaivism.
11 A Medieval saint and scholar who wrote the famous book Tantra Alok.
12 The kundalini power that prevails through human existence for many ages, many generations and many dynasties.
13 'Nonflock', an epithet of Lord Shiva.

Tapa of Matsyendra Nath

In another story, it so happened that the great Matsyendra Nath journeyed to the Himalayas and carried out intense *tapa* and meditation there. Then Adi Nath, Lord Shiva was pleased and appeared to Matsyendra Nath, to ask him what he needed. The great yogi asked Shiva to give him a disciple greater and more perfect than himself. The Lord answered and said, "You are already perfect and have attained to the final enlightenment." But Matsyendra Nath insisted, so Lord Shiva said that he would himself manifest as his disciple. Then, from the heart of Shiva (who is the Eternal Shiva Goraksha Babaji) burst forth an irradiant flame of splendor and Shiva Goraksha Babaji was manifest in the Divine realm. Later, by the power of Kriya Shakti, he involuted to pull around himself a vesture composed of Astral *tanmatras*[14] of light, creating an avataric body to manifest on the Celestial plane and then gathering the subatomic particles of light to manifest on the Terrestrial plane. The supreme Guru called Shiva, had assumed the form of Shiva Goraksha Nath to play the role of disciple to his disciple Matsyendra Nath.

Chowrangee Nath (10 BCE-103 CE)

The Immortal Naths, although fully enlightened, spurned *Brahma Nirvana* to remain on earth for the instruction and guidance of humanity to Divinity. They took on the most heavy and awful karma of large sections of society and humanity to remove their obstacles and give them a boost on their spiritual paths. These were certainly great sacrifices for which these great *vibhutis* (divine beings) wanted nothing in return. They were motivated to lay their life on the line for the evolution of human consciousness. Amongst such saviours, one of the foremost names is Gyan Swaroop (knowledge form of Chowrangee Nath).

---

14 'Fine matter', the subtle aspect of the material elements (*bhuta*) which may be seen in the form of light during yoni-mudra (also jyoti-mudra); the potentials of sound (*shabda*), form (*rupa*), touch (*sparsh*a), taste (*rasa*), and smell (*gandha*).

Gyan Swaroop Chowrangee Nath, sacrificing *Nirvana* for Humanity

Chowrangee Nath, also called Puran Bhagat, was the son of King Shalivahan of the Rajput[15] Pamars of Sialkot in the then northern Punjab bordering Afghanistan. The King had two queens, the older of whom was Queen Archan, the Mother of Puran. The other queen, who was much younger, was barren. She made advances to Puran, which he refused, and so she brought false charges against him, which the King believed. Then cutting off Puran's hands and feet, he threw him into a well to die. This was the well in the village of Karol, five miles from Sialkot. It is now called Puranwala.

Goraksha Nath happened to pass by to drink water and found the body in the well. Knowing Puran's innocence, He rescued the body from the well, brought it back to life and restored its limbs. Puran became a Goraknathi and followed the path of Yoga. He was given the name of Chowrangee Nath. Such was his power and compassion that later he even granted his former betrayer, Queen Lunan, a boon. She bore a son named Rasalu, the legendary hero who con-

---
15 A princely clan of Rajasthan.

quered most of the cities in Afghanistan. Rasalu had a chequered life of romance, adventure and intrigue. His conquests in India and Afghanistan were due to the blessings of Goraksha Nath, whose ardent disciple he later became. He was the legendary hero conqueror and king whose name is mentioned with awe in Muslim history and documents.

It is interesting to note that it was during the reign of Emperor Kanishka of the Kushan dynasty that these incidents and exploits occurred. The emperor himself was keen to combine the ancient Indian, the modern Greek and the Buddhist philosophies and revel in that knowledge. At that time, 10 BCE-70 CE, there happened to be, at Kashmir, the Bodhisattva Ishanath today called Jesus. Jesus, who had come to India to study Yoga, and Chowrangee Nath, already a great yogi, attended the great Buddhist council of Haran near Sri Nagar. There the collection of Buddha's work *Lalita Vistara* was formulated, which shows striking similarity with the New Testament.

An account of the meeting of King Shalivahan with Jesus is given in the ancient Indian text called the *Bahavishya Purana*. This is a historical account, which continues to be updated as historical events happen on earth. The Purana means ancient book. It is the historical accounts of a day of Brahma lasting 4 billion 320 million years. It is mentioned here that King Shalivahan met Jesus in Kashmir where the two exchanged views and Shalivahan later advised Isha (Jesus) to get married since he had finished his mission, which was announced in the year 54 CE. The Nath Tradition of Yoga, by the time of Jesus' advent, was of hoary antiquity. It had a deep influence on Jesus' yogic and meditative practices. Tutored by his Guru Chetannath, Jesus went by the name of Isha Nath.

King Guga Nath - The Chauhan[16] (970 CE - 1000 CE)

Born on the eighth day of Bhadon (Shravan Bhadrapad)[17], he was the son of King Jewar and Queen Bacchal of the Agni Vamsha[18] lineage of the Chauhan clan of Rajputs. By the grace and blessings of the Divine Guru Goraksha Nath, at Guga Nath's birth a naga appeared and he was later worshipped as a naga god. To this day, in my family temple at Gwalior, victims of snake and scorpion bites are cured. Still, women desirous of good children pray to Guga Nath and their prayers are granted.

I was born on the 10th of May, in 1944, by the blessings of Goraksha Nath Babaji, through the grace and holy ash of my family Guru, Guga Nath. Babaji blessed me with his presence and is ever guiding me in my service to humanity, giving through me the path of yogic meditation for the evolution of human consciousness. My whole life, during my Himalayan travels and my teachings in India and America, I am breathed through by Guga Nath and Goraksha Nath's inspiration.

The temple my grandfather, the late Raja Shitole Deshmuk of Pune, built in Gwalior is dedicated to Guga Nath. The sanctum sanctorum (the holy of holies) is dedicated to his great Guru Goraksha Nath. Even today, a *Guru Darbar* (royal court of the Guru) is held every Monday at Mahal Goan in Gwalior, in the state of Madhya Pradesh, and attended by my family. We are welcomed and honoured by the beating of drums as we enter the temple marking the family status of a Raja (King). By tradition and the wish of King Guga Nath, our family is made to sit on the left outside of the inner sanctum of Shiva Goraksha Babaji. To the right side sits the officiat-

---

16 Chauhan means Lord, as Nath means Lord. The Chauhans are a clan from the Rajput dynasties, and are called Agni-Vamashas, meaning families who descend from the source of the fire god, c.f Sisodias (Surya-Vamashas) descending from the source of the sun god, cf. the Yadhavas (Soma-Vamashas), who descend from the source of the moon god.
17 The monsoon rainy season.
18 Ancient rishi, son of Mithra

The Immortal Naths

ing priest, and directly in front of the Goraksha Nath altar room, a throne of flowers is laid for King Guga, the Chauhan.

After some time, the *Mahant* (head priest) of the temple, who is infused with the holy spirit of Guga, sits in front of the sanctum. Before the ceremony, a sacred fire, infused with the holy Spirit of Guga Nath, is lit by the priest to invoke and honor the Maha Guru, Shiva Goraksha Babaji. Camphor, clarified butter, incense, saffron and sandalwood are used to invoke the presence of the Divine Goraksha. Petitions are made as the priest brushes the petitioner with a brush of peacock feathers (*morchal*). The Mahant loses all body consciousness as he is inspired by the great Soul of Guga Nath, who uses his body as an instrument to deal with the victims of snake and scorpion bites. The body with the spiritual entry (*avesh*) of great Guru Guga grants boons to the faithful. All wishes that are worthy of being granted are granted by the Chauhan Guga Nath. This is done in witness of the sacred fire of Goraksha Nath. Barren women are granted children, sick people are given health, snake-bitten people receive their cure and their string bonds (*bandhas*) are cut in front of the Goraksha fire. The yogis are granted their spiritual success and an everlasting love for God and Goraksha (Guru Maharaj).

I had been witnessing the Monday *Guru Darbar* my entire childhood, until I grew up and finally met both of these legendary Gurus. They have graced my livingness and made it worth living for others, making me realize that in serving humanity, I serve my larger Self, and above all them!

When Takshaka Naga, the Chief of the King Vasuki Naga, asked Guga the Chauhan about his ancestry, Guga replied, "I am the grandson of King Amar. I come from the village Gard Darera in Bikaner. I am the son of King Jewar Chauhan. My mother is Queen Bacchal. My name Guga is given to me by my Maha Guru Goraksha Nath. By the blessings of Goraksha Nath will be my marriage to Princess Sharada of Assam." Indeed Goraksha materialized a grand marriage party with elephants, horses, men and jewellry to marry his disciple King Guga with unparalleled pomp and splendor.

Babaji Blessing Guga Nath

His mother Bacchal, who had formerly left her King, went to her home in Fort Gazni, which was located in Kabul. So this would connect Guga Nath with the Rajputs reigning in Kabul before the Mussalman (Muslim) rule there. The Ratan Nath shrine also is near Kabul and so is the Khwaja Khizra shrine located in upper Sindh in Uderolal. This would also connect to the shrine of Kwaja Moin Uddin Chiste in Ajmer[19], both of whom were disciples of Shiva Goraksha. There is a Gazni in Gujarat, which may have been the home of Queen Bacchal.

---

19 A city in Northwest India.

Gyan Nath – Lord of Wisdom (13th century CE)

The saint Jnaneswar (Jnan Nath or Gyan Nath) was truly called the king of mystics in that he completed his famous book in his teens, the *Jnaneshwari*, a marvelous translation of the holy *Bhagavad Gita*[20] of Lord Krishna. After having completed this work, Gyan Nath took *sanjeevan samadhi* at Alandi, a small village near the town of Pune in India. When he went into his final samadhi; he was only twenty-one years of age.

Gyan Nath - disciple of Shiva Goraksha Babaji

---

[20] 'Lord's Song', the most popular book on the science of Yoga, embedded in the epic Mahabharata and containing the teachings of Karma Yoga (the path of self-transcending action), Jnana Yoga (the path of wisdom), Bhakti Yoga (the path of devotion), and Raja Yoga (the supreme path of meditation) as given by the Avatar Krsna to Prince Arjuna on the battlefield of Kurushetra.

Gyan Nath, alias Gyaneshawar, was a disciple of Shiva Goraksha Babaji. It is the same family yogic lineage from which I also descend. He was an adept in the Nav-Nath tradition of yoga by which he achieved his *nirvikalpa samadhi* and *sanjeevan samadhi* states of final liberation. His spiritual lineage is from Goraksha Nath Babaji, whose disciple was Gahari Nath, whose disciple was Nivritti Nath, who was the Guru of Gyan Nath. Therefore his teachings are very much of the Nath lineage, even to contemporary yoga practitioners. He authored *Amrita Anubhava* (Experience of Immortality), which shows his spiritual roots lie in the teachings of Goraksha Nath, who is a living embodiment of immortality and an incarnation of Shiva himself. His philosophical stance was *Sphurti Vada*, understood as the doctrine of spontaneous manifestation. He believed deeply in the excellence of the Nath Yoga doctrine which added bhakti or devotion instilled with wisdom; it was to him a composite whole.

The Lord Jnaneswar has extolled yoga as the supreme path to self-realization. At the same time he understood that the most excellent of these yoga practices were not possible for the simple and common masses to perform. So, out of his compassion, he encouraged and showed the people the path of devotion (bhakti). This later took the form of the bhakti movement in Maharastra state. The masses embraced this movement and were called the *"Varkaris."* The path of devotion, although slower than the classic yogic path, is nonetheless easier, and more people tend to be attracted to devotional chanting. Of course, it is best to combine both yoga and devotion (the main component of the bhakti movement) for the optimum spiritual progress.

When Jnaneswar was a child of twelve years, he was being ridiculed and doubted by the people of his village concerning his spiritual yogic practices and powers. During those times, there lived a great Nath Yogi called Chandeva, and he, having heard of the harassment to little Gyan Nath, went to bless and certify the boy saint's spiritual status. The Nath Chandeva is said to have then been over fourteen hundred years old and since he had no enemies in the world, the wild beasts of the jungles served him. He rode on a tiger to meet Gyan Nath and his family. Upon seeing him, the villagers were terrified; but he told them to be calm. The great Chandeva told the people that Gyan Nath was a true son of God and a Nath Yogi and then blessed the whole village. The Nath Chandeva raised the kundalini power latent in Gyan Nath, which made the wall on which he and his brothers and sister were sitting move. This convinced the doubting villagers of Alandi as to the spiritual prowess of Gyan Nath. Then Chandeva, having blessed the village, left for his jungle abode near the town, which is today called Saswad.

It is ironic that in Medieval times, due to the ignorance of the Nath Yogic tradition among the masses, some fanatic cults of the bhakti movement tried to belittle and falsify the spiritual stature of the lofty Nath, Chandeva. This was irresponsible jargon by partisan cultists. The yogi must be seen in his proper perspective. Jnaneswar never ceased to extol the excellence of yoga and gave bhakti to the masses out of compassion.

"The Avatara of Wisdom" was born in the village of Alandi (Maharashtra, India) in the thirteen century. He is called the king of mystics by the high initiates of the secret circles of the Nath Mandala. His MahaGuru was Babaji Goraksha Nath himself, who initiated the young Gyan Nath into the mysteries of Nath Yoga and the ultimate realization of *Nirvikalpa* and *Sanjeevan Samadhi*. Having successfully accomplished the Nath yogic practices, he however found them too demanding for the normal people and householders. As a result, he advocated the simple devotional pathway to God. From this evolved the bhakti tradition of the *Varkaris*. Gyan Nath's miracles were not intended to aggrandize his spiritual stature, but to instil faith of the Divine into the hearts and minds of the then-sceptical masses. However, his mahasamadhi also known as the *Sanjeevan Samadhi* (*Saroub Samadhi*), meaning the preservation of his rainbow-body of light in life and death, clearly points to his Nath knowledge. This more than shows us that in his avataric stature and mission, not only is his Consciousness immortal, but the body and mind too, a distinct feature of immortality of the Siddha-Nath yogic tradition.

Sundarnath - Origin not Known, 21st century

It is said that when Sundar Nath undertook his *tapas* in a cave near Badrinath temple, the Badrinath vibrated with his spiritual intensity. One day, some miscreants (they were just boys we were told) went into the cave and found Raja Sundar Nath in samadhi. To test his yogic state of trance, they placed a burning charcoal on his thigh. The king of yogis didn't budge, for he was totally out of his body in samadhi, so the burning coal went deep into the flesh of his thigh. On descending from his heightened state of awareness, the yogi realized that there were burns covering his thigh. With compassion, he blessed the boys, for they had created a context whereby yogi Sundar Nath knew that he could never be shaken or diverted from his practice and communion with God. It is said that this great master traveled into the solitudes of the higher regions of the Himalayas, to the legendary city of Alkapuri. This spiritual centre near the Indo-China border is where he is today, lost in communion with God.

Nobody knows for how many thousands of years this monumental Siddha Nath yogi has been meditating in the Himalayan snows. It was necessary to mention his awe-inspiring name as he was a direct disciple of Shiva Goraksha Babaji; not only this, but in recent times he descended to the haunts of men to participate as being a *Mahant* in the Gorakhpur temple in the Gorakhpur temple in North Central India. His name may be found mentioned in the government office of the Garhwal Gazetteer, Rudraprayag, Gopeshwar and Badrinath. A magnificent photo of his adorns the temple of Badrinath as we encircle the outside of the temple. He was not only affiliated to the Babaji Goraksha Nath lineage, but was His disciple too.

CHAPTER 14

THE ANCIENT OF DAYS

Shiva Divided Himself – Root Races

In the *Skanda Purana* it is written that the Complete Shiva divided himself into two portions and still remained Complete. Bursting forth from the heart of the Complete Shiva, with irradiant splendour came forth the other Shiva who was also complete. This Shiva, who came into manifestation at the beginning of time, was known as Shiva Goraksha Babaji.

Om Purna Mada Purna Midam
Purnasa Purna Mudachataye
Purnasya Purna Madaya
Purna Meyva Vashishyate

From the Complete if the All is taken
The Complete still remains the Complete

   He is the Ancient of Days, and the forefather of all adepts of esotericism, the greatest king of the divine dynasties called the earliest and the last. In his symbolic dance of creation, he is depicted as Nataraja. In one of His many hands, He is shown as holding the *damru*[1], a drum in which one side narrows down to the vanishing point of the black hole of the disillusion of creation. The damru expands again into the white hole which explods forth the infinite creation. The *damru*, shaped like an hourglass, also depicts the sound of the Causation of Creation. One of the hands is in a gesture of blessing which depicts the steady state Space of Preservation and finally in the last of his hands, he holds the great fire, which depicts the Transformation of Creation into *Laya* (Zero). In his hands, he holds the thunderbolt with three-forked lightning (the *Trishul*[2]) which depicts three fundamental gunas of the *sattva* of luminosity, the *raja* of activity and the *tama* of inertia. These three qualities form the underlying factor of Creation, which later mutate into the electron, the proton and the neutron respectively.

The Birth of Goraksha Nath

---

1 The drum of Shiva in the shape of an hourglass, depicting both Sound and Time Eternal of Creation, Preservation and Dissolution.
2 Trident.

The Eternal Now

Babaji, the Eternal Now, broods over the humanities and the world cycles. By His mere looking down from on higher awareness, He pulls the whole evolutionary process of humanity, progressing it towards divinity. The cosmic manifestation of Shiva Goraksha Babaji is without beginning or end; it is eternal. That is why He is called the Aja Purusha, meaning, one who has no birth and therefore, no death. In his cosmic body, Babaji is working on a grand scale in the universal cycle of the spiritual hierarchy. This concerns the realm of devas, angels and rishis, called the "inconceivable" realms by Shri Yukteshwar who was in the line of discipleship of Shiva Goraksha Babaji. There is little knowledge as to the means and methods whereby the gods evolve themselves into higher states of awareness. There are however, ancient Puranas and scriptural texts that speak about the evolution of the secondary gods, the angels and even i*shwars*, meaning the supreme rulers who ruled as Manu Swayambhu and Manu Vivasvat[3], who is our lord the Sun.

The celestial manifestation was in the beginning of the *Shweta Varaha Kalpa*[4], from the heart of Shiva burst forth a flame of irradiant splendor and the eternal Shiva Goraksha Babaji was manifest in the celestial realm to carry on His inconceivable work (*lila*). He, who is ever-present in the cosmic and causal spheres of relativity, came to our astral globe for the first time eighteen-and-a-half million years ago, bringing with him the Sages of the Fire Mist. This was the beginning of the planting of the first seeds of the spiritual hierarchy of our septinary globe and beginning of an intelligent humanity[5]. The divine spark was then planted by the Sages of the Fire-mist as a seed in the human phenomena. The seed has now grown in this present age to see us human beings flowering into the likeness

---

3 The victorious sun.
4 'World-Cyle of the White Boar'.
5 Prior to this was the pre-Atlantian emotional race, and going further back hundreds of millions of years ago, there was the Lemurian age and even before this, there was the Hyper-Astral era. At that time, human beings wandered as astral shells called bhutas with instincts but no intellect. Perhaps they had rudimentary feelings too...

of our own Divinity.

The Terrestrial Manifestation of Babaji was about seven hundred years ago, which is a duration of approximately five human kalpas, each kalpa lasting one hundred and twenty years. This information was given by Yogavatar Lahiri Mahasaya to his disciple Pranabananda. Babaji is ever the same in His full omniscient consciousness whether absorbed in His cosmic consciousness, in celestial body of lightless light or appearing on our terrestrial globe. The difference between His manifestation as the Mahavatar and the manifestations of an avatara are that the avatara wears a vesture of light as His body form and may express his powers as per His avataric mission, whereas the Mahavatar adorns an apparent body of lightless light and is unlimited in His omniscient, omnipresent, and omnipotent expression. All glory to Babaji Goraksha Nath, all glory to the Sages of the Fire Mist, the Agnishvattha Rishis. Many times later, He manifested from the cosmic to our terrestrial plane as and when the need arose.

Rudra Kumars

The *Rudras* and *Kumars* are the virgin angels to whom Varun, Mitra, Indra, Yama, Michael and Gabriel all belong. They are the divine rebels who preferred the curse of incarnation and long terrestrial existence to seeing the misery of human beings who were evolved as shadows through the semi-passive energy of their too spiritual creators. "If man's use of life should be such as neither to animalise nor spiritualise, but to humanise the self," to do so he must be born human, not angelic. Hence tradition shows celestial yogis offering themselves as voluntary victims to redeem humanity by descending on our globe. They thus exchange their personal individuality for individual personalities and take up their abode on earth for the whole cycle of a *kalpa*. They sacrifice the bliss of *Bramha Nirvana* for earthly life. This sacrifice of the Great Avataras called the *Rudra Kumars* is higher and of a more in depth duration than the Bodhisatvas, who also perform such a sacrifice on a smaller scale of a *maha-yuga*⁶.

Viswakarma is one such Kumars who sacrificed himself for the sake of humanity. His story later spread to ancient Greece as the god Prometheus who stole the sacred fire of the mysteries of heaven and gave it to man for which he had to pay the price.

Sanat Kumar

Babaji Goraksha Nath, "the Lord of Irradiant Splendour," is also called Sanat Kumar, meaning "the eternal virgin youth." He came to be by direct manifestation from *Nilalohita Shiva* (blue void of absolute Consciousness) infused in Brahman⁷ who is *viraj-vaak* (light-sound) and in some mysterious way has gone beyond the evolution of the rest of the thirty-three *Kumars* (the Sages of the Fire Mist).

The deeper nature of his own work is beyond our comprehension though the *Kalki Purana*, the *Bhavishya Purana* and the *Chandogya Upanishad* give us fascinating insights into the nature of this divine Shiva Kumar, loftier in spiritual stature than even the *Purna Avatara*. "There He stood, 'the youth of sixteen summers,' Sanat Kumar, the 'eternal virgin youth,' the new ruler of the world, come to His kingdom. His pupils, the three Kumars, with Him, His helpers around Him; thirty mighty Beings, great beyond Earth's reckoning, in graded order, clothed in the glorious bodies they had created by Kriya Shakti. This was the first spiritual hierarchy."

---

6 One complete cycle of all of the four yugas, name Satya, Dwapara, Treta, Kali.
7 'That which has grown expansive', the Ultimate Reality of Atman, Purusha.

33 Lofty Beings

Accompanying Shiva Goraksha Babaji are thirty-three lofty beings, the Shiva-Kumars, the immortal virgin youths. Babaji is Jaggan Nath (Lord of the Universe), the head of the spiritual hierarchy of the Sages of the Fire Mist with their rainbow bodies of light, all in graded order, to assist him in his divine evolutionary work. The *Kumars* are the true progenitors of spirit in humanity and because of these incomprehensible beings, the holders of the sacred flame, the spiritual evolution of humanity was and is continuously made possible. In ancient texts, they incensed the devas (the celestial beings) for imparting the secrets of the Divine to mortal men. Wonderful accounts about this wondrous Being and His Divine assistants are given in the *Markandeya Purana*, and the *Samkhya Karika* of Ishvar Krishna.

Difference between Kumars and Goraksha

The difference between the *Kumars*, the mind-born sons of Shiva and Shiva Goraksha Babaji, the direct manifestation of Shiva is the duration of their work in the relative spheres of manifestation; the work of the former lasts for a kalpa, the world cycle called a day of Brahma, whereas, the direct manifestation of Shiva, the Mahavatar Goraksha Nath, exists for a *Mahakalpa*, which is the duration of God Brahma's Creation in being.

He is Jaggan Nath, the lord of our universe for this world cycle and a vaster reality when he leaves for a longer Isness of being. His work is incomprehensible even to the devas and archangels.

Shiva Goraksha Babaji is the collective consciousness of the seven primordial Sages of the Fire Mist born at the beginning of time. As I have mentioned before that Babaji and Goraksha Nath are one and the same Being, whom I refer to in this book, freely interchanging their names according to the context in which they are placed.

Mahabhinishkaran – The Great Sacrifice

Babaji's consciousness is of such an extended nature that it comprehends the life and livingness on our globe, our galaxy, and our universe all at once. This nameless one is known as Shiva Goraksha Babaji, Isvara Sanatana and Mahavatar Babaji. He is the deathless Master of eternity, who has sacrificed himself for the redemption of humanities for a whole world cycle, a *mahakalpa* of 4,320,000,000 years (Four billion three hundred and twenty million years), which is not even a wink of an eye in His Consciousness. Because He stays in the universe for the whole life span of its creation, assisting in the evolution of all sentient and non sentient beings by sacrificing Himself and infusing His spirit in every atom of creation, He is therefore called Mahabhinishkaran or "The Great Sacrifice." These are eternal sacrifices made by lofty divinities in the ceaseless cycles of creation, preservation and enlightment.

Babaji is the total light of the highest Elohim and yet in His unfathomable compassion, has left behind a finite portion of His infinite Consciousness to evolve humanity into the likeness of Divinity. This finite and immortal portion of His Divinity manifests amongst the haunts of men from time to time as the need arises. Throughout eternity, this Eternal Now watches over the evolution of humanity until it is liberated. Truly, He is called the Visible – Invisible Saviour of Mankind.

Shiva Goraksha Babaji's Cosmic Isness is without beginning or end, the source of all truth and the head of all divine hierarchies. His celestial form appeared on earth eighteen-and-a-half million years ago in the middle of the *Shweta Varaha kalpa* (world cycle of the White Boar). His human form composed of sub atomic particles of light, has appeared on our planet Earth time, and again as the need arose. He took the latest avataric form six human kalpas ago, approximately 720 years ago. He intends to keep this form - so it is spoken in the mystic circles - till the coming of the Kalki-Maitreya Avatara. He shall then bless and advise the avatara in his future mission, and then merge into his celestial or cosmic form which only he knows. This transition of descent from His cosmic to His celestial and then to His terrestrial form is a matter of mere convenience for this lofty Being, depending upon the spheres of consciousness He would like to bless with His enlightened wisdom.

He is now the Eternal Now who by His mere presence directs all Avataras and Prophets in their evolutionary work and mission. He is called The Great Initiator, who taught the sacred mysteries of Godrealization to Agastya Rishi, Hermes, Orpheus, Zarathustra, Buddha, Melchizedek, Bhogar Nath (Bo Yang), Matsyendra Nath, and so on and so forth. In more recent times, Babaji gave to Yoga-Avatara Lahiri Mahasaya, the Kriya Yoga teachings adapted to complement the evolution of today's peoples. The eighteen South Indian Siddhas, the eighty-four North Indian Siddhas, the Nav-Nath (Nine Maha Siddhas), are all emanations from this Supreme Being, incomprehensible and great beyond the reckoning of mortal and celestial Beings.

Babaji Goraksha Nath has given us this truth of practicing the various ways and means of speeding up our spiritual progress. He is the great "*Lakulish* of the lilac lagoons." The lilac lagoons are the depths of our own soul consciousness. He holds in his hands the *lakulish*, which represents the thunderbolt club of evolutionary lightning, surpassing life and death. This evolutionary lightning is called the kundalini. In the individual sense, the *lakulish*, which is the lightning club itself, represents our spinal chord with the brain as the club, and kundalini as the lightning.

Far beyond the reckoning of not only mortal man but even of the Gods, this Nameless One, this visible, invisible Saviour of mankind, whose consciousness is spread throughout eternity, is called "the Lightning Standing Still."

He is the Great Initiator of past, present, and future.

As Swayambhu

Celestial Devas, Angels and Yogis worshipping Him

The Mahavatar (Swyambhu) is specifically the great unborn, Self-manifestation of Shiva and has a much loftier work than the Avatara. The Cosmic Being called Shiva Goraksha Babaji will not incarnate from age to age, but is perpetually present until the world cycle is over. He broods over humanity, His children, from eternity to eternity. His work is far beyond the comprehension of mortals. He stands at the ninth level of Cosmic Consciousness, in the realms of His Cosmic, Celestial, and Terrestrial presence and work are concerned. In so far as his spiritual depth and realization are concerned, it is beyond the ninth level; His spiritual stature is inconceivable beyond the reckoning of both human beings, the Celestial Devas and Gods.

The Nath yogis are the greatest Hatha and Raja yogis that ever walked the earth and are no doubt the authorities on the subject of rejuvenation and *Kaya Kalpa*. Even the celestial angels and devas worship and acknowledge their wisdom. It was to these forms of

The Ancient Of Days

yogic practice and philosophy that I was most drawn. Traditionally, there are eighty-four Siddhas, and over and above them, nine Mahasiddhas called the Nava-Naths. The term Siddha means a perfected being, totally liberated from *samsara* (the world wheel that turns by the power of ignorance). They are adepts who, having transcended the fifth degree of initiation, have moved up the evolutionary ladder and expanded to serve humanity as their larger Selves. The nine Mahasiddhas are those adepts who have achieved the seventh degree of initiation and beyond to the eighth and ninth degree of divine Isness. The siddhas and their *sangh*[8] are the core foundation of the systems of yoga and *yogachara* (yoga teaching). Their ways of yoga are pre-Vedic, predating Buddhism, Jainism and even Hinduism. Gautama, who later became the enlightened Buddha, not only learned from them but he was also one of them. He later went on to found his own school and philosophy, born of the ancient Siddha and Nath tradition. Such also was the case of the great Mahavira (a contemporary of Buddha, who expounded the Jain philosophy). Their followers later corrupted their teachings as is often the case.

The Siddhas may choose their dwellings at will, roaming the cities like the Siddha Trailanga Swami who resided at Manikarnika Ghat in Varanasi. However, they are mostly found in the Himalayan ranges, silent and away from public gaze, as in the case of Siddha-Avadhoot Raja Sundar Nath who chooses the snowy abode of Alkapuri beyond Badrinath. They are the guardians of the Himalayan peaks, established in *Sanjeevani Samadhi* for thousands of years in undecayable bodies of light for the salvation of the world.

In their selfless service, the Siddhas and Mahasiddhas (the nine Naths), form what is known as The Guardian Wall of Humanity. They have denied themselves the highest state of salvation, remaining incarnate until the time their lesser brothers come to self-realization. Their Great Spirit permeates the evolutionary impulse of humanity and their force drives our infant race along its evolutionary journey towards divinity.

---

8 A collective body of like-minded people

The Hatha-Raja Yoga system of Goraksha Nath holds, within its power, humanity's hope for physical immortality combined with divine liberation. The tradition of Hatha Yoga has an immense wealth of hard won gold, including information about the potentials of body and mind. Modern medicine, psychology, and advanced scientific methods are rediscovering some amazing facts that the Nath yogis have taught and demonstrated in their lives for thousands of years.

Rishis Breathe the Love-Breath

There are people called rishis and yogis in the Himalayas who are giving love of a much higher quality by nature of which we breathe. They are breathing our breath for us. I have demonstrated and shown to those who attend my *satsangs* worldwide that a Master can breathe through your breath, suffusing your body with life-prana. So how much more could the Grand Masters do? How much more would the Divine Masters do? It gives you reason to think sincerely, intently and inwardly from your Soul (not from your mind), but to knowingly know that this is the Truth, because you have experienced a Master breathing through your breath. Am I right? That is the form of love that is given. This does not mean that those unknown Great Masters, away from the sight of mortal human beings are not great in their greatness. Their song was never sung on this earth and yet they are dying for us. By their every breath, they give us New Life Awakening.

Nath Yogis: Janus-Faced Transformers

I longed to be like those great Nath yogis, the colossal Janus-faced transformers who with one face absorb the mighty cosmic currents of the Universe to save humanity from harm's way, and through the other face transmit benevolent radiation to humanity for the spiritual evolution of their Consciousness.

If it had not been for these Masters and Siddhas, not only would this world have been a poorer place to live in, but humanity itself would be unable to withstand the stupendous cosmic kundalini surge which would have wiped it off the face of the Earth. This is the inconceivable work of the mighty Siddhas, the monumental Avadhoots and ineffable Avatarnaths by whose very breath we live. It is in the aura of these Nameless Ones, far beyond the reckoning of mortal man, that we live and move and have our Being.

Cosmic Man: Unfolding of the Septenary Man

There are seven cosmic beings known as the *Sapta Rishis*, the seven primeval sages of our galaxy. They are our *Ishvars* and informing spirits. *Ishvars* are secondary Gods below Parameshwar, the Lord God. Their biographies are not only written in the *akashic*[9] records, but they are also written in the ancient archives of India, the great libraries of the Himalayas.

The Rishis are those great cosmic beings like Vashishta and Vishwamitra who came during the Lemurian times, the Atlantean times, and the early Aryan times, where Lord Rama prevailed as the Avatara of Vishnu. There were two gurus teaching him. One was the Rishi Vashishta, his family guru, who wrote the treatise called the *Yoga Vashishta*. Then we have the other guru, Vishwamitra, who taught Rama the life supporting and liberating *Gayatri Mantra*. He also taught him the art of self-defence and noble warfare.

The Seven Great Sages are the informing spirits of the seven stars of the *Sapta Rishi* Constellation (the Great Bear constellation)[10]. Have you ever seen, on a clear night, the stars of the Great Bear? They're now known as Ursa Major in modern classification. From ancient days, the Seven Primeval Sages were known as the Sapta Rishi. The first is Marichi, then Atri and Pulastya, then Pulaha Angiras, Vashishta and Vishwamitra.

---

9 The thoughts imprinted in the homogenous radiant ether of the cosmic mind.
10 Mysteriously, the Rishis of the Great Bear connect to a form of Shiva Vastuspati, the hunter Vyad, which the Egyptians later called the Dog Star. The "Mrug Nakshatra", the deer, later called Orion in the west is hunted by this Great Hunter-Vastuspati Shiva. From Him sprang all the Vastushastra, the essence of geomancy, later influencing heavily the Chinese science Feng Shui.

Fifth Level Initiation: Siddha Nath Yogi

The hierarchy of the Siddha *sangh* comprises the Guardian Wall of humanity – this is the great Nath mandala.

> *Then stiller than stillness itself*
> *With bated breath, I do behold*
> *The rising Self-Sun's nectar gold*
> *I dissolve in that mystery untold.*
>
> Yogiraj Siddhanath

The Siddhanath yogi is dedicated to the *Fifth Declaration of Human Rights for World Peace*:

By virtue of being a world citizen it is one's inalienable right to attain the consciousness of natural enlightenment, leading to the realization that your expanded consciousness and humanity's consciousness is one. Further realize that humanity's consciousness as the World Disciple is to be bridged with Divinity's Consciousness, and the Siddhanath yogi is the bridge, the *Tirthankar*, who not only builds the rainbow bridge between humanity and Divinity but sacrifices himself to be it!

As he lies across the chasm to form the bridge, human souls walk over him and pass through his aura of light to enter the realization of their Divinity. Such is the work of the Nath yogi and Nath mandala – to help evolve this World Disciple and bridge the gap between humanity and Divinity. The Siddhanath yogi gives directly the consciousness of natural enlightenment, the "Here Now" state of *sahaja samadhi*[11].

These great Nath Masters are one with the Divine will and they

---

[11] 'Together-born', natural enlightenment; the fact that the transcendental reality and the empirical reality are not truly separate but coexist, or with the latter being an aspect or misperception of the former; often rendered as 'spontaneous' or 'spontaneity'; the sahaja state is the natural condition, that is, enlightenment or realization.

are ever in the waking consciousness of enlightenment. When out of the body, the Siddhanath rises to still higher states of Divine Consciousness. The experience is practically impossible to describe. Their service to humanity is the evolution of human consciousness leading to the realization that one's expanded Consciousness and humanity's consciousness are one. This is the fifth declaration of human rights for world peace which I have given. At all times, the Siddha *sangh* generates spiritual power, sacrificing it and putting it to the service of humanity, using it for lifting the heavy burden of the world. Metaphorically, the Siddha is said to be Janus-faced, with one face absorbing the cosmic forces of other worlds and spheres of consciousness, transforming their potent effects into love and harmony. With the other face, transmitting to humanity the much-needed healing spiritual energy at a reduced and beneficial level, for their growth and evolution, thereby transforming them.

Sixth Level Initiation - Avadhoot-nath Yogi

The *Avadhoot-nath* yogi means he who has completely cast off all limitations of body and mind. He is the Lord who has the power to grant boons, give protection, and bring about liberation. *Avadhoot-nath* is the Lord of ceaseless and persevering devotion, kept alive by the power of yoga and sacrifice. The Seven Mighty Beings who have passed the sixth level of initiation have the power to focus within themselves the essence of all seven heavenly spheres of consciousness. These mighty *avadhoots*, these seven Naths are the sun rays of the *Sapta Rishi*, the Seven Sages of our constellation called the Great Bear. Each is an overlord of one of the seven races, seven planets, and seven galaxies. You will see as the evolution of these Souls proceeds that they expand to become one of the Sages of the Fire Mist, and one of the seven sages of the Great Bear, which are only their physical bodies. Their informing spirits are way beyond the comprehension of all mortal beings and even beyond celestial Beings or devas.

Seventh Level : Vishnu Avatara – 1 of 7 Primeval Flames

I am bringing to light that the Avataras of Vishnu are considered to be his direct emanation of one of the seven primeval flames, called the Seven Rishis of the ancient of days, the archangels of the heavenly host and collectively the sacred Elohim of eternal living fire. Lord Krishna, for example, was a direct emanation of Sanatana Rsi Naryana. He is, however, the descent of Deity in form (*mayavi rupa*) of individuality. His appearance to man on earth is objective but in sober fact is not so. His illusive form has no past or future, nor does he have reincarnations due to karma, which has no hold on him.

Eighth Level: Rudra Nath Yogi - (Shiva Kumar) The Sages of the Fire Mist

Four mighty Beings preside over the inner government of our galaxy and four pillars of the universe. Tradition whispers what the *Gupta Vidya*[12], the secret knowledge, affirms. Reference is made in the *Linga Purana*[13] of "the Inner Man," who only changes his body from time to time. He is ever the same, knowing neither rest nor nirvana, spurning the seven heavens and remaining constantly on earth for the salvation of humankind. Such are the seven virgin Sages of the Fire Mist, the *Shiva Kumars*. Four sacrifice themselves for the sins of the world and instruction of the ignorant, until the end of this world cycle (*manvantar*). Though unseen, they are ever present. Their bodies are composed of other-worldly lightless light. They are the undying, immortal ones, great beyond the reckoning of mortals. You should never speak their names in vain or before an uninitiated group of people, nor the names of the disciples of these great ones. The wise alone will understand. These sacred four have

---

12 Secret wisdom.

13 One of the ancient texts of the episodes relating to Lord Shiva. The linga is an oval sphere, which represents Shiva. It symbolizes Him to be everywhere and nowhere at the same time. Shiva has his center everywhere and circumference nowhere. In tantric aspects it is also used as the symbol of rejeneration and procreation.

been allegorized in the *Linga Purana* as the "Angels of the Face of God." The same holy text states that Shiva as the supreme Sage of the Fire Mist is born in each kalpa as sixteen virgin youths: four white, four red, four yellow and four brown. These are the sacred Sages in whom Shiva's Spirit of Divine wisdom and chaste ascetism incarnates. They are infused with his power. This connects with the epitaph of Babaji Goraksha Nath, "The Youth of Sixteen Summers."

These mighty Beings came to Earth because our world was at the stage of evolution where we could receive the divine spark whereby the intellect or *buddhi*[14] could be made possible. Without the guidance of these sages, the human mind would have plunged into a world of passion and animal nature. Because of these sages (the *Shiva Kumars*), the evolution of human consciousness was given a great impetus. They are the wondrous rulers of our spiritual government and dwell in *Shvetdeep*[15], a spiritual location beyond the Himalayas, in the aurora borealis of the northern lights. It is said that they brought the Sanskrit language to our planet from Venus and Sirius. A clearer understanding may be had of these beings by meditating on Shiva, so say the yogis.

The balance of the universe is rooted in reciprocity, and the foundation of the evolution of the world is sacrifice. Even at the high level of the Sages of the Fire Mist, the Rudranath Yogis, sacrifices are made to prepare great sages to undertake a greater work in the world.

Shiva Kumars

Avataras of Shiva. Also called the manifestations of Lord Shiva, the Shiva Kumars stand at the eighth level of Cosmic Consciousness, they are usually invisible and unknown. However, they incarnate specifically for the yogic and spiritual evolution of human consciousness. They are not limited to the *yuga* cycle as are the avataras

---

[14] 'That which is conscious, awake', the higher mind, which is the seat of wisdom (jnana); manas.
[15] White Island.

of Vishnu, but manifest when the need fo spiritual evolution arises. They are also called the Agnishvatta Rishis (the Sages of the Fire Mist).

The Goraksha Nath Babaji yogic tree has twelve branches, Sat Nath being one of them. They say the lineage descended from Adi Nath (Shiva himself), who gave it to Parvati Nath (his consort), who gave it to her two sons Kanthad Nath and Kartikeya. This divine science of yoga was further passed onto Vishnu, who initiated the spirit of our sun called Vivashvat, and from there it descended to the kings of the solar dynasty who guarded and preserved this science from age to age. From Vivashvat Surya, Vaivashvat Manu got the initiation and then gave the science of the evolution of consciousness to Ikshavaku. It was then passed on to Raghu[16], then Dilip[17] and later to Harischandra, and then to Rama, thirty-seventh in descent from Ikshavaku.

---

16 Name of one of the Kings of the Solar Dynasty.
17 King of the Solar Dynasty, 16th descendent from the sun, the son of King Ikshavaku.

CHAPTER 15

KALKI AVATARA AND BABAJI MAHAVATARA

Everybody speaks of the avataras and their work; but very few have portrayed the mysterious and evolutionary work done by the Mahavatar Shiva Gorakhsha Babaji concerning the evolution and destinies of nations and humanity. This lofty being holds in His consciousness the blueprint of creation and the action plan of our world, which He executes through His mind's eye. For He ever lives in the present and as far as He is concerned what was, *is,* even now. The future for Him has already been revealed. It is all in the present. Nothing is hidden from His omniscient gaze.

Their Special Work and Mission

The two lofty Beings—Mahavatar Shiva Goraksha Babaji and Kalki Avatara Maitreya—are working in close co-operation and understanding. Together they are sending out vibrations of love and evolution for the redemption of humanity. Mahavatar Babaji is working on the *atmic* level of the Divine Consciousness of humanity. Kalki Avatara Maitreya is working upon the *buddhic* level of the divine mind of humanity.

It is not given to us to know what arrangement or spiritual impetus humanity shall be given at the beginning of the new age, but it is said that a tremendous Being, a manifestation of Shiva Himself, shall incarnate at the end of the millennium, in one or many souls, and do as great a work on the spheres of the inner consciousness of humanity as the Kalki Avatara will do on the outer, at the junction of the Leo–Aquarius zodiac.

This slow, careful and gradual evolution of the minds and souls of humanity is being done to prepare the people at large to be more compatible to receive the blessings and transformation given by the Kalki Avatara when he incarnates upon Earth during the Leo–Aquarius age. The *Atmic* Consciousness of the people shall then be further transformed and evolved to a deeper realization, by the blessings and awareness given by Babaji.

Although these benedictions will be at a subtler level of human receptivity, more people shall avail and be evolved by this higher alchemy of total transformation, since more people will be spiritually prepared as previously mentioned. But besides the positive work, the battle against the negative forces in the world is one of the hallmarks of the Kalki Avatara—to destroy the evil on the inner plane of the negative mind and also on the outer plane of evil and negative forces.

The sixth avatara of Vishnu was Parashurama. He worked on the plane of *tapa*, which was self-directed discipline to destroy the ego that was embodied in the warrior class of humanity at the time. He brought about a balance of the then psycho-social order. The seventh avatara of Vishnu, Lord Rama, worked on prana, or life-force control. The eighth avatara of Vishnu, Lord Krishna worked on bhakti or *manomaye*, and the emotional body to bring about balance, love and harmony. Then the ninth avatara Buddha did his work on *vijyanamaye*, the mental sphere of humanity. Now the tenth avatara of Vishnu Kalki-Maitreya works on the *buddhic* or intuitional body and Babaji is always working on *atma avastha* (no work, no mind). The Kalki will first work on the negative forces of the mind and intellect which obstruct the evolution of humanity, and then will later to go on to bring about the age of enlightenment. Babaji will be the Eternal Presence all around the world cycle and always guide the prophets and avataras guarding humanity from age to age. He represents the beyond-mind called the *Atma* and has no work. He is the PRESENCE which guides the plan of the evolution of humanity.

Lord Krishna says:

Partrinaya sadhunama vinasaya ca dushkritam
Dharama samsthapanarhtaya sambhavami yuge-yuge

To protect the righteous, to disintegrate the dark forces
To establish the dharma, I am born from age to age

Bhagavad Gita
Chapter 4 Verse 8

Babaji's relation to the Kalki Avatara is very deep and very old. We could compare it to the relationship between a master and his disciple on the outer plane. Babaji would be the master who, remaining in the background, would be assisting the evolutionary work of the Kalki. In the inner spheres of one's universal consciousness Shiva Goraksha Babaji is the Christos who projects His spirit to animate the Christ called the Kalki Avatara. This brings us to the question of whether the second advent of Christ is the same as the coming of the Kalki Avatara. I would get to the point directly and opine in the affirmative that both these events and these spiritual beings are one and the same. In my experiences and visions I see this, and if we study closely both the prophecies in the *Kalki Purana* and the Bible, we shall see the similarities in the advent of the Kalki and the second coming of Christ.

It is said of the Kalki Avatara that he shall be riding a white horse, called Devdatta[1], with glory all around him. He shall wield the meteoric Sword of Knowledge called Ratna Maru (Shiva's sword given to Kalki by Gurudeva Parashurama) to cut asunder the bonds of ignorance. In the biblical book of Revelations' description of the Second Advent it is said that the Christ shall come riding on a white horse surrounded by an angelic host; He shall wield the

---
1 Granted by God.

flaming sword to bring about justice and righteousness on Earth.

Inner Government of the World

In the Indian pantheon, the four horsemen shall be as follows: on the first horse shall be Vikramaditya (El Morya), the ideal king; the second horse shall be of king Devapi (Kuthumi), the ideal world teacher; the third horse will be ridden by Lord Vaivaswat Manu (the present spiritual king to be succeeded by Vikramaditya, who incarnated as Gyanavatar Sri Yukteshwar, and will incarnate as the next Manu called Savarni); and riding upon the fourth horse shall be Maitreya, the Kalki Avatara, who will begin and accomplish his mission and pass on to higher realms. He will be succeeded by the World Teacher Devapi, who is none other than Yogavatar Lahiri Mahasaya.

It is of great value to know that our present lord, Vaivaswat Manu, wrote and expounded the celebrated scripture called the *Manav Dharma Shastra*. It is also called the *Manu Smriti*, the fabric upon which is based the code of ethics, spiritual evolution and its guiding principles. This lofty being, although embodied as an individual manifestation, is also the spirit of the Aryan fifth root race[2]. He holds office for a good 300 million years in the spiritual hierarchy of the inner government of the world[3]. His term is now coming to an end, where he will hand over the reins of government beginning from 2012, to his successor, the Savarni Manu.

In the Prophecies they say that there will be three horsemen preceding him and his, the fourth white horse will be the one on which Kalki Maitreya will be riding. He is said to be the *Maseeha* or the Messiah, the savior of mankind. Babaji, the immortal Metatron (the Angel so close to God that He is God), shall be a witness to this divine drama, and merely by His presence this *avataric* work shall be accomplished.

---

2 The noble race from the country of Aryavarta, presently called India.
3 The Vaivaswat Manu had already prepared the causal, mental and emotional bodies and when evolution produced the human body, then the Spirit of man (as the Sages of the Fire Mist), through the Lunar ancestors, entered the human form of flesh.

In the Indian pantheon of rishis or sages we see that the Kalki Avatara is no lesser a person than the ancient sage Maitreya meaning 'friend'. His spiritual father is rishi Parashara, the great divine astrologer, whose father is the rishi Shakti, and his father the ancient rishi Vashishta, seen as the last-but-one of the seven stars in the Great Bear. The father of Vashishta is the ancient rishi Varuna. Such is the grand spiritual ancestry of rishi Maitreya, the Kalki Avatara to be. Kalki is presently residing as a *bodhisattva* in the Tushita Heaven[4], and is known as Manjunath/Maitreya, disciple of Shiva Goraksha Babaji.

The Indian pantheon, which is the source of the Buddhist hierarchy, accepts the Indian rishi Maitreya as the fifth secret Buddha who is to come as the Kalki Avatara. By then Gautama, the fourth secret Buddha, whose spirit still pervades the Indian continent, shall have moved on to vaster and more incomprehensible realms of kingship and being. Kalki will do just as Krishna and the preceding three Buddhas did in former lifecycles.

The time of his coming is chosen to balance *dharma,* and to set straight those who think that by creating *adharma* (unrighteousness) they can imbalance the gunas and *dharma*. When there is an upsetting of the laws of *dharma*, and equilibrium in nature and man has to be restored, hence, the inner government of the world takes it upon itself, at the appropriate time, to restore this balance. In 2012 our Sun, situated in the arm of Orion, was in alignment with its brother bipolar star, called Maghayanti[5] (Alcyone), situated in the Pleiades cluster in the constellation Taurus. With this alignment commenced the work of the balancing of the gunas and that of restoring righteousness on Earth. Of course along with the good work, there are bound to be certain upheavals like the tilting of the Earth's axis, the shifting of tectonic plates and global war-like situations.

These natural and man-made calamites will not wipe out the

---

4 A heavenly sphere where the Kalki *avatar* is preparing for his second advent on Earth; therefore, it is connected to Shamballah from where the Kalki is to appear.

5 One of the seven sisters of the Pleiades

whole of humanity but only those portions of the Earth and of humanity which are a hindrance and blocking the work of the great balancing act of nature and the spiritual evolution of humankind. Those souls that need treatment shall be dealt with appropriately and, for some, bodies and minds will be reoriented during this time. Those bodies unfit for the change shall be disposed into the elements and their minds transformed in the fires of celestial Gnosis. It is these great Presences in the form of the four horsemen of the apocalypse who shall enter into the spirit of humanity and of nature, and work with the genomic transformation of the bodies and minds of the future races to come, drawing a lot of DNA material from the parent fifth root race passing on to higher spheres. These great beings guided by yet higher Presences will bring about a future evolution of all sentient and non-sentient beings. They will work to bring to a spiritual head an egalitarian society and a more evolved human citizenry. The four spiritual beings represented mystically as riding on their horses (representing purity, light and harmony) are mentioned below.

The Four Horsemen of the Apocalypse

BABAJI THE LIGHTLESS LIGHT
DOTH SHINE UPON THE HORSEMEN'S FLIGHT
COMPASSIONATE AND HEALING LIGHTS
FOUR HORSEMEN IN THEIR SPLENDID FLIGHTS
AWAY OH DARKNESS, FLY OH NIGHT
THE YOGIS COME IN RADIANT MIGHT

Yogiraj Siddhanath

1st horseman on black horse:	World king to-be, Vikramaditya/ Gyanavatar Sri Yukteshwar
2nd horseman on yellow horse:	World Teacher to-be, Bharthari Nath / Yogavatar Lahiri Mahasaya
3rd horseman on brown horse:	World king, Vaivaswat Manu
4th horseman on white horse:	World Teacher, Kalki Maitreya

The four horsemen of the apocalypse depict a very in-depth secret doctrine of the evolution of the human races and their progress towards harmony and peaceful coexistence with one another. Each of the horses that the great beings ride, does not represent the races according to color, but the work that is to be done in improving the color of the spiritual aura. Here, the white horse means showing them the clarity of inner light of their souls; the black horse represents the unfathomable darkness beyond which lies the Star of Liberation that has to be understood; the brown horse represents a stability and balance of the Earth with the spirit; and, the biscuit-yellow horse represents the ability of the future developed races to maintain conscious awareness from birth, right through the passage of death to an enlightened dimension. These are inner meanings of the spiritual work the four horsemen have to do. Any attempt at a deeper explanation would require the reader to go into a deep meditation, because words fail to convey the realization of the work of these divine four horsemen.

Three Lords of the World

During each world period there are three successive Lords of the World. The present holder of the office is already the third (*Sanat Kumar* aspect of Shiva Goraksha Babaji). He resides with his three pupils or Naths in an oasis called *Svetdeep*[6], the white island of Shamballah, in remembrance of the time when it was an island in the central Asian sea. These four greatest of adepts are often called "The Virgins of the Fire Mist." They belong to an evolution entirely more advanced than ours. Their bodies though human in appearance differ widely from ours in construction being rather bodies assumed for convenience rather than ordinary bodies. Their body vestures are of an undecayable quality as other-worldly light. They require no nourishment and remain unchanged for eons of millions of years.

---

6 From sveta (white) dvipa (island). In this island is the celestial city of Shamballa (Sambalpur) wherein reigns the King Sanat Kumar. The Sages of the Fire Mist and the Kalki Avatara are also said to reside on this spiritual island.

The three Lords of our world who assist our World King Manu are called *Prateyaka Rudras*[7] / Buddhas. They are themselves destined to be our three Lords of the World when our humanity is occupying the planet Mercury. It is on the first ray that the greatest progress for man is possible within the hierarchy of our globe, for there are on it two initiations beyond that of the Manu. The *Pratyeka Rudras* / Buddhas who stand at the eighth degree of initiation are above the Lord Manu Vaivasvat who stands with the Lord Maitreya at the seventh level of initiation. These silent meditators are greatly misunderstood by some writers who have described them as entirely selfish beings that refuse to teach what they have learned and pass away into the highest supreme liberation, called Kaivalya[8] (Brahma Nirvana). It is true that these God-like initiates do not teach at even the highest levels and that they will leave our world only to carry on their glorious work in inconceivable dimensions and spheres at the behest of Lord Shiva (The Supreme Manu).

The Lord Vaivasvat Manu has crossed the seventh level of initiation and is known as Noah in the Bible, where he gathered the seeds of humanity, a pair of every kind of living being, before the flood holocaust and brought them safely over to seed our earth with the Aryan fifth root race and animal life. On the higher levels of the three Lords of the World (Dattatreya, Ganesha and Kartikeya), the task of the third Lord of the World (ninth degree initiate) is far greater than those of the first and the second Lords (eighth degree initiates). Because it is Third Lord, Kartikeya's (an aspect of Shiva Goraksha) work to round off satisfactorily the period of evolution and to deliver over countless millions of souls and evolving jeevas into the hands of the seed Manu Ganesha, who will be responsible for the souls over inter-planetary nirvana. This is most probably the work at the end of the *manavantar*[9] and at the end of the kalpa. The seed Manu will hand the souls over in turn to the root Manu of the next globe. The third Lord of the World (Jaggan Nath),

---

7 High rishis of the Fire Mist of the eigth degree.

8 'Isolation', the state of absolute freedom from conditioned existence, as explained in Ashtanga Yoga; in the non-dualistic (advaita) traditions of India, this is usually called moksha or mukti, 'release' from the fetters of ignorance (*avidya*).

9 A reign of one manu.

having fulfilled this duty, takes another initiation entirely outside of our world and its hierarchy and attaining the level of the "Silent Watcher." In that capacity, he remains in office for the whole period of the round and it is only when the life wave has again occupied our planet and is again ready to leave it, that he abandons his unique self-imposed task and hands it over to his successor.

The evolutionary work of sub and root races, chains and planets belongs to the various Manu Kings of loftier and loftier hierarchies. This present Lord Vaivasvat Manu is the seventh out of the fourteen Manus and is the evolutionary spiritual king of our Aryan fifth root race. So we are halfway through the world cycle called the Great White Boar cycle (the *Shweta Varaha Kalpa*), which lasts 4 billion 320 million years.

The Lord Krishna-Maitreya, who is to descend upon earth as the Kalki Avatara, is in the Christian scriptures called The Second Coming of Christ. The eternal spirit of Maha-Vishnu who inspired through Parashuram, then came as Ram, then came as Krishna, after which he came as the Christ, and then incarnated as Matsyendranath. This Nath in his celestial form is also called Avalokiteshwar, who in Maharasthra, India, is worshipped as Vitobha, symbolizing the man crucified in space, like the eternal Christ; he is also called Panduranga. A similarity in all incarnations is the sacrifice made by the Krishna-Christ. In Buddhist scriptures also, you see Avalokiteshwar, crucified with the marks of the stigmata on his hands, and in Christianity, Jesus was also crucified with the marks of the stigmata on his hands. This gives us a great link to the similarity between the Krishna consciousness, Avalokiteshwar, the Christ consciousness and Vitobha (Krishna). In the Middle-Ages when Matsyendranath / Avalokiteshwar incarnated, he prayed to Lord Shiva to give him a disciple greater than himself. The result was the birth of Goraksha Nath as his disciple in the earthly sense, and his Supreme Guru in the divine sense. This is the mystic relationship between Shiva Goraksha Babaji and the Lord Maitreya Krishna.

Work and Mission of Babaji and Kalki

These two Beings - the Mahavatara Babaji Goraksha Nath and the Avatara Kalki Maitreya together are evolving humanity, Babaji awaring and expanding the Atmic level of Divine Consciousness and the Kalki working upon the Buddhic level of Divine Mind. The Krishna, Maitreya and Vasudeva are the same person. The mystery of the Vasudeva-Mantra lies in the fact of its liberating quality. All souls that are caught up in the transmigrating cycle of birth and death resort to this mantra, which liberates them. In his aspect of Vasudeva, Krishna is the guardian of all the souls that have to pass through him to get *moksha*. In initiated circles, it is well experienced that the Vasudeva mantra purifies the devotee striving for liberation and more often than not, this mantra succeeds in giving the due result, for each individual soul is screened, balanced and blessed by Vasudeva Krishna to go into higher dimensions and then to salvation. Millions and billions of such souls are being prepared for such enlightenment and would later come back accompanying the chosen one *lakh*[10] forty four thousand Rishis and Siddhas to serve the Kalki Avatara in his divine mission on earth, when he comes at the time of the Second Advent. The Second Advent is the same as the Coming of the Christ.

Shiva Goraksha Babaji, with the great manus, avataras and *avadhoots* is working on the divine consciousness level of humanity. This slow, careful and gradual evolution of the minds and souls of humanity is being done to prepare the people at large to be more compatible to receive the blessings and transformation given by the Kalki Avatara on the Buddhic level when he incarnates upon earth during the Leo-Aquarius Age. The *Atmic* level of Consciousness of the people shall then be further refined and evolved by the blessings and awareness given by Babaji. Babaji's benedictions will be at a subtler level of human receptivity, hence there will be relatively less people who shall avail of and be evolved by this higher blessing.

---

10 Hundred thousand.

The special work and mission of Kalki: Love (Bhakti Yoga)

As I have said before, the work of the Kalki Maitreya is more on the Buddhic (intuitional) plane of the human soul. The work of Babaji Goraksha Nath is on the Atmic (spiritual) plane of the human soul. It is interesting to note that Sri Krishna also makes a mention of Kriya Yoga in the Gita Ch. 6, 24-26. to protect the righteous by giving them soul liberating techniques such as Kriya and Raj yoga, bhakti yoga of devotion and Karma Yoga of enlightened action which teaches us to perform selfless actions bereft of desires thereby creating no new karma. This is one of the famous definitions of yoga as skill or dexterity in action – *Yoga Karmaneshu Kaushalyam.*

Besides the positive work the battle against the negative forces in the world is one of the hallmarks of the Kalki Avatara, to destroy the evil on the inner plane of the negative mind and also on the outer plane of evil and negative forces.

Evolutionary Boost – Kalki Avatara

Shiva Goraksha Babaji is the deathless presence of eternity who keeps in His aura even the coming of the Kalki Avatara and all of the divine manifestations. It is not given to us to know what arrangement or spiritual impetus to humanity shall be given at the beginning of the new age, but it is said that a tremendous Being, a manifestation of Shiva himself shall incarnate at the end of the millennium, in one or many souls, and do as great a work on the spheres of the inner consciousness of humanity as the Kalki Avatara will do on the outer, at the junction of the Leo-Aquarius zodiac. Why this apparently premature spiritual boost is being given, only God knows.

Remember that humanity at large is not ready to awaken from its slothful, sweet slumber of delusion, illusion and error. Although a galvanic spiritual surge shall come from this great manifestation of Shiva, it will not damage the spiritual system of humanity, or its astral chakras, corpus callosum and brain system. The evolutionary surgery by this lofty Being is to prevent the extinction of humanity from the face of the earth, while spiritually enabling it to make the paradigm shift to a more enlightened state of awareness!

This immortal Being was never born. He is *aja* (deathless). He is the source of the Nath tradition of yogis, the great "*Lakulish* of the Lilac Lagoons," originating from the night of pre-history. The yogic tradition of the Nath yogis predates the *Vedas* and is *Shramanic* effort-driven in its essence. At that time the ancient Babylonian, Egyptian, Chinese and Mayan civilizations existed only in their embryonic stages.

Who is Kalki Avatara?

The Kalki Avatara is mentioned by various different names in different faiths and religions. The Christians know him by the name of Christ and his second advent. In the Nath tradition, he goes by the name of Matsyendra Nath. In the Buddhist tradition, they call him Avalokiteswar. In the Vedic scriptures of India, he is called the Rishi Maitreya, also destined to be the fifth secret Buddha. In the Bhakti movement of devotion in Maharashtra, India, he goes by the name of Vithoba, which signifies the cosmic man, cruxified in space. In the Sufi tradition, many believe him to be the Imam Mahadi.

The above names refer to one and the same spirit of Vishnu consciousness, variously known as the Krishna consciousness and Christ consciousness.

The Buddha of the past was glorified in the Rishi Kashyap. The present Buddha is glorified in Gautam, the Buddha. The future Buddha is to be Maitreya, also known as the Kalki Avatara. It is interesting to note that in the description of Imam Mahadi, he has imbibed the qualities of both the Kalki Avatara and the future Manu Savarni called Vikramaditya.

Former incarnations of the World King and World Teacher

Avataras retain their consciousness life after life. This is not so with normal people who forget their past lives totally at birth; though some people do retain partial past life memories. The Great Ones, through the power of *tapa* and yoga, are fully conscious through the ages in their celestial bodies. Normal peoples' veils are subject to their former karma while for masters, *avadhoots* and *bodhisattvas*, the veil of maya is often self-taken. At the dawn of the new era, at the *avataric* level of spiritual awakening, will stand two monumental Beings—King Vikramaditya, descended from the Solar Dynasty of the house of Ikshavaku Rama and the World Teacher Nagarjuna, descending from the house of Yadav Krishna of the Lunar Dynasty. The Spirit of Vishnu descends into all *avataric* world teachers just as the spirit of Shiva descends into all *avataric* spiritual kings. The *Mahavataric* descent of Lord Shiva is Shiva Goraksha Babaji who plays His role for the whole of existence.

Former Incarnations of our World King and World Teacher	
World King Manu Maharaja	**World Teacher *Maha* Guru**
Bhishma	Devapi (Uncle of Bhishma)
Karna (3102 BCE) (Born to queen, found in bulrushes by a poor man)	Balrama (3400 BCE)
Moses (1270 BCE) (Born poor, found by a queen in bulrushes)	Abraham (1800 BCE)
Arya Morya (340 – 298 BCE Reign) (Vikramaditya 1)	Arya Chanakya (350 – 288 BCE) (Partial avatar of Vishnu)
Vikramaditya (57 BCE)	Bharthari Nath (70 BCE)
Chowrangee (Puran) (90 CE)	Shalivahan (18 – 102 CE)
Aaryasangh (200 CE) (disciple of Nagarjuna)	Nagarjuna (150 – 200 CE) (disciple of Goraksha Nath)
Shamz Tabrizi (died in 1249 CE)	Kabir (1440 – 1518 CE)
Maharana Pratap (1540 – 1597 CE)	Yogi Sri Chandra (1494 – 1644 CE) (said Maharana his brother in past life)
Shivaji Maharaj (1666 – 1709 CE)	Ramdas Maha Guru (1627 – 1680 CE)
Gyanavatar Sri Yukteshwar (1855 CE)	*Yogavatar* Lahiri Mahasaya (1828 CE)
Agni Surya Yogi	Shiva Bala Yogi (1940 CE)
Yukteshwar as Manu Savarni (successor to Manu Vaivaswat)	**Maha Guru Lahiri Mahasaya** (successor to Kalki Maitreya)

Avataric descents of Lord Vishnu

1. Bhagvan Matsya
2. Bhagvan Kacchha
3. Bhagvan Varaha
4. Bhagvan Narsimha
5. Bhagvan Vamdeva
6. Bhagvan Parashurama (whose Guru was Jamadagni)
7. Bhagvan Ramchandra (whose Guru was Vashista)
8. Bhagvan Krishna (whose Guru was Narayana)
9. Bhagvan Buddha (whose Guru was Kashyap)
10. Bhagvan Kalki (whose Guru is Parashuram) - yet to come

The World King

A certain mention must be made of the spiritual world kings of our Earth called the Manus. The Manus are spiritual initiates of the highest order, in the direct line of Shiva Goraksha Babaji. They are the archangels presiding over and above the gods who, through their infinite compassion, have spurned the highest nirvana in order to assist in the evolution of physical and astral beings. They take upon themselves the task of guarding and guiding the races of humanity for a period of 300 million years. It is Babaji who directs and guides their lofty work and provides the necessary impetus for evolving humanity.

Within each Day of Brahma (also called a *kalpa*) are fourteen smaller world cycles, each of which is presided over by a spiritual Manu[11]. Six such world cycles have already elapsed and ours is the seventh over which Vaivaswat Manu presides as the spiritual king. This is therefore called the *Vaivaswat Manavantar* of which 300 million years have elapsed, almost completing his reign. He is succeeded by the next Manu called Savarni. The first indications of

---

11 We are presently in the universal cycle of the *Shweta Varaha Kalpa* (White Boar Cycle), which constitutes a day of Brahma (four billion, three hundred and twenty million years). We have finished one *parardha*, that is one half day of Brahma of the present universal cycle.

this transition on the astral sphere appeared upon the completion of the year 2012.

The year 2012 struck a new note of evolution in the lyre of Apollo, who in India is the great Manu Vivasvat (Father of Vaivaswat), our Sun God. Out of the seven strings of his lyre, he has struck the fourth string, which is the fourth round, and a lot of work needs to be done on the astral chakras and the kundalini energy of the whole human race, and of higher celestial beings. In this, the first Manu (Swayambhu), the seventh Manu (Vaivaswat), and the eighth Manu (Savarni) have an important role to play.

The seventh Manu, Vaivaswat who is the king of the inner hierarchy and inner government of the spiritual world, will hand over the reins of his kingdom to his successor, the incarnation of Gyanavatar Sri Yukteshwar, who in his former life was Vikramaditya. He is to be the future king of the inner spiritual world and will go by the name of Manu Savarni. In the same way, the world teacher of the hierarchy of the inner government of the world, the Lord Kalki Maitreya, will hand over the spiritual teachings to his successor, Yogavatar Lahiri Mahasaya. He was the king Devapi in his former life and is destined to be the future World Teacher.

Lord Vaivaswat, this mighty God-essence is the same and stays on guard in compassion to evolve the infant humanity for 300 million years, which are completed, and whence he has handed over this great office to his successor, the Manu Savarni.

Vikramaditya in his former life was El Morya, an ancient Emperor of India, the grandfather of Emperor Ashoka, and Bharthari Nath was the king Devapi. Vikramaditya El Morya, an ancient Rajput prince, stands to serve humanity and the new and upcoming race with great strength and serenity. Those who have a powerful Mars and Sun aspect in their astrological charts, favorably express the qualities of valor, courage and military genius as well as Raja Yoga practice. The king Nath Vikramaditya will evolve into the future Manu Savarni of the sixth root race. He is destined to be the future spiritual king of our world. Presently, he is at work in both his physical and celestial bodies on the coast of California as well as the entire west coast; it is an India-California connection. He teaches Raja Yoga and is connected with Lord Shiva's power, majesty, and spiritual glory.

The Coming World Teacher

He is to be the great world teacher and has to do with wisdom and Jnana Yoga. He is destined to succeed Maitreya, the present world teacher, and disciple of the supreme sage Parashara. It is prophesied in the *Kalki Purana* and *Vishnu Purana*[12] that these two mighty Beings, Vikramaditya of the Solar dynasty and Nagarjuna of the Lunar dynasty, by their power of *tapa* and yoga, are alive throughout the ages and shall establish a spiritual world beginning from the dawn of this millennium. Nagarjuna's work is to do with the vibrations of the planet Mercury and the Moon. The divine work of both these lofty beings shall reach its zenith when the zodiac signs of Leo and Aquarius shall be maximally activated upon the Earth approximately 2499 CE.

---

12   Ancient text according to the Vaishnava philosophy.

Seventh Level Initiation: Avataranath Yogi

They are the true world teachers and Divine rulers of all the humanities, past, present, and future. There are three mighty Avatara Nath yogis who are at present governing our spiritual world:

1. The Avataranath Vaivaswat Manu: The seventh Spiritual King, son of the Sun Vivasvat Manu, from whom descends Ikshavaku and then Rama Chandra (thirty-seventh in descent from Ikshavaku). The Vaivasvat Manu will hand over the reigns to Savarni Manu.

2. The Avataranath Maitreya: He whose spiritual ancestry is from the Avatara Parshuram whose successor was the Avatara Rama who was then succeeded by the Avatara Krishna, then Siddhartha. Then comes the Avatara Kalki called the Maitreya. All along, the spirit of Maha-Vishnu incarnated as these great Saviours of humanity. In esoteric circles, he is called *Sapta-sapti*, meaning he is the seventh spiritual Sun and with the seventh Manu Vaisvata will bring about a change for the new age.

3. The Avataranath Agastya: The son of the ancient Rishi Mitra, is the teacher of Karma Yoga and activity of Brahma; expansion, generation, and procreation of all species and especially the human race. He came from Kailash, the abode of Shiva, in the Northern Himalayas of India. He then resided in middle India and is now finally the father of the South Indian fraternity.

The Avatara Kalki Maitreya is the fifth secret Buddha and should in no way be confused with the Purna Avatara Krishna. This mistake is committed by many writers and needs clarification, although the spirit of *Krishna Atma* informs Maitreya Buddha, the latter will soon be merged to his parent source Krishna, who is Divinity itself. The expounders of spiritual philosophy should be able to discern this fact. The five secret Indian Rishis whom the Buddhists call the Buddhas are Marichi, Kashyap, Krishna, Gautam and Maitreya.

The Kalki Avatara and His Assistants

The coming of the Kalki Avatara is also called the second advent, or by some, Judgment Day. This is the time when all people shall be judged according to their karma and perfect justice meted out. Negativity itself shall be punished, and goodwill and peace shall rule the earth. Mighty shall be the descent of these Beings in their chariots of spiritual fire. It is to be remembered that when so supernal and lofty a Being as Kalki, descends on earth he is a Purna Avatara, that is a full Avatara (for details refer to the *Bhavishya Purana* and *Kalki Purana*).

The Kalki Avatara will be accompanied by two mighty assistant Avataras. The first will be the Manu Savarni, whom people know as the King Vikramaditya (victorious Sun). Some know him as El Morya and to some he is known as the Divine Sisodia Gulablal Singh. But there is a mystery in this, which try as we may, we cannot resolve. Hence, we are not making the endeavor to do so. However, this is the ideal king who will be accompanying the lofty Kalki Avatara. Also accompanying him will be the divine Priest who was in his former lives the King Devapi mentioned in the classic Indian epic *Mahabharata*. Devapi was also known as the Rishi Koothumi who is destined to be the spiritual preceptor and World Teacher.

It is also interesting to know that the great Kalki Maitreya is abiding in the Tushita Heaven awaiting the appropriate time for his avataric descent on earth at the beginning of the Leo Aquarian age. It is said in the mystic circles that presently he is in the company of the sixth Avesh Avatara of Vishnu called Parashuram. Maitreya is in a state of samadhi and the learning of the skill of Divine Arms, which may be the use of mantric power such as the *varuna astra*[13] or the *brahma astra*[14] *vidyas*[15] to be employed to eradicate the negativity of evil which exists on earth. And then transform the negative and the

---

[13] A mantric hydro-missile used for elimination of negative forces.
[14] A lethal weapon composed of mantric vibrations, which is infused into a missile and then used against the enemy. Eg: Varuna Astra (water missile) and Agni Astra (fire missile).
[15] Inner wisdom.

imbalance of the gunas to their equilibrium state.

The Tushita Heaven is a sub-plane of the God Varuna's *Sukhavati*[16] heaven. The Lord Varuna (Neptune) is one of the Sages of the Fire Mist. The four great kings or the Maharajas of the four directions are given below. They are the *Lipika*, thelords of our karmic deeds and future destiny.

North: Rudra (Mithra) Apollo (Kailash Heaven)
East: Indra - Mars/Aries (Amaravati Heaven)
West: Varuna - Neptune/Posiedon (Sukhavati Heaven)
South: Yama - Pluto/Hades (Yamaloka Heaven)
Centre (of Gravity): Brahmanaspati - Zeus/Jupiter

In order to assist in the evolutionary work that Kalki and Babaji as saviours of humanity are ordering, we the Hamsa Yoga Sangh must take our stand under the great *Siddha Sangha*, which is the Guardian Wall of Humanity. We must serve humanity as our larger self and dedicate ourselves to the furthering of human awareness by teaching the Babaji Kriya Yoga. We must enable everyone to experience the unified field of consciousness, thus making all human beings realize that at the level of consciousness Humanity is One; so that we may all live on this planet in peaceful co-existence.

This would enable people to take the quantum leap into the great reality when the ever-present Babaji Gorakshan Nath gives that Truth, and to later flow in the evolutionary process of the removal of all negativity and then its transformation to a balanced state of peace and bliss when the Kalki Avatara comes at the beginning of the Leo-Aquarius Age.

---

16 Of Lord Varuna as Amravati Heaven is of Lord Indra.

The Inner Work of Vikramaditya and Bharthari

Even now on the inner spheres of the conscious minds of humanity, the two great kings are at work. Devapi, the king of the Lunar dynasty and El Morya Vikramaditya, the king of the Solar dynasty, at the behest of Kalki Avatara and Babaji Mahavatara are at work on the western coast of America. The Californian border is very receptive to this transformative spiritual work being done by those masters very patiently and carefully.

These two lofty initiates of the inner government of the world are themselves being evolved to take on a higher office in internal world affairs. El Morya shall succeed the former king Vaivaswat Manu to become the next king Savarni Manu. Devapi shall succeed the Kalki Avatara to become the next world teacher, the sixth Secret Buddha[17].

King Manu Savarni shall incarnate on Earth to restore the Kshatriya race of the Solar Dynasty, to which Lord Rama, the seventh Avatara of Vishnu, belongs. The world master Devapi shall simultaneously incarnate on Earth to restore the sacred race of the Lunar Dynasty, to which Lord Krishna, the eighth Avatara of Vishnu, belongs[18].

---

17 As the Kalki *avatar* Maitreya is from the Tushita Heaven of *rishi* Manjushri, the king Devapi too traces his source thence.
18 The whole of humanity belongs and falls under these categories of Solar, Lunar and Fire. The latter has completed its work as its guiding lord Parashurama of the Bhargavas has already incarnated.

Kalki Avatara and Babaji Mahavatara

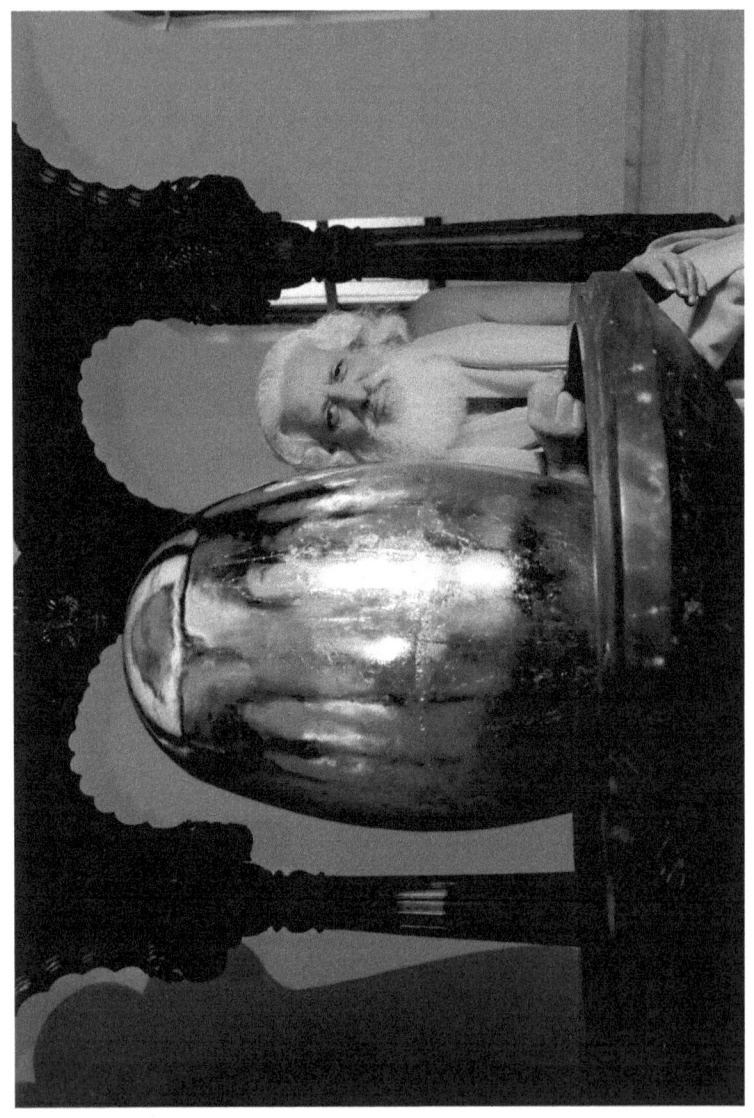

CHAPTER 16

THE ORIGINAL KRIYA YOGA
ITS SECRET AND PERFORMING ART

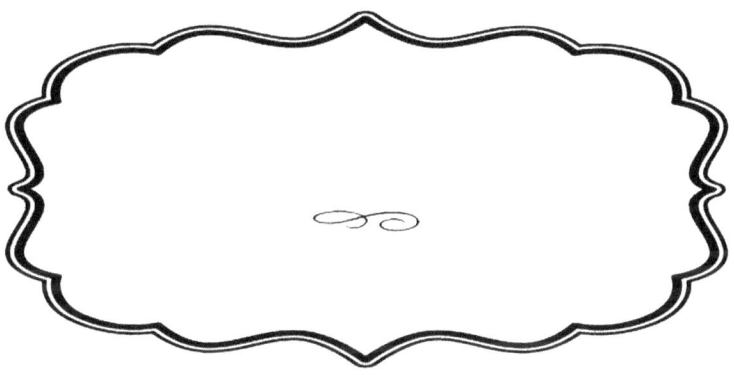

Goraksha Shataka and Kriya Yoga[1]

This timeless yoga of the evolution of human consciousness is handed down to us from the Ancient of Days—the great rishis and royal sages of the Solar Dynasty. This grand science went into obscurity in the Middle Ages and almost went into oblivion. It was rediscovered, clarified and given to humanity again at this time by the compassionate Shiva Goraksha Babaji, who eternally guides the evolution and destiny of all nations and world cycles.

This is the sacred fire ceremony of the yogi, whereby he symbolically offers the oblations of pranic breath into *apanic*[2] breath

---
1 Goraksha Shataka 2v 10-22
2 The downward flowing current as opposed to upward flowing pranic current.

and vice-versa, to equalize the two life currents, enter the *sushumna* (central channel in spinal cord), and enter *kevali*[3] *kumbhak,* a samadhi of the ecstasy of expanded consciousness.

There never has been, nor will there be, a time when man's own nature shall cease to demand his best and foremost attention. The science of yoga commends itself to the foremost minds of east and west. So vital is this inner science for the evolution of human consciousness that beside it, the greatest of human achievements pale into insignificance.

By the neutralization of the two life currents of prana and apana, the practice of the science of Kriya Yoga pranayama[4] results in the arresting of decay and aging in the body. This is done by rejuvenating the blood and body cells with life energy (prana) that has been distilled from the breath and moved into the spine and the brain. The Kriya yogi arrests all bodily decay, thereby quieting the breath and heart. This renders the purifying actions of the breath and heart unnecessary as they gradually slow down through persevering practice.

The Bhagavad Gita and Kriya Yoga

The *Bhagavad Gita* mentions this science of Kriya Yoga (*4:29*). The Kriya Yoga pranayama called the prana-apanic fire rite by the yogis, teaches man to untie the cord of breath that binds our soul to the bodily cage. The soul is then released to fly and expand into the super-conscious skies of omnipresent spirit and come back at will into the little body cage. No flight of fancy is this, but a true experiencing of divine bliss.

---

3 'Pot-like', in the science of Yoga, the retention of and constriction of the locks (*bandhas*) to usher vital energy (prana) into the spinal cord (*sushumna nadi*) for the awakening of *kundalini*.

4 'Life-breath extension', breath control and expansion, the fourth limb (*anga*) of Patanjali's eightfold path, consisting of conscious inhalation (*puraka*), retention (*kumbhaka*), and exhalation (*rechaka*); at an advanced state, breath retention occurs spontaneously and for prolonged periods of time.

Pranayama is derived from its Sanskrit roots, prana (life) and *ayama* (control). So pranayama is therefore life-force control and not breath control. In the larger sense, the whole world is filled with the universal life-force energy called prana. Everything is a differentiation of the modes of expression of this universal force. Therefore, universal prana is *Para-Prakriti* (pure Nature). This eminent energy is derived from the infinite spirit and permeates and sustains the universe.

Individual prana is an intelligent force but has no consciousness in the empirical or transcendental sense. The soul is the conscious unit and prana is its basis. The consciousness through mind-ego dictates terms and prana follows the dictate. Neither grossly material nor purely spiritual, prana borrows from the soul its power of activating the body.

There are two main life currents in the body. One is that of prana which flows from the coccyx to the point between the eyebrows. The nature of this life current is soothing. It introverts the devotee's attention during sleep and the wakeful state, and in meditation unites the soul with the spirit in the third ventricle of the brain, in yogic parlance called the *shivanetra* or third eye.

The other main current is that of *apana* which flows from the third eye to the coccyx. This downward flowing, extroverted current distributes itself through the coccygeal centre to the motor-sensory nerves. It keeps man's consciousness delusively tied to the body. The *apana* current is restless and engrosses man in sensory experiences.

In the *Bhagavad Gita*, Lord Krishna extols the yogi in glowing terms:

> *Greater is the yogi than body disciplining ascetics, greater even than the followers of wisdom's path. Greater than the path of action. Be thou Arjuna a yogi!*
>
> *Bhagavad Gita, chapter 6 verse 46*

Kriya Yoga pranayama arrests bodily decay connected with apana, manifesting in the exhaling breath, by fresh inhalations of life-force (prana) distilled from the inhaling breath. This prana enables the devotee to do away with the illusion of decay and mutation. He then realizes that his body is made of 'lifetrons' of congealed light. The body of the kriya yogi is recharged with extra energy distilled from the breath and energized by the tremendous dynamo of energy generated in the spine. The decay of body tissues decreases. This ultimately lessens the work of the heart by assisting blood cleansing functions. The heart pump becomes quiet, owing to the non-pumping of venous blood and exhalation and inhalation of breath are evened out.

The life energy unites in the currents in the spine. The light of pure prana scintillates from the six chakras to all the bodily cells keeping them in a spiritually magnetized condition. Kriya Yoga is referred to in yoga treatises as *kevali pranayama* or *kevali kumbhaka*. This is the true pranayama that has transcended the necesssity for inhalation (*puraka*) and exhalation (*rechaka*); breath is transmuted into inner life-force currents under the complete control of the mind. When the breath stops effortlessly without either *rechaka* or *puraka*, it is called *kevali kumbhaka*. (Hatha Yoga Pradipika[5] II-73). Of the various stages of pranayama (such as breathlessness), *kevali* is extolled by adept yogis as the best or highest (remember that Kriya Yoga is not breath control but life-force control). When one gets to the advanced state of Shiva Shakti Kriya, the breath ceases. Duly, the cool ascending *pranic* current and warm descending *apanic* current are felt flowing in the *sushumna nadi*[6] (spinal cord). This is an *avasta* (state) of *kevali kumbhaka*. Though in principle it may be equated with Kriya Yoga, *kevali pranayama* is not as explicit as the specific Kriya Yoga science and techniques expounded by Shiva Goraksha Babaji:

---

[5] Literally, 'Light on the Yoga of Sun and Moon' compiled by Svatmarama Yogi, inspired by and dedicated to Shiva Goraksha Babaji. This work comprises 389 couplets and integrates the practices of Hatha and Raj Yoga.

[6] Literally, 'Very gracious channel', the central prana current in or along which the serpent power (*kundalini shakti*) must ascend toward the psycho-energetic center (*chakra*) at the crown of the head in order to attain liberation (moksha).

The Lord surrounded man's soul first with an idea body. Then he encased the idea body with a very subtle light, the astral body. The third or final encasement was the electro-atomic dream body, the illusion of a fleshly form.
Bhagavad Gita, p. 306, Vol. I, Paramhansa Yogananda

The *Gita* advises us to practice pranayama (life-force control) to enable us to realize that we are not made of flesh, but of life-force condensed from the thought of God!

Babaji's Kriya Yoga is *Goraksha Shataka*

Kriya is a process of converting breath into life-force and realizing the body as light. In the authentic text of *Goraksha Shataka* (*II: 14*; as enlightened by Shiva Goraksha Babaji), by the perfect performance of 12 Kriya pranayamas, the yogi gets to the internal state of *pratyahara*[7]. By practicing 144 Kriya pranayamas, he enters the state of concentration. By practicing 1,728 *Omkar Kriyas*, he expands into the state of meditation. As he goes on to practice 20,736 Kriya pranayam, he enters the ecstasy of expanded consciousness called samadhi. These exact numbers have been taken by Yogavatar Lahiri Mahasaya, which he has mentioned ad verbatim in his instructions for the practice of Kriya Yoga (ref. his book, entitled *Commentaries on the Bhagavad Gita,* chapter eight, verse fourteen). They have been given to today's world as a standard measure for the practice of Kriya Yoga. This undoubtedly shows that not only is Shiva Goraksha Babaji the founder of the original Kriya Yoga, but is also the direct Guru of Yogavatar Lahiri Mahasaya.

However, it is important to note that Kriya cannot be practiced so many times by a beginner. When the body and mind of the yogi are prepared to accommodate the high voltage of so much Kriya Yoga, his guru will advise him that he is ready for the experience of samadhi. If the Kriyas are broken into several sittings, there is no harm; it will just take longer.

---

7 'Withdrawal', sensory inhibition, the fifth limb (*anga*) of Patanjali's eightfold path.

Kundalini Kriya Yoga
Goraksha Samhita chapter 1 verse 47-51

Kundalini is the electro-magnetic pranic energy, which means 'coiled spiral' and stems from an earlier root *kund* meaning 'fire pit'. It is coiled three and a half times around the *swayambhu linga* at the base of the spine. Kundalini is represented by a cobra snake and can move a yogi from static state to kinetic activation in a split second. The kundalini is intensified spiritual prana. If the pranic energy is to be compared to an atomic bomb, the voltage of the kundalini energy benefits the guided yogi like a benevolent hydrogen bomb. The *kundalini shakti* (force) is activated and awakened during the Kriya Yoga pranayama, which I call the kundalini breath. It is hidden and latent within all human beings in their nervous systems.

When Kriya Yoga pranayama is performed as per the satguru's guidance, the pranic life-force in one's spinal cord (*sushumna*) builds up to generate a great spiritual magnetism and voltage. By the ceaseless movement of the Kriya life-force breath, one's prana, breath, vital fluid and mind become one to form the evolutionary life-force energy called kundalini. Its most effective application, insofar as one's spiritual evolution is concerned, happens only when it enters the central channel of the spine called the *sushumna nadi*. This dynamic process is best brought about by the practice of Kriya Yoga. This awakened kundalini is one of the most potent boosts for the out-of-body experiences and evolution of any spiritual practitioner. The out-of-body experience helps the yogi shift his awareness from the physical body and mind to pure Consciousness. Repeated experiences of such a shift establish the yogi in the self-realized state of an ecstatic expanded consciousness.

Kundalini Meditation
by Yogiraj Siddhanath

Hiss kundali, sting ego-mind
With nectar-poison so sublime
Penetrating my rainbow lotus shrines
Making me to myself divine!

Kundali bless me with thy blaze
Delusion suffering fear efface
Spine darkness with they lightning light
Fragrance me, negative karma ignite!

You are Life, its livingness you keep
Oh mother of the mystic deep
Remove shadow of death from me
In Shiva deathlessly to be!

Alakh Niranjan Om Shiv Om!
Alakh Niranjan Om Shiv Om!

According to the Nath tradition in India, the kundalini is revered as the divine virgin, the consort, the divorcee and the widow, all in one. She is the universal life-force of sustenance and evolution. At the base of the spine, the sleeping beauty Shakti awaits Her Lord Charming Shiva's kiss of consciousness, which releases Her to ascend up the spine and unite with Him in holy communion at the thousand-petalled-lotus in the crown chakra. Shakti–kundalini is the bride Cinderella, the 'lady of the cinders' who when fanned by the alchemical fire of Shiva–Shakti Kriya, ignites as kundalini, blazing up the chimney of the spinal *sushumna* to unite with immortal Lord Shiva in the crown chakra.

The Raja Yoga process of awakening the kundalini is done by entering the *unmani* state of still-mind expanded awareness. It is so utterly simple, the naked truth; and man by mind is so complicated that it is difficult for him to be absorbed in this profoundly still state called *Sahaja Samadhi*, which is the natural state. Therefore, if one practices it, it will take him twelve years to thoroughly de-complicate his mind. It would mean going into or melting into a state of awareness, bereft of any residual traces of karma, or thoughts. *Patanjali's Yoga Sutras*, the *Bhagavad Gita*, and the philosophy of Goraksha Nath, were not only the greatest expositions of yogic philosophy and literature, but their authors were also the greatest givers of truth the world has ever witnessed.

Khechari Mudra[8]
Goraksha Shataka Part 2 verses 43, 44, 63, 68

> *An inverted well in the inner sky*
> *Where the yogi drinks his fill to fly*
> *In khechari realms beyond death and die*
>
> *But the uninitiated thirsty go*
> *Because they miss life's vital flow*
> *To the realms of moksha they cannot go*
>
> Yogiraj Siddhanath

The above sutra is given by Shiva Goraksha Babaji regarding the *khechari mudra*, where He says that those who have mastered this mudra can penetrate their tongue up the hollow of the throat to near the midpoint of the eyebrows. Above this is the third ventricle in the brain, which is like an inverted well, dropping the nectar on the tongue. All people initiated into advanced Kriya Yoga can avail of this nectar to retard the aging process of their body cells and simultaneously attain the state of samadhi. We must understand that in the true Kriya Yoga teachings, the *khechari*

---

[8] Space-walking seal'; facilitates astral travel. The yogic practice of 'swallowing the tongue in order to seal the life energy (prana) to be given by a bonafide guru; the seal of the tongue beyond the uvula, stimulating the pituitary gland to drink of *amrit*.

mudra is a must because it blocks the *ida-pingala*[9] channels and assists in the opening of the *sushumna* channel, forcing the pranic breath to enter the central channel and bestow self-realization on the practitioner of Kriya Yoga. It is also one of the mudras, which sets apart the true Kriya Yoga teachings from that of other teachings of yoga which are not the true Kriya Yoga. In all Kriya Yoga practices, the *khechari mudra* is always used to ensure the rapidity of spiritual evolution.

Yoni Mudra[10]
Goraksha Shataka Part 2 verses 16, 71

> *Sitting in siddhasana having inhaled the prana*
> *Let the yogi block the ears, eyes and nasal passage*
> *With the thumbs, index and middle fingers. And then*
> *withdraw and concentrate himself in the third eye*
>
> Goraksha Shataka Part 2 verse 16

This is a very important technique for the evolution of spiritual consciousness, but later on, as the yogi evolves in spiritual stature, the technique drops away on its own, and he is able to see the star of soul consciousness without it. People must not imagine, which they often do, that they see the Star whilst they are only hallucinating. Seeing the Star comes at a very advanced stage.

Sit during evening time in Siddhasana posture facing North. Begin to practice Kriya Yoga, after which you do the *Yoni Mudra* (*Jyoti Mudra*). Throughout the practice, the tongue is kept in the *Khechari Mudra*.

---

9 'Pale conduit', the prana currents or arcs ascending on the right and left side of the central channel (*sushumna nadi*) associated with the sympathetic and parasympathetic nervous system and having a cooling and calming effect on the mind when activated.

10 Also known as *jyoti mudra* and *shanmukhi mudra*, the blocking of one's ears, eyes, and nostrils with one's fingers where the inner sound, *anahata nada* (*Omkar*) is heard and the soul is seen as a spot of light at the third eye. This technique will not enlighten without the initiation of a living kriya master.

1. Sitting in Siddhasana if possible, or then in any other comfortable position. Raise your hands and close your eyes with your index fingers, with a quarter of the index finger on the eyelashes and three-quarters on the curvature of the eye socket.

2. Then with your thumbs, close your ears, putting the pressure of the thumbs directly above the earlids where the skull and jawbone join. This ensures a complete closure of sound.

3. Further shut your closed mouth with your ring and pinky fingers.

4. After this, focus your consciousness at the base of the spine, do the rectal lock and the chin lock.

5. Then, block either side of your nostrils with both of your middle fingers. While these seven orifices of your senses are being shut, hold your breath as long as you comfortably can (about thirty seconds).

ATTENTION PLEASE: The details of pranayama and yogic breathing may be learned only from a Living Master who will enlighten this technique. Some western authors have tried to make this technique public but have misfired and have not been able to give people enlightenment through their unauthorized efforts, for the inner spirit of the technique has been left out.

When the ideal Third Eye develops within you, it will be seen by all Yogis and practitioners as a pale gold intense ring of light with the deep blue centre, and after long years of practice, you will see and then be your Soul as the scintillating white star.

Yoni Mudra for Penetrating the 'Stargate'

In Kriya Yoga, the *yoni mudra* is essentially a technique to master the art of *pratyahara*, which means the withdrawal of mind and prana (life-force energy) from the objects perceived through the five senses. The advanced technique with *khechari mudra* leads one right up through the states of concentration and meditation, so that the yogi penetrates the 'star-gate' of the third eye to enter into omnipresent bliss of samadhi.

Yoni means 'womb' or 'source'. It is also called the *jyoti mudra*, meaning 'inner starlight seal'. A third name is *shanmukhi mudra*, because *shan* means 'six' and *mukhi* means 'orifice' or 'mouth', and in this technique, the six orifices are sealed so that the inner star of the soul can be perceived, passing through which the conscious seer experiences Cosmic Consciousness.

With *yoni mudra*, your mind is brought into a state of relaxed absorption, whereby *pratyahara* (sense withdrawal) ensues. This state of sense withdrawal occurs because of the pressure of the fingers upon specific nerves and acupressure points.

There are also physical benefits of *yoni mudra* because it stimulates the vagus nerves through pressure on the ear canals with the thumbs. The stimulation of these nerves brings about a dominance of the parasympathetic nervous system, lowering the metabolic threshold. Consequently, the heart rate is reduced and the heart is rested. One's blood pressure is brought to a calmer state, and with regular practice, the digestive system is toned and improved and the nervous system is rejuvenated.

Yoni mudra brings about an equipose of body and mind.
Yogiraj Siddhanath
Wings to Freedom, chapter 10

Shiva Shakti Kriya Yoga - The Yogic Science of Love

As Shiva–Shakti Kriya Yoga deals with the highest evolution of humanity, it is rightly called the 'Science of all Sciences'. Nevertheless, it is rooted in divine love, without which, it flowers not. We practice the Shiva–Shakti Kriya through sound, light and vibration. One becomes so absorbed, that one becomes these divine emanations. The sound must be made with love and joy; the vibration becomes the expression of Divine Selfless Love.

The upward and downward currents spiritually magnetize the spinal column, thereby transforming the seeker into a perfect receptacle of divine light and love. The yogi becomes the process of yoga. The yogi becomes the yoga. The pilgrim, the path and the goal become One ... Love. Shiva–Shakti Kriya Yoga reveals that by practice alone, and not by blind belief, one progresses and walks upon the 'Royal Path to Self-realization'. This Awakening stills the mind and allows one's Divine Self to be revealed. Amongst the pathways to self-realization, Shiva–Shakti Kriya Yoga is peerless.

Patanjali's Yoga Sutras and Kriya Yoga — Chapter 2

Kriya Yoga consists of the three basic virtues, *Tapa, Swadhyaya*[11], and *Ishvara Pranidhan*, which are of great assistance in the evolutionary journey of the practitioner. We can sum up the authentic Kriya Yoga with 3 factors:

Tapa - self-directed discipline and austerities which lead to rapid spiritual progress.

Swadhyaya - self-directed yogic study of the mind and consciousness. Yoga is an inner ascent through ever more refined and ever more expanded spheres of mind to get to the divine consciousness which lies at the core of our own beings. Kriya Yoga is the best practice of *swadhyaya*.

Ishwar Pranidhan[12]: humble surrender of one's ego to God and guru. No doubt sincere Kriya practice helps in the evolution of consciousness, but ultimately it is the personal relationship with God and

---

11 'Going into one's own self'; self-study, important to the yogic path, listed among the practices of self-restraint (niyama) in Patanjali's eightfold Yoga; recitation of mantras.

12 'The Lord as priority', total surrender to the Lord; in Patanjali's eight-limbed Yoga one of the practices of self-restraint (*niyama*).

your master, your dedication and devotion to them, that opens the doors of salvation. *Ishwar Pranidhan* is unconditional devotion to God and the Master.

Tapa - Self directed austerities

The word we have rendered as discipline is wrongly translated as "mortification;" and has primary reference to fasts and other bodily penances. A slightly older word is closest to the meaning of *tapa* - the word 'askesis'.

> *"The admitted purpose of bodily austerities is to break the fixity and automatism of habit at the physical level, and to make the body more amenable to the dictates of the will."*

The true meaning of *tapas*, or self-discipline is to treat the body in such a way as to overcome its demands, and to induce a relaxation of the grip of bodily desires; so that the mind and spirit are no longer hampered by the those bodily desires.

> *Just as gold when heated (tapa)*
> *comes clear of the slag*
> *shining in its pristine purity*
> *so Jivatma by Tapa of Pranayama*
> *is cleansed of vishaya vasna*[13]
> *and shines in its pristine glory!!*
>
> Yogiraj Siddhanath

> *Niyam, Yama discipline the conduct of a person*
>   *Asanas discipline the body*
>   *Pranayama purifies the emotions*
>   *Dharana*[14] *shapes the mind.*
>   *Dhyana furthers the Awareness of Mind*
>   *Samadhi "Is" the ecstasy of expanded consciousness*
>
> Yogiraj Siddhanath

---

13 Attachment to material desires.
14 'holding', concentration, the sixth limb (anga) of Patanjali's eight-limbed (ashtanga) system of Yoga.

Swadhyaya – Self Directed Study

This second requisite or study is a shaping and purifying of the mind, and simultaneously becoming more and more aware of your indwelling consciousness. A shaping of the mind is done by concentration, which is called the faculty of exclusive attention. This is necessary for any great undertaking. The word study should not be taken in the sense of collecting information from books, but rather of tuning in the whole nature of one's being to a given wavelength, thereby letting the mind become absorbed with the subject at hand. This means that by the power of concentration, the subject and the object become one (*samyama*).

> *Kriya Yoga is an inner ascent through ever*
> *more refined, and ever more expanded spheres*
> *of mind, to get to that Consciousness*
> *which lies at the core of our own being.*
>
> Yogiraj Siddhanath

The yogi who is deeply yearning for self-realization, devotes himself heart and soul, day and night, to that aim, and subordinates all else to it. He sacrifices leisure, luxury and personal pleasure. He sees all events as furthering or stopping his goal!

Pranayam with mantras are ancient formulas, so devised as to be effective not only in meaning, but also in sound. When recited in correct and traditional intonation, they are said to assist the yogi in detaching from the preoccupations of ordinary worldly existence, clarifying and stilling the mind.

Ishvara Pranidhan – Self offering to divinity

This is the resignation to the will of God and Guru. Apart from the necessities for acceptance of and submission to the teacher, there is also involved a profound acceptance of the conditions of Individual

Life. The ambitious or resentful person is never sufficiently at leisure from himself to achieve the recollected concentration for a calm mind, which may expand into infinite awareness A calm mind is the basic faculty required for undisturbed yoga practice. There is, however, a much subtler reason why acceptance is the one of the fundamental necessities. For all loftier achievements of living an unimpeded flow of life force or libido, spiritual energy is necessary. It is possible to exist with the life-force dammed, but creative awareness demands a freeflow; a flow of being afloat upon the stream of being.

> *An experience of union with life is not possible where there is nonacceptance of life's conditions; a resentful wish to be otherwise or have otherwise or an attitude to things and people as they are.*
>
> *The Yogi has to be so intent upon the creation of a new self that he has no leisure for grumbling at his environment.*
>
> Yogiraj Siddhanath

The Hallmarks of the Original Kriya Yoga (and What is NOT the Original Kriya Yoga)

The original Kriya Yoga for the modern era was given by Mahavatar Babaji to Yogavatar Lahiri Mahasaya in a cave at Dronagiri[15], Ranikhet in the autumn of 1861.

There are people teaching many types of yoga and calling it Kriya Yoga. I have highlighted certain points to show the difference between the true Kriya Yoga of the Babaji–Lahiri Mahasaya lineage and certain 'yogas' taught by others. All other imitations and copies of this original Kriya Yoga came a good ninety years later. The other yogas called Babaji's Kriya Yoga have nothing to do with the original Kriya Yoga with which I am concerned. The other yogas were introduced to the public after the mahasamadhi of Paramhansa Yogananda in

---
15 A sacred mountain which is in the Kumaon range of the Himalayas.

1952. This statement is merely to clarify in the minds of the people as to the original Kriya Yoga taught by Lahiri Mahasaya and the much later yogas introduced by various people called Babaji's Kriya Yoga. The Kriya Yoga that others teach does not corroborate with the true lineage of Kriya Yoga, passed down from Shiva Goraksha Babaji through the Yogavatar Lahiri Mahasaya–Gyanavatar Sri Yukteshwar–Paramhansa Yogananda lineage, which is the authentic Kriya Yoga, and that which is intended when we refer to Kriya Yoga taught by Babaji.

It is imperative to make a clear-cut distinction between the original Babaji's Kriya Yoga as given to Lahiri Mahasaya by Babaji Himself, which is not to be confused with the Kriya Yoga taught ninety years later by people who chose to ride the wave of the original Kriya Yoga and called their yoga Babaji's Kriya Yoga. The clarification I am making between the two is very necessary to clear the confusion in the minds of millions of seekers, between the original Babaji's Kriya Yoga, as was first taught to Yogavatar Lahiri Mahasaya at Ranikhet in the autumn of 1861, and the Kriya Yoga propounded by others after the mahasamadhi of Paramhansa Yogananda in 1952. That they chose to teach this, ninety-one years later, under the same name of Babaji's Kriya Yoga and confuse the people, is certainly not a welcome move. This deludes and bifurcates truth-seekers to two spiritual paths of the same name.

This clarification will prevent the misguided adventures of devotees and a lot of wasted time for those who truly want to come directly to the original Kriya Yoga of Mahavatar Babaji's, Yogavatar Lahiri Mahasaya's, Gyanavatar Sri Yukteshwar's and Paramhansa Yogananda's lineage. It was prophesied by the great Yogavatar, Lahiri Mahasaya, that Kriya Yoga propagated by him would encircle the globe by the grace of none other than the immortal Babaji, the supreme initiator of all the angels, yogis and prophets of the past, present and future.

Another pertinent point of the authentic Kriya Yoga of Shiva Goraksha Babaji is that the life energy is concentrated in the *sushumna nadi* of the central spinal cord. A 44-second cycle of Kriya breath gives the practitioner one year of natural spiritual unfoldment. This is what qualifies the original Kriya Yoga to be called The Lightning Path. Since the South Indian and Canadian schools of 'Babaji Kriya Yoga' have no such specific practice of *sushumna* central channel breathing, they cannot give the lightning evolution of a year in a 44-second cycle. Therefore, these are not the authentic Kriya Yoga of Babaji and Lahiri Mahasaya. They are a type of yoga, but not the original Kriya Yoga as mentioned in *Autobiography of a Yogi* or Babaji's enlightening Kriya teachings.

Salient Features of Original Kriya Yoga

We begin with the *Omkar Kriya*—hearing and becoming the inner sound of Om. Then we do the Ham-Sa Kriya, witnessing our breath and inner self. Simultaneously, the practice of *khechari mudra* is given on the accomplishment of which kundalini shakti ascends up the *sushumna nadi* and Shiva's grace begins to descend. Then as this process goes, we do the regular Kriya Yoga pranayama for a 44-second cycle. Then we move on in the sequence to practice the *Nabhi Kriya*[16] to even out the breaths of [and apana. Then next in order is the practice of the *Thokar Kriya* with the Vasudeva mantra, after which the *Mahamudra*[17], meaning the posture of the great liberation, is done. The spine becomes flexible. Then we go on to the *Yoni mudra*, also called the *Jyoti mudra* to form the star-gate, which is to be penetrated. Then only the experience of *nirvikalpa samadhi* may be had and the doorway to moksha is opened. *Paravastha* is the last of the techniques to be practiced. It is called 'the after-effect poise of Kriya'. In the original Kriya Yoga, there must be the proper perineum pressure during the practice of *mahamudra* and kriyas.

These are the hallmarks of original Kriya Yoga which distinguish it from other yoga kriyas, misleadingly called Babaji's Kriya Yoga. These other yogas have led to a great confusion for the seekers who are

---

16 A yogic technique to join *pranapana* at navel (*manipur chakra*) and get steadiness of mind.
17 The posture of the great liberation.

searching for the original Babaji's Kriya Yoga, the hallmarks of which I have given above. It's a shame that nowadays, Kriya Yoga and Babaji's Kriya Yoga have become a very elastic and generic terminology, used for all sorts and types of Kriya Yoga, except the Original Kriya Yoga. One of my intentions is to wean, from the yogic fabric of generic Kriya Yoga, the genuine and original Babaji's Kriya Yoga, and place it before the thousands of disillusioned and wandering seekers lost in the dazzle of today's supermarket of yoga.

One of the Sequences

1. *Omkar Kriya*: listening to the *Omkar* with the divine sensation of light, vibration and sound.
2. *Ham-Sa Kriya*: witnessing our breath and inner self (*Vai-upasana*) misappropriated as *vipassana*.
3. *Kriya Yoga Pranayam*: also called Kundalini Kriya Yoga, is spiritual spinal breathing in the *sushumna* (central spinal channel), whereby with the constant friction of the ascending and descending breath, the kundalini light rushes up the chimney of the spine to meet Her Lord at *Sahasrara* (or the thousand-petalled lotus at the crown chakra).
4. *Nabho Kriya*: steadies the mind, improving the digestion.
5. First *Thokar Kriya*: awakening chakras and kundalini.
6. Second *Thokar Kriya*: penetrating kundalini through chakras.
7. *Mahamudra*: the posture of the great liberation.
8. *Jyoti Mudra*: penetrating the star-gate.
9. *Paravastha*: ecstasy of expanded consciousness.

KARMIC REPERCUSSIONS: Teaching something as what it is not certainly involves the justifiable karmic repercussions. Whether you mislead knowingly or in ignorance, the repercussion, good or bad, will be there. So wake up! Make the restitution. Do not teach Babaji's Kriya Yoga when it is not Babaji's Kriya Yoga. This statement is not directed to any particular person or yoga system, but given as a pertinent warning to false, ego-oriented teachers and those who teach without authorization.

Modus Operandi of Kriya Yoga
In Relation to Spiritual Nadis (Meridians)

As we practice the Kriya Yoga pranayama, our *dharana* (concentration) deepens and we enter the *sushumna nadi* channel. There, the yogi works his prana (life-force) to a subtler dimension of *dhyana* (meditation), where he enters into the *vajra nadi*[18] channel. As he goes on practicing hour after hour and day after day, his meditation deepens and he finds himself moving in the *chitra nadi*, where he expands into the experience of the *savikalpa samadhi*. As the yogi's desires fall away by Kriya, he 'awares' himself into the *brahma nadi*[19] channel where he experiences the ecstasy of expanded consciousness called *nirvikalpa namadhi*. When the yogi by Kriya Yoga practice crosses the threshold of concentration to enter into meditation, his *brahma granthi*[20] dissolves at the base of his spine. As he progresses further and goes deeper into meditation, he dissolves his *vishnu granthi*[21] at the heart centre (where he would apply the technique of *Thokar Kriya*). Then his consciousness 'awares' into the *savikalpa samadhi* where his final *rudra granthi*[22], situated at the midpoint between his eyebrows, begins to dissolve. The *rudra granthi* could remain unresolved right up to the point where he enters the *brahma nadi* to experience the ecstasy of expanded consciousness of *nirvikalpa samadhi*.

After long years of dedicated practice, the yogi dissolves all the three *granthis* (negative pranic knots); then and then alone he may experience the final beatitude of constant *nirvikalpa namadhi* which yogis call the *nirbeeja* (seedless) *samadhi*. The yogi, who by the practice of advanced Kriya Yoga blends into Raja Yoga[23], is then

---
18 The second of the psychic nerves. First is *sushumna*, second is *vajra*, third is *chitra* and fourth is *brahma*.
19 The subtlest psychic nerve, e.g., *sushumna, vajra, chitra* and *brahma nadis*.
20 A psycho-generic plexus located at the base of the spine.
21 The heart plexus *chakra* where this Vishnu knot is located, which has to be loosened and penetrated like the *brahma* and *rudra granthis*.
22 Pranic plexus situated in the third eye.
23 Raja Yoga cannot be successful without the preliminary foundation and practice of the vital Kriya Yoga bridge.

said to have dissolved all his karmas. This constitutes his mind-stuff composed of *vrittis*, meaning whirlpool of thoughts, his *pratyaya*, which are thought-forms of his mind, and his *samskaras*, which are called 'remembered experiences' or 'stored impressions' latent in his memory banks. With the ceaseless practice of Kriya Yoga and persevering in Raja Yoga by 'awaring his consciousness', the yogi is successful in disconnecting his soul-consciousness from his mayic mind. He then wins his wings to freedom, becoming a free soul. This is the modus operandi of how the yogi experiences enlightenment by the sacred practice of Kriya and Raja Yoga.

Bhagavad Gita in the Light of Kriya

Lahiri Mahasaya gives the central point of the *Gita* in the light of Kriya Yoga.

First is Omkar Kriya: Listening to the Sacred Sound
Second is Pranayama Kriya: Evens itself out into Kevali Kumbaka
Third is Khechari Mudra: Attending to the star in Yoni Mudra
Fourth is Paravastha: The state of expanded consciousness
Fifth is doing all works without expectation for fruits – this means, performing your daily Karma without an agenda, as desire stifles spiritual progress

The *Yoni mudra* is the beatific inner revelation of Kriya, which assists in the termination of every desire before it originates and helps, just as Kriya pranayama helps us, in the freeing of all thoughts. Lahiri Mahasaya also emphasizes that holding on to the *Paravastha*, which is the after-effect pose of Kriya, greatly accelerates the evolution.

Paravastha

To attain the still or poised state of breathing in natural cause, I am of the certain experience that every time the *Paravastha* is practiced, it disconnects the link between the karmic desire-mind and the consciousness and frees the soul consciousness to make extremely rapid progress towards self-realization. This is the reason why the Yogavatar Lahiri Mahasaya emphasized 'holding onto the still state of tranquility', the awareness of the Zero not Zero, as I call it. This is the great charm and beauty of the *Paravastha*, which in other systems of yogic practice may be described as a form of the *unmani avastha*, meaning the no mind state of enlightened awareness.

I have made many humble endeavors to give to all sincere seekers and disciples the *Shivapat* awareness during my United Consciousness Conferences, which I hold the world over. *Shivapat* is the 'awaring' of my consciousness into the restless minds of all receptive seekers, whereby they experience my Universal Soul Consciousness as a clear-mind state of thoughtless awareness. This in Kriya Yoga is called *Paravastha*.

This is my working hypothesis, number one:

If any mind is attuned to an undifferentiated consciousness (the master) then that mind shall gravitate itself out of light-mind existence and aware itself into that consciousness, to the degree of its attunement with that consciousness.

Yogiraj Siddhanath

This is my working hypothesis, number two:

The undifferentiated consciousness of the master gravitates itself into the light-mind existence of the thought-mind of the seeker, thus transforming the seeker's mind to his own consciousness; to the degree of the attunement of that mind with the master's consciousness.

Yogiraj Siddhanath

Kriya Yoga and Surya Yoga vis-à-vis 2012

The coming new age will see a great change in the awareness and evolution of all receptive souls who are making the effort to contact their Higher Selves. In this regard, the carbon based human body must be detoxified by the science of Kriya Yoga to receive the message of the Rishis, Manus and Sages of the Fire Mist. The practice of Kriya Yoga will increase one's capacity to hold extra prana and light. If sufficient people practice the sacred science of Babaji's Kriya Yoga, Surya Yoga and ingest sufficient light from our Sun Vivasvat Manu, its bipolar central sun, Maghayanti (Alcyone) and the yet larger central sun Vastushpati (Sirius), then a metamorphic transformation in the collective consciousness of the World Disciple shall take place.

Kriya is the magic elixir for the new age where the transformation of large oceans of humanity will be the cause of mitigating and diverting a world war like situation. By the practice of Surya Yoga, which I have given freely in the Akashic Records and on "YouTube" as well, the people may increase their spiritual solar light and charge their body batteries to overcome certain negativities resulting as an outfall due to the cataclysmic changes occurring before and after the year 2012. The effects of Kriya and Surya Yoga will be to raise the collective consciousness of humanity, giving them a more holographic awareness; whereby they will be able to use their psychic, telepathic and intuitive abilities with greater facility to contact their spiritual guides and Mahagurus.

It is said that during this time will take place the changing of the Divine Guards of the spiritual hierarchy. The year 2012 will be the beginning of the work of the King of the inner government, Lord Vaivaswat Manu; his successor, Lord Savarni Manu; the World Teacher, Lord Kalki Maitreya and his successor, Lord Devapi.

During this time, certain planetary upheavals as the tilting of the axis, the shifting of tectonic plates and world war like situations could be a probability for our human family. In order to mitigate and even prevent such cataclysmic effects, it is necessary for all truth seekers and yogis to raise their body, mind and soul vibrations to a higher frequency; thereby matching the "Magneta" vibrations, whose photon-belt surrounds our great central sun called Vastushpati (Sirius). If we are to intake a larger quantity of sunlight, then we must practice the Siddhanath Surya Yoga and the Kriya Yoga pranayama. In the sacred India scripture, the *Bhagavad Gita*, it is mentioned that whenever there is an imbalance in the human phenomenon and the planet, the divine avatara incarnates on Earth to restore the balance; save the righteous who live in harmony with nature and to destroy the negative forces of the Earth that create disharmony and imbalance.

It is a known fact that our sun, Surya, revolves around a dual central sun, called Maghayanti (Alcyone), and both in turn circumambulate around the yet bigger central sun, in Vedic Astronomy called Vastushpati (Sirius), which in turn revolves around the galactic centre. Prophets, seers and astronomers have seen that it takes approximately 280 to 300 million years for a smaller revolution of our Sun around its immediate bipolar sun. This corresponds to the end of our Lord Vaivaswat Manu's reign called a Manavantar.

Now there is going to be an alignment between the three suns, namely Vivasvat Manu (our Sun), Maghayanti (it's bipolar sun) and Vastushpati (the biggest sun). This alignment, some feel, would be in a straight line and others calculate, it would be triangular, but at the same flat level. Whatever the case may be, this will cause changes for the better because humanity is evolving; and for the worse because of the passing phase of minor cataclysms. These can be seen as our Mother Earth experiencing growing pains as she prepares to give birth to a more evolved humanity, namely our present sixth sub-race growing into the sixth root avataric race 499 to 700 years hence.

As I have said before that out of the 6 billion 700 million souls that populate our planet, those that attune themselves to the higher vibrations of the coming age and capacitate in them the light radiated from the three suns, will be the ones who have a better chance to adapt and survive the pre-2012[24] upheavals. This does not mean that other good souls will not come through. The geological cataclysm and human holocaust will not be of the magnitude it is depicted to be because we have the grace of the Eternal Messiahs, Babaji, the Kalki, the central Sun Sirius and the Seven-Sages, called the *Sapta Rishis*, who have saved our planet from the deluge before and will do it again.

This passage from a hymn comes to mind:

> *Ye Fearful Souls Fresh Courage Take*
> *The Clouds Ye So Much Dread*
> *Are Big With Mercy And Shall Break*
> *With Blessings On Your Head*
>
> William Cooper

---

24 The pre-2012 cataclysms are notable. The great tsunami which occurred in Sumatra in 2004, the devastating earthquake which occurred in Pakistan occupied Kashmir and hurricane Katarina in Louisiana are definitely the cataclysms associated with the changes predicted for 2012. After 2012, there will be more positive effects, spiritually and otherwise for this earth in comparison to its negative effects. I am speaking here mainly of the good spiritual and evolutionary effects by Kriya Yoga and Surya Yoga after the year 2012 has past.

> *Change happens at the critical moment.*
> *Change happens at the turning point!*
>
> Yogiraj Siddhanath

This is as much of a spiritual noumenon as it is an astronomical phenomenon. The powers of the divine wizards of humanity are working for its welfare only if humanity opens its hearts. Let us face with courage the coming of the brave new world and the coming of a utopia, which would bring us into a dimension akin to the Golden-age, called Satya Yuga, as is in *Shamballa*. We are now in the larger cosmic cycle of Kali Yuga, the iron age, within which is a smaller cycle of Dwapara Yuga, the copper age, and contained in the copper age is the the yet smaller cycle of Treta Yuga, the silver age. It is said by people of inner vision that the smallest cycle of Satya Yuga will be ushered in by the year 2012, which will culminate in the year 2700, where a quantum leap will be taken in the evolution of human consciousness. At this time, the future Man Savarni, will choose from the sixth sub-race, the flower of humanity called the sixth root-race. These will be those people who are at present engaged in the diligent practice of the science of Kriya Yoga, called the sacred fire right of the yogi and the practice of Surya Yoga.

The two lofty grand masters of humanity, who gave this soul saving science to the world, are none other than the Lord Gyanavatar Yukteshwar, who is the future Manu Savarni, and the Lord Yogavatar Lahiri Mahasaya, who is the future World Teacher. As I have explained before, it is mainly these four divine Beings, who will be the driving force for the evolution of our humanity. It is they who are the inner controllers (*antaryamis*) of the celestial hierarchy of the inner government of our humanity. This inner government is established in the celestial realms of the white island of Shamballa, so mystically spoken of in the *Kalki Purana* and other Indian scriptures. But above these four is the one mysterious Being. They call him by many names. He is the visible-invisible saviour of all humanities and world cycles. Called *Sanat Kumar*, he is an aspect of the unfathomable Shiva Goraksha Babaji and the true King of the celestial hierarchy of the inner government of our world.

Babaji The Lightning Standing Still

CHAPTER 16

GORAKSHA SHATAKA
AN AUTHENTIC SOURCE OF KRIYA YOGA

Om Sri Shiva Goraksha Shataka

Babaji's Kriya Yoga is the Goraksha Shataka

The hundred verses of *Goraksha Shataka* given below connect beautifully to the original Kriya Yoga which is given to us by Shiva Goraksha Babaji, Yogavatar Lahiri Mahasaya and Gyanavtar Sri Yukteshwar. Some of the instructions of Kriya Yoga have been taken verbatim from the *Goraksha Shataka*. This only goes to make clear that Babaji of *Autobiography of a Yogi* and Goraksha Nath, who wrote the *Shataka*, are one and the same person.

The *Goraksha Shataka* is veiled in mysticism, not so as to withhold it from sincere truth-seekers but to protect it from being abused by the profane and uninitiated masses. The Master had scooped from the slush, the seed of human life and caused it to evolve into the blooming lotus of immortality. Such pragmatic alchemy has influenced the culture of yoga and dharma the world over

By virtue of my experience, I have put reason to rhyme as the *Goraksha Shataka*. In other words, I penned the verses through the experience of my *Nath Sadhana*. This rendering is thus inspired, not intellectual; therefore it is not as a pundit would have written, but as a yogi has experienced.

This poetic rendering is as Shiva Goraksha Babaji would have it for the benefit of all on this path of evolution.

GORAKSHA SHATAKA POEM PART I
BY YOGIRAJ SIDDHANATH

1.
Namo Namah Guru Supreme
Thy presence shatters maya's dream
Thy glory, us knowledge to know
Transforming us in bliss to grow!

2.
Constant in thy *swayambhu* light
Raj hamsa[1] in thy splendid flight
Beyond causation space and time
Homage Meen Nath guru sublime

3.
With devotion having homage paid
Goraksha opens liberation's path
Secret fusion of head and heart
Yogis whereby to bliss depart

4.
To benefit yogis of all kind
Nath unveils the mindless mind,
With hundred gems beyond all price
Dispelling ignorance in a trice

5.
This *gyan* inverts the senses five
From mayic pull to spiritual hive
Beyond the gates of death he glides
Yogi who in Gorakh confides

---
[1] The king's swan.

6.
Oh valiant yogi striving free
Practice yoga and Siddha be
Benedictions of yogis divine
Dispelling sorrow, on you shine

7.
Asan and pranayam gems sublime
Pratyahara Dharana jewel the self
The fifth the diamond *dhyan* divine
Then flowers samadhi beyond time

8.
Asans many as beings there be
Beyond the ken of humanity
Shiva alone knows the family tree
Whose blossoms blooming set us free

9.
Eighty-four lakh the *asans* they say
Expounded by Nath in every way
But He specially selected eighty-four
To pave the way, salvation's door

10.
Then He further selected *asans* two
For collecting of the honey dew
The first the *Siddha* perfect stance
The second yogi's lotus trance

11.
Siddhasana opens salvation's door
Left heel against perineum floor
The right against the *kanda*[2] squeeze
Eyes in *bhrukuti*[3] and then freeze

---
2 Bulb or root.
3 The third eye called Kuthastha Chaitanya.

12.
Kamalasan[4] conquers death disease
Right foot on left thigh with ease
With left foot do the same as this
And steady glide into the Bliss!

13.
How can yogis Yogis be
Who know not centres; *Nadis* three?
Sixteen *adharas*[5] and sheaths five
Must know to in divinity dive

14.
This body temple with doors nine
Upheld by spinal pillar fine
Presiding *shaktis* five sublime
Yogis know them to be divine

15.
The *mula* is four, *swadhisthan* six
Manipur has ten petals fixed
Emblazoned in the heart of prana
Twelve *anahata* petals shine in *dhyan*

16.
Vishuddhi sixteen petalled blue
Agyana quicks — *Hamsa* flight anew
Sahasrara the thousand-petalled Sun
In its splendors second to none

17.
The *muladhara* is base and root
Followed next by *swadhisthan*
Between them *kamrupa yonisthan*
Place for *kula kundalini dhyan*

---

4 Lotus posture, also known as padmasana.
5 The supports (the six chakras).

18.
The *chatur*[6] prana chakra *adhara*
The root and rhythm of *Sangsara*
Above which doth the *yoni* be
Praised by adepts as 'lover's eye'

19.
Irradiant *linga*[7] midst *yoni* stands
Bejeweled splendor facing back
Yogis who actualize this light
Are masters of immortal might!

20.
Yonisthan of molten gold
Triangular lightning flash!
Doth house of kundalini fold
Whose virgin radiance never old

21.
Having seen the light supreme
Yogi transforms the mayic dream
With *Alakh!* Samadhi now he glows
Beyond the birth death cycle goes

22.
By word of Sva doth *pran* arise
And raises Hamsa to the skies
The resting prana in *Swadhisthan*
From which is named the *Medhra sthan.*

---

6 Four.

7 'Mark', the pillar or penis as the creative principle; a symbol and popular icon of Lord Shiva; a symbol for the universe.

23.
To *Sushumna* the *kanda* is strung
Like a threaded jewel hung
This region of the navel called
Manipur where *samana*[8] installed

24.
The soul doth wander till it finds
Anahata nada beyond the mind
Then rested in the self remains
Beyond merit demerit twain

25.
The seventy-two thousand *nadis* born
From the *Kanda yoni* pran,
Located twixt the navel and
The *Linga Yonisthan*

26.
Among the thousands of *nadis*
Seventy-two are selected chief
From them the most important *sthan*
Given to ten vehicles of prana

27.
Ida, Pingala[9], *Sushumna* three
Chief *nadis* of evolutions tree
Then *Hastajivhava*[10], *Gandhari*
With *Pusa* and *Yashasvini*[11]

---

8 A prana of a green hue connected with digestion.
9 'Reddish conduit', the prana current ascending on the right side of the central channel (sushumna nadi) and associated with the sympathetic nervous system and having an energizing effect on the mind when activated.
10 A subordinate nadi.
11 One of the sub-nadis in the body.

28.
Alambusa Kuhus[12] and *Samkhini*
Are the vital *nadis* ten
All yogis having knowledge of
Should learn their location then

29.
Ida runs left *Pingala* up right
Sushumna in mid-region reigns.
Awaiting kundalini's light
Left eye *Gandhari* Moon of night

30.
Hastjiva the sunlight in the right eye
Pusha hears *pranava*[13] in the right ear
While *Yashasvini* resides left ear
Alambusa gives *vaak siddhi* clear

31.
Kuhus nadi joins *linga sthan*
Samkhini carries *mula prana*
Such are the vital *nadis* ten
Giving us light again and again

32.
Conductors of prana are *nadis* three
Ida, Pingala and *Sushumni,*
With their presiding deities three
Sun, Moon, and Fire kundalini

---

12 A sub-nadi.
13 Another name for the sound of Omkar.

33.
Prana inhales, apana exhales
Samana digests, *Udana* regulates
Vyana, Naga Kurma[14] in body flow
There *Devdatta*[15] *Krkara Dhananjay*[16] glow

34.
Hridaya[17] prana *Gudadal*[18] apana
Positive negative poles of *dhyana*
Navel *samana* the throat *udana*[19]
And spreading the body rosy *vyana*

35.
Prana is life, apana is death
Samana stores food assimilates
Udana is life's metabolic key
Vyana flows throughout our body free

36.
Then comes secondary pranic life
Naga, Kurma and Krkara[20] energy
With *Devdatta* second to prana
And *Dhananjay* following *Vyana*

37.
And though the body lifeless be
Dhanajay leaveth not the tree
These pranas ten, and *nadis* ten
Match one another in all men

---

14 Turtle (the one on land).
15 One's pranic life forces.
16 A victor over wealth and materialism, one of the five upparanas.
17 The heart.
18 Rectal passage.
19 Metabolic prana, concerned with the lymphatic and metabolic systems; one of the five main life forces namely Prana, Apana, Samana, Udana and Vyana.
20 A sub-prana.

38.
Soul is struck by prana apana
Spines up and down salvation's path.
The life of breath is death indeed
Upon whose victory yogis feed

39.
The *jiva*[21] controlled by prana apana
Is restless with no *samadhana*
Moving in *Ida Pingalasthan*
It cannot be perceived in *dhyana*.

40.
As a Hamsa soars in azure blue skies
Our consciousness to the heavens flies
But bound by the gunas three
Prana apana hold wings of liberty!

41.
The Prana Apanic *Anusandhan*[22]
Mastered by yogic pranayama
Brings union of these *Vayus* two
Sets free the Hamsa's flight anew

42.
The *Jiva's* prana inhaled with 'Sa'
And apana exhaled with 'Ha'
Ever doth the soul breath say
The Hamsa mantra night and day

43.
Yogis in *dhyana* become aware
How breath at birth did them ensnare
Twenty-one thousand thirty score
Japa leads soul to salvation's door

---

21 'Individual self', the individuated consciousness, as opposed to the ultimate Self (param atman).
22 Kriya Yoga is also called Pran-Apan Anusandhan.

44.
Hamsa is *Gayatri's ajapa japa*
The opener of yogi's *moksha dvar*[23]
So with sincerity let him strive
And let not him his animal drive

45.
This knowledge is all supreme,
Its practice melts the magic dream
The experience of the 'Hamsa Still'
Makes us know the cosmic will

46.
From *kundali* is *Gayatri* born
Who then becomes the prana
Yogis uniting prana-apana[24]
Are true adepts in *sama*[25] *dhyan*.

47.
Above our *kanda* in coils eight
Kundalini seals the yogi's fate
With head resting at *Brahmadvar*[26]
She our salvation's *taranhara*.

48.
Having blocked with Her face
The path leading to Shiva's shrine
Awake! Oh sleeping splendor mine
And lead me to my home divine!

---

[23] Smaller Kriya called Hamsa Ajapa Japa sets the soul hamsa free.
[24] Kriya Yoga consists of uniting the Pran-Apanic breath currents.
[25] Balanced.
[26] The door at the crown of one's head, sahasrara chakra.

49.
The yogic prana ablaze unites
With kundalini to ignite
Mano–buddhi then penetrates[27]
Sushumna chakras living light

50.
She like a hissing serpent goes
Glistening kundalini upwards flows
By magnet heat of pranayam
Awakens She! Our wisdom grows

51.
Oh valiant yogi striving free
By *pranic kumbhak* break the seal!
The brave by storm the heavens take
Nirvana through kundalini they make

52.
In *padmasana* do triple *bandh*
Focus on *kundali* in *kanda*
Do the Hamsa pran apan
Gain precious kundalini *gyan*

53.
Hard practice, beads of sweat form,
Rub them into the body form
Then yogi must of milk avail
Avoid all food acid and stale

54.
Yogi immersed in yog *abhyas*
Must channel senses and be chaste.
Dwelling far from worldly *bhog*
Makes yogi master of Yog

---

27 In Sanskrit 'bhedana'.

55.
Food is fodder for the mind
And goes to mental making
Eat sweet and soft *mithahar*
At every fast of breaking

56.
Eight coiled *kundali* on *kanda*
Gives *mukti* to yogis sincere
And bondage to the *manda*
So those who practice need not fear

57.
Yogis who, ready for *mukti*,
Khechari, Mahamudra masters be
Jalandhar[28], *Uddiyan*[29] and *Mula*[30] bandh
Adepts be, to break *mayic skanda*

58.
With all the *nadis* purified
The moving of both Sun and Moon
And all the humors in us dried
Is perfect *Mahamudra* done

59.
Pressing perineum with left heel
Inhale then stretch the right side foot
Hold breath go forward and touch toe
Repeat left centre each breath let go.

---

28 Chin lock.
29 The abdominal lock.
30 Rectal lock.

60.
Having practiced with *jyotsna*[31] Moon
And then equal with *bhaskar*[32] Sun
This *mudra* should be done
By daily practice our well being

61.
For him no food is good or bad
Who does the *Mahamudra*
Food poisoning, foods of defect
Will on him have no ill-effect

62.
Ills like consumption, leprosy
Away from such a yogi flee
Who true to *Mahamudra* be
In regular *sadhana* practice

63.
The bringer of success to those
Whom *Mahamudra* is so close
Must only be to the wise disclosed
Souls sincere calm and reposed

64.
Daily eat cow flesh yogi pure
Get lost in wine and revelry[33]
When dazed and dazzled in the eye
Be free! by *khechari* roam the sky

---

31 The moonbeam.
32 One of the splendid names of the Sun god.
33 This is a mystic expression; 'eat cow flesh' means swallow the tongue in khechari mudra. Wine and revelry refers to soma rasa, the immortal nectar which flows down the tongue as a result of khechari mudra.

65.
By Allakh! Gorakhia's magic touch
Disease hunger nor sleep assail
Yogis who rent maya's death veil
Victors who in *khechari* prevail

66.
By afflictions is he troubled not
Nor tainted by his fruits of karma
Is not troubled by sting of death
Deathless He, conqueror of breath[34]

67.
Precious and prized by all adepts
The *chitta* enters *Khe* the sky
Tongue frees mind of bondage thoughts
Unmani brings to all souls lost

68.
By *Bindu* our body composed
Of flesh and blood and bone
By *Bindu* it is decomposed
When essence withdraws home

69.
Who seal by *khechan Bindu* gem
Embraced by damsels of the spheres
Their *bindu* falleth not to waste
For they immortal *soma*[35] taste

70.
So long as *khechari mudra* done
The *bindu* falls not down
As long as *bindu* up remains
Death dies, yogi immortal reigns

---

34 He being Mrityunjay, 'Conqueror of Death'.

35 The elixir which is God, from the practice of khechari mudra in yogic practices; it is also taken from plants and connected with the Moon; anti-aging ambrosia may be extracted from Moon plants.

71.
By chance, should *bindu* descend
And move towards the *yoni sthan*
It is arrested and returned
By shakti of *yoni mudra dhyan*

72.
The vital *bindu* is two kinds
Pure white and blood red
The first is called semen virile
The blood red, menstrual

73.
Rajas the female flows from Sun
Bindu the male secretes from Moon
Difficult fusion of these two
Evolves you to dimensions new

74.
Bindu of Shiva, *rajas* of Shakti
Bindu is *Indu*[36] and *rajas Ravi*
Unite these elements by alchemy
In *Alakh Niranjan* be ever free!

75.
Then by shakti *chalan*[37] *vayu*
Rajas impelled to join *bindu*
Volatile wonderful the union be
Then you Yourself as divinity see

76.
Then *bindu* with *Chandra* is one
And *rajas* with *Ravi* unites
But a yogi true is only he
Who marrying both gets karma free

---

36 The feminine energy of the Moon.
37 Making a vacuum of the stomach and moving it in and out.

77.
Kala the great *Garuda* keeps flying
Past barriers of decay and death
So *uddiyan* immortal lion slays
Breath elephant to make Pranic days[38]

78.
Practice then the *uddiyan bandh*
Awaken *kundali* of *kanda*
By ceaseless study of this art
Yogis to *mukti dham*[39] depart

79.
Jalandhar is the chin lock
And practiced to prevent the Moon
Letting its nectar flow to waste
Giving yogis *sanjeevani's* taste

80.
By closing the throat in *Jalandhar*
The nectar in the head contained
Unconsumed by body's death fire
And life serene in the self remains

81.
Third lock is called *Mula Bandh*
Apana withdraw then rectum close
Press *yoni* with back of left heel
And then enter the yogic pose

---

38 This means that the pranic life-force of the Lion slays the Elephant of breath to move to a longer life; when prana moves individually independent of breath, it leads the yogi to immortality.

39 Place of rest, also meaning a sacred place of worship; home.

82.
By pran apanic[40] *anusandhan*
Purified are inner body *sthans*
Even the aged and the old
By *mula* get young and bold

83.
Take *padmasana* perfect pose
In lush serene surrounding
Shivnetra yogi lost in *Om*
Know self as *nada*[41] resounding

84.
Om thou supreme light divine
In worlds *bhur*[42], *bhuva*[43], *svaha*[44] shine
Light of light that lights all lights
Sun Moon and fire you ignite

85.
Father of the triform time
Of past present and future
Contained in thee all Gods and worlds
Om's light doth feed all nature

86.
In thee desire and knowledge grow
Rudri, Brahmi, Vaishnavi flow
Such art thou ineffable light
Om splendor of the lightless light

---

40 Name for Kriya Yoga, connecting inhaled with exhaled life-force.
41 'Sound', the inner sound of Om, as it can be heard through the practice of Nada Yoga.
42 This is a dimension of the terrestrial sphere as Bhuvar is the astral sphere and Swaha, the heavenly sphere.
43 An emotion, or Bhakti, devotion.
44 The wife of Agni Abhimani, father of the three sub-fires (pavaka, pavamana, shuchi).

87.
In the blueprint of creation
Emblazoned is thy cosmic seal
This whole drama of life,
A projection of your magic dream

88.
Om with every breath and thought
Sets yogi free from karma
Giving nirvana to those who strive
As per their personal dharma

89.
Even the evil chanting Om
Are tainted not by karma
Would like a lotus lying,
In water unwetted and undying

90.
Absorbed in *nada*, the *Bindu* still!
By ceaseless *ayam* of prana
When prana is still, *bindu* is still
Then conquer death, new life fulfill

91.
As long as prana in body flows
Jivatma doth therein reside
Prana leaves, the *Jiva* also leaves
So live for God! Do pranayam

92.
Yogi deathless, fearless bold
Prana between the eyebrows hold
By *kevali* in Shiv *Netra* be!
Oh death, where is thy victory?

93.
From fear of *kala* death they say
Gods, Sages in pranayam stay
But we must put this fear away
And live in prana the *kevali* way

94.
The human prana by *rechaka* goes
Thirty-six fingers it outflows
Same length it takes to be inhaled
The living mystery still unveiled

95.
By prana the *nadis* purify
Toxins cleanse secretions dry
Then only can, you hold breath's gale
Mystery of life and death unveil

96.
In lotus posture yogi stay
Do Sun Moon prana of night and day[45]
Sushmana Spinal Breathing called,
Victor of death be breath enthralled

97.
Meditate on nectar crescent Moon
In third eye enter mystic star
Absorbed in Self Samadhi be,
Find peace for Self and for humanity

98.
Through *surya nadi*[46] having filled
The prana of life in *dhyan* inhale
By *kumbakh* fill in stomach hold
By *Chandra* left apana exhale

---

45 Inhaled prana of Sun and exhaled prana of Moon is Kriya Yoga.
46 The life-force flowing through the right nostril.

99.
Meditate on radiant mass of light
In *manipur* the navel chakra
The mystic Sun and Moon unite,
Find peace in Hamsa's deathless flight.

100.
Merging our prana in His all Prana
Sun, Moon and stars He holds
Our lives fuse with His Livingness
Ourselves as Om in Him behold!!!

Om Tat Sat Om!

GORAKSHA SHATAKA
INHERENT SOURCE OF KRIYA YOGA

SINCE BOTH ARE THE SAME BEING,
THE KRIYA YOGA WILL ALSO BE THE SAME.

Their Essential Oneness:

Goraksha *Kriya*	Babaji *Kriya*
Omkar Kriya verses 83 to 86	*Omkar Kriya*
Hamsa Sadhana verses 42 to 45	*Hamsa Sadhana*
Kriya Yoga Pranayama (Shiva *Shakti*) verses 41, 46, 49, 93 to 96	*Kriya Yoga Pranayama*
Nabhi Kriya verse 99	*Nabhi Kriya*
Mahamudra verses 59 to 63	*Mahamudra*
Yoni Mudra verse 71	*Yoni Mudra (Jyoti Mudra)*
Unmani (Par Avastha) verses 67, 100	*Par Avastha (Unmani)*
Taraka Raja Yoga verse 97	*Taraka Raja Yoga*
Thokar Kriya verses 49 to 51	*Thokar Kriya*
Shad-chakra Bhedana verses 49 to 51	*Shad-chakra Bhedana*
Khechari Mudra verses 64 to 69	*Khechari Mudra (Jivho Granthi Bhedana)*
Siddhasana verse 11	*Siddhasana*
Padmasana verse 12	*Padmasana*

CHAPTER 18

THE ANCESTRY OF KRIYA YOGA

In the Ancient of Days, *Mahankal*, the Great Beyond Time, also called Lord Shiva, the Lightless Light, illumine-exploded this soul-liberating science to his consort, Uma, the first virgin light (also called Padma Matri, the Transcendental Matrix of creation), by virtue of which, Shiva, the Eternal Lord of Everything and Nothing, divided his Self of Lightless Light in half. But in spite of the division, both halves still remained complete. One of those complete Beings was called Shiva Goraksha Babaji, whose work was to give the science of yoga to the world and to liberate it from its delusion, illusion and error. He came to ceaselessly involute, permute and evolute the spirits of countless humanities through the school of life and then to take them back to their eternal home in the Divine. He was all the while the Great Moving Spirit in every soul of humanity, and His divine energy called *Mataji*, the Lightning Kundalini, is still the crucial factor in the evolution of all human souls.

Simultaneously, Uma passed on the science of yoga (the unity of Soul with Spirit) to the centripetal inward flow called *Sanat Kumar,* or Kartikeya and the centrifugal outward flow of creation called Ganesha. There was also Vishnu, the all-pervading one, personified as Vishnu-Krishna, who received this Truth for the salvation of all sentient and non-sentient beings. And he, along with Shiva Goraksha, passed it down to the kings of the Solar Dynasty, the first of which was the Lord Vivasvat Manu, our Sun. Lord Vivaswat Manu gave this science of evolution to Lord Vaivasvat Manu, the Father of our

The Ancestry of Kriya Yoga

Aaryan Root Race, approximately 300 million years ago. He in turn gave it to the kings of the solar dynasty, Ikshavaku (Apollo), Saturn (Sabatheal, Shanni), and Yam (Zadkeal). Then it was later passed on to Raghu, then to Dilip, then to Malchizedek, and later to Harischandra, and then to Rama, the thirty-seventh in descent from Ishkavaku.

Then as the science spread, Abraham practiced it, and later Moses got it from the burning bush from Babaji as Yah-weh (Jehova), Therafter the science spread and was known and practiced by Vikramaditya, who was akin to the King Arthur of India, and Chowrangee Nath, who was directly initiated by Shiva Goraksha Babaji. It was later known to the Christ himself when he incarnated in the body of the man Jesus. And then later came Nagarjuna and Aaryasangh also practiced this science to perfection. The King Arthur, who was like the Vikramaditya of England, also practiced this sacred science of Kriya Yoga.

It was later handed down in the Middle-Ages to Kabir and then to the King Shivaji[1]. Kabir incarnated as Samarta Ram Das, and then as YogAvatar Lahiri Mahasaya and the King Shivaji incarnated as GyanAvatar Shri Yukteshwar. They are the future World Teacher and World King respectively. They are responsible for the inner governing of the world. And when the Judgment Day arises, Lahiri Mahasaya shall don the robes of the World Teacher, and Shri Yukteshwar shall don the robes of the Spiritual King.

The Kriya Yoga is mentioned in the *Patanjali Yoga Sutras*. It is also mentioned in the *Vaivaswat Manu Smriti*. But the detailed modus operandi is given by Shiva Goraksha Babaji in His *Goraksha Paddhati* consisting of *Goraksha Shataka* in its first part and *Yoga Shataka* in its second part (*Shataka* means 100 verses, so there are 200 verses in *Goraksha Paddhati*). The sacred knowledge of Kriya Yoga, which deals with the evolution of human consciousness was passed down many millions of years ago, by Shiva Goraksha Babaji to Lord Vaivaswat Manu and to Kalki Krishna. The lofty Manus and

---

1 The Medieval Marhata King who repelled the Mogul forces and restored India, saving it from total invasion and returning it to its Hindu glory.

their work are specifically concerned with the evolution of our root race by the predominant application of one's *Atmic* will, just as the evolutionary work of the World Teacher is done by the predominant application of one's *buddhic* intellect. Kriya practiced through desire begets karma. Kriya practiced through consciousness is desireless and creates no new karma; whereby the disciple rapidly moves towards self-realization. This yoga, when practiced with total surrender to the Master, moves the spirit of the Masters themselves in the spine of the practitioner.

Yogavatar Lahiri Mahasaya, the World Teacher to succeed the Krishna-Kalki Avatara, has extensively referred to the latter's sacred works from the *Bhagavad Gita*, relating them to the original practice of Kriya Yoga. As a matter of fact, he has written a whole commentary on this, called *Commentary on the Bhagavad-Gita*. He has also referred to the *Vaivaswat Manu Smriti* while teaching the advanced Kriya Yoga. The *Manu Smriti*, given in its original form, is properly called the *Manav Dharma Shastra*, which means human religious code of conduct, comprising the whole of the social, yogic and ethical code of humanity and dealing with the genomatic and conscious evolution through Kriya Yoga. This monumental compendium of knowledge will be handed over to the next law giver, called Moses, who later incarnated as El Morya and then as Gyanavatar Sri Yukteshwar. His work it is to upgrade and update the old "Manava Dharma Sashtra" intended for the fifth root race to suit our contemporary sixth sub-race, which will flower into the sixth root race. The Ten Commandments were but a spark of Manu's compendium of moral and ethical codes. They were but a drop in the ocean given to Moses to suit the then-evolving humanity.

Here it is Parashara, the Indo-Aryan Hermes who instructs Maitreya, the Indian Asclepious (the son of Apollo, the Sun God) and calls upon Vishnu in his Triple Hypostasis as Brahma, Vishnu and Shiva.

Krishna is known as Christ in the west; the same Christ who took Jesus' body as a vehicle to fulfil his ministry, Krishna-Maitreya Christ, call him what you may, for they are all the same World Teacher. He will hand over the spiritual knowledge of evolution to Yogavatar Lahiri Mahasaya, who is the World Teacher to-be.

Lord Vaivaswat Manu, also known as Noah in the west, will pass the great laws of the *Manava Dharma Sashtra* to Lord Yukteshwar, who was Moses the law giver in his former incarnation and will be the Manu Savarni in the future. The new commandment will begin with the keyword of unity of humanity and its consciousness.

Sri Yukteshwar is currently working in his celestial body in *Hiranyaloka* (the golden heaven), to advance souls beyond the *nirvikalpa samadhi*. He is simultaneously working in another body and mind to initiate Kriya Yoga and evolve all terrestrial beings. He is presently working incognito on the western coast of California and is in no way concerned whether people know him or not, but is absolutely certain that Kriya Yoga, the sacred science of evolution and peaceful co-existence will encircle the globe. It is he in future who will don the mantle of the Manu Savarni (Spiritual King) when the Kalki Avatara descends for his work approximately 499 years hence.

CHAPTER 19

THE SAGE OF ALL AGES

Presently we are now in the *Vaivasvat Manavantar* world cycle of the *Shweta Varaha Kalpa* (4,320,000,000 years), which constitutes a day of Brahma (God as Creator). We have finished one parardha that is one half of the *Shweta Varaha Kalpa* (white boar world cycle). Until the whole world cycle is complete, the Eternal Babaji shall remain with us as the Visible-Invisible saviour of mankind. Later he will move on in his incomprehensible ways.

The Mahavatar is ever-present for the duration of Creation. He continues to be in full omniscient consciousness manifest on the grosser terrestrial planes as and when the need arises; and then He withdraws himself into His own latent Cosmic Consciousness. So like the Sun, which sets at night and appears to be born the next day but in fact ever remains the living light, so also it is with the immortal Shiva Goraksha Babaji. It appears as though he manifests and then disappears, but in reallity, He is ever-present either in the celestial or terrestrial spheres.

This is the reason why historians are confounded as to the dates of appearance of this great Visible-Invisible Saviour of mankind called the Mahavatar Shiva Goraksha Babaji because the mortal researchers have taken mortality and death for granted. In their confined and cramped up minds they cannot even imagine that bodily immortality is possible for every human soul, the atma inhabiting the impermanent body is of course already immortal.

How can westernized authors with a mind coloured by thought judge a colourless mind, a contentless consciousness, and a pure vigilant awareness? It can't be done because judgmental thoughts are biased by the three gunas (primal characteristics) and differ from person to person. To expound the works of Goraksha Nath or to take another example, the Buddha, is surely beyond the scope of their self-opinionated views. Their judgment is disturbed by thoughts. Only samadhi can experience samadhi. Only a Buddha can merge in Buddha. The scholar has reference books for crutches. The yogi flies free in search of his experiences and knows the suchness of things as they are!

Babaji's Dream Bodies

Babaji takes on many dream bodies of various subtleties. Rarely does he chose to adorn a terrestrial body, a human form composed of atomic particles and molecules. If in His compassion, He decides to bless or to appear to some denizens in the astral and celestial spheres, then He would wear the celestial mantle composed of *tanmatras*, the subatomic particles of light composed of the fabric of electro-protonic matter.

Although the great Presence called Babaji does not have to necessarily work even in the causal or buddhic spheres, He out of His great compassion may chose to bless the greatest of avatars and tapasvis. Then he would wear the undifferentiated rainbow fabric of electronic radiant ether which is at times called the *Boddhisatvic* body or the *Buddhija* or at a yet higher level, there is the *Atmaja* body difficult to describe in human terminology. Here is an attempt to describe the *Atmaja* body: undifferentiated fabric of homogeneous light - Shiva's Mahavatars divine unlimited infinite consciousness without beginning or end - paramatmic formless attributeless infinite presence - Lightless Light which Lights that Light, which Lights the Light of all our Souls.

Blessings by Avatartic Descent of Bodies

The very word "Ava" means descent and "tara" means to cross over. So the avatara descends in compassion and crosses over into the ocean of *samsara* and relativity to save the drowning souls deceived by the web of maya and caught in the quagmire of materialism.

Babaji may choose to create by the power of His Kriya Shakti, any of the bodies composed of the varying combinations of the sub-atomic particles of *sattva*, *raja* and *tama*. But at times He directly takes His formless body of Lightless Light, transcending all human understanding and the laws of physics, He appears to the infant humanity in his majesty inconceivable. This is totally different than the avataric body, clothed in an apparel of light; the *Mahavatric* body has no such direct effect on the evolution of human bodies or consciousness. If it did, its power would do more harm to the delicate human body and soul. Therefore, Babaji's power has to be channelized by a step-down transformer. They are firstly the Purana Avataras, then Babaji's power is further lessened through the avatara, it gets even lesser through the Aunsh avatara and then in its least spiritual voltage, it is distributed in love and compassion through the *avadhoots* and siddhas the worldover. This is the compassionate love of Babaji distributed in diminishing progression. People for whom even this spiritual blessing is too much, are guided by normal people of wisdom through devotional chants and spiritual story telling. So, His blessings do not miss any of the billions of souls striving for evolution as the collective consciousness, we call the *world disciple*.

It is to be noted that even the bodies of Shiva Goraksha Babaji are so powerful that they have the capacity to bless and liberate. What to say of his *Paramatic* essence and Himsef !! These bodies are Cosmic (causal), Celestial (astral), and Terrestrial (earthly). The transition from His Cosmic to His Celestial and then to His human, Terrestrial form is a matter of mere convenience for this lofty Being, depending upon the sphere of consciousness He would like to bless with His enlightened wisdom. If He does appear to any person in his

Celestial or Cosmic body, He then pulls that individual's spiritual essence up and expands it to a higher state of awareness.

Pulling the veil of maya by his own will, He reconfigures his formless body of lightless light to appear to the infant Humanity in a lightbody composed of sub-atomic particles. He then withdraws himself back into his own latent Cosmic Consciousness. So it merely appears as though He manifests and then disappears. In reality, He is everpresent either in the subtler or grosser spheres. This deeper phenomenon is beyond the comprehension of the linear mind of historians and scientists alike. Therefore their historical dates chopped up into years and decades and centuries, cannot conceive of an "Eternal Now" running through the pages of history and all the scriptures of humanity. So little is our understanding, so limited our vision, that even my writing of this ineffable truth would fail to convince the hard-boiled eggs of limited thinking.

The power by which man is bound to the three-dimensional world was known to the Rishis and Sages of India's antiquity, it is known as maya. Maya, the great deceiver, is the power by which dualities coexist: good and evil, pleasure and pain, wax and wane, birth and death. Yogis, realizing the universe to be composed of opposing sub-atomic particles of light and sound, have severed the bonds of maya to evolve themselves to even more refined and evermore expanded spheres of Consciousness, thereby transcending the laws of physics and conquering death. Though He is composed of Lightless Light, Babaji, by his supreme command over maya, creates a light body (*mayavi*) to incarnate among men and carry out His Divine work.

The difference between the manifest bodies of the Mahavatar[1] and the avatara is that the avatara wears a vesture of light as his body form and may express his powers as per his mission whereas the Mahavatar adorns an apparent body of lightless light and is unlimited in his omniscient, omnipresent, and omnipotent expression.

---

1 A *Swayambu,* meaning a Self-born manifestation of Lord Shiva, the Supreme Ascetic and meditative Consciousness of the manifested universe and more beyond.

From Poem *Reality*

This world our sages did perceive
Is mind stuff materialised
In relative sequence it is built
Deceiving mortal eyes
This world is but a thoughtfulness
Of Mayaic atomic intertwine
Whose electrons are energy
Of light essence sublime

        Yogiraj Siddhanath

The Sage of All Ages

Like the spiritual sun, Babaji walks through the pages of all the great scriptures, revealing himself to only the few He chooses and usually remaining invisible. He appears on the grosser terrestrial planes as and when the need arises and guides humanity through the work of his disciples from whom his divine mission continues to manifest. He then withdraws himself into his own cosmic Consciousness. Babaji's presence is magical and confounds the human mind, for being present, He appears to be invisible and even when He is invisible, He can be perceived by those who enter the depths of samadhi. Therefore, it is more a question of their state of awareness and clairvoyance, which Babaji graces rather than Babaji himself appearing and disappearing. This is one reason why historians are confounded as to the dates of this great Visible-Invisible Saviour of mankind called the Mahavatar, Shiva Goraksha Babaji.

He took the form of Adi Nath Shiva himself, then of Rudra of the ancient of days. It was He as the angel of the Lord who walked with Adam and Eve in the Garden of Eden. As Babaji's consciousness has within it the *Trimurti* (trinity), one of his forms is the Lord Krishna, who in occult circles is called Shambhu Chaitanya (Shiva of Irradiant Consciousness). We see this great Being walk through the pages of the great scriptures of the world. He came approximately seven thousand years ago to bless through his samadhi the seventh avatara of Vishnu, Lord Rama, at his coronation in Ayodhya. As a physical token of his blessings, his disciples came with 'prasad' as the Guru's holy blessings. Then He came in 3102 BCE, that's about 5000 years ago, to bless and to be with the people during Lord Krishna's time while He was the eighth avatara of Vishnu.

It is a well understood fact amongst the initiated circles that it was Shiva Goraksha Babaji who orchestrated the birth of Karna and the five Pandavas. It was He who gave the sacred mantras of the Sun and all other elements to Queen Kunti[2] who then conceived the six celestial sons born of the informing spirits of the Sun and five elements. First born was Karna, but being immaculately conceived before her marriage to King Pandu, He was not counted among the five Pandavas, but spiritually a Surya Putra (Son of the Sun). Then were born the five sons of King Pandu: Yudishtira of Yama (God of Death), Bhima of Vayu (the Wind God), Arjuna of Indra (God of Heaven), Nakul and Sahadeva of the Ashvin Kumars (Twin Solar Gods of Healing).

In the ancient of days, when Krishna was on his excursions, he happened to come to the ashram of the great Garga Rishi. In his *satsanga* with the great Sage, the topic of the immortal Being called Goraksha Nath came up, in which the Krishna got very interested in knowing more about this mysterious and immortal Being called Shiva Goraksha and he asked the great Rishi, "Who is this God called Goraksha Nath? By what mantras and means may He be propitiated? And what type of meditation is to be done? Please do tell me." In response, the Rishi Garga went on to tell the following story. "In times of yore, the Devas (gods) and the Sages asked the Lord Shiva to expound to them the mystery of Goraksha Nath. They further beseeched Mahadeva (the Great God) to tell them how this great omniscient Yogeshwar was born. The Lord replied that the Lord Goraksha Nath is of the nature of *Alakh-Swaroop* (the es-

---

[2] Wife of King Pandu, mother of the Five Pandavas.

sence of lightless light). His mother is the great Void and His father is the Eternal Consciousness. Goraksha Nath was born from Himself (*Aja*), meaning birthless and hence deathless. Then Lord Shiva unveiled the great mystery saying that Shiva Goraksha Babaji was Himself who had incarnated in the haunts of men to spread the true yoga and end the suffering of humanity. The mantras of Goraksha Nath are *swayama-siddha*, means self activated to be put into action for protection, prosperity and peace."

So legendary and holy had Goraksha Nath become, that a *Goraksha Sahastranam* (thousand names) and a *Goraksha Gayatri* mantra was composed by the Rishis of yore to make clear to all devotees that He was ranked amongst the highest Gods and Rishis of the time.

He took the form of Adi Nath Shiva Himself, then of Rudra of the ancient of days. He then manifested in 6000 BCE as Kalagni Nath. Subsequently, He came in 5000 BCE in the holy city of Kashi as Dakshinmurti, during which time He initiated himself. In 1400 BCE, He appeared to Moses in the burning bush as the great Yahveh (Jehova). In the year 70 BCE, He manifested himself as Goraksha Nath, at the time of King Bhartari Nath and his younger brother Vikramaditya. Then continuing His divine play, He came to King Shalivahan and blessed his elder son Chowrangee Nath, whom He initiated into yoga. Babaji is mentioned in the *Autobiography of a Yogi* as having initiated Adi Shankaracharya. In this story, he was to defeat Mandal Mishra's wife in a debate. He was asked about the experience of married life. In order to accomplish this, he had to enter the body of a dead king, animate him and experience such a life. Here he clearly mentions, and it is also well documented in Shankayacharya's annals, that he would enter the body of the king by the process of *parkaya-parvesh* taught to him by his Nath Gurus and mentors, Matsyendra and Gorakhsha Nath. This reveals to us that Babaji of *Autobiography of a Yogi* and Goraksha Nath are one and the same Being. The ever-present Babaji had even journeyed north to Nepal where He conquered the Nagas and was called Nagaraja. The Nagas are a certain type of yogi practitioners who assumed the form of nagas (cobras). They hold the mystic knowledge of kundalini awakening. In the same ever-present body, He later appeared as Shiva Goraksha Babaji in the ninth century CE to Guga Nath. This was during the time of Guga Nath, whom He empowered to have complete mastery over the Nagas (his passions) and ultimately be worshipped as a Naga God himself, a full blown Nath Yogi who has mastered his body, mind and soul.

Neophytes, Nagas and Naths

The serpent has ever been the symbol of the adept, powers of immortality and Divine Knoweldge. These qualities are inherent in the rising kundalini. The serpent casting of its skin shows the dual nature of mind after it has conquered and defeated lust. In the Cosmic scenario, the Sun defeats the dragon Rahu. But the dragon serpent kundalini is triple in nature and must cast off three negative coats before it can become a fully enlightened Nath Yogi.

When the Neophyte defeats passion, he is a Naga.

When the Naga overcomes mind, he is a Nath.

When the Nath overcomes intellect (*buddhi*), he is merged in *Kaivalya*, the incomprehensible freedom from earthly bonds and all relativity.

As each successive skin of the yogi is shed from passions to emotions to mind to intellect, the evolving yogi is stripped to bare spirit. He finally evolves to Nath and then to No-Thing! God!

Matsyendra Nath Prays to Shiva

In 740 CE it so happened that the great Maha-Yogi Matsenyndra Nath journeyed to the Himalayas and carried out intense tapa there (self-imposed austerities), immersing himself in ceaseless samadhi. Then Adi Nath, Lord Shiva was pleased and appeared to the Nath and told him to ask of him what he needed. The great yogi asked

Shiva to give him a disciple greater and more perfect than himself. This is regarded as the greatest triumph of humility of the Master in Indian culture, though this is not the very highest state of total disappearance from the face of the earth and of creation, because in such a case, even the desire for *Brahama Nirvana* must vanish. The Lord answered and said, "You are already perfect and have attained to the final enlightenment." But Matsenyndra Nath insisted, so Lord Shiva out of compassion agreed that He would himself manifest as his disciple.

After he beseeched Lord Shiva for a disciple, Shiva Goraksha by the power of Kriya Shakti involuted to pull around Himself a veil of maya, a vesture composed of sub-atomic particles of light, creating an avataric body to descend from His already established cosmic state before creation, which was one with Param-Shiva and then He descended to His already established causal state, 13.75 billion years ago at the beginning of creation. Then by further mutation He descended to the celestial realm (astral plane) 4.32 billion years ago as the primeval Sage of the Fire Mist to create the first spark of global self awareness, and then finally to the terrestrial plane 300 million years ago (the seventh Vaivaswat Manu) to guide, bless and evolve humanity, then withdraw into the celestial and causal realms to guide the higher initiates and evolved souls, and finally appear again and again to guide our present humanity and so the cycle of evolution goes on ad infinitum with succeeding Manu Kings of Shiva's Spirit and Vyas Gurus of Vishnu's Spirit. Ultimately both unite as one.

He has also spoken to some more of His advanced initiates and avataric disciples that He will stay in His physical body till the coming of the Kalki Avatara, guide and assist Him through his mission, and then withdraw into His own celestial cosmic Self. He has also interestingly said that He will always remain visible to a few people on this planet earth. It is however being theoretically explained by me, it is like the reflection of the complete Sun being in a drop of water which represents our planet earth, and the complete reflection of the Sun also being in the sea which represents the celestial sphere, and also the ocean which represents the infinite cosmic realms. Though Babaji's image is complete even in the smallest particle to the vastest infinity, but how He could do this and yet withdraw into His cosmic splendor is the mystery of all mysteries. That is why Babaji is called The Mystery of all Mysteries, the Great Sacrifice and the Sage of All Ages. So in the true sense Shiva Gorksha Babaji is first the guru of Matsyendra Nath on the cosmic realm and later became His disciple on the terrestrial realm.

CHAPTER 20

THE DIVINE ALCHEMIST
And His Alchemy of Total Transformation

The science of the alchemy of total transformation was first given to this world by the Divine Alchemist Shiva Goraksha Babaji. The first we know of it was during the time of Atlantis, when India went by the name of Aaryavarta[1]. Then we have the science coming down along the corridors of time, where all the great yogis and siddhas practiced it to transform their bodies into immortal bodies and then into the rainbow light bodies. The alchemical portion to do with mercury, which in India is called the *Paras Mani*[2], meaning the philosopher's gem, was a science as old as the transformation of the body by yogic means. So we have two streams of thought and practice, in so far as the alchemy is concerned:

1. The first is to do with the transformation of the decayable body into light by yogic means.

2. The second is to do with the transformation of the decayable body into light by alchemical means.

This chapter covers the modus operandi of both these techniques. The solidification of the philosopher's gem was also called *Paras Mani*. This alchemy brings about the magical transformation of a corruptible body into its rainbow form of immortal light, but Shiva Goraksha also gave us the knowledge of the direct transformation

---

[1] An ancient name for the land known as India. He wrote the book *Arya Siddhant*.
[2] 'Mercury gem'; consolidated mercury.

The Divine Alchemist

of the physical into the spiritual body by the practice of the mystical yoga of the Nath yogis. In today's methods of practice, to begin with, we understand that there are two processes of consolidating mercury—one is called the Patanjali Process of hot fusion and the other is the Goraksha Process of cold fusion of mercury.

One of the pertinent contributions of Babaji to humanity was the *Bindu Rahasaya*[3]—the transformation of sexual energy into spiritual light. This secret doctrine has not yet been fully expounded nor exposed to the general public in its deeper sense, but remains in the safe custody of the mystic circle of Nath yogis. This, when properly followed bestows rapid evolution of the body, mind and soul, but gives negative explosive results if improperly done.

The great Bhogar Nath Siddha (Bogar Nath) went to China, where he was known as Bo Yang and later became the celebrated Chinese siddha called Lao-Tze. He taught them the Yin-Yang Yoga of the Indian system (Shiva–Shakti Yoga). He also later wrote some occult treatises on the alchemy of mercury and other metals, and their uses. However, somehow some uninitiated neophyte Chinese practitioners of alchemy got a hold of stray scraps of vague and nebulous data floating here and there, and have given an incomplete picture of this Alchemy of Total Transformation. Beginners must beware of dabbling in this science unless it is taught by authentic Nath yogis of India, and not any uninitiated Chinese version, which is a quick fix of half-knowledge.

I am now here specifically referring to the ultimate transformation of the vital fluid in human beings to a spiritual essence called *Ojas*[4], which ultimately assists in the preservation of body and immortality. We must understand that a condensed drop of sperm is a wonderful phenomenon. If transformed with proper knowledge, it can lead you to enlightenment. If abused, it can set you ablaze. Such is the

---

3 A treatise written by Shiva Goraksha on the conservation of vital energy and its subsequent transformation into divine energy by a yogic process.
4 'Vitality', the subtle energy produced through practice, especially the discipline of chastity (*Brahmacharya*).

power of the sexual drive. The purely yogic techniques given by Babaji Goraksha Nath, such as *vajroli*[5], *sahajoli*[6], and *amaroli*[7], must be cautiously practiced under the proper guidance. These are advanced techniques of yoga that deal with the transformation of sexual and other bodily fluids into spiritual energy.

Mercury, Magical Formula of Healing and Wholing

There are a lot of yogis spread over the Garhwal region of the Himalayas who practice the making of the alchemical *shivalinga* for their yogic practices and meditations. Mercury, when in a fluid state, represents the elusive mind and is difficult to grasp. It also has contents of sulphur and arsenic, which are poisonous. However, when that same mercury is solidified through an alchemical process, it represents the steady and still mind. The process of solidification expels all of the poisons in the metal and gives it a nectarine effect, which it radiates on the body and mind of the practitioner, arresting the aging process of his body cells.

In chemical terminology, mercury has the symbol Hg and is described and experienced as a very heavy liquid (quicksilver). This element cannot be divided but may be distilled at 370° C. It is a slow volatile liquid that evaporates gradually under the Sun's heat. In ancient times, it was both successfully and unsuccessfully used in the medical world, but due to the dangers of its toxicity, it was discarded. This was due to a lack of understanding regarding how to alchemically transform the poisonous effects to its nectarine effects after it is solidified. However, the art of extricating the poisonous sulphur and arsenic from the liquid substance and transforming it into a nectarine solidified mercury tablet has been known to Indian alchemists since the dawn of history. To grasp the unique and stunning potential of this metal, mercury

---

5   A *tantric* technique for men to transform sexual into spiritual energy.
6   A *tantric* technique for women to transform sexual into spiritual energy.
7   A *tantric* technique of auto-urine therapy.

needs to be understood in its alchemical aspect.

Now the difference between chemistry and alchemy is that the former does not acknowledge the idea of Divine play or Consciousness as the origin of creation and sadly regards consciousness as a by-product of matter. Alchemy on the other hand has its foremost concern with the spirituality of matter and tries to understand it as emanating from universal consciousness. So any immediate hopes of uniting the ideology of chemistry with alchemy is a far cry because chemistry only considers that which is tangible, and seen to the eye and perceptible to the senses. But alchemy is divine and takes the cosmic forces, for man and for matter, as the source of the manifestation of our worlds.

The pioneering yogi-alchemist experiences man as made of spirit who, by permutations and beautiful combinations, becomes the soul and then the mind, then the emotions and then the body. The chemist, on the other hand, looks to the material side of man and mistakes the effect for the cause, and in his mistaken identity he imagines the body to be the real self, and the consciousness an emanation from the body.

In the sacred compendium of the Nath yogis, the minerals and their evolved metals were considered to be connected to, and a part of the seven planets of our Sun's system. To begin with, gold was associated with Surya, the Sun; silver with Chandra, the Moon; mercury with Budha, the planet Mercury; copper with Shukra[8], the planet Venus; iron was associated with Mars; tin with Jupiter; and, lead with Saturn. Of course we are talking of alchemy and not gemology, but the precious stones of the Earth were also connected with the planets and their metals, e.g., ruby with gold and the Sun, pearl/moonstone with silver and the Moon, emerald with mercury and Mercury, diamond with copper and Venus, coral with iron and Mars, yellow sapphire with tin and Jupiter and the blue sapphire with lead and Saturn.

---

8 The planet Venus, symbolizes life and also the vital fluid.

The Alchemical Chart

Rishis	Marich	Attri	Parashara	Bhrigu	Bharadwaj	Angiras	Surya
Deities	Surya	Chandra	Budha	Shukra	Mangal	Guru	Shani
Planets	Sun	Moon	Mercury	Venus	Mars	Jupiter	Saturn
Metals	Gold and Mercury	Silver	Mercury	Copper	Iron	Tin	Lead
Gems	Ruby and Diamond	Pearl	Emerald	Diamond	Coral	Yellow Sapphire	Blue Sapphire

The Alchemy of Mercury as Trinity

There is a secret of opening up and expounding a metal by alchemical means. It is said in the secret doctrines of Goraksha Nath, that when metals are taken apart, they liberate a mercurial spirit, a sulphurous soul and a saline body. It is said that these three chemicals mercury as Shiva, sulphur as Vishnu and salt as Brahma constitute the *Trimurti* (mercury as trinity). Even plants emit these three principles of the body, soul and spirit. When we divide and lay open any plant, at first it exudes a mercurial spirit contained within the alcohol of the plants. Then the plant gives off a certain oily sulphurous soul, which can be sensed and is the essential oil of the plant. This would be like the *Bindu* or the procreative seed of the plant. Lastly the plant yields its basic salt. This is the salt that fixes the two spiritual volatile principles of spirit and soul which makes it a plant as it appears to us. The building sap and material are all included in the above description.

As the great masters of alchemy like Parashara, Hermes, Nagarjuna and Nitya Nath have confirmed, when you alchemically expose or lay open a metal after its purification, it releases the spirit of the metal and then its mind, followed by its procreative salty essence. It is said by the great alchemists and the people who I have been working with that all the various metals potentially exist in mercury just like a great tree exists in a seed. All metals can be absorbed into mercury and the same flowing mercury can be absorbed into other metals by processing with herbs, hot and cold fusion and mantras. This is one of the reasons why mercury is celebrated by all alchemy traditions as that which converts base metals into gold.

In the burning cauldrons of the Earth's bowels, all the metals are coagulated into the Earth's crust. They also exist in a state of fission and fusion, constantly stirred up by the central fire of the Earth and bound by its amalgamating salt of the mineral. As it rises further from the physical, it goes to the astral soul of sulphur, which is a partial fiery element of the soul of the minerals of the Earth. Then above it rises the bubbling and most volatile quicksilver known to us as mercury, which is the spirit of all the metals. We must bear in mind that to alchemically solidify mercury, we must not use just any available raw materials; the virgin mercury found in a cinnabar and natural ore is very pure and is the one to be used in the process of solidification, even though there is a great effort in removing the toxic sulphur and arsenic content. This is deeply in contrast to the base mercury found in the market because the nascent mercury is alive; it is much easier to coagulate and solidify virgin mercury because it contains more sulphurous and metallic properties that congeal it. The virgin mercury found in the mines has either a Solar (gold) or a Lunar (silver) inclination, or it is found in balance of the two constituents of gold and silver. This is most desirable for forming the sacred *shivalinga* of solid mercury. This balanced mercury is called the *Ardhnarishwar* or Hermaphrodite metal.

The magic of mercury is such that it is a metal in cold fusion liquid. The temperature is very low which makes it a superb agent and easy to use in the alchemy of metals. Mercury, at room temperature, is in its liquid state because its inner sulphur is in lesser proportion and its mercurial/quicksilver spirit is dominant. Mercury contains the four elements: the Earth represents its density, water its fluidity, sulphur its fire, and air its volatility. From these four magical qualities, only two may be normally perceived, namely its density and fluidity. The fire and the air are the mystic qualities, which the yogi uses to bring about a spiritually charged *shivalinga* of mercury.

The spiritual effects of mercury, when solidified, impact meditators and devotees through radiation. It has the power of purging minds of negative thoughts and raising the consciousness to tranquility. All this depends on how powerful the yogi in charge of the *shivalinga* happens to be. The kundalini qualities of mercury are that it is an up-streaming process and tends to rise as it goes through the physical, emotional and mental bodies. The works of the divine alchemist Goraksha Nath state clearly the remarkable qualities of purified mercury and have categorized its power of assimilation to eighteen basic *samskaras*, and further to twenty-two *samskaras* (impressions).

Magic of Mercury Solidification

Before we proceed to make a solidified mercury *shivalinga*, we must get down to purifying it and taking out its toxins of arsenic and sulphur. When certain salts are used to purify mercury, it becomes a powdery substance. It appears to be like a silvery veil when thrown on water, like a silver milky skin floating atop the surface. It is then reanimated into flowing mercury. When this process is repeated three times or more, they call it fainted mercury. Then a leeching of the burning arsenical sulphur takes place in the form of greasy black soot. After this, to solidify mercury, it is processed with concentrated herbal extract and mineral ashes, which are from plants of cold nature. The next process is killing the mercury, which then gives life to the practitioner. It itself takes on a nobler form through death. Then it is taken through a process of resurrection (in humans, akin to the self-resurrection of Yogavatar Lahiri Mahasaya, the Christ, and Gyanavatar Sri Yukteshwar). While performing each process, certain mantras have to be chanted and herbs infused to bring the proper impressions and *samskaras* of a truly spiritual product capable of awakening the yogi's evolutionary force.

Once mercury has been completely purified of its arsenic metallic sulphur, it takes on remarkable properties, because due to the removal of negativity and toxins, an empty space remains in the soul of the mercury where its memory can be housed. That is to say, the empty space in the mercury becomes its memory. This space is open to the receiving of impressions, emotions and even the motivation to walk and talk—but such cases are rare. This memory holds the spiritual charge and Shakti of the yogi who does the prana *pratishta*[9] (infusion of life-force kundalini) in the mercury *shivalinga* from which he later radiates this 'Earth Peace Through Self Peace' force for the welfare of all human beings. In a lesser sense, he also uses it to assist all practitioners of yoga in their meditation or to heal any obstacles that come in the path of meditation.

The Mystical Effects of Mercury

The making of the alchemical *shivalinga* is one of the main features, and the legacy left behind by the immortal Goraksha Nath. Its main purposes are as follows:

1. Transformation of sexual into spiritual energy
2. Separating the astral from the physical body
3. Awakening the kundalini
4. Used in *Yoga Vidya*, it rejuvenates body cells
5. Enhancing intellect (*buddhi*), as Mercury (Budha) is its planet
6. In *Yoga Vidya*, it results in expansion of consciousness

The mercury is considered to be the vital fluid of Shiva, and

---

9 To infuse life-force energy into a deity or a *shivalinga* and make it responsive to your prayer and yogic necessities.

correspondingly has potent effects on the physical and astral body such as transforming the sexual into spiritual energy, and vice versa. Silicon is considered to be the feminine element, and the unity of mercury with silicon promises conception and new life or *sanjeevani*, the power to raise dead cells to life, to rejuvenate body cells and thereby bring forth immortality. To reveal more than this in a book intended for the general public is not appropriate. In order to learn the deeper details of the science of immortality through mercury, a pupil must first approach the *ayurvedic* schools of teaching. When done with, he must learn from the appropriate yogic master this highly advanced alchemical science.

Yoga, The Alchemy of Total Transformation

I am here speaking of the yogic transformation of one's body and mind to its ultimate state of light, love and consciousness.

Yoga, the spiritual evolution of consciousness, has as such integrated within its womb the alchemy of total transformation. It reorients and transmutes our body and its chemistry. The ancient Nath yogis have passed down to us the legacy of how to create and mix our body energies of air (prana), fire (*tejas*[10]) and water (*ojas*) in the right way and finally transmute ourselves into radiant light, awaken our kundalini energy, and become enlightened.

The yogis and rishis were the most ancient of doctors too. They developed the science of *Ayurveda* (often called the fifth *Veda*), which bases its cures and remedies upon the three biological *doshas* (humours) of *kapha* (phlegm), *pitta* (bile), and *vata* (wind). They are the biological counterparts of the three elements of water, fire and air. If we go deeper into the science of yogic transformation, we will see that the vital fluids of our body gradually become *ojas*, the nectar of sustenance, the bile and its heat becomes *tejas*, the fire of kundalini and wind, which is *vata* becomes transformed

---

10 Yogic brilliance along with *ojas* and prana.

into prana, the 'Livingness' of life. When heightened and worked upon, the three vital essences speed up evolution. But in order to fully actualize the essence of our Beings, the yogi works on the seven vital essences of his being, Earth, water, fire, air, ether, mind and *Omkar*[11]. He climbs up the ladder of the elements, imploding and transforming in his meditation the grosser into the subtler and merging into the final nirvana, his natural state of Enlightenment.

Tattwas / Elements	Humors/ Doshas	Essences	Qualities	Truths
Nectar	Fluid / Kapha	Ojas	Nectar	Love
Kundalini	Bile / Pitta	Tejas	Kundalini	Light
Hamsa	Wind / Vata	Prana	Hamsa	Livingness

Now we shall go deeper and look into the Yogic Meditations, what the functions of the three essences are and how they may be developed and finally transformed to higher faculties to assist us in the process of self-realization.

---

11 I call *Omkar* the birthing hum of Creation. Before creation began, *Omkar* was smaller than the nucleus of the atom within which was contained the mind and matter of the universe. At the beginning of time, the *Omkar* burst forth with an inconceivable light and sound, and the creation was born in relative sequence.

Functions of Prana

Prana is the universal life force energy, which becomes individualized in each one of us. It is the life current of air, the healer and guiding intelligence behind all psycho-biological processes. It subdivides itself into the five constructive energies in our bodies, which are:

1. Prana - on the meditative level it governs the unfoldment of all higher states of awareness.
2. Apana - helps in the throwing out of all the toxins and negative elements of our body, it eliminating all waste
3. *Samana* - helps the body with all the digestion and assimilation
4. *Udana* - assists in all the metabolic activity of body and mind providing the balancing of physical, emotional and mental states
5. *Vyana* - is the life current which circulates all over the body and mind to give it health and Vitality

The sub-pranas are *devbatta, dhananjay, alumbusha, visvodhara,* and *krikara*[12] which assist in the minor functions of body maintenance. Prana in our deeper consciousness sustains us throughout our cycles of birth and death and rebirth imparting life to all the different bodies of our incarnations.

Development of Prana

Pranayama is the most effective way of developing prana. The fact of the situation is that man breathes 21,600 times in 24 hours. In order to increase his prana, he must conserve it and simultaneously generate it, and this is done by lengthening the breath so he takes less breaths in 24 hours, say 10,000 then he takes less till he gains the breathless state of samadhi, conserves his 21,600 life currents of breath and transforms them to keep his body cells in a spiritually magnetized condition, but here we are getting into the alchemy of prana, which

---

12 Triple sound of creation, preservation and dissolution. A. U. M.

shall be discussed later. Pranayama of course means the *Ayama* or the extension and cessation of prana by breathing in such a way that one's body and mind, filled with Pranic Oxygen, are saturated with Life and Light, so that there is no need to breathe; Prana ceases and breath stills. The body, mind and soul in samadhi find breathing superfluous and unnecessary. Pranayama, the *Ayama* of prana has been mastered and *Kevali* begins to operate. The process of Pranic Meditation here referred to goes by the name of Shiva-Shakti Kriya Yoga. It is an ancient meditation with pranayama used by the Great Nath Yogis and Sages of Yore. The Nath Kings of the Solar Dynasty passed it down through the corridors of time to our present humanity – a great gift for the evolution of our consciousness. The other practices of developing prana through meditations on space and sound are called 'Nada Brahm[13]' meditation. The Raja Yogic System of the Nath Yogis, *Koti Surya* Meditation, techniques of *Vajrayana*[14], *Anumeena Pranayama*[15], and other Raja Yoga systems, have Shiva Shakti Kriya Yoga as an integral practice.

Another system worthy of mention is the famous Hatha Yoga way of the Nath Yogis called *Anuloma-Viloma Pranayama*[16]. It is alternate nostril breathing. The right nostril breath is Ha (*tejas*, fire), the left nostril breath is Tha (*ojas*, water). Balancing both *tejas* fire of right and *ojas* water of left nostril increases prana (life energy).

Shiva-Shakti Prana Meditation develops prana and also purifies the vital fluids in the body, taking their psychic essence to the higher centres (chakras) in the brain to transform it into *ojas*. The *Khechari Mudra* is a great assistant in true pranic movement and in availing of the *ojas* and *Soma*. The Shiva-Shakti creates *tejas* and *ojas* to develop prana.

Koti Surya Meditation is done on the Super Nova explosion of a countless suns merging in the implosions. Consequently a great

---

13 The unheard sound of the Omkar during the Omkar Kriya.
14 The Lightning Path of which the Shiva-Shakti Kriya is the crest jewel.
15 A Nath yogic technique of internal pranayama.
16 Pranayama of alternate nostril breathing.

space of Nothingness is experienced and since *Akasha*/space is the mother of prana, wherever or by whatever means space is created in one's mind as consciousness, there shall be created prana. But this is an implosive way of generating the Universal Livingness force in oneself, and must not be practiced without the guidance of a True Master. Hence, the technique is not given and not advised. There are gentler meditations to create space in one's mind and body and as a result develop prana.

The combining of Raja Yoga and Bhakti Yoga practices develops prana. Raja Yoga is fire – *tejas* and Bhakti devotion is *ojas* and they combine well to produce the *Marut Prana* so dear to yogis for the attainment of samadhi, the contentless Consciousness called *Samrasya* or Total At-one-ment.

It is truly difficult to give an exact rendering of this transformation of *vata*, or wind, of the body into prana. It is life-force for spiritual development which transforms prana (by the process of Shiva-Shakti Kriya Yoga and Hamsa Yoga) into Divine Consciousness. As prana itself is used as a path in the process of the Ham-Sa breath chant as well as in the Shiva-Shakti, I am at a lack of words to make you understand how the path becomes the goal. An imperfect example would be like men of ice in an ice boat rowing down the river of prana towards the ocean, which is the goal. On reaching the Ocean of Godessence, the boatmen of ice, the river of prana and the Ocean of Godessence become one. But by the same token, this experience has already happened, only you weren't aware of it then; you are aware of it now. For each individual boatman, the time of his Now, his Enlightenment, is when ever the ice of his Ego melts to make him realize his oneness with his boundless ocean of Consciousness.

But to transform prana in its highest form of the immortal Life Energy, it needs to be married to the *tejas* of lundalini and united to *ojas* the nectar (*amrita*[17]). This fusion of kundalini as Light and nectar as Love is what enables the lifeforce of prana to be transformed into

---

17 The nectar of immortality that flows from the psycho-energetic center at the crown of the head (sahasrara-chakra) when it is activated by yogic means, transforming the physical body into a divine body (divya-deha).

a divine force: a hamsa breath, a Shiva-Shakti happening, which has the power to create higher samadhis (spiritual absorptions) dissolving deep seated conditionings in our consciousness. These conditionings form what is called the chain that binds us to the cycle of births and deaths. All glory be to the hamsa prana that forces us from the bondage of birth and death. This chain of karma is called "*Karma Shrinkala*[18]" which is dissolved by the practice of Shiva-Shakti Kriya and Hamsa Yoga, the way of transforming prana to free your flight into Divinity.

Transformative Process of Prana

A) By Shiva-Shakti Kriya Yoga purifying vital fluid and transforming it to *ojas*.
B) Transforming *tejas*, the gastric fire, to kundalini and visa-versa.

The transformative process of prana into *Marut Prana* and ultimately into Divine Consciousness is by working with prana in the *sushmna nadi*, in which the prana enters after the *Khechari Mudra* is mastered. As in Hatha Yoga, prana may enter by the Raj Yogic method of the *Unmani Avasta*, where the mind and breath are both still and the life current of prana transforms to immortal *Marut Prana* to enter in the subtler *vajra nadi*. Then, *Marut Prana* distilled by spinal movement and devotion, is transformed to a *savikalpa* consciousness and begins to move in the *chitnni nadi*[19], a channel connecting the Cave of Brahma, the third ventricle. Then by deeper states of yogic absorption, prana is transformed from *savikalpa* into *nirvikalpa* consciousness; it makes its presence felt in the b*rahma nadi*, the third and lateral ventricles called the Hamsa swan where true knowledge is experienced by the yogi. This means that at the samadhi levels of our evolution, not only does prana govern all our higher states, but it is transformed into those states of samadhi.

---

[18] The chain of events which binds the soul to the cycle of reincarnation.
[19] The third of the four psychic nerves.

Transformation	Avasta States	Channels of Expression
Prana	Khechari Avasta	Sushmana Nadi
Marut Prana	Unmani Avasta	Vajra Nadi
Chaitanya Prana	Savikalpa Samadhi	Chittni Nadi
Brahma Prana or Kundalini	Nirvikalpa Samadhi	Brahma Nadi

Thus the alchemy of the subtle transformation of prana into Consciousness happens by inner spinal ascent through ever more refined and evermore expanded spheres of consciousness until prana, with *ojas* and *tejas*, merge with the Divine Indweller at the core of our own Being. When prana transformed into kundalini becomes of the essence of our Indwelling Spirit, then we awaken to and become aware of our Divine Selves.

Before I proceed further I must clear the misconceptions, of some half-informed readers, that the yogi secures an immaculate body of light free from the ravages of time not for the sake of immortality but for the sake of God!

To be in a perfect rainbow-body, free from disease, decay and death to achieve God-realization, undisturbed in one body in one lifetime – what a grand transformation! What a splendid truth!

Functions of Tejas (Gastric Fire)

The quality of *tejas* is distilled from the psychic heat of the *pitta*/bile in us. *Tejas* is the subtle energy of gastric fire. It is the radiance of the vitality through which we digest our thoughts, our impressions and even the air we breathe. On the inner spiritual level, *tejas* governs the development and unfoldment of intuitions, precognition, clairvoyance, clairaudience, premonitions, and all psychic and perceptual phenomena. *Tejas* is important for the *Siddhis*, which are acquired during yogic practices. Unlike the *Ayurvedic* humours, which cause disease in excess, the yogic essences of prana, *tejas* and *ojas*, distilled and purified forms of wind, bile and phlegm, do not cause disease when increased or heightened by spiritual practices; they support one another.

Development of Tejas

The power of *tejas* is developed by control of speech – that is, avoiding aimless talking and gossip mongering. To intensify the power of *tejas*, observing periods of silence is very good. The energy of *vaak* (speech) is conserved; the sound is conserved and transformed into *tejas* radiance, the internal energy of insight. The goddess kundalini is said to be wearing a garland of sanskrit letters around her neck, implying it is effectively made of the resonant frequency of sounds/mantras. Therefore, mantra yoga[20] is an excellent way of developing *tejas*. The chanting of the *Gayatri Mantra* would go further to transform *tejas* into the kundalini energy itself; another king of mantras is the *Mrityunjai Mantra*, which awakes *tejas* into kundalini to give the practitioner *moksha*. Then we have certain *bija* seed mantras such as Om, Hrim, Ham Sah, Shrim Klim, which generate *tejas* in us. The process of Mantra Yoga is to begin chanting it loudly for a short time in *Vaikhari Vaak*. Then muttering it in *Madhyama Vaak*, a *sthavan* in a whispering sound. Then for a longer period, the mantra is chanted mentally as in *Pashyanti Vaak* and finally, when the *sadhak*[21] does it in *Para Vaak*, he dissolves into the Here-Now silence. Any mantra given by the Guru is more effective than on your own.

<u>Raj Yoga of the Nath tradition</u> - involves the focusing one's eyes on the flame called *Trataka*. This greatly helps to develop the inner fire

---

20 The yogic path utilizing mantras as the primary means of liberation.
21 A spiritual practitioner.

of *tejas*. The Patanjali Yoga also has similar practices of focusing the mind on an object.

Jnana Yoga[22] - The quality of *tejas* is generated through the Yoga of Knowledge using one's discrimination to distinguish the eternal from the transient and to know the unchanging truth behind the superfluous changing names and forms. This discrimination called *vivek buddhi* brings *tejas* to life.

The Practice of Self-Inquiry - Asking oneself – Who Am I? With singular attention, holding the mind to sharp inquiry generates *tejas*.

Transformation of Tejas

The heightened energy of *tejas* transforms it into kundalini energy. But when the kundalini rises in the spine, it requires adequate sperm-oriented *ojas* to sustain it; hence the importance of sexual control during the process of transformation. When *tejas* is moved in the spine by pranayama it converts itself to kundalini. So we can say that the combination of *ojas*, *tejas* and prana make a formative kundalini. The factor of mind absorption plays a crucial role while *tejas* is being transformed into the kundalini, which is the heart and Internal Fire responsible for all inner transformation.

Yoni Mudra of Nath Yogis

The Raj Yogis developed Hatha Yoga. The Nath Yogis focus on the inner eye of Shiva by a technique called the *Yoni Mudra* and the *Shanmukhi*. This develops tejas and transforms it to kundalini, which is the residual light-sound vibration lying coiled 3½ times around the *swayambhu linga* at the root of our spine. The three coils represent the Light Sound Aum: creation (A), preservation (U) and dissolution (M). The half-coil represents the crescent *Nada* sound of *Gandhar* and *Bindu*, the Light of the primeval atom. Yogis meditating on this inner sound of *Gandhar*, called the *Anhad Nada*, can solve

---

22 Yoga of wisdom.

the mystery of existence and reincarnation to reabsorb themselves with the Divine. Here the kundalini formed of the sanskrit alphabet of AUM liberates the practitioner from the cycle of rebirths and karma. Such is the power of the transformed *tejas* called kundalini. Kundalini is Yoga Shakti, developed by *Agni-Sar, Chalan*[23], *Jyoti Mudra*, Shiva-Shakti, and Kundalini Yoga. This power of yoga is necessary to catalyze the higher evolutionary potential within us. The energy is the Universal Life force and the key to yogic alchemy, but it has related and evolutionary results. Hence the importance of the Yogacharya Guru to guide the disciple on his evolutionary journey. This is the story of the spiritual evolution of one's consciousness.

Functions of Ojas

Although *ojas* is distilled and extracted from the reproductive fluid, it gives the human body the power to sustain itself and the endurance to progress not only sexually, but through all forms of exertion. It lines and lubricates our *nadis* and preserves the nervous system. *Ojas* gives us the basic capacity to defend our immune system against all disease and weakness. It gives resistance and endurance against disease. It absorbs the pranic life while breathing and helps store prana. Like the pranic force in the mind, it gives balance and movement. The *tejas* force assists the mind to perceive and determine. So the *ojas* force in the mind endows it with patience and endurance, giving it the strength to resist stress and disturbance. *Ojas* in our deeper consciousness is the power through which the soul produces all its various bodies. As Soul Consciousness, prana, *tejas* and *ojas* are Livingness, Light and Love.

Development of Ojas

Through *Brahmacharya*[24] *ahara*, Raja, Bhakti and Hatha Yoga.

---

[23] An exercise of the tongue done during practice of kechari mudra.
[24] The discipline of chastity for the channelisation of vital energy (prana) and transformation into ojas and tejas by the practice of Shiva-Shakti Kriya Yoga and Mahamudra.

Hatha Yoga - The control of sexual energy by the reduction of sexual activity and subsequent discharge of the vital fluid would enhance the *ojas* in oneself. The lesser the discharge of the seminal fluid, the more the chances of its transformation into *ojas*. Let me make it clear at the outset that the conservation of the sexual fluid is not a question of morality but of vital energy. Therefore in many yogic and tantric disciplines, *vajroli* (sex without orgasm) is taught, but this requires a high quality of continence both mentally and physically and is not practice which may be undertaken by the common lot. Instead a moderation in sexual indulgence is encouraged, and then the build up of *ojas* is slower but more easily attainable.

Raja Yoga – The process of *Prathyahara* is the withdrawal of the electrical flow of prana. The withdrawal of the senses from their objects as mentioned in the *Yoga Sutras of Patanjali*. When the five senses are inward-turned and controlled, the amount of energy expended through them is lessened and helps build up *ojas*. The abstinence of sensory indulgence in mass media entertainment is also a good conservation of *ojas* energy.

Bhakti Yoga or Devotional Bhajans – This is the best way to develop *ojas*, for this involves the sublimating and redirecting of our emotional energy inwards through the Love of God. Various forms of devotional worship and chanting, then service to Guru and the Divine are some of the ways that *ojas* may be built up in us. This helps the devotee to control his senses and his sexually transforming human emotions into Divine feelings.

Diet – The right diet for developing *ojas* is vegetarian and nutritive like milk, ghee and natural sweets, the whole grains such as wheat, rice, seeds, nuts, dry fruits and fresh fruits. There are *Ayurvedic* herbs and tonics that develop *ojas* such as *Chyvan Prash*[25] – *Amla*[26] (*Emblica officinalis*), *Ashvagandha*[27] (*Withania*

---

25 A tonic in India made of wild gooseberries (amla).
26 The Indian wild gooseberry.
27 Indian ginseng, an ayurvedic herb used for stress relief and various other remedies.

Somnifera), *Shatavari* (*Asparagus racemosus*), *Bela-Shailush*[28] (*Sida codifolia*). Then there are invigorating tonics such as *Shilajeet*, and gems like red coral and pearls crushed to make tonics for health. Gold and silver are used in the Alchemy of Total Transformation. Then two vital chemicals of mercury and sulphur are of a very enhanced nature and are used in the build up and rejuvenation of the body, which shall be discussed later.

Transformation of Ojas

This is variously called *Amrit* or *Soma*, the Shiva energy. It descends from the crown chakra, *sahasrara*, and feeds and sustains kundalini energy as she ascends up the spine and chakras. *Amrit* is the purified *ojas* energy of the subtle body, which has been extracted and distilled through the yogic practices of the Naths. It has been experienced as the subtler male energy, which, through surrender, *Isvar Pravidhan*, sympathy to fellows and protection (*raksha*), brings about the descent of grace, *Guru Kripa*. *Ojas* provides healthy bodies to sustain the evolution of the reincarnating souls, life after life. It transforms to nectar of immortality (*amrit*) and gives immortality.

Now the process of the transformation of body fluids, semen to *ojas* to nectar and finally to Love is given. By a healthy diet, the body fluids and semen, the vital fluid, is enhanced. Then a transformation of vital fluid into *ojas* takes place with the practice of *Pratyahara* – withdrawal of the vital fluid from the senses by *Brahmacharya*. A further purificatory transformation from *ojas* into nectar (*amrit*) takes place by Bhakti Yoga (devotion) with Love until the very devotion of Love transmutes the nectar of our body into the emotion of Love.

There is of course an advanced method for the transformation of sexual fluid to ojas and then to nectar (*amrit*). In the deep practices of yogic and tantric disciplines *vajroli* (sex without orgasm, reversal of the vital fluid to the spiritual energy) is taught but this requires a high quality of excellence both mentally and physically and is not

---

[28] Wood apple, a fruit loved by Lord Shiva.

for the masses. Therefore a moderation in sexual activity and sincere devotion (bhakti) is the slower but safest way for the transformation of *ojas* to *amrit* to *Prem* (Love).

The process of *pratyahara* (withdrawal of electrical flow) of *ojas, tejas, and* prana (essences of water, fire and qir) into the *sushumna* channel is done after the *Khechari Mudra* under the Guru's guidance. Here, a spiritual osmosis between the essences of *ojas*, vital fluid, *tejas* fire and pranic air takes place to rejuvenate into nectar of Love, Light of kundalini and Consciousness of prana.

Bhuta Shuddhi (Purification of the five Elements comprising our body)

First of all, the yogi engages in a process called *Deha Shuddhi*, the purification of his body. This is done by *Yogasanas* to keep the body fit and healthy, thereby maintaining a strong immune system. Simultaneously he eats the proper food called *Sattvic Ahar*[29]. The diet here varies from person to person depending on the Yogi's constitution – the *kapha, pitta* and *vata* proportions in him. Basically, without being over fastidious about diet, the yogi should predominantly eat vegetables, drink milk and eat fruits of the season, along with whole grain products. This will keep his body healthy. Drinking fresh lime and other citrus juices helps strengthen the nervous system and purify the body. The ideal quantity of food a Yogi should eat is scant: 50% food, 25% liquids and 25% empty stomach for *Saman Prana* to efficiently digest and convert the food he eats into energy.

Fasting once a week has been found is the best purifier of the body and eliminates much disease. The dietary system is rested and body renewed. Fasting is not starving, but a medically proven way to keep a healthy body and a clear mind. When you fast, your body fat and sluggishness is burned, keeping you healthy and alert; but when you starve this eats into your muscles and brings weakness,

---

29 A diet which is pure and predominantly of sarrva gunas.

which is not good. We must know when to stop and draw the line.

Advanced yogis, out in the caves and jungles meditating, do not always get food regularly, so they fast, and by certain *mudras* and pranayamas like the *Khechari*, *Seetali*[30] and *Sitkari* are able to assimilate the Solar Life-giving energy through the medullary plexus.

A healthy body depends upon three factors – circulation, assimilation and elimination. So the Yogi engages in good exercise of the bowels. *Basti*[31] and *Shakha Prakshalan* are effective yogic ways to cleanse the bowels with water.

The taking of preventive nutrients such as *Chavan Prash*, *Amla* and *Shilajee*t are anti-oxidant tonics that retard and later arrest the aging process of the body. Some of the *Ayurvedic* tonics and herbs, which retard the aging process of the body keep it healthy and pure are given as follows. The alkaline based tonics like *Gajar*/Carrots and grape seeds containing Vitamin E are also complimentary to longevity.

Let us go on to see where the *Shad Ripus* fit into the scheme of *Bhuta Shuddhi* and where the *Panch Kleshas*[32] fit. The *Shad Ripus*, or six obstacles of *kama* (lust), *krodh* (anger), *lobha* (greed), *moha* (attachment), *matsar* (jealousy), *abhimana mada* (pride), are very low order of emotions lodged in the *Kama Deha*[33] and their cleansing or transformation is done by wilful determination of *Yama*

---

30 Form of yogic pranayama where you breathe through the tubular shape of the tongue.

31 Hatha yogic technique of sucking water through the rectum, then abdominal churning and finally throwing it out.

32 Five afflictions of delusion (*avidya*/ignorance, asmit/thinking oneself to be a body and not the divine soul, raga/attraction, dvesh/repulsion, abhinivesh/clinging on to bodily existence and its temptation).

33 The body of desire.

(*Kul Dharma*[34]), *Niyama*[35] (*Kul Achara*[36]), Pranayama and Mantra Yoga.

A) *Chitta Shuddhi*[37] – (Cleansing five negativities of mind)

All this purification of the negativities of the mind is done till there is no-mind (*Unmani Avasta*) is obtained after the *Chitta* is cleansed. The *Chitta* is the lower desire mind, and the thinking mind and intellect called the *Mano-Buddhi-Ahamkar*[38]. The mind, intellect and ego also called *Suksham Sharir*, with its desires; the *Manas Sharir*, with its false identity; and *Karan Sharir*[39], with its *Ahamkar*[40] – I-am-ness and its Karmic Records – *Karma Shrunkhala*.

The Five Ignorances of *Chitta Shuddhi* are:

1. *Avidya* – Ignorance of the True Self
2. *Asmita* – Feeling of I-ness of body consciousness arises (the fallacy of mistaken identity of being body and not Soul)
3. *Raga* – Being attracted by objects of the five senses
4. *Dvesh* – Being repelled by objects of five senses.
5. *Abhinivesh* – The lust for bodily life. Innate urge for procreation of one's own species.

These five *kleshas* or obstacles are lodged in the causal body and their transformation may be done by self-directed discipline and self-directed study, by Kriya Yoga, Omkar Techniques and Mantra Yoga.

---

34 The behaviors and traditions of the family.
35 Self-restraint', the second limb of Patanjali's eightfold path, which consists of purity (shauca), contentment (samtosha), austerity (tapas), study (svadhyaya), and surrender to the Lord (ishvara-pranidhana).
36 Carrying out the behaviors and traditions of the family.
37 Mind purification (by meditation, mantras and chanting).
38 Mind, intellect and ego.
39 The causal body.
40 'I-maker', the individuation principle, or ego, which must be transcended; see also asmita, buddhi, manas.

B) *Nadi Shuddhi* – (Cleansing 72,000 Psychic Nerves)

This is done by pranayam. The different types of pranayam do different degrees of *Nadi Shodhan*[41]. To assist in the purification of psychic nerves, and the physical purification of the nerves, drinks of fresh lime and other citrus juices can be taken, which also act as a good nervine tonic.

Sun and Moon – The left nostril called the *Ida* is the moon's nerve source and the right nostril called the *Pingala* is the sun's nerve source. The left *Ida* moon nerve is connected with the *kapha* in our body and the right *Pingala* sun is connected with *pitta*. When we do the alternate nostril breathing called *Anulom-Viloma Pranayam*, these two humours of our body are balanced and distilled to *ojas* and *tejas* respectively. Then by the advanced process of the Shiva-Shakti Kriya, that *ojas* and *tejas* is further purified into nectar and Light. This transformation of the grosser into the finer elements I have experienced during the course of my *sadhana*. The *Pranava* and *Omkar Sadhana* is essential (according to *Goraksha Paddhati*) in transforming *ojas*, *tejas* and prana into Love, Light and Livingness Joy.

Nadi Shodhana

Nadi Shodhana is a classical way of transforming the body humours of fluids, bile and wind into *ojas*, *tejas* and prana. The left *Ida* moon nerve is connected with the body fluids in our body, the right *Pingala* sun nerve with gastric fire, bile, and the central *sushumna* with the breath. When we do the alternate nostril breathing called *Anuloma-Viloma*, the three humours in our body are balanced and distilled. Vital fluids turn to nectar, gastric fire turns to Light, and breath turns to life. By advanced practice of Shiva-Shakti *Anusandhan*, *Omkar Kriya*, and *Mahamudra*, - *ojas*, *tejas* and prana are evolved into nectar, light and life.

---

41 'channel cleansing', the practice of purifying the conduits for higher evolutionary states of Yoga, especially by means of breath control (pranayama).

Anuloma Viloma Pranayama - The Magical Formula of Purification

This is to purify the 3 humours in the body and is done as follows.

Meditate on the Primeval Guru Shiva-Goraksha Babaji in the solar heart; contemplate on the seed mantra Yam of the Wind element. Then keeping your attention on the solar heart centre, do the following meditation:

1. Inhale through the left nostril, mentally repeating the mantra YAM 4 times.
2. Hold the breath and repeat the mantra 16 times,
3. Exhale the breath, saying mentally the mantra 8 times.
4. Then raise the Agni (fire) from the navel towards the heart.
5. Inhale through the right nostril mentally repeating the seed mantra of fire RAM 4 times.
6. Hold breath for 16 repetitions
7. Exhale through left nostril, mentally repeating RAM 8 times
8. Contemplate the moon (Chandra), inhale through left nostril repeating the seed syllable THAM 8 times.
9. Hold breath 16 repetitions while in the forehead.
10. Exhale through right nostril while repeating the seed syllable LAM 8 times.

This pranayam is best done in Siddhasana.

The other ratios of this pranayam are - 8:32:16, 6:24:12, 5:20:10, 4:16:8, although the shorter you make your pranayam, the safer it is.

The Hermetic Mysteries

Shiva Goraksha Babaji was the one who taught the ancient mysteries to one of His disciples; who in the east is known as the Brahma-Rishi Prashara, and in Greece was known as Hermes. These mysteries were later taken to Greece and were called the Hermetic mysteries. They spread to Europe and also simultaneously to China, Russia and Mongolia. In fact, for a clearer understanding, Parashara or Hermes is the informing spirit of the mystery planet Mercury. Therefore, the great initiate Parashara and Hermes are connected not only with the planet Mercury but also with its fluidic metal called Mercury. Mercury is the magical fluid which goes by the name of quicksilver, the art and the magic of the consolidation of which forms one of the pillars of the Hermetic mysteries. Solidified mercury rejuvenates life and expands the consciousness of those who know its mysteries.

In the year 1910, the Supreme Master Shiva Goraksha Babaji initiated our mighty solar Vivasvat Manu into one of the incomprehensible mysteries of the Divine. Babaji also made corrections with the planet Mercury and with the Hermetic mysteries and their magical formulas. The mantras, which were formulated by the Sage Parashara, the Indian Hermes, were difficult for western disciples and initiates to pronounce and they usage became the great challenge for the western world to succeed in. Consequently, the mother mantra called The Omkar or Om was put as the final symbol of the great deep from which sprang forth the Hermetic and all mysteries relating thereto. The word Om gives us the vital clue that the Hermetic mysteries also began in India. They later spread to Greece and Rome and Europe and China and the world at large, the outer names being different but the inner essence being the same.

The Rectifications

The first rectification commanded by Shiva Goraksha Babaji was that He told Hermes to correct the grand symbol of the Hermetic Hierophant, that the jewel in the lotus of his crown chakra should not be red but should represent the Quicksilver colour of Mercury.

The second rectification which was made was to enlighten disciples that the five elements of Earth, Water, Fire, Air and Æther must be shown as the subtler interpenetrating and enveloping the grosser element and not surrounding the initiate as is presently depicted. This mistake can have dire consequences, which may lead the disciple to confuse vibrations and subtlety of one element's relation with the succeeding element and therefore, may lead to a confusion of mantras, which are to be applied to each of the elements in their proper sequence.

The third rectification was that the artefact of *Ardh-Narishwar*, which means half Shiva and half his feminine Shakti, should be given more importance in the balancing of the left and right brain of the disciple. This is the form of Shiva - the male principle, and Shakti - the feminine principle, the intellectual and the emotional. After the ancient symbology of *Ardh-Narishwar*, there is an interesting story that Parashara, the Indian Hermes, descended from the heavens to unite with Matsyagandha, the fish women of the waters, representing Aphrodite, the Greek goddess of the water form. From the union of the Parashara with Matsyagandha was born the Guru Vyasa[42] representing Mercury and wisdom. Later in history, this symbol was taken from India and grafted in Greek mythology where they told the story of Hermes and the Goddess Aphrodite who united to balance the male-female principles of creation and like India's Ardhinareshwar artefact were represented as Hermaphrodite, the half-man half-woman symbol. This symbol was commanded to be higher up in the hierarchy of the Hermetic mysteries, which is not so as of today. This must be done immediately and exchanged with the top symbol of the man and woman in human harmony and relationship.

Presently, there is a plethora and a growing number of self-styled "masters" who want to teach the the *Parasharic* mysteries and the schooling of the body, mind and soul. But I would like

---

[42] 'arranger', the name of several great sages, but specifically referring to Veda Vyasa, who arranged the Vedic hymns in their current form and who also is attributed with the compilation of the Puranas, the Mahabharata, and other works, including the commentary on the Yoga-Sutras of Patanjali, the Yoga-Bhashya.

to caution and to guide the new age people that three things are absolutely necessary if one is to delve into the magical mysteries of the solidification of liquid mercury, of Parashara the Rishi and Hermes the high Initiate, all three being connected in the deeper alchemical sense. The first would be to find a true Master (Satguru Yogi), the second would be to master the art of consolidation of mercury (*Paras-mani*), and the third factor would be the successful application of this magical mercury to bring about an Immaculate Body coupled with self-realization. I have given a fairly good idea of how mercury is processed in the pages gone by.

Because of a lack of patience and an attitude of humility to learn from the eastern Masters of India, the magical mysteries of the Parashara/Hermes' secret doctrine must remain a closed chapter until sufficient humility is cultivated and magnetism of the disciple increased so that he may come in the divine aura of the true Master. Of the many people who practice the art of the solidification of mercury, the art of weather-magic and body-immortality, they succeed only to a partial extent and then fall back to square one. The new age enthusiasts are very intrigued by the magical formulas of the mysteries, which are no longer available to the western word in the potency of their seed sounds called mantras. So they are compelled to concoct false intonations, feeble invocations and ineffective spells because they lack the support and spiritual charge of the ancient sages and founding fathers of the science.

Tantra holds the original keys

The original name for the magical feats is called *siddhis* and the original name for the magical chants is called mantras. The whole gamut of the Solar mysteries, Hermetic mysteries, Martian mysteries, Venusian mysteries and many more are detailed in the various tantras and secret doctrines of India. But the initiates of the new age like Aleister Crowley and Franz Bardon were unable to bring about their effective and constructive usage because of the lack of the contact with the True Masters and the non-availability of the true magic formulas called mantras. Now instead of banging one's head on a brick wall and trying to squeeze out of the Hermetic mysteries the magic and *siddhis* by pseudo chants, it would be better to go to the land of India and search where the Hermetic mysteries originated and are still preserved in papyrus scrolls wrapped up and kept in the sacred monasteries of India. By originated I don't only mean literature, but the living fact and the operating skills to bring Divine magic into the actual realms of our day to day lives so that they may help and assist in the healing and evolution of humanity at large. There are people in the length and breadth of the land of India who perform true magic and not for the sake of self-aggrandizement or any outward show, but they work silently for the alleviation of the obstacles which confront a pilgrim's progress and for the spiritual progress of humanity.

I would like to end with a very interesting note that one of the highest forms of the magical treatise of the ancient yogis of India goes by the name of Kriya Yoga, which Shiva Goraksha Babaji gave to the world as a soul-saving science. If this divine science is practiced with sincerity, it is bound to give you the knowledge, not only of the Hermetic mysteries, but of all the mysteries of the world. The word magic has been grossly abused in these modern times. The true meaning of magic is The Great Spirit.

When a Master performs the sacred magical art, all the *siddhis* (magical powers) and magical formulae stand before him with folded hands. But when a student who is trying to be a siddha, aspires after these magical powers called *siddhis*, then the *siddhis* may grant their hand of blessing on his head.

Now here lies the danger, for the *siddhis* and nature spirits, can be volatile in nature, and turn against the aspirant performer of this magic art called *siddhi*. This could lead to serious karmic repercussions. Therefore, amongst the highest initiates, it is said that we leave the *siddhis* alone, and wait for them to spontaneously serve the grand Siddha. Many a wannabe-siddhas and lesser magician has been tempted and fallen into the trap of acquiring magical powers and *siddhis* for self-aggrandizement. Consequently, they have fallen from grace and have had to struggle back upon the purely spiritual path.

So here's a warning for the neophyte, student and aspirant: do not go after evanescent magical *siddhis*. You must practice pure spirituality such as Raja Yoga, Kriya Yoga, and/or Bhakti Yoga, and wait for these *siddhis* to automatically sprout their fruits from your own soul power, just as mangos appear fully ripened in their season. In this way the *siddhis* and magical powers must be a slave to the Master adept. The aspiring adept and neophyte must not hanker after magical powers nor *siddhis*.

Hear this, oh disciples! For this is the voice of the Silence from the Himalayan yogis of the ancient of days.

The Solar Mysteries
Who is Surya, Our Spiritual Sun?

The spiritual sun is the seventh sun behind our Lord, the Sun. All the Suns are enveloped and interpenetrated by It; the subtler interpenetrating and enveloping the grosser, breathing the Hamsa life into the vastness of creation, animating every atom of our universe. Surya, the Central Spiritual Sun is the Godessence enshrined in every Human Soul. The Sun is the fact that enlivens the Livingness of Humanity.

Below are given the names of the Seven Spiritual Suns called the supreme Manus or Kings right down to the progenitors of our humanity, in descending order:

The seventh and highest is the Lord Shiva himself.
The sixth next to him is Shiva-Goraksha Babaji.
The fifth is Marich, the ancient Rishi.
The fourth is his son, Kashyapa Aditya.
The third is the spirit of our sun, Vivasvat Manu.
The second is his son, Vaivasvat Manu of the fifth root race.
The first is Savarni Manu, the king of our future sixth root race.

The Manus and Kings who are the powers of our spiritual sun further divide themselves into smaller and smaller rulers, administrators and caretakers of our human race, our communities, right unto the heads of our individual families. In the inner spiritual world, this is a subconscious and well-formed administrative system. Now each individual in any human race, past, present and future, is destined to evolve - even if it takes millions of years of lives and deaths - to the head of a certain community, a race and ultimately a humanity, and to be called the embodiment and Manu, that is Spiritual King, who represents that community race or humanity. This is done through the science of Surya Yoga, the evolutionary path of the Solar Initiate.

The Sun Our Immediate Deva

The sun is the one in whom we live and move and have our being. In Sanskrit, the word *Deva* means "shining one." We drink its life and float in its radiant plasma. All human beings are saturated with the life giving essence of the Sun. Neither humans nor plants would survive without its light and energy. Therefore the sun (Surya) is our immediate *Deva* (God) whom we must love, adore and worship every day to lead and guide us to the Supreme Lord God! The virtues of the Sun qualify it to be our *Deva* and immediate archangel who sustains all life on earth.

The life of every living creature on our planet is ultimately dependent on the Sun. It is the primary source of nourishment, responsible for life itself. Similarly, it is our lineage to the divine source of knowledge via the cosmic entity of prana. This is the universal life force that awakens us and evolves us to our divine indwellers.

The ancient Indian solar technique of pranic healing connects the solar heart of the individual and the giver of this life-energy for our planet, the Sun. This is the spiritual absorption of pranic healing-light through the act of submerging oneself in the cosmic current that sustains the whole of creation. From the astral body, the entire network of subtle nerves (*nadis*) and physical nerves are fed with the luminosity of pranic light.

The solar prana is the link between our limited consciousness and "He About Whom Naught May Be Said." That is why I say that our only immediate *Deva* is the Sun, the source of pranic life, the very fabric of the universe that leads us to the Non-being Essentiality by which creation itself is sustained. This is the Truth with which Mahavatar Babaji Goraksha Nath has enlightened saints and sages since time immemorial.

The Science of Bioluminescence
Solar Osmosis

Prana is described in the Indian yogic texts and treatises as "the breath of life" or "life force energy"; a subtle element or entity underlying the fabric of all of creation, animating sentient beings with consciousness and life. It is the vibratory power that sustains us throughout our cycles of reincarnation, imparting life to all the different bodies we incarnate in. It is our soul-potential, expressed in the human being as one's individual vitality. Knowledge of this majestic undercurrent and the science of channelling its awesome power, for pranic-healing and advancement along the evolutionary path to enlightenment, is the most cherished undertaking, unlocking the inner mysteries of soul and Divinity.

Prana is "life" and pranayama is the yogic extension or control of the living impulse animating every atom of our universe. Prana is conveyed to our planet from the light of the Sun and congealed in material form. Thus, for our planetary system, the Sun is the source of prana. Likewise, in the course of pranic-healing, prana may be most effectively availed of through the rays of our Sun since the highest concentrations of prana are found in sunlight. Prana is the life of oxygen, however this life-force is something more subtler than oxygen. Just as photosynthesis occurs in plants, a bioluminescence occurs in our bodies through the focused absorption of sunlight whereby we inhale and ingest the salubrious rays of the sun through the medulla oblongata called "the Mouth of God," and the third eye of Shiva, thereby rejuvenating ourselves.

India's Influence of Solar Pranic-healing on the World

Pranic Healing is originally an Indian science and prana is a Sanskrit word meaning Universal Life-force Energy mentioned in the yogic text and *Vedas* (e.g., *Atharvaveda*). Famed Chinese philologist and author of *Wisdom of India* Lin Yutang once said: "India was China's teacher in religion and imaginative literature and the world's teacher in philosophy. A trickle of Indian religious spirit overflowed to China and inundated the whole of Eastern Asia."

The techniques of pranic healing are yogic in origin, not Chinese or Filipino as some have been lead to believe. In India, Pranic Healing was originally known as *Prana Chikitsa*, and the *Reiki* technique was called *Sparsha Chikitsa* meaning, "healing by touch". Both techniques of *pratyaksha* and *uproksha chikitsa* (hands-on and distance healing), have been used by the people of India to heal themselves and others, long before *Reiki* and the later Pranic Healing came into existence.

The simple fact of the matter is that the science of Pranic Healing migrated from India to China, Japan, the Philippines, and other parts of the world where, over a period of time, it took on new names and forms; *Prana Chikitsa* was given the name "Pranic Healing", *Sparsha Chikitsa* was given the name "*Reiki*." This is like putting old wine in new bottles. Some contemporary *Reiki* healers claim this knowledge to have been taken from the *Lotus Sutras* of Gautama the Buddha, who lived in India in 500 BCE.

Retarding the Aging Process
The Third Eye Centre

Though prana is inhaled and ingested through the lungs and skin, the greatest amounts of pranic energy are taken in through the astral third eye centre (*agnya chakra*), an area referred to in yogic parlance as the Cave of Brahma. Physically the third eye is the third ventricle, a hollow space located in the centre of the brain. Aside from the ingestion of prana at the third eye centre, stimulation of this area of the brain helps in improving functions of the endocrine system such as metabolism, blood pressure, digestion, functions of the immune system, and balance of hormones. It is also linked to the aging process, which is retarded and even arrested during the advanced techniques. This is, however, a result of the luminosity of prana, and not the manipulated functions of the endocrine system.

Absorption of sunlight and prana into the third eye centre also affects the secretion of melatonin in the pineal gland, a hormone activated during deep sleep and directly linked to the amount of sunlight a person is exposed to. Melatonin decreases in production after youth and eventually stops with old age. Therefore, the practice of Surya Yoga, by increasing production of melatonin, improves the body's natural capacity to heal itself during deep sleep, even in old age.

> *Healing the apparent self*
> *Of the ignorance of the true self*
> *Is the ultimate source of all healing*
>
> — Yogiraj Siddhanath

Alchemical Mercury *Shivalinga*
In Honour of Shiva-Goraksha Babaji

At a convocation held on the auspicious day of *Maha Shivaratri*, the Hamsa Yoga Sangh inaugurated the Earth Peace Temple at the Siddhanath Forest Ashram near Pune on the 8th of March, 2008.

The Earth Peace Temple has been established to bring about unity and abiding peace amongst all peoples of the Earth. We teach no religion. People from all climes and times, races and religions are welcome with open arms. This is a closely guarded mystery vortex.

The temple houses the world's largest solid (*akhand*) mercury *shivalinga*. Mercury when purified and brought to a solid state is referred to as the elusive 'Philosopher's Stone' or '*Paras Mani*'. Meditating in the radiance of this *shivalinga* rejuvenates and transforms the meditator. Its nectar-like effects have been experienced by meditating Nath yogis since time immemorial and used for *kaya-kalpa* and *sanjeevani* (rejuvenation).

The creation of this type of alchemical mercury shivalinga is a closely guarded secret of the Indian spiritual culture blessed by Shiva Goraksha Babaji. This rare *shivalinga* is now ours to avail of and to use for the purpose of Earth Peace Through Self Peace.

Over the past thirty years I, along with my wife Shivangini, have with loving care in the gentle valley of Sita Mai, set up this powerful centre for spiritual-seekers. Disciples and evolved souls from all over India and the world come to learn the evolutionary techniques of Babaji's Kundalini Kriya Yoga.

The Ultimate Healing is Realizing God
The Ultimate Magic is Knowing God
The Ultimate Yoga is Becoming God

Yogiraj Siddhanath

CHAPTER 21

THE MANUS AND MANAVANTARS
THE COSMOLOGY OF THE MANUS

Vaivasvat Manu, the son of Surya (Vivasvat Agni), and the saviour of our race is infused with the seed of life physically through Brahma and spiritually by Shiva Goraksha Babaji, the Supreme Manu (ref. *Goraksha Rahasaya*). Shiva divided himself into two Beings and both remained complete, one as the Incomprehensible Nothingness and the other, Shiva Goraksha Babaji for the ceaseless involution-evolution and ultimate nirvana of humanities. He enters into the relativity of all creation through the Lightless Light which lights that light which lights the light of all our souls. This great sacrifice, though being in the core of every electron, still remains free from it. An infinitesimal portion of Himself further descends through Brahma to the Sages of the Fire Mist, the mind-born sons, and works through them at the ninth level of initiation.

Rig Veda / Shiva Rudra

The Supreme Manu and Great Yogi Shiva Goraksha-Babaji, the forefather of all adepts in esoterism is one of the Greatest Kings of the Divine Dynasties. He is called "The Earliest and the Last!" and is the patron of the third, fourth and fifth root races in His partial aspect. For in His earliest character, He is Ascetic-Dig-Amber clothed with the elements. Then he is Tri-Lochana (the three-eyed), Panchanan[1] (the five-faced) - an allusion to the past four and present

---
1 A name for the five headed Shiva.

fifth Aryan Root Race. Though five-faced, He is only four-armed as the fifth race is still alive. He is the "Great Beyond-Time" and Saturn is his partial aspect of Time, as Saturn-Kronos[2]. His *Damru* in the shape of an hour-glass shows that He is the Great Beyond-Time who also holds the *Trishul*, meaning the triple-forked-lightning. With it, He creates causation, space and time through His Shakti, the Great Mother Mataji. He is depicted of having cut off Brahma's fifth head leaving him with only four; it is an allusion to a certain degree in cosmic initiation, and also to the races. Shiva in His infinitesimal aspect is also called Panchanan, the five-faced of the fifth root race, who will hand over the sixth root race to the six-faced Kartikeya as Sanata-Kumara, the Lord of our World, under whose guidance the Lord Vaivasvat Manu and Savarni Manu shall be working and blessing the fifth and sixth root races respectively.

This third root race coincides with the coming of the Sages of the Fire Mist (Shiv-Kumaras) with Sanat Kumar, an aspect of Shiva Goraksha Babaji, to establish the spiritual hierarchy in our world system. This is the duration of time whence the Devas and secondary gods descended from the celestial spheres to marry the daughters of men to thereby improve the genetic evolutionary process of humanity. A good example is when Divine Parashara (Hermes) married a human girl called Satyavati. The reverse was when Divine Ganga married King Shantanu, father of Bhisma, the ultimate warrior of *Mahabharta*.

Creation of Sacred Fires

Earth and Man are a product of the three fires whose three names in Sanskrit are *Pavaka* - which is electric fire, *Pavamana* - which is solar fire, and *Suchi* - which is fire by friction. In esoteric explanations, Brahma the Cosmic Being had his eldest son Agni Abhimanin[3] married to one of Daksha Prajpati's daughters called Swaha. (In the metaphysical sense "The fire of friction" means the union

---

2 The planet connected with time.

3 Name of ancient fire god married to Svaha from who there are three fires, Pavak, Pavaman and Shuchi.

between Abhimanin, which is *buddhi*, the sixth principle of intuition, and Swaha, which is *manas*[4], the fifth principle of mind; the fifth merging into the sixth *buddhi* and becoming one with *Atma*, the seventh and highest principle. In the physical sense, the fire of friction between Abhimanin and Swaha relates to the creative spark or germ which, fructifies and generates us human beings who are the lesser Manus or Manus in the making. The three sons of surpassing brilliance produced by the two were *Pavaka* - the electric fire, *Pavamana* - the solar fire, and *Suchi* - the fire by friction.

In the Indian pantheon, the three brilliant sons, who were the three fires, were cursed by the sage Vashista to be born again and again upon this earth. This apparent curse was a blessing in disguise to humanity, for upon it was made all the progress, progenation and evolution of the evolving races on our Earth.

Daksha and Santatii[5]

The name Daksha means the adept and intelligent Sage with an undercurrent of Creative Power. He is the son of Brahma and Aditi, agreeable to other versions a self-born power. He is the chief of the *Prajapatis* (Lords or Creators of Beings). *Vishnu Purana* says, "In every kalpa, Daksha and the rest are born and absorbed. Rig Vedas says, "Daksha sprang from Aditi and Aditi from Daksha" – a reference to the eternal cycle of rebirth of the same divine essence, a True Sacrifice repeated for the evolution and redemption of humanity and Santatii, meaning its progeny.

So it goes to show that all these ancient spiritual beings were not fictitious but embodiments of the scientific elements of creation and were creators themselves.

---

4 'mind', the lower mind, which is bound to the senses and yields information (vijnana) rather than wisdom (jnana, vidya).
5 Offspring.

Sanat Kumar (Lord of our World)

This Sage of the Fire Mist is the present Jaggan Nath. He is also one of the great Manus who has taken upon himself to look after the vast numbers of humanities and their souls to evolve and to round them off and to hand them over to the next seed Manu. This is the stature of the work that Kumar Kartikeya will do as a King Manu and hand it over to the next seed Manu called Ganapati (meaning, The Lord of Humanities). Sanat Kumar has crossed the ninth level of initiation, which none can give but is an incomprehensible mystery. The eighth degree Sages of the Fire Mist ultimately evolve to this status, which puts them on the level of the "Lord of the World," an office that is held first for the shorter period of a first or second Lord on one world and when that has been achieved, for the longer responsibility of the third upon some other world.

The task of the third Lord of the World is far greater than these of the first and second Lords. Therefore, it is his duty to round off satisfactorily that period of evolution, and to deliver over countless millions of souls and evolving souls into the hands of the seed Manu who will be responsible for the souls during the inter-planetary nirvana. This is most probably the *Pralaya*[6] at the end of *kalpa* and not *manu-antar* (the gap between the reign of a seed and a root Manu) and will hand them over in turn to the root Manu of the next globe.

The third Lord of the World, having fulfilled this duty, takes another initiation entirely outside our world and its hierarchy, attaining the level of "The Silent Watcher." This is the tenth degree initiation on par of that of a solar planetary creator (Brahma). In that capacity He remains on guard for the whole period of the round, meaning the whole septenary world cycle of the evolution of humanity; and it is only when the Life-wave has again occupied our planet and is again ready to leave that He abandons his strange self-imposed task, handing it over to His successor.

---

[6] Partial or total delusion through cataclysms and/or holocausts.

Sacrifice of the Sages of the Fire Mist

The fire Devas, the Rudras, the *Kumaras*[7], the Virgin Angels (Michael, Gabriel, etc), the Divine Rebels as misnamed by the Jews and the Church are the Sages of the Fire Mist. But the *sanatana dharma* and yoga say that these lofty Beings preferred the curse of incarnations and long cycles of times that existence and rebirths to seeing the misery of those beings, evolved as shadows out of their brothers through the semi-passive energy of their too spiritual creators.

Hence tradition shows the Celestial Yogis offering themselves as voluntary victims in order to redeem humanity; to endow him with human affection and spiritual aspirations. To do this they had to give up their natural status and, descending on our globe, take up their abode on it for a whole cycle of a *Maha Yuga*, thus exchanging their impersonal individualities for individual personalities – and the bliss of nirvana / *moksha* for the curse of terrestrial life.

The true meaning of this that those Divine Yogis who underwent this trial or sacrifice, were prepared by Lord Shiva for even a higher responsibility in the world and cosmic order. For a greater Bliss unwanted or wanted but which was to become their ultimate State of Being.

Manus the Divine Kings

Our Supreme Sun, sitting on his *Surya Rath Simhasana*, which means the bejeweled fire chariot-throne driven by seven splendid white horses, each representing an important planet of our solar system, rides through the twelve signs of the zodiac, dispensing justice and propelling evolution to human and celestials alike. The four wheels represent the four gods Yama for earth (death), Varuna for water (regeneration), Kubera for fire (life) and Indra for aerial-life force (prana).

---

7 A youthful man from the age of sixteen to twenty-one.

The gods are the turning wheels of time of the chariots which are called the Rings-Pass-Not, the effects of which no mortals, except divine yogis, may transcend. This is clearly the *Merkabah*, the fire chariot-throne described variously in other schools of thought. There is more than one *Merkabah* operating at various levels, enthroned upon the *Cosmic Merkabah* is the supreme Shiva Goraksha.

King Vaivasvat Manu the son of Surya (called Vivasvat Agni) and the Saviour of our Race is connected with the Seed of Life both physically through Brahma and spiritually through Shiva, The Supreme Manu.

A Manu is the Spirit of Shiva in Humanity, or a race or a sub-race or the entirety of all humanities past, present and future in a day of Brahma (*kalpa*) or the entire life of Brahma (*maha kalpa*). Each cycle of humanity is represented by a personification called the personal King Manu of that sub-race, race or humanity, leading up to the entire humanities of all the *maha kalpa* whose Manu is Brahma (Swayambhu) himself.

The Manus, The Indras, The Seven Rishis

The reason why I am giving these details in this book is because Babaji is Shiva and hence the very essence of the above mentioned Manus and Rishis and celestial host.

In the *Vayu Purana*, in the chapter on *manavantars*, here Lomaharshana tells the sages about the various *manavantars* (eras). You will remember that each day of Brahma is called a *kalpa* (cycle) and there are fourteen *manavantars* in each *kalpa*. Each *manavantar* is ruled over by a Manu and lasts for a duration of 306 million 720 thousand years. The gods, the seven great sages and the individual who holds the title of Indra change office from one manavantar to another. In the present *kalpa*, six *manavantars* have already passed. We are in the seventh Vaivasvat *manavantar*.

The first Manu was Swayambhu at the beginning of our *kalpa*. *svayambhuva* means "the self-born." During this Manu's reign, the records of the corresponding seven sages have been lost.

The second Manu was Svarochisha. Then the Indra who ruled heaven was Vaidha and the seven great sages were Urjja, Stambha, Kashyapa, Bhargava, Drona, Rishabha and Angira.

The third Manu was Outtana.

The fourth Manu was Tamasa. Then king Shibi held the title of Indra in heaven; the names of the seven great sages were Kavya, Harsha, Kashyapa, Prithu, Atreya, Agni and Jyotirdhama.

The fifth Manu was Raivata. Vibhu was the Indra of this period and the seven great sages were Poulastya, Vedavahu, Yajuh, Hiranyaroma, Vedashri, Bhargava and Urddhavahu.

The sixth Manu was Chakshusha. The title of Indra was held by Manojava and the seven great sages were Havirdhana, Sudhama, Vashishtha, Viraja, Poulastya, Poulaha and Madhuratreya.

The seventh Manu Vaivasvat is the king of our present fifth root race and this is the seventh *manavantar* of the present *kalpa*. Purandara holds the office of Indra and the seven great sages are Vishvamitra, Jamadagni, Bharadvaja, Sharadvata, Goutama, Atri, Vasumana and Vatsari.

There will be seven more *manavantars* in the future before the end of the *kalpa*.

The eighth Manu of the sixth root race will be Savarni. The title of Indra will be bestowed on Vali, the son of Virochana. The seven great sages then will be Galava[8], Bhargava, Dvaipayna, Kripa, Dipitimana, Rishyashringa and Ashvatthama.

---

8 Ancient rishi after whom the city of Gwalior was named.

The ninth Manu will be Merusavarni or Dakshasavarni. Adbhuta will hold the title of Indra then. The seven great sages will be Skanda, Medhatithi, Vasu, Jyotishmana, Dyutimana, Havyavahana, Sutapa and Vasita.

The tenth Manu will be Dharmasavarni. The title of Indra will be held by Shanti and the seven great sages will be Havishmana, Sukriti, Atri, Apamurti, Pratipa, Nabhaga and Abhimanyu.

The eleventh Manu will be Bhavasavarni (alternatively known as Rudrasavarni). The Indra will be Vrisha and the seven great sages will be Havishmana, Vapushamana, Varuni, Bhaga, Pushti, Nishchara and Agniteja.

The twelfth Manu will be Ritasavarni. The title of Indra will vest with Ritadhama and the seven great sages will be Kriti, Sutapa, Tapomurti, Tapasvi, Taposhayana, Taporati and Tapomati.

The thirteenth Manu will be Rouchya. Divaspati will be the Indra and the seven great sages will be Dhritimana, Pathyavana, Tattvadarshi, Nirutsaka, Nishprakampa, Nirmoha and Svarupa.

The fourteenth and final Manu will be Bhoutya.

(The names of the fourteenth *manavantars* are given in other *Puranas* as well. But the names tend to differ, particularly for the future *manvantars*.)

Selection of Manus, Indras and Rishis

Manu means the divine thinker who knows that he is not the body but the soul divine. He is a highly evolved soul who more often than not is an enlightened being. If such be the case, then his love's labour as a Manu King to guide and to evolve humanity is a choice of his own undertaking. Usually such lofty beings are enlightened souls who sacrifice themselves for the evolution of human kind and the evolution of the planets they dwell on. But at times the office of

Manu need not be held by a liberated soul, but are selected according to their karmic merit to reign over a human race. Such beings are wise and enlightened but not necessarily liberated (*moksha*). This may be due to them being bound by the last shreds of their karma or due to a self-imposed refusal to enter nirvana. Making the sacrifice, they direct the evolution of humanity on the physical terrestial sphere.

The Indra, or "celestial king", is also selected according to his karmic merit and evolution. It is not a criteria for a celestial king such as Indra to be fully enlightened or liberated, but he is a highly evolved soul who by his good deeds has risen to the position of the celestial king of heaven and the denizens thereof. This also does not mean that an enlightened soul cannot take up this heavenly office for the welfare of the souls thereon. But more often than not, he prefers the bliss of enlightenment to the pleasures of paradise, which are a natural way of life in the astral celestial spheres.

The seven Rishis are enlightened beings in the causal divine sphere. And all these seven sages although liberated from karma themselves chose to remain in the realm of causal relativity to do the work of the evolution of the world at the command of the Supreme Creator. But most of the time, this lofty office of the seven sages, that is called *Sapta Rishis*, is a self-taken sacrifice because they have refused to enter the liberating state of *Nirvana-Moksha* and instead, chosen to work for the denizens of the causal sphere by evolving them to the enlightened state, which they themselves are on. They work for long durations of time to serve the human, the astral and the causal spheres out of compassion which arises from the core of their own realization. They sacrifice their final state of awareness of the highest God-bliss and such enlightened beings, whether they be the Manus, the Indras or the Rishis; they are all worthy of being called "The Heroic Sacrifice". Their work is to evolve the beings in all the heavens and on earth so that the great *Kala Chakra*, the wheel of time, moves on.

As the Rishis also evolve on a yet much loftier level, they move

The Manus And Manavantars

on to works which are of a more lengthy and responsible nature. But the moment any enlightened Manu, Indra or Rishi chooses to enter the final liberation called *Brahma-Nirvana* or *Nirvana-Moksha*, they are free to do so after having completed their cycle of service to God and man. It appears that the turning wheel of time and evolution of humans and gods and devas and rishis depend upon two factors - the first the law of karma and the second the greater law of Sacrifice, which a brave soul even after finishing his own karma and fit for the final liberation stays back upon earth to help the suffering humanity and even the Devas. So engrossed are they in the suffering of humanity that they become this suffering; so immersed are they in the joy of humanity that they have not time for their own joy. Such are the great beings called the Manus who represent the spirit of humanity and guide it to its final haven of joy. This lofty work is done on the celestial spheres by great enlightened Devas (demi gods) such as Indra, Yama, Varuna and Kubera. They mark their period of time during which they have sacrificed to serve the celestial beings and help them in their onward journey. However, those souls of great merit who are wise but not enlightened and yet hold such an office as Indra and Kubera merely do their work, enjoy the merits of heaven and then return to earth to finish their karmic obligations. Having done this, they can enter the final liberation (*Nirvana-Moksha*) from the earthly sphere.

Given below in respective order to cycles of time and duration of races is the sequence of the reign of each Manu, the planets they are on and the races to which they will to evolve, genetically, emotionally, intuitionally and spiritually. The first round is shared by a root Manu and a seed Manu who reign for 300 million years each, which is 600 million years. So fourteen Manus reign for 4,320,000,000 years which make a day of Brahma called a *kalpa*. But it is interesting to note that each of the planets have seven sub-spheres or astro-causal *lokas*. The seven heavens or *lokas* on each planet with their terrestrial, astral and causal denizens are included in all root races. This makes a total of forty-nine spheres in a whole chain of seven planets. Here, when the seventh Root Manu Vaivasvat is finished with the evolution of the fifth root race on three of the planets and halfway through the fourth planet, a changing of guard will take place as he rounds up the seeds of the fifth root and sixth sub-race in the making, passing them onto his successor, the eighth seed Manu Savarni. He will go on to physically and spiritually evolve this seed souls of the fifth and sixth rub-races on three and a half planets to bring forth a full blown sixth root race, leaving behind the old fifth root race, which has gone on to higher spheres. This process of evolution continues so on and so forth, living the life of creation goes on until all the fourteen Manu Kings have completed their self-imposed or divinely appointed tasks. At this point they themselves go on to higher states of evolution and take on loftier offices of responsibility in creation.

Table of Cycles and Rounds

1st round – 1 Root Manu Planet 1 – Swayambhuva (Hyper-borean)
1st round – 1 Seed Manu Planet 7 – Swarochisha (Lemurean)
2nd round – 1 Root Manu Planet 1 – Uttama (Lemurean)
2nd round – 1 Seed Manu Planet 7 – Thamasa (Atlantean)
3rd round – 1 Root Manu Planet 1 – Raivata (Atlantean)
3rd round – 1 Seed Manu Planet 7 – Chackchuska (Aryan)
4th round – 1 Root Manu Planet 1 – Vaivasvat (our Progenator, fifth root race) (Aryan)
4th round – 1 Seed Manu Planet 7 – Savarna (seed Manu of sixth root race)
5th round – 1 Root Manu Planet 1 – Daksha Savarna
5th round – 1 Seed Manu Planet 7 – Brahma Savarna
6th round – 1 Root Manu Planet 1 – Dharma Savarna
6th round – 1 Seed Manu Planet 7 – Rudra Savarna
7th round – 1 Root Manu Planet 1 – Rouchya
7th round – 1 Seed Manu Planet 7 – Bhoutya

Vaivasvat – thus though seventh in order given, is the primitive Root Manu of our fourth human wave (The reader must always note that Manu is collective humanity and also personified in a single man as its representative. Our Vaivasvat was but one of the seven Manus presiding over the seven races of our planet. Each of these has to become witness to one of the periodical recurring cataclysms (by fire, water or ice) that close the cycle of every root race).

And it is this seventh Vaivasvat Manu who is the Hindu ideal embodiment of the Aryan fifth root race. (also including Noah, Enoch, Deucalion). He is the Being who rescued our race when nearly the whole population of one hemisphere perished by water, while the other hemisphere was awakening from its temporary obscuration. It is elsewhere said that he along with Vishnu as Matsya avatara rescued the seeds of a past humanity and brought them from the moon to seed our earth. Refer to the story of Matsya avatara in the "Ten Avatara Series" of Matsya, Kacchha, Varaha[9], Narsimha, Vamana[10], Parshuram, Rama, Krishna, Buddha and Kalki).

The Major Vaivasvat Manu (Swayambhu) was the Manu of the Great Cosmic Flood when life and seeds were shifted in the great ark from the Moon to the Earth with the spirit of the Maha Vishnu towing the ark with the seeds of all humanitiy, the seven sages and Vaivasvat himself protecting and guiding the ark of the covenant.

Vivasvat Manu (our Sun) The King of the Solar					
Mother Sandhya			Mother Chaya		
Yamuna (daughter)	Yama (son) God of Death	Vaivasvat Manu (son) King of the 5th root race	Savarni Manu (son) Successor 6th root race	Shani Planet (son)	Tapti (daughter)

---

9 The third boar-faced avatar of a series the ten avatars of Vishnu.
10 The fifth dwarf avatar of a series of the ten avatars of Vishnu.

In the Vishnu Purana, Book II, Ch 3

The reigns of God Manus, lower God Kings, Manus and Men are all given in the descriptions of seven islands, seven seas, seven mountains, each ruled by King Manus and each said to have seven sons, referring to the 7x7 minor Manu Rulers and Law-givers.

In Manu Smriti I, 32, 33 - Manus The Creators

The great Vivasvat Manu Surya is the same as Vaishvanara, the living Magnetic Fire (Agni) that pervades the manifested Solar System, which is (The Informing Spirit of the Sun) (The Homogenous Fabric of Radiant Ether of our Solar System). The Vaivashvat Manu is the son of Vivasvat Manu, the Sun himself. The name Vaivashvat, however, seems to be of a generic nature and there could be the greater and smaller Manus who govern the larger and smaller cycles of creation even to the point of even human Manus, who are the world Emperors and Kings on our Earth. So the reigns of the Manus and Kings are cycles within cycles, and the gyrational teeth of the turning wheels of time give to each King, Leader and Chieftain their karmic due.

Manu declares Himself created by Viraj[11] or Vivasvat Agni, who is the homogeneous fabric of radiant ether infused with divine spirit, which means that his *Atma* emanates from the never resting principle in the beginning of every new Cosmic activity. That universal *Atma* – collective Elohim that radiates from within himself all these cosmic *Atmas* that become the centres of activity – progenitors of the numberless solar systems as well as of the yet undifferentiated human *Atmas* of planetary chains as well as of every being thereon. Each cosmic *Atma* is Swayambhu, the self-born which becomes the centre of force from within which emerges a planetary chain (of which chains there are seven in our system) and whose radiations become again so many Manu Swayambhus (a generic name mystery) each of these becoming as a host – The Creator of His Own

---

[11] The masculine aspect of light-sound, whose feminine aspect is Vak Saraswati.

Humanity. (See Manus and Mahavataras in the *Manav Dharma Shastra*)

Shiva-Goraksha Babaji and Vishwakarma

One of the greatest mysteries which baffle both the human and celestial minds, is how the deep spirit of the inconceivable Shiva Goraksha Babaji moves through the great Being called Vishwakarma. We are dealing with the astronomical and astrological cycles, wheels of the evolution and events in the great almanacs of causation, space and time. These are wheels within wheels with the bigger wheels moving the smaller wheels includig causation within them. The gyrational and gravitational teeth of the wheels fix themselves into one another to met out the justice to man and devas. Karma grinds in justice and karma grinds exceedingly small, giving the just reaction for the minutest action. And yet there always remains a window of escape for evolution and everlasting peace within. The karmic pattern of the astrological calendar and its astronomical cycles are governed by a great force and the law of laws which is personified beautifully in the being called Vishwakarma, who is the architect of the Gods and who moulds both human and celestial actions according to their deeds. He is the one in-charge of the tri-form karma of the moving wheel of time.

Evolution of Planets and Manus
From the Secret Compendium of Manav Dharma Shastra of Lord Vaivasvat Manu

This evolution of Manus and their process of evolving other beings is taken and inspired by accounts given in the ancient Hindu scriptures by Brahma Rishis Brhigu, Vasistha and Parashara and later, by the latter's reincarnated self Varaha-Mihir[12], who detailed the astronomical cycles and astrological events to their minutest logical conclusion. These Great Rishis, who were like the Manus themselves in

---
12 One of the greatest astronomers and mathematicians who is said to be a direct incarnation of the even greater rishi Parashara, who is the Indian Hermes (Mercury).

realization, had a major role to play in these *Puranic*[13] dissertations and calculations of the individual, planetary, solar, galactic and cosmic cycles.

Our humanity is the wiser today for the contribution of the above wisdom given to us by the Great Vaivasvat Manu, Savarni Manu, and the likes of Brhigu, Parashara and Varaha Mihir. Along with them, we pay homage to the great Aaryabhat[14] of India, who gave to the world the zero and the numericals, without which, the computer that we are typing on would be naught. They show us the astronomical cycles of how the evolution of life proceeds on the seven globes in seven rounds.

They also give us knowledge of how the seeds of a future evolving humanity are transferred from one Manu King to another, until both humanity and the planet descend into matter and then evolve from the fifth root race back into Eternal Spirit. So lofty were the calculators of our world cycles that the Gods and the Manus themselves were the calculators of their own world cycles and the evolvers of their own humanities, of which they were the spirit.

1) Everything in the metaphysical as in the physical universes is septenary. Hence every planet, visible or invisible, is credited with six companion globes. The evolution of life proceeds on these seven globes from first to the seventh in seven cycles.

2) These globes are formed by a process called the "Rebirth of planetary chains (Rings)." When the seventh and last cycle of one such chain has been entered upon, the first globe "A" followed by all the others, instead of entering a period of rest – or "obscuration" as in their previous cycles – begins to die out. The planetary dissolution (*Pralaya*[15]) is at hand. The hour has struck and each globe has to transfer its life and energy to another planet (See diagram The

---

13 of the *Puranas*, an ancient text.
14 A famous Indian astronomer and mathematician who discovered the numerical zero.
15 Parashara describes the three types of *Pralayas*: *Naimittika* - Individual; *Prakritika* - Partial; *Atyantika* - Absolute

Moon to Earth).

3) Our Earth is the visible representative of his invisible superior fellow globes, its "Lords," and has to live as have others through seven cycles. During the first three, it descends from Spirit and consolidates. During the fourth, our Earth settles and materializes. During the last three, the Earth returns to its ethereal form and is then spiritualized into its parent source.

4) Its humanity develops only in the fourth – our present cycle. Up to this fourth life-cycle, it is referred to as humanity. Evolution is like the grub which becomes chrysalis and butterfly. Man, or That Which Becomes Man, passeth through all forms and kingdoms during the first cycle, then through all human shapes during the second following cycle, arriving on our Earth at the commencement of the third. In the present series of the fourth life-cycle and races, man is the first form that appears thereon – preceded only by minerals and vegetables that have to depend on man for further development and evolution through man. During the three rounds to come, humanity, like the globe on which it lives, will be ever-tending to assume its primeval and spiritual form (Ascending Ark), that of the Divine Angelic Host. Man tends to evolve his consciousness to perfection like every other atom in universe.

5) Every life cycle on globe D (our Earth) is composed of seven root races. They commence with the ethereal and end with the spiritual on the double line of physical and moral evolution, from the beginning of the terrestrial cycle to its close. This is a globe cycle of the seven *lokas* (spheres). The seven *lokas*/heavens are Bhur, Bhuvaha, Svaha, Maha, Jana, Tapa and Satya. The other is a planetary round from globe/planet A to G, the seventh.

6) The first root race is the first men on Earth, who were the progeny of celestial men, called rightly in Indian philosophy the "Lunar Ancestors / *Pitris*[16]", of which there are seven classes or hi-

---

[16] Our lunar ancestors from whom humanity is thought to have descended and ascended until they evolved out of the lunar cycle.

erarchies.

Babaji is the collective consciousness of the hierarchy of the heavenly host, including both the Lunar Ancestors and the Solar Sages of the Fire Mist, and is incomprehensibly more. That's why Sanat Kumar is merely an aspect of him, although he is the Supreme Manu and King, called the Lord of the World who resides in Shamballah, the White Island.

The essence of the souls of these lofty Beings must not be mixed up with the temporary terrestrial and celestial offices they hold, no matter how long they may appear to us mortals. The soul essences of these celestial beings are immortal and extended in relativity to the duration of their realization. Does this mean that the more self-realized a Being, the longer the duration of his office in the world?

The duration of the office he holds depends upon the degree of his sacrifice. These lofty renunciations are made for the redemption and evolution of humanities and other world-building (masonic) work which each high initiate decides to take upon himself, because the curse of terrestrial office is definitely a sacrifice in comparison to the bliss of celestial heaven. These decisions to sacrifice themselves for the redemption of humankind are either self-taken or at the behest of their higher superiors.

The truly Catholic (literally meaning "universal") ideology which is based on the universal life principle of humanity, with their six billion and three hundred million gods, representing each soul of our present population, is Hinduism, which may rightly be called Hinduanity/Humanity. All other religions, such as Buddhism, which is based on Buddha-teachings; Christianity, which is based on Christ-teaching; Islam, which is based on Mohamed's teachings; Zoroastrainism, which is based on Zoroastrist's teachings; Sikhism, based on Nanak's teachings; and Judaism[17], which is based on Moses' teachings, follow a particular figurehead.

---

17 The religion of the Jews/Yahudins, the father of whom is Abraham.

India's Guidance to "the Church vs. the Darwinists" Controversy

The ancient philosophy of India dissolves the quarrel between the Darwinian theory of evolution and the Orthodox Church. The answer comes from the great Manu, Lord Vaivasvat who gives us the knowledge that the terrestrial involution of humanity takes place along Darwinian lines where the elements provide the gross material body and Lunar ancestors provide the emotional, mental and intuitional bodies of man and the spiritual evolution provided by the Shiva element, which is the *Atma* spirit in every soul. The spiritual soul with its spark of divinity, is given to it by the Solar Archangels (called Agnishvattha the Sages) of the Fire Mist.

The crux of the problem, regarding the controversy between the Church and the Darwinists, is that both imagine the true man to be a physical entity and not a Divine Spirit. Hence they connect him with the passage of terrestrial evolution, which naturally brings forth minerals, plants, reptiles, apes and man. But Indian wisdom differs sharply and is emphatic on its stand that man is truly a spark of the the immortal Spirit-Self, and not a terrestrial mortal body-mind. This puts to rest an inconvenient dilemma and an uncomfortable delusion that our True Selves came from the apes. Therefore, I would exhort all scientists to humble themselves and introspect that their True Selves and origins are Divine and not coming from the delusive slush of matter and the limitations of an egotistic mind. Oh humanity, let us pride ourselves in the fact that we are immortal spirits and rejoice that our origins are Divine.

Herein lies the reconciliation between the religionists and the scientists, that the physical form of man could evolve from the the animal form right through the human form, then to the emotional and mental faculties. But the true man, the Spirit that he is, definitely comes from the Gods. Hence, in the deeper sense, Indian wisdom states that man in his truest essence is descended from the Divine, only his physical vestures are from evolutionary matter, including the form of his past incarnations where he has to pass through the first form of the apes, then to Afrikanas man, the Robustus, the Erectus, the Sapiens, the Neanderthal, then to modern man. This which we call the modern man, is but a garment or a temple erected to honour the incoming Eternal Spirit. So the whole journey of evolution is just so that the Divine Spirit, our True Self, can express itself in its truest form. The sweet nurse of nature unrolls itself so that the Spirit of man can express itself to perfection through the ever improved models of its physical temples.

Whether the Spirit Self inhabits its physical vehicle at the beginning of evolution or at a particular point thereof is not the issue. WHAT IS, OF CRUCIAL IMPORT, IS THE FACT THAT THE ETERNAL SPIRIT, WHICH EXPRESSES ITSELF THROUGH TRANSIENT AND VARIOUS EVOLUTIONARY FORMS, IS NEVER TOUCHED, CONTAMINATED OR ASSOCIATED BY THOSE FORMS AND YET IS THE SOURCE AND SPIRITUAL DRIVE OF TERRESTRIAL EVOLUTION WHICH EVOLVES INTO THE MATERIAL BODY THAT OUR SPIRIT SELVES INHABIT! Matter is lifeless without the informing spirit of God which uses the human body of matter to express its will in ever evolving cycles, rounds and and globes of creation. The very spirit of the divine spark motivates all matter and mind of the universe to evolve into its likeness and permeates it through and through without which the whole of creation is lifeless; and yet creation can never comprehend its creator, the Divine, but rather, gets lost in it.

So we must make the paradigm shift and not mistake ourselves to be born from apes, which is merely the physical garment but know by deep introspection, that our true Self is born from the Divine and our origin is Divine. From my poem, *Autobiography of the Self*:

> *And all along Evolution's path did I travel,*
> *My outer coats were different,*
> *each one more expressive than the first,*
> *but essentially I was the same*
> *And finally awaited me the crucial temple of man*
> *But it was only a man of clay, until I entered my ray*
>
> Yogiraj Siddhanath

The source of your material body is the Divine Mind and the source of your Spirit-Self is the Divine Consciousness. Therefore this is the humble request that the Church and the Darwinists do not ram their heads like two goats on a one-way mountain bridge and both fall down and perish with no results, but try to perceive the amicable solution in the philosophy of the wise Sages of India. When we go to the Indian time cycles, we now understand that calling Egypt the cradle of civilization and Africa the cradle of humanity is a very misleading and childish concept and their timelines seem to be a flash in the pan as when compared to the Great Indian Calendar of astronomical cycles and globes and creation.

Elemental Kings, Four Directions

God of Ether manifesting as Akash[18], Jupiter, Guru (Brahmanaspati[19])
God of Air manifesting in the tempest as Mars, Vayu (Indra)
God of Fire symbolized by thunder, Venus (Jove, Kubera)
God of Water symbolized by the Flavia Bull, Neptune (Varuna)
God of the Earth, who appears in earthquakes as Pluto (Yama)

	Kuber Agni	
Varuna Parjanya	Brahmanaspati Akasha	Indra Vayu
	Yama Prithvi	

---

18 'Pather Æther" (father space), the first of the five cosmic elements of which the physical universe is composed; also used to designate inner-space, that is, the space of Consciousness (cid-akasha).
19 An ancient name for the informing spirit of Jupiter (Zeus).

The above are not the *Lipika*, the Cosmic Maharajas (ref. chapter 15, page 209). But here they are the Planetary Guardians and Maharajas of the four quarters of the Earth.

CHAPTER 22

THE GREAT INDIAN CALENDAR

THE COMPUTER, THE COMPUTATIONS AND THE COMPUTED ARE ONE AND THE SAME BEING

The pertinent question asked by many a deep thinker and philosopher is, "How old exactly is our Earth, our Moon, the Sun and our existing creation?" And it is for this reason that I am detailing here the length and duration of the Great Indian Calendar of Creation, the calibrations of which were formulated by the great rishis Narada and Asuramaya and even loftier Beings like Vivasvat Manu (our Sun, also called Kashyap Aditya[1]), Vaivasvat Manu (son of our Sun and the father of our present humanity, the fifth root race), Bhrigu, Parashar, Agastya, Vishwamitra, Ravana and Varahamir. It is said of them that they were the greatest of astronomers India ever knew. It is interesting to note that the astronomer Rishi Parashar himself, to complete a vital portion of his astronomical and astrological calculations, reincarnated later as the genius astrologer Varahamir. Asuramaya was a great astronomer, was called GyanBhaskar[2], the Sun of Knowledge. He was said to have been the most powerful sorcerer of the White Island. There are many other legends concerning him, and it is popular belief that he was a pupil of the Sun God called Lord Vivasvat Manu who was a disciple of Shiva Goraksha himself. Asuramaya is said to have lived at Romaka-Pura[3] (city of the sweat-born), in the western quarter of Shamballah on the White Island.

---

1 Born of Aditi. One of the names of our sun.
2 The sun of knowledge; a title given to the Rishi Yagnavalka and the great astronomer Asurya Maya.
3 A city in the western part of Shamballah where the great astronomer Asurya Maya lived.

Here Sanat Kumar, an aspect of the eternal Shiva Goraksha Babaji, reigns as King even till today.

Now the question arises that what has this great Indian calendar got to do with Shiva Goraksha Babaji and who is this mystery of mysteries? Well on the face of it, I can tell you that Shiva Goraksha Babaji is the great Indian calendar itself. Not only is He the great Indian calendar but He is beyond its cycles of time and space. It is said that Shiva Goraksha Babaji is not an avataric descent but Shiva himself manifested of Himself. He is called Mahankal, The Great Beyond Time. And therefore this stupendous Being is the head, the heart and the soul of undying knowledge and is the One who truly inspires other Manu and Rishi astronomers to write about time and duration of the great world and cosmic cycles. He is one of the highest and innermost Beings, who in his mind's eye computed the whole of the cycles of Time and Creation from the existence of creation itself called Brahma, to the minutest iota of creation and time.

The *Puranic* scriptures are an account of the duration of a one-day-cycle of Brahma our Creator, lasting four billion, three hundred and twenty million years, detailed to the, let us say the present semiminutest duration of a nanosecond cycle. The time taken by light to travel one foot, is a billionth of a second, called a nanosecond. If we further divide time to its ultimate vanishing point, we get to a timespace continuum called no-time. And when you get to no-time, which is the speed of light, time stands still. But Babaji is the Great Beyond Time and therefore faster than the speed of light. Therefore, time ticks back to the future faster than light. So Shiva Goraksha Babaji is the time-reversed phenomenon along with the Creator. Since Babaji is the Great Beyond Time, He is also called the ETERNAL NOW, because for Him, there is no past, present or future, everything is in the Now! Because he who can play with time is as equal unto the Creator of causation, space and time. It is the Creator that can play with time and space, so Babaji plays with causation, space and time as a child plays with soap bubbles (ref. Gurunath's YouTube video "Soap Bubbles" or "Life is nothing more than this").

Another great Sage was Brahma Rishi Parashara, who laid down great astronomical time-cycles and astrological predictions. He was the one who guided the Indian Rishi Maitreya and, along with Avatara Parashuram, is grooming him as the Second Coming of Christ, known to the mystic circles and spiritual world as the Kalki Avatara. Then the great astrologer called Varaha-Mihir made phenomenal contributions to the world treasury of astrology and astronomy. He was the incarnation of his predecessor Rishi Parashara. The calendar to be given here is what modern science knows nothing of, and besides which the Mayan and ancient calendars pale into insignificance.

The length of duration of the astronomical figures given in this calendar dovetails closely with the secret works. The initiated yogis know of these esoteric cycles of the divisions of the *yugas* into racial cycles, which I have already given before in the chapter of the Manus. The Puranas contain references to some of them and have to be clearly spelled out. These sacred astronomical cycles are lost in the night of prehistory and most of them pertain as stated to the calculations of Lord Vaivasvat Manu, Sage Bhrigu, Narada, Parashara and Asuramaya. The latter had a reputation of a giant and a sorcerer, but the Antediluvian Giants were not all bad sorcerers. As a matter of fact, Asuramaya has done more good to the world as a White Wizard of Humanity, otherwise our modern generations would be lost in the deep spaces of the starry skies of eternity, not knowing whither to go and whither to turn or what to do with the wealth of the universe and its time cycles that the good Lord has endowed us with.

Human Cycle Calendar
By GyanAvatar Yukteshwar

Lord Yukteshwar as Manu Savarni, is the successor to Lord Vivasvat Manu of the fifth root race. He will be the King and Father of the sixth root race. This computation refers to the solar and planetary Creator, and is to do with the personal evolution of humanities and races.

360 days of mortals make a human solar year	1 One solar year
Satya Yuga contains (Sun passes through 4/20th of its orbit in each the descending and the ascending arc)	4,800 4 thousand 8 hundred solar years
Treta Yuga contains (Sun passes through 3/20th of its orbit in each the descending and the ascending arc)	3,600 3 thousand 6 hundred solar years
Dvapara Yuga contains (Sun passes through 2/20th of its orbit in each the descending and the ascending arc)	2,400 2 thousand 4 hundred solar years
Kali Yuga contains (Sun passes through 1/20th of its orbit in each the descending and the ascending arc)	1,200 1 thousand 2 hundred solar years
The total of the said four Yugas constitute a Maha Yuga	12,000 12 thousand solar years
The total pair of four Yugas constitute two Maha Yuga The ascending and descending arcs	24,000 24 thousand solar years

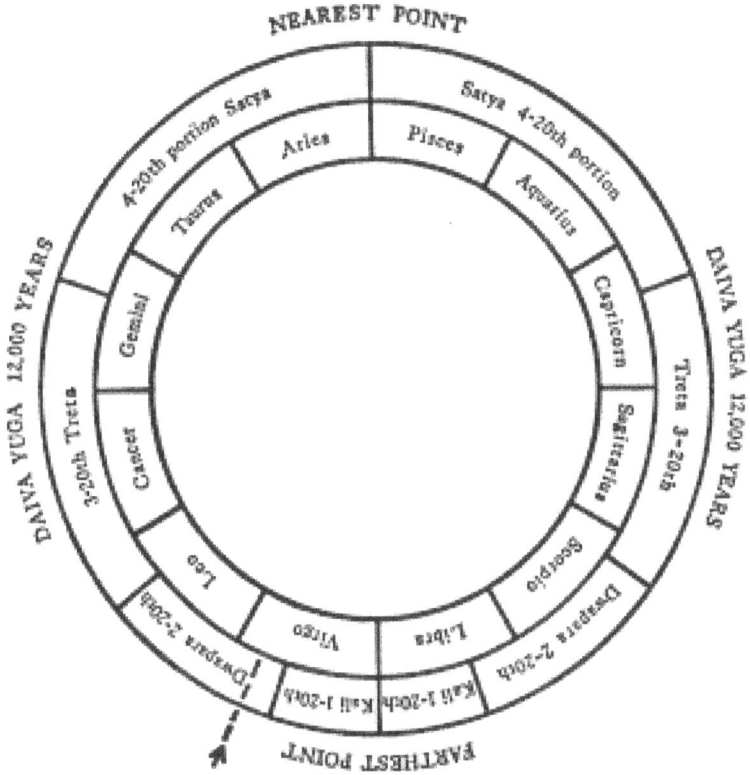

Sri Yukteshwar's 24000 year cycle

Virgo is the sign opposite Pisces. The Autumnal Equinox is now falling in Virgo; the opposite point, the Vernal Equinox, is perforce now falling in Pisces. Western metaphysicians, who consider the Vernal Equinox to have chief significance, therefore say the world is now in the "Piscean Age".

The Equinoxes have a retrograde movement in the constellations; hence, when the Equinoxes leave Pisces-Virgo, they will enter Aquarius-Leo. According to Swami Sri Yukteshwarji's theory, the world entered the Pisces-Virgo Age in A.D. 499, and will enter the Aquarius-Leo Age two thousand years later, in A.D. 2499.

Planetary Cycle Calendar

I have endeavoured here to build upon Sri Yukteshwar's twenty-four thousand years human cycle, going on to the planetary and solar cycle, treating the informing spirits of the planets as celestial Devas/angels, whose chief life giving father is the informing spirit of our sun, variously called Lord Vivasvat Manu, Agni Kashyap Aditya, and Agni Vaishvanar.

> *"Such is the great influence of Time which governs the universe. No man can overcome this influence except him who, blessed with pure love, the heavenly gift of nature, becomes divine; being baptized in the sacred stream Pranava (the holy Aum[4] vibration), he comprehends the Kingdom of God."*
>
> Gyanavatar Sri Yukteshwar
> *The Holy Science*

The extension after the *yugas* into the *maha yugas* and *kalpas* has been calculated by me, in my humble endeavour to show the racial, the human, the global and geological cycles of our planetary system and its Kings and Rulers, the sub-minor Manus. They, along with the minor and major Manus, rule the spiritual hierarchy of the inner government of our world. There is no conflict or disharmony in the management of the inner organization, as the sub-Manu works under the greater Manu in ascending order and dons and discards his official mantel according to the appropriate time cycles. I am deeply indebted to the great *Vedic* scriptures and to the *Manav Dharma Shastra* (a volume comprising the Kriya Yogic, spiritual and social codes) of the Lord Vaivasvat Manu, King of our world. He of course belongs to the greater cosmic cycle given in the previous charts.

---

4 The birthing hum of creation from the beginning of time, containing the far limits of the mind and matter of the universe.

One hundred and forty two of such Maha Yugas form the period of the reign of two minor Manus with their corresponding cycle	1,704,000 1 million, 704 thousand solar years
The reign of fourteen Minor Manus embraces the duration of 994 Maha Yugas, which is equal to	11,928,000 11 million, 928 thousand solar years
Add Sandhis, i.e., intervals between the reign of a Minor Manu, which amount to six Maha Yugas, equal to	72,000 72 thousand solar years These are only the rest intervals of Manus
The total of these reigns and rest intervals of fourteen Manus, is 1,000 Maha Yugas, which constitute a Kalpa, i.e., one Day of Minor Brahma (Universal Cycle - a day of Creation is the length of life assigned to each planetary chain)	12,936,000 12 million 936 thousand solar years Total reign of 14 Manus A Kalpa of the Minor Manu Brahma's Geological Day
As Brahma's Night is of equal duration, one Day and Night of Brahma would contain	25,872,000 25 million 872 thousand solar years
360 of such days and nights make one Year of Brahma, equal to	9,313,920,000 9 billion, 313 million, 920 thousand solar years Minor Manu Brahma's Geological Year
100 such Years constitute the whole period of Brahma's Age, i.e., Maha Kalpa (Minor Manu Braham's Geological Lifespan of Planetary Chain)	931,392,000,000 931 billion, 392 million solar years

Highlights of Cosmic Calendar
Geological History of Planets and Manus

I. The beginning of Earth's Evolution, up to the Hindu years Tarana (or 1887) ... 1 billion, 955 million, 884 thousand, 687 years.

II, The (astral), mineral, vegetable and animal kingdoms up to Man, have taken 300 million years to evolve which constitutes approximately the reign of one Major Manu.

III. Time of the first appearance of our first "Humanity" (on our Planetary Chain) ... 1 billion, 664 million, 500 thousand, 987 years. This is beyond any of the minor humanities or races referred to in our history or palaeontology reference books.

IV. The number that elapsed since the "Vaivasvata Manavantar – or the Human Period – up to the year 1887, is just ... 18 million, 618 thousand, 728 years.

V. The full period of one Manavantar is ... 308,448,000 years.

VI. Fourteen Manavantars, plus the period of one Satya Yuga make one Day of Brahma, or a complete Manavantar, or ... 4,320,000,000 years. Therefore a Maha Yuga consists of ... 4,320,000 years.

VII. The age of the present universe until now is 13.75 billion years; which is still in its infancy as compared to the total life span of the universe which is 311 trillion 40 biillion yearrs approximately.

Indian Cosmic Cycle Calendar
From the Works of the Brahmanical scriptures

This includes the astronomical and astrological calculations of the stupendous rishis and luminaries. So great were they in their wisdom that they ranked amongst the hierarchy of the Devas and star angels. It is to these great rishis and yogis we are eternally thankful for all the knowledge and wisdom they have imparted to our human kind. Without this knowledge, we wouldn't have had a clue as to who we are and in which direction the great warp and weft of creation is leading us.

To the Supreme Manu Shiva Goraksha Babaji, Brahma (our Creator), his mind born sons - the Lord Marich, Atri, Angiras, Pulastya, Bhrigu, Vashishta and Vishwamitra, we offer our ceaseless salutations. We are also indebted to Lord Vivasvat Manu our Sun, Sage Parashara, Agastya Muni, Deva Rishi Narada, Asuramaya and Varahamir for their priceless contribution to the great cycles of creation and its calendar.

Last but not the least, we must not forget the invaluable knowledge given to humanity by Lord Vaivasvat Manu in his *Manav Dharma Shastra* (the *Manu Smriti*), and his successor Lord Savarni Manu, who incarnated as Lord Yukteshwar and gave us the knowledge of cosmic astrology and his astronomical cycles of the human calendar which I have detailed from his book *The Holy Science*.

The Great Indian Calendar

360 days of mortals make a solar year	1 One solar year
Satya Yuga contains	1,728,000 1 million, 728 thousand solar years
Treta Yuga contains	1,296,000 1 million, 296 thousand solar years
Dvapara Yuga contains	864,000 864 thousand solar years
Kali Yuga contains	432,000 432 thousand solar years
The total of the said 4 Yugas constitute a Maha Yuga	4,320,000 4 million, 320 thousand solar years
71 Maha Yugas form the period of the reign of 1 Manu	306,720,000 306 million, 720 thousand solar years
Reign of 14 Manus embraces the duration of 994 Maha Yugas, which is equal to	4,294,080,000 4 billion, 294 million, 80 thousand solar years
Add Sandhis (intervals) between the reigns of 14 Manus which amount to 6 Maha Yugas, equal to	25,920,000 25 million, 920 thousand solar years
Total of these reigns and rest intervals of 14 Manus, is 1,000 Maha Yugas, which constitute a Kalpa (one Day of Brahma) (Universal Cycle - a day of Creation for each planetary chain)	4,320,000,000 4 billion, 320 million solar years
As Brahma's Night is of equal duration, one Day and Night of Brahma would contain	8,640,000,000 8 billion, 640 million solar years
360 of such days and nights make one Year of Brahma, equal to	3,110,400,000,000 3 trillion, 110 billion, 400 million solar years
100 such Years constitute Brahma's Age, i.e., Maha Kalpa (Life span of one of the successive Universes, called.. The Jagat)	311,040,000,000,000 311 trillion, 40 billion solar years

Daring to Conceive the Age of God

I know this endeavour is a non-endeavour in hopelessness. Nevertheless, to give the reader a feeble idea of a dream nano-second of the Lord God, I make this endeavor!

It is said in the circles of the high initiates of the world that one such Age of Brahma, our creator, constitutes but a day of Vishnu, the cosmic preserver. One hundred such days, which is thirty one quadrillion, one hundred and four trillion years (31,104,000,000,000,000 years), constitute his year. One hundred such years, which is three quintillion, one hundred and ten quadrillion, four hundred trillion years (3,110,400,000,000,000,000 years), constitute the duration of his office in existence. It is further whispered amongst the high initiates that this would constitute a day in the life of Mahadeva, the Great God Shiva. One hundred such days, which is three hundred and eleven quintillion, forty quadrillion years (311,040,000,000,000,000,000 years) would constitute but a year in his fancy. One hundred such years, which is thirty-one sextillion, one hundred and four quintillion years (31,104,000,000,000,000,000,000 years), would comprise one of his many Creations, which he dreams out after for ineffable infinities and yet remains the same. He is the Being About Whom Nobody Knows Nothing!

We must realize that here we are talking about God, who is very sacred to even God, and as you and I and all of us know, this is but a day in the life of a yet greater Creator, Brahma, and one hundred such sextillion days, which is which is three septillion, one hundred and ten sextillion, four hundred quintillion years (3,110,400,000,000,000,000,000,000 years), would form but a year of this lofty Creator, in which our Creation would merely be one of the decillion galaxies. Then we go on to one hundred such years, equal to three hundred and eleven septillion, forty sextillion years (311,040,000,000,000,000,000,000,000 years), which would comprise his Dream Creation. Now this, as we all know, with the high initiates, that 100 such days is a day in the life of Vishnu, the all Preserving infinite essence, which is thirty-one octillion, one hundred and four septillion years (31,104,000,000,000,000,000,000,000 years). Vishnu's year is comprised of one hundred such days, which is three nonillion, one hundred and ten octillion, four hundred septillion years (3,110,400,000,000,000,000,000,000,000 years). Then his existing presence in being would be three hundred and eleven nonillion, forty octillion years (311,040,000,000,000,000,000,000,000,000 years). Then it is said in the highest mystic circles that this is but a day in the life of the ineffable Mahadeva. One hundred such days would comprise one year, which is thirty-one decillion, one hundred and four nonillion years (31,104,000,000,000,000,000,000,000,000,000 years).

But let me tell you, dear readers, that this is just the beginning, for Who in the heavens and the infinite infinities are we trying to fathom? Are we trying to fathom Him for whom all these figures are but a wink of an eye? And so His creations go on ad infinitum, to the infinite googols, which man has created and will ever create until He is pushed out of existence in infinite numbers of times with his tin-ticking mind ever to fail to comprehend the infinite glory of the eternal infinite infinities for ages to come and ages to go. All Glory be to the ineffable, unspeakable one, who is beyond the comprehension of the mortals, the immortals, the Devas and the Celestials, the Angels and the Archangels! Even the Gods of Creations bow down to this infinite process of the ever-creating universes of googolplexes of infinities BEYOND THE COMPREHENSION OF ALL THAT IS AND IS NOT. This is what has been understood by the greatest of Rishis and Hierophants of all time. How can a finite mind comprehend the incomprehensible, ineffable and inconceivable beyond-mind? Close your eyes, smile and it is good to feel humble and know that ALL THAT WE KNOW IS THAT WE KNOW NOTHING.

Babaji The Lightning Standing Still

APPENDIX

DECLARATION OF HUMAN RIGHTS FOR EARTH PEACE

If Earth Peace is to herald the Dawn of the New Age, realize 'The Soul Cry'

**Humanity Our Uniting Religion
Breath Our Uniting Prayer and
Consciousness Our Uniting God!**

To serve Humanity as our Larger Self by Earth Peace meditation on full-moon days, absorbing its peaceful rays within while radiating them to the world without.

Use the way of the Peaceful Breath, which flows equally in all, as a means for attaining Earth Peace, thereby diffusing individual and international conflicts.

One's inalienable right lies in the furthering of the **Evolution of Human Consciousness** for World Peace, by exercising one's will to good for making one another's lives on this planet a celebration.

By virtue of being a World Citizen, it is one's inborn right to attain the **Consciousness of Natural Enlightenment** leading to the realization that one's expanded consciousness and humanity's consciousness is One.

As we evolve, we live less and less in our bodies and more and more in our consciousness. Hence, fusion of our positive awareness with that of nature's cultivates an improved and balanced ecosystem. **Help to evolve Nature with your Nature, because Nature is the Nature of Man!**

Allow yourself to heal and be healed of the negativity of your mind by letting go of the negative mind, which covers the splendor of your soul.

India's Gift to Humanity

> INDIA WAS CHINA'S TEACHER IN RELIGION AND IMAGINATIVE LITERATURE, AND THE WORLD'S TEACHER IN PHILOSOPHY... A TRICKLE OF INDIAN RELIGIOUS SPIRIT OVERFLOWED TO CHINA AND INUNDATED THE WHOLE OF EASTERN ASIA.
>
> Lin Yutang, author *Wisdom of India*

Not through trumpets nor clarion calls, but as silent as the morning dew, has India's gift of spiritual knowledge seeped into the hearts of humanity. The very people who conquered them by means of war, themselves were conquered by India's spirit of peace and philosophy of love. The mindset and courage of our people to sustain wave after wave of foreign invasion, and yet engulf them in our culture is unique amongst the peoples of the Earth. As though this was not enough, India went on to teach humanity the ultimate lesson of peace. They broke the shackles of British rule and went on to win their political independence in 1947. This was done by the totally peaceful means called *satyagraha*—a non-violent reaction against injustice, returning love for hate. This unique political movement was headed by the Indian Mahatma and saint, Mohandas Karamchand Gandhi.

In its expertise in the evolution of spiritual consciousness, India stands second to none. Its deep yogic insights and profound philosophies have greatly influenced European, Asian and now, even Western thought. India dominated Tibet's and China's philosophies and cultures for 20 centuries. The contemporary techniques of today, such as pranic healing, sudarshan *kriya*, tai-chi, chi-gung, and reiki are like little whirlpools and eddies in the great river of ancient Indian yoga and spirituality.

As early as 500 BCE Bhog Nath was initiated into the Kundalini

Appendix

Kriya Yoga by the immortal Kalagni Nath of Kashi, a holy city of Northern India. He belonged to the Nav Nath tradition of yogis. He then took Nath yogic and healing knowledge to China where he was called Bo Yang and later, as the legendary Lao-Tzu, he established the Taoist movement in China and gave as a gift to the people the sacred Kundalini Yoga which went by the name of *Yin-Yang Yoga*. Yin stands for Shakti, the female divine principle, while Yang is Shiva, the male divine principle. He taught them the balance of pranayama that is Tai-Chi, by breathing to unite the two male-female principles atop the head and enter the golden yoga state of samadhi. Bhog Nath also taught thousands of Chinese disciples tantra, the yoga of transformation of sexual to spiritual energy.

Later in 300 CE, another Indian yogi, the Buddhist patriarch Bodhidharma established the Shaolin temple in China. He established the *Dhyana* (Zen) school of Chinese and Japanese Buddhism. He also taught the martial art of *Mushti Prahara*, the technique to strike at the vital centers (*marmasthana*) and temporarily cripple the enemy, but specifically warned his disciples never to use these arts for aggressive purposes, only for self-defense. This later became the Shaolin Kung Fu, the Tai Chi Chuan and the Japanese Karate.

India has been the source of the sacred wisdom and healing knowledge to the whole world since time immemorial. This selfless service from the enlightened yogis has largely been erased, forgotten or ignored by those peoples who have benefited so much spiritually, physically and culturally. However, during historical times, there have survived records of the spiritualizing impact of these selfless yogis.

In the present time, there is an East-West exchange: as the West values nothing that is free, the compassionate Shiva Goraksha Babaji has decreed that there should be an exchange of Western material wealth for India's spiritual wealth. In all my travels the world over, I have realized that in spite of its shortcomings, India is the spiritual dynamo of the world. It shall lead humanity in wisdom's ways more and more as time flows on.

One of the wonderful gifts that India has given to the world is its yogic philosophy of death. The body is the apparent perishable self and the soul is the immortal self. When a body gets old, it is cast off like a worn-out garment. The soul lives on to transmigrate into a new-born body and family which will help it to work out its remaining karma. This philosophy of putting in its proper place one's mistaken identity has greatly eliminated the fear in the hearts of countless generations of peoples all over the world. It has given them a purpose to live for and a purpose to die for, with courage and confidence, knowing that:

They're not this house of flesh and bones
Which sleeps decays and dies
They are immortal consciousness
Lord of the earth and skies

COSMOLOGY
THE DOCTRINE OF DIVINE EYE

A REAL experiential exposition of creation (*utpatti*), preservation (*sthiti*) and dissolution (*laya*) - they represent expanding Brahma, pervading Vishnu and dissolving Shiva respectively.

At the beginning of time, an inconceivable phenomenon took place in the bosom of the Great Deep from where were born the three Lords of Light/Causation, Space and Time, spreading across the face of Nothingness for eons of billions of years. The Light preceded the Sound by a few eternities and gradually retarded its velocity to mutate into sound so the Light-Sound was the mind of Brahma, the Creator and his creative energy, the sound of Om. The Light-Sound was the potential homogenous fabric of the radiant ether of the mind and matter of the universe to be. Through eons of billions of years, creating the ripple effect on the waters of eternal space, Causation Light and Duration Time, carved out the destiny of Creation, humming all-the-while, their favorite tune of Omkar, which was the background tune of the birthing hum of Creation, the song of the Great Mother herself. In this Birthing Hum of Creation, Saraswati, the Creative Light of Brahma who later transformed into Lakshmi, the Preserving Light of Vishnu. Then finally, Uma, the virgin light of the dissolution of the mind and matter of the universe, the consort of Shiva.

So, through all the livelong days of the lengthening mind of Brahma through various permutation combinations, the jigsaw of the whole of creation began to be put in place. The vast galaxies and stars and clouds of incandescent vapor all took their place as though being ordered into a pre-planned situation. By this Great Creator, Brahma, called The Expanding One. Then the Lords of Light and Darkness were born and there begun an evolutionary battle for supremacy between the *devas* and the *danavas*, *adityas* and *daityas*, the *manus* and the *rakshasas*. Each evolving being and place pushing from within outwardly to find its own glory in the Sun. Through the passage of eonic time, the Sun and the Moon and the Stars, they were born, each one of which, mind you with their special informing spirit who did guide and direct the planets to effect the world's situation on its onward journey. Billions of years later to effect the karmic blueprint of the human being in order to make him grow and learn as per the expansive awareness that our Lord Brahma the Creator had infused into the whole of existence. The history of Creation is so vast that if we were to squeeze it in a 24-hour time span, the whole evolution and existence of man would be a mere two seconds. Creation then mellowed and matured into its next phase.

Then the all-pervading Vishnu took the place of the expanding Brahma and brought creation into what we call the steady state. As the world cycles and galactic cycles took their rounds, spinning and whirling - and - rotating and revolving in the vast eternities of Space, Creation was at its best, singing the song of eternal Love, to love itself and the driving force of Love, ever-expanding and balancing creation with another balancing force of negativity and apparent dissolution. This Supreme Lord, called The Steady State who in ancient India was known as Vishnu, the All-Pervading Intuitive Awareness, who will ultimately be transformed into the great dissolving liberator, Shiva—and then Vishnu's intuitive awareness will further refine and expand itself into Shiva's super-conscious *Paramatmic* State.

But as for now, the great dancing veil of Maya, the veil of the eternal fabric of radiant ether thrown over creation, was to remain until all human souls in creation, with their self-effort could penetrate this great veil called Maya and win their final gold of self-realization. So, the steady state of the great delusion of Maya was designed by Vishnu the preserver himself in order to strengthen the will of the human souls travelling through the university of life and death so that in the final outcome they may emerge victorious and strong and full of love and compassion. Then having realized themselves to be the immortal *Atma* (Spirit of God) and not a corruptible body, they in turn would stretch their limits too to lend their brothers a helping hand to achieve the same realization of Oneness with the divine. During this whole process of the evolution of human souls, and the preservation of human creation, God's aspect of Vishnu descends as a Saviour from age to age to assist humanity in its upward evolution to Divinity. This saviour in India is called an avatara. Ava means downward and tara means stretching out to those souls drowning in the Maya of materialism and the veil of delusion. Of course there are many successes and failures in this process but those who fail, take another minor round of reincarnation and keep trying until they succeed.

However, the great Lord of Preservation had not only the human element to evolve but his was the vaster work of evolving the planets the stars and the galaxies—and the great informing Spirits therein, although they were a part of his larger self. He played the game of Creation and put them to the test by evolving them through vaster and vaster responsibilities unto his own self and therein to His final Self, who is called Shiva, Mahankal, the Great Beyond Time. We have to remember that God is the Great Trinity of Creation, Preservation and Destruction, working simultaneously in relativity; only one aspect of the Trinity dominates the other at a particular given space/time frame. From a nanosecond until eternity, the eternal process of creation, preservation and dissolution is going on.

Pratiprasava, the Great Inward Turning

Now the process of the great process of Shiva, the great Dissolution begins to dissolve, both on an individual and a cosmic scale. The Great Creation matured and celebrated through all its victories and glories and failures now itself desires to make its paradigm shift from time to Timelessness called Mahankal Shiva. Trillions of years having passed, and Spirit and Light having descended into the *pravritti* path (the descent of Spirit and Light into matter) constantly metamorphing into sound, energy and matter, now decides to take the upward arc of ascending from matter to energy to sound to Light into Spirit; this is called the *nivritti* path, where the soul efforts to disengage itself from the trammels of the senses, identifying with its own soul-spirit, it makes a beeline for the Final Reality. Similarly in the cosmic paradigm, the vedic sage Parashara explains to his disciple Maitreya, who is coming as the Kalki Avatara. He goes on to relate how through a series of cataclysms the earth is transformed and swallowed up by water, water by fire, fire by air, air by *akasha* (*Pater Æther*) and *Æther* finally resolves into the light-mind of Brahma and then the great Brahma transforms into his higher self, Mahavishnu its ultimate matrix, the cosmic light-sound of Omkar.

It is from Omkar, the primal *Viraj-vaak*, which means the primordial light-sound of creation, that the great introverting process of Lord Mahanakal, Shiva, the great time, begins. It is necessary to remember that there are broadly four light sounds created from Omkar.

• The grossest sound of Omkar is called *Vaikhari-Vaak*, which are those vibrations which can be heard. Here the energy is Saraswati herself.

• The medium sound of Omkar is called the *Madhyama-Vaak*, which is softly heard as the mumble of creation. Here *Saraswati Vaak* is transforming into *Lakshmi Vaak*.

• The still subtler sound of Omkar is called the *Pashayanti-Vaak*, which is the mental sound of the mind of creation. Here *Saraswati Vaak* has transformed into *Lakshmi Vaak*. At this speed and velocity of the mental sound, the *anahad nada*, transforms into light-sound. This is where the particle electron transforms into the wave of light[1].

---

[1] If lord Time, lord Light and lord Space are the true Rings-Pass-Not and the far limits of the mind and matter of universe are contained in them, therefore, the three lords are also in relativity. No matter how subtle they may be, they are still composed of the finest matter. Because the light-space-time continuum dissolves ultimately into the great black vortex, i.e., the Great Time Mahanakal, therefore, this proves they are something and not nothing, otherwise, the space-time-continuum would not be dissolved into the super-massive black vortex (*Ahirbudnya*). Sound is neutro-protonic matter, Radiance is proto-electronic matter and Light is a released corpuscular electron called a wave.

The critical state where the subtlest matter called the electron becomes light is when the

• The fourth stage of the Omkar sound is the *Para-Vaak*. Here the sound is pure light. At this stage, *Lakshmi Vaak* has become *Uma Vaak*. *Uma* means the virgin light, bordering the stage of the Lightless Light, with her source *param-gurutva-akarshana* (supreme gravitational attraction), Mahankal Shiva.

Spiritual Insight into the Lightless Light and Shiva Mahankal

I have explained above the process of transformation on a scientific basis from the gross terrestrial elements to the subtlest stage of matter, which is light. If we are to proceed further according to the Indian line of awareness, we must remember that there is a huge gap between light, which is the subtlest matter, taking the colossal quantum leap to Divine Consciousness, which is no matter, no light, no space, no time. Scientists have not been able to bridge the gap of introducing Consciousness into Einstein's general theory of relativity which is $E = mc^2$. Therefore, as a working measure, I have taken the liberty to bridge this gap between light, the subtlest matter and grosser Consciousness by the phrase, "the Lightless Light." In order to make light touch Consciousness, there has to be a bridge and this bridge is called the Lightless Light, which lights that light which lights the light of all our souls. For lack of a better word, I'd call this Lightless Light, "a more descending Consciousness."

There is a huge huge gap. We cannot say whether the light takes the leap to the Consciousness or the Consciousness descends to the light. I would understand this to be a mutual ascent-descent process and the facilitator of this process of the highest realization is none other than an aspect of Babaji, "The Lightning Standing Still." In the lower microscopic sense, celestial lightning mutually descends

---

particle of the corpuscular electron is transformed into the wave of light. We must remember that the electron travels one mile slower than the speed of light. And if the velocity is increased, the particle electron must become the wave of light. This is the crucial happening or transition from matter to light. We then go on to explain the crucial transition from light to Lightless Light (grosser consciousness) and then to Consciousness itself. This transition is explained in my Damru Philosophy.

to fuse with the ascending terrestrial lightning of the earth. This also takes place in the human body where the kundalini lightning arises from the root chakra to be mutually met by the Divine descending lightning at the crown chakra and in the third eye. This is how everybody gets *chaitanya darshan* of Babaji as The Lightning Standing Still.

Enthroned as the Trinity Itself is Babaji, follwed by His Mahavatar Christos and then His Christ. Babaji is the ever appearing and disappearing Star of Salvation to all human and celestials alike. He is the Lighting Standing Still, who transforms himself into the star each time a soul is enlightened. This is the Doctrine of the Divine Eye, experienced as the star.

At the cosmic lever, it is this essential truth, which divine Satgurus and the denizens of the celestial spheres have experienced; it is this essential experience of lightless light which bridges the gap from light to Consciousness. The denizens of celestial dimensions experience not only the spectrum of the seven-fold light, but also go beyond into the higher states of seedless samadhi, where they experience the "lightless light." When the terrestrial ascending light meets the celestial descending light, it becomes the Lightning Standing Still. This can happen at the individual as well as the cosmic level where it is called the Lightless Light, or, to be more accurate, the Star of Lightless Light seen in the singularity of the vortex of the Great Deep, which the wisdom tradition of Indian Rishis calls the *Krishna Vivar*, meaning the dark vortex of the Great Deep.

Now we further go into the workings of the great Shiva, the dissolver, the emancipator and the illuminator of our creation. As the spirit of His nothingness, which is *Ahirbudnya*, the unfathomable serpent of the Great Deep, sucks the whole of creation into His dark mystic vortex of The Non Being Essentiality, there comes a critical state where light, space and time stands still. And when the light, space and time stands still, the great zero called "the Rings-Pass-Not" has been transcended. And karmic light, with creation stamped upon it, is resolved to zero and quivers before the super massive

Gravity of darkness of intense light. Lord Light, lord Space and lord Time also bow their heads dissolving into an intense gravity (*Shiva Gurutva Akarashana*) and being absorbed into the timeless majesty of the unknown called the Mahankal Param Shiva, the great beyond time (there is a process that happens in the mystic black vortex of the great goddess Kali awaring into the depths of darkness, for Kali is the great black void of the universe which along with Causation, Space and Time is awared into Mahankal making them realize themselves as originated from and dissolved into Him). Kali is esoterically the consumer of negative and dark matter, who facilitates the soul into the bliss of the Lightless Light. The continuum of light/causation, space and time have been resolved into their essential oneness with the great void black-hole. As it resolves these gods of causation, space and time into their essential essence, only the naked truth remains, which we call *Nagna Satya*, which means "the naked singularity."

So intense is the unfathomable darkness, that inconceivable gravity dazzles the deepest opacity of the darkest hell of the unknown singularity invoking a brilliant star at its centre. And therefore, in the singularity of the super-massive dark hole vortex, there shines the star of the Lightless Light. When the whole universe is compressed into a dot and goes on to vanishing point, when light, space and time are pushed out of existence and *Kaivalya* Consciousness is still far away, then steps in the Lightless Light, through which the illuminating star shines forth. What is this star of Lightless Light? What is this star, which shines in the darkest depths of consciousness when all the mind and matter and light of the universe have been swallowed up? This is the cosmic star of liberation called the Lightless Light, which bridges the grosser consciousness to the light. Let us know that through this star of cosmic salvation that entire universes may transit into the ineffable state of Godessence – Cosmic *Kaivalya*. So, this star of Lightless Light, which survives beyond the light, space and time of our earthly knowledge, is the star of the cosmic eye of Shiva, which has the power to enlighten entire creations or to project them back through Omkar light into light, sound, ether, air, fire, water, earth and make a new material creation. Please note that here

I am only speaking about the grosser consciousness and nothing has been said about Supreme Consciousness.

Mass distorts space-time to intensify into Supreme Gravity. Supreme Gravity enhances mass to transform into light, space and time, absolving matter and relativity into no-matter and Divinity. Matter transforms to light, light expands to space and space disappears into timelessness which is absolved into a Supreme Gravity whose mass is infinite and is of the qualiy of OMNIPRESENT NOTHINGNESS.

If the Earth were compressed to the size of a marble and gravitational omnipresence were compressed to the size of a marble, theoretically, the omnipresences marble would outweigh the Earth marble, because gravity/omnipresence in its intensity is everywhere and nowhere at the same time, and also because gravity has pushed matter out of existence and likened matter onto itself to be everywhere and nowhere at the same time. Gravity's center is everywhere and circumference nowhere. This is the Isness of Lord Shiva preceeding His higher inconceivable state of the omniscient Param Shiva.

Damru Hypothesis

So, to my understanding, the whole picture of creation, preservation and dissolution of the cosmos appears to be in the shape of a double drum which is thin at its waist, or as I would put it, to be in the shape of a *damru* which Shiva holds in His hand. And at the narrowest funnel point of the end of the black hole and the beginning of the white hole shines this ineffable star of Lightless Light.

A series of diagrams of the time-drum *damru* with a tube space of equal length between creation and dissolution will show that the *utpatti*, *sthiti* and *laya* (that is creation, preservation and dissolution) are an infinite process. Existence lasts a duration of 311 trillion years including creation, preservation and dissolution. Our existence is presently in its infancy and only 13.7 billion years old. So, according to the Indian brahmanical calendar, the whole process of one cycle of creation, preservation and dissolution takes approximately

311 trillion 40 billion years. There is yet a greater cycle where only creation lasts 311 trillion 40 billion years, preservation the same and dissolution the same. This makes a vaster existence of approximatey 933 trillion 120 billion years, which for the holder of the time-drum is but a wink of an eye. There are Holders of mightier and mightier time-drums ad-infinitum. O little mortal man with a limited mind, do you dare to know His Ineffable Majesty?

In honor of what this insight is, I can never hope to complete it because it is endless and human words have ended long before I have even begun. Such is the paucity not only of human intellect, but even of the Divine intellect of those who have tried before me. For thousand of years, people have tried to prove DIVINE REALITY and have failed. And for thousands of years, people have tried to disprove DIVINE REALITY and have also failed. Divine reality is of experience and not of the written word. It would be well to say here once again, YOU ARE GOD TO THE EXTENT YOU KNOW GOD, BECAUSE GOD FULFILLS ALL INDIVIDUALS, HUMANITIES AND INFINITE ETERNITIES, BUT THEY IN TURN CANNOT FULFILL HIM, FOR HE IS THE NON BEING ESSENTIALITY. HE IS EVERYWHERE, NOWHERE AND NOW HERE!

Maya, the great illusion of the world, feels solid if each atom is 99.9% space. The reason for this is energetics, it's just like a football net with 90% space and only 10% matter. But still, the ball can't go through it. Similarly, the atomic structure of our body is held together by subtler and subtler forms of energy such as prana, tan-matras, and the three gunas, which comprise creation.

RISHI SANGH IN SHAMBALLAH

Describing what happens at Shamballah, the 'Celestial City':

I am a foreigner to this land, I belong to that land where there is no life nor death. I am drunk every day; I'm drunk all the 12 seasons with the ambrosia where the ego is dead and the Atma is alive.

I am a foreigner to this land, a traveler. I belong to that country, to that land where there is no winter; it is spring all the time. There is no winter of sorrow nor death, and there is a new life awakening of the spring. It is spring every moment and at all seasons. In this garden of my body, the seven lotuses bloom to their fullest capacity. The spring garden of my body makes the seven lotuses of the chakras bloom with which I adorn the feet of Shiva Goraksha Babaji.

I'm a foreigner to this land, I belong to the land of Shamballah, the sacred White Island, where every day is a festivity of colors. We throw beautiful rainbow colored paint and water on each other.

In that island where I belong. The sacred island of Shamballah, of Sambalpur, there's the festival of Holi, where we spray colored water upon one another. Seven-colored waters spinning in the seven colors of this festival and I become colorless. I have no colors of attitude or emotion. I've become the colorless one, the egoless one as I spin in the mystic whirling dance[2]. I spin and spin and spin and while spinning I dissolve into the great bliss.

---

[2] This is the spiritual whirling dance of the rishi mandala (representing the evolution of the planets around the sun god, tater enacted as the rashi mandala dance in Rajputana, in the land of India).

I am a foreigner to this land, I belong to that land where the thirty-six types of music, called ragas and raginis, are played all the time.

The whole world is composed of music and octaves. The walls are music, the people are music, the food is music, the light is music, the love is music. So, I belong to that place where everything is music. Every person is music, every place is melody, everything is symphony, and the thirty-six tunes are played all the time. And the naubath, the great drum, beats out the creative sound of great Omkar. Ommmmm!

This is the great White Island, the Shamballah, the white haven of bliss. My identity is:

My haven is within me, my identity is that I belong to the country of Paramadham, the highest state of spiritual awareness and the name of my village is the Nectar Lagoon. It is a lagoon of nectar in which I reside, which is the upper third eye where there's the inverted third ventricle. This is my identity, and my name is Siddhanath and I belong to the paramadham.

I am a foreigner to this land; I belong to that land where Goraksha Nath, Shiva Goraksha Babaji, is the Supreme Soul of Creation.

He is the great divine Atma-Rama and he is the one who is breathing through me, Ham–Sa, Hong–Sau, So–Hum, whilst I sit at rest. So I have practiced His name so much that even without me having to take His name of the Ham–sa and the So–ham, He is doing it for me and asserting in every breath Ham–Sa, That thou art, I am He, and He is me.

So this is my beloved town of the White Island, where within my own body and at the location of Shamballah and Shvetdeep, I attain my final goal.

I attain my self-realized state and know myself to be the divine indweller; and then move on to God-realization.
This is the description of the island of Shamballah and Shwetdeep, which can go into higher and higher spheres even beyond Shamballah. This place is beyond the terrestrial, even beyond the celestial, making its way to the ineffable divine.

ARYANS
Original Inhabitants of India

Arya-Varta (India) has ever been known as the Land of the Rishis, and its Himalayas, the Abode of the Gods. Time and again, India has come forth to show the beacon of spiritual light to all countries and is, no doubt, an unfathomable dynamo of spiritual light in our world of today. This most ancient of civilizations in the Land of Arya-Varta, or "Land of the Aryans," has survived the ravages of time where other ancient civilizations like Mesopotamia, Egypt, Babylon, and Ur of the Chaldees have faded away. India lives on today because the spirit of its people is rooted in the practice of divinity called Yoga; also because of the flow of its ancient wisdom towards Divine Knowledge, called *Atma Vidya*. So potent is this Divine Yoga that a tickle of it influenced the whole of Asia, and today it has flowed and inundated the whole world of receptive souls.

The very name Arya-Varta shows where the Aryans originated and why their land was called so. There is no other place on earth that was called Arya-Varta except India. Therefore, it surprises me how people could take such an unsubstantiated and controversial stand regarding this word "Aryan," which itself comes from the ancient Indian language called Sanskrit. The Hindus and their Sanatana Dharma (literally, "eternal religion"), were a very advanced culture, whose people interacted with one another in peace and joy. Many a foreign scholar has written about the highly developed ancient Indo-Gangetic civilization in 3000 BCE, and the yet more ancient Indo-Saraswati civilization which flourished 6000 to 7000 BCE. The noble Aryan dwellers of the land of Arya-Varta lived in peaceful co-existence, being its original dwellers, and had developed good roads, organized housing and fine draining facilities.

The historical accounts of Arya-Varta have no mention whatsoever of any foreign people invading its land. Neither is there any mention of a foreign invasion or influence of any type in our oldest texts called the *Vedas* and the *Manav Dharma Shastra*, which is the ancient code of ethics and history written by Lord Vaivasvat Manu. The Aryan invasion is a misconception and a concocted story to divide India and strip it of its own knowledge and culture, giving the credit of India's wisdom to foreigners. Where are the burnt fortresses, the weapons and relics of mangled armor? Where are the smashed chariots, and bodies, and invaders and defenders? Despite extensive excavations at the Harappan sites, there is not a single bit of evidence that can give us unconditional proof of any ancient foreign invasion. Any skeletal or artifact proofs that were and are being found, are of totally indigenous Aryan and Dravidian origins.

Aryan Invasion Theory, a Total Misconception

It should be noted that, to date, no hard evidence has proven the Aryan invasion theory to be a fact. The recent emergence of new evidence over the last couple of decades has debunked the validity of the Aryan invasion theory. The origin of this theory is nowhere to be found in Indian historical records of the *Vedas*, *Puranas*, and *Itihasas*. It is only mentioned in nineteenth and twentieth century politics and German nationalist propaganda.

In the year 1853, Max Mueller was commissioned by the British to write about the Aryan invasion theory in order to promote their divide and rule policy. He created a rift by creating his Aryan race theory as opposed to the Dravidian race. When challenged in 1888 by eminent scholars, he saw his reputation was at stake and backpedaled from the word "race," explaining that he meant to include only those who speak the Aryan language. The original Sanskrit meaning of the word "Arya" is "the noble one who is righteous," and it was commonly used in addressing a gentleman as "arya-putra" (noble son). It has nothing to do with race, cast, or color - it simply connotes a noble inhabitant of Arya-Varta, the land of India. So when the bluff was called, Max Mueller spilled the beans and admitted that his theory of an Aryan invasion was concocted, and there was no Aryan invasion and "subjugation" of Dravidian people.

A study conducted in 2009 by the Centre for Cellular and Molecular Biology[1] (in Hyderabad, India) in collaboration with Harvard Medical School, Harvard School of Public Health and the Broad Institute of Harvard and MIT, analyzed half a million genetic markers across the genomes of 132 individuals from 25 ethnic groups, from 13 states in India across multiple caste groups. The study asserted and demonstrated that there was no trace of any foreign invasion in the Indian Sub-continent, but that the very indigenous Aryan people were themselves, their own Aryan race.

---

[1] "Reconstructing Indian Population History," by Reich et al., *Nature*, 461, 489-494, 24 September, 2009.

GLOSSARY

A

Abhaya: fearless

Abhimana: pride

Abhinav Gupta: a medieval saint and scholar who wrote the famous book Tantra Alok.

Abhinivesh: the lust for life.

Abrahama: a name of Abraham, the Father of the Jewish, Muslim and Christian races, connected with father of creation, Brahma.

Achalchambu Nath: signifying a cycle of time, identified with Shesha Nath, the serpent of infinity.

Achambay Nath: see Achalchambu Nath

Adharas: the supports (the six chakras)

Adi Shakti: the primordial goddess energy.

Adi Shankara: the first spiritual pontiff of the Shiva order of acharyas.

Adi Nath: 'Primordial Lord', the founder of the Nath Yogis, Shiva Himself.

Adi Shesha: The first serpent, signifying one of the seven cycles of infinity.

Aditi: the name of the goddess signifying space and the wife of the rishi Kashyap.

Aditya: born of Aditi. One of the names of our sun.

Advaita: 'nonduality', the truth and teaching that there is only One Reality called Atman or Brahman, especially as found in the Upanishads; see also Vedanta.

Advaita Vedanta: culmination of the Vedas in monism.

Agastya: ancient rishi, son of Mithra.

Agni: presiding deity of the element of fire.

Agni Abhimanin: name of ancient fire god married to Svaha from who there are three fires, Pavak, Pavaman and Shuchi.

Agni Vamsha: ancient rishi, son of Mithra

Agni Yogi: he who practices the fire yoga, which is also called Kriya Yoga, sacred fire rite of the yogi.

Agnisar: abdominal movement to raise kundalini fire.

Agni Shvatha Rishis: Sages of the Fire Mist

Agya Chakra: 'command center', a yogic appellation for the third eye center; center of Divine Presence located at the midpoint between the eyebrows.

Ahamkara: 'I-maker', the individuation principle, or ego, which must be transcended; see also asmita, buddhi, manas.

Ahirbudnya: 'Unfathomable, Inconceivable and Ineffable Serpent of the Deep', epithet of Lord Shiva. This word refers to the infinite Shiva in the scripture, Ahirbudnya Samhita.

Aja: 'the unborn', a term used for the primordial Divine as well as its universal energy called Kundalini.

Aja Ek Pad: 'The Unborn Standing on One Foot', it is an epithet given to Lord Shiva, giving us to know his awesome infinity. It is mentioned in the scripture, the Ahirbudnya Samhita.

Aja Purusha: the Supreme Man who was never born and can never die.

Ajapa Japa: Also called Ajapa Gayatri, not chanted but observed with the silent mantra of the Hamsa-Soham.

Ajmer: a city in Northwest India.

Akarma: 'actionless action', karmaless action.

Akasha: 'Pather Aether" (father space), the first of the five cosmic elements of which the physical universe is composed; also used to designate inner-space, that is, the space of Consciousness (cid-akasha).

Akashic Records: the thoughts imprinted in the homogenous radiant ether of the cosmic mind.

Akhaada: a school of discipline in the nath yogic tradition.

Akula: 'nonflock', an epithet of Lord Shiva.

Alakh: the Lighltess Light; a name for God.

Alakhnanda: name of a river flowing from the Himalayas joining with other rivers to become the holy Ganges.

Alakh Niranjan: 'The Lightless Light which lights that light which lights the light in all our soul'; a name for God and a greeting, voiced by Nath Yogis.

Alkapuri: legendary city in the Northeastern Himalayas.

Allah: A name for God.

Alam Prabhu: a saint who existed 150 years after Babaji Gorakshanath who blessed him in a vision. The story of the physical meeting of both these masters is not a historical fact.

Alumbusha: One of the five sub-Pranas.

Amar Nath: the sacred pilgrimage of Lord Shiva in north India.

Amaroli: a tantric technique of auto-urine therapy.

Amba: 'Great Deep', appellation for an aspect of the Divine Mother. The waters of the unfathomable deep. Also known as the goddess Bal Tripura Sundari.

Amla: the Indian wild gooseberry.

Amrita: the nectar of immortality that flows from the psycho-energetic center at the crown of the head (sahasrara-chakra) when it is activated by yogic means, transforming the physical body into a divine body (divyadeha).

Amrita Anubhava: amrita means nectar and anubhava means experience. This is a scripture written by Saint Jnaneswar.

Anahada Nada: means the unstruck sound, usually heard in the heart/Anahata chakra.

Anahata Chakra: 'wheel of the unstruck sound', the twelve-petal lotus of the heart. The heart has since ancient times been viewed as the secret seat of Vasudeva and the location where the immortal sound Om can be heard. Its seed syllable (bija mantra) is yam pertaining to the element of wind.

Ananda: 'bliss', the condition of utter joy, which is an essential quality of the ultimate reality (tattva) described as sat-chit-ananda.

Anandmayi Ma: the joy permeated mother; she was a 20th century saint/avatar.

Annamayee Kosh: the intuitional body of bliss; 'sheath composed of food', the lowest of the five 'envelopes' (kosha) covering the Self; the physical body.

Angiras: one of the seven rishis who holds an office in one of the planets of the Great Bear/Dipper constellation.

Anuloma Viloma: pranayama of alternate nostril breathing.

Anumeena Pranayama: A Nath yogic technique of internal pranayama.

Anusandhan: an inner connection of mind with deity.

Apana: the downward flowing life-force energy in the spine. In Kriya Yoga it is used for dissolving karma.

Apanic: the downward flowing current as opposed to upward flowing pranic current.

Aradhya Kalam: one of the spiritual gurus of Gautama the Buddha.

Archangel Gabriel: the Archangel next in command to the Archangel Michael.

Archangel Michael: the first Archangel of the face of God.

Ardhnarishwar: half-Shiva and half-Shakti, akin to the later Greek god, Hermaphrodite, half-male, half-female respectively, showing to us that the balance of the universe is rooted in reciprocity.

Arjuna: 'fair', one of the five Pandava princes who fought in the Mahabharata War; disciple of the Avatar Krishna whose teachings can be found in the Bhagavad-Gita.

Artha: money or finance (ref. the four efforts-kama/desire, artha/money, dharma/religion, moksha/salvation).

Arundhati: the wife of the great rishi Vashista who is the penultimate rishi of the Great Bear/Dipper.

Aryabhat: a famous Indian astronomer and mathematician who discovered the numerical zero.

Aryan Root Race: is the noble race from the country of Aryavarta, presently called India.

Aryasangh: the great Medieval alchemist and philosopher of advocating the Taraka Raja Yoga system of Maitreya-Krishna.

Aryavarta: an ancient name for the land known as India.

Asamprajnata Samadhi: the yogic ecstasy of expanded consciousness equivalent to the vedantic ecstasy of nirvikalpa Samadhi.

Asana: seat', a physical posture (see also anga, mudra); the third limb (anga) of Patanjali's eightfold path (asthanga-yoga); originally this meant only meditation posture, but subsequently, in Hatha

Yoga, this aspect of the yogic path was developed further; also the seat upon which a yogi sits durng meditation.

Ashram: 'where work or effort is made', a hermitage; also a stage of life, such as brahmacharya, householder, forest dweller, and complete renunciate (samnyasin).

Ashivagandha: Indian ginseng, an ayurvedic herb used for stress relief and various other remedies.

Ashwatthama: Son of the rishi Dronacharya, one of the eight Chiranjeev's (immortals also including Kripa, Hanuman, Vyasa, Vibhishana, Parusharama, Mahabali, Markandeya); he was present during the time of the great Mahabahrata war, about 3102 BCE.

Ashwini Kumaras: the twin surgeons of the gods.

Asmita: delusion of maya, which makes you forget that you are the soul and not the body.

Assam: a state on the northeast of India famous for its tea.

Asso Pat: a sacred plant similar to basil given by lord Dattareya to Queen Pingala, the wife of king Bhartari.

Asta Bhuja: name for the goddess Durga with eight arms.

Astral Body: inherent in the astral body is the emotional body and also the higher celestial body of which the subtler human being is composed.

Astral Chakras: the chakras corresponding to the astral body.

Atmadarsani: one who gives soul enlightenment or divine spiritual insight self-knower)

Atma Monads: a whole unit of consciousness containing the mind, the soul and its Spirit/atma-buddhi-manas.

Atman: 'self', the true Self, the individual spirit or soul, which is eternal and super-conscious; our true nature or identity; sometimes a distinction is made between the atman as the individual self and the parama-atman as the transcendental Self; see also purusha, Brahman.

Atmaswaroop: of the form of the soul.

Atri: the second of the great rishis of the Sapta Rishi (Great Bear/Dipper Constellation).

Aulia: a mendicant; a God-intoxicated yogi.

Aum: the birthing hum of creation from the beginning of time, containing the far limits of the mind and matter of the universe.

Aunsh Avatar: A partial avatara that manifests only the degree of Divinity necessary to fulfill a specific mission.

Aura: the astral/celestial radiance round the body of a meditating yogi and a saint, the nimbus/halo predominantly emits from around the head area.

Autobiography of a Yogi: a spiritual classic written by Paramahansa Yogananda in the 20th century.

Avadhoota: 'cast-off', he who has shed everything; a Nath Yogi who having gone through the 6th stage of initiation, by both his individual effort and Divine grace, achieved the Consciousness of the avatar.

Avalokiteshwara: this is a Buddhist name for the great yogi called-Matsyendra Nath in Maharastra; he is identified as Vithoba

Avasta: 'condition', the super-conscious states of Yoga distinguished according to the level of refinement of God Realization.

Avatara: 'descent', the descent of the Divine into a terrestrial lightbody for spiritual work and the salvation of the world; identified outwardly by specific signs, such as the tendency of the avatara to cast no shadow.

Avesh: the entry of the spiritual essence into a human being, which makes him a partial avatar for that lifetime (example Parshuram).

Avidya: 'ignorance', the root cause of suffering (dukha); also called ajnana; cf. vidya.

Ayama: the cessation, ceasing to be (example: pranayama).

B

Baba: revered father; a generic term

Babaji: 'revered father', in the Nath tradition, the name denoting Shiva Goraksha Babaji; 'The Youth of 16 Summers'; 'The Ever-Youthful Immortal Yogi'; also mentioned in Yogananda's book, Autobiography of a Yogi. Balak Nath: a disciple of Babaji Gorakshanath and the Nath Yogi who lived during the middle ages.

Bal Tripura Sundari: an epithet of the divine feminine energy as the beauty of the three worlds.

Balrama: the elder brother of Krishna.

Banaras: the sacred city of the pilgrimage to Kashi Vishwanath (Lord Shiva).

Bandha: a yogic lock (mulabandh, uddiayanbandh or jalandarbandh).

Basti: hatha yogic technique of sucking water through the rectum, then abdominal churning and finally throwing it out.

Bela-Shailush: wood apple, a fruit loved by Lord Shiva.

Bhagavad Gita: 'Lord's Song', the most popular book on the science of Yoga, embedded in the epic Mahabharata and containing the teachings of Karma Yoga (the path of self-transcending action), Jnana Yoga (the path of wisdom), Bhakti Yoga (the path of devotion), and Raja Yoga (the supreme path of meditation) as given by the Avatara Krishna to Prince Arjuna on the battlefield of Kurushetra.

Bhadon: the rainy monsoon season.

Bhairav: the masculine classical melody; the first raga created by Lord Shiva.

Bhairavi: the feminine classical melody, consort of the raga Bhairav.

Bhairva Nath: an aspect of Lord Shiva

Bhajan: rom the root bhaj 'to divide', devotional song whence the devotee is separate from Deity and does not fuse with God as does the yogi in samadhi.

Bhakti: 'devotion' or 'love', the love of the bhakta toward the Divine or the Guru as a manifestation of the Divine.

Bhakti Sutra: 'Aphorism of Devotion', an aphoristic work on devotional Yoga authored by Sage Narada.

Bhakti Yoga: 'Yoga of devotion', a major branch of the Yoga tradition utilizing the feeling capacity to connect with the ultimate reality conceived of as a personal Divinity.

Bharat: the land whose people are wedded to the light of the Soul; the land of India.

Bharatvarsh(a): Present-day India – the land whose people are wedded to the Divine light.

Bhartari Nath: one of the nath yogis, 70 BC; the elder brother of Vikramaditya.

Bhaskar: one of the splendid names of the sun god.

Bhava: an emotion, or Bhakti, devotion.

Bhavani: the feminine aspect of Shiva dwelling in the seven heavens (bhavanas) of Bhur, Bhuva, Svaha, Maha, Jana, Tapah, and Satya (seventh heaven).

Bhavishya Purana: an ancient text prophesying future events.

Bhima: second of the Pandava brothers.

Bhisma: the great grandsire

Bhoga Nath: a disciple of Kalagni Nath of the Nav Nath tradition; he hailed from the pilgrimage city of Kashi Vishwanath.

Bhrigu: one of the seven rishis of the Great Bear, ancestor of the Bhargava race and the father of rishi Markandeya and Shukra, the informing spirit of the planet Venus.

Bhrukuti: the third eye called Kuthastha Chaitanya.

Bhumi: Mother Earth

Bhur: this is a dimension of the terrestrial sphere as Bhuvar is the astral sphere and Swaha, the heavenly sphere.

Bhuta: 'to become', the material elements, also called pancha bhuta, or five elements of earth (prithvi), water (apas), fire (agni), air (vata), and space (akasha).

Bhuta Shuddhi: 'purification of the elements', transformation of the gross physical body into a Divine body, by dissolving the five elements.

Bindu: 'seed-point', the creative potency of anything where all energies are focused; the red dot worn on the forehead as indicative of the third eye. Bindu means focal point or dot, the one compressed nucleus of cosmic energy, which bursts forth as the Naada, the cosmic sound of Omkar, the birthing hum of creation.

Bindu Rahasaya: a treatise written by Shiva Goraksha on the conservation of vital energy and its subsequent transformation into divine energy by a yogic process.

Bo Yang: His original name was Bhog Nath who went from Benares to China to teach the people the science of the Yin Yang Yoga (the Shiva-Shakti Yoga). Later came to be known as the celebrated Lao-Tzu who also wrote the Tao Te Ching.

Bodhisattva: 'enlightened being', the Chiranjeev immortals and avadhoots who's bodhi-chitta (buddhi) are purfied to such a degree of compassion that they spurn Nirvana (moksha) to serve humanity.

Bogar Nath: ref. Bhog Nath

Brahma: 'he who has grown expansive', the creator of the universe, the first principle (tattva) to emerge out of the ultimate reality (brahman). Brahma – The Creator, also called Vidhata, the God of the destinies of all nations and humanities.

Brahma Astra: a lethal weapon composed of mantric vibrations, which is infused into a missile and then used against the enemy. Eg: Varuna Astra (water missile) and Agni Astra (fire missile).

Brahma Dvar: the door at the crown of one's head, sahasrara chakra.

Brahma Granthi: a psycho-generic plexus located at the base of the spine.

Brahma Nadi: the subtlest psychic nerve. Eg: sushumna, vajra, chitrini and brahma nadis.

Brahma Nirvana: merging in the transcendental core beyond the universe and being everywhere and nowhere at the same time. Highest state of enlightenment.

Brahmacharya: the discipline of chastity for the channelisation of vital energy (prana) and transformation into ojas and tejas by the practice of Shiva-Shakti Kriya Yoga and Mahamudra.

Brahman: 'that which has grown expansive', the Ultimate Reality of atman, purusha.

Brahmanaspati: an ancient name for the informing spirit of Jupiter (Zeus).

Brahmanda Purana: one of the ancient texts of the universe

Brihaspati: refer to Brahmanaspati

Buddha: 'awakened', a designation of the person who has attained enlightenment (bodhi) and therefore inner freedom; term designating Gautama, the founder of Buddhism, who lived in the 6th century BCE.

Buddhi: 'that which is conscious, awake', the higher mind, which is the seat of wisdom (jnana); manas.

Buddhism: after Gautam Buddha, a Hindu prince who attained enlightenment and his followers who were called Buddhist. Buddha was not a Buddhist but followed the traditional Hindu/Indian lifestyle.

C

Chaitanya Prana: means Soul Life Force

Chakra: 'pranic wheel', the psycho-energetic centers of the subtle body (sukshma-sharir). Classically seven of such centers are given: muladhara chakra at the perineum, svadhishthana chakra at the base of the spine, manipura chakra at the navel, anahata chakra at the heart, vishuddhi chakra at the throat, ajna chakra in the middle of the head, and sahasrara chakra at the top of the head.

Chalan: an exercise of the tongue done during practice of khechari mudra.

Chanakya: a partial avatar of Vishnu, 350 BCE, called Kautilya, wrote the Niti Darpan. He assisted Chandra Gupta Morya to become the first emperor of India.

Chandogya Upanishad: one of the oldest scriptures written in 200 BCE; it's contents elaborate on the nature of Om and prana.

Chandra Nadi: the lifeforce energy flowing through the left nostril.

Chandrasoma: moon nectar

Chandravat: a clan of the ancient moon dynasty.

Charan Paduka: charan means, the holy feet and paduka means sandals.

Chatrasal: the Medieval king who assisted the King Shivaji with King Govinsing to regain the lost Indian Empire.

Chatur: means four or it could also mean clever.

Chauhan: Chauhan means Lord, as Nath means Lord. The Chauhans are a clan from the Rajput dynasties, and are called Agni-Vamashas, meaning families who descend from the source of the fire god, c.f Sisodias (Surya- Vamashas) descending from the source of the sun god, cf. the Yadhavas (Soma-Vamashas), who descend from the source of the moon god.

Cherubim: these are the divine child angels and the other name is Seraphin.

Chetan Nath: a Medieval nath yogi who was said to be one of the masters who taught Jesus the science of yoga.

Chinna-masta: the name of a tantric goddess.

Chiranjeev(a): There are eight immortal Beings of a particular world cycle. They are Hanuman, Ashwatama, Parusharama, Mahabali, Sage Vyasa, Kripacharya, Vibhishana, and Markandeya. There have been many more Yogis prior to and later than these classical eight who have become immortals. These are the souls who live continuously for one world cycle.

Chitrini Nadi: the third of the four psychic nerves.

Chitta Shuddhi: mind purification (by meditation, mantras and chanting).

Cittars: originally pronounced as Siddhas, perfected beings of the fifth degree initiation.

Chola: an ancient dynasty in Tamilnadu of the lineage of the fire descendants.

Christ: the 7th degree initiate; the World Teacher; an avatar such as Kalki Avatar, Maitreya, Matsyendra Nath, Avalokiteshwara, Vithoba (the man crucified in space).

Christos: the Divine higher-Self called Archangel Michael, Narayan 'the Lord of Irradiant Splendor', and Amitabh. The Christos has crossed the 8th degree of the great initiations. Above them there is only one, 'The Eternal Now,' Shiv-Goraksha Babaji.

Chola: is here referred to the physical, apparent body of a Yogi, which he can change at his own sweet will, when his former body garment becomes decrepit and old. This may be done by the process of entering another's body or by the process of Kayakalpa (body rejuvenation). Or he may choose to maintain the body in perfect health by the Sanjeevani (rejuvenating) process of Kundalini Kriya Yoga.

Chowrangee Nath: a disciple of Shiva Gorasksha, an elder son of King Shalivahan, 10 BCE to 70 CE.

Chyvan Prash: a tonic in India made of wild gooseberries (amla).

Cit: 'consciousness', the super-conscious ultimate reality (see Atman, Brahman,Chaitanya).

Citi: 'shakti', kinetic energy; see kundalini.

Citta: 'mind-substance', ordinary consciousness, the mind, as opposed to cit.

Cittargiri: a place in southern India also known as the hill of the Siddhas.

Count St. Germain: a Hungarian ascended masters who controls tantra and the beneficial rays of the moon. Ref. Racokzy.

D

Dabisthana: an ancient book on mysticism written by a Kashmiri scholar Moshan Fani.

Daksha Prajapati: an ancient sage known as the first and the last. He is also the father of Parvati. When Shiva was not invited to his fire ceremony, he upset the cosmic law and the result was a war in which his Yadnya was foiled and his head cut off. This refers to a mystic type of initiation.

Dakshinamurti: a name for Lord Shiva, facing the South. It is said that this Sage was a youth and taught his disciples in silence.

Damru: the drum of Shiva in the shape of an hourglass, depicting both Sound and Time Eternal of Creation, Preservation and Dissolution.

Dars(h)an: 'vision' or 'sight', divine vision in the literal and spiritual sense; the seeing and receiving of blessings from a Divine Guru or spiritual Being; of a system of philosophy, such as the yoga-darshana of Patanjali. In a general sense, blessings pouring out from the eyes of the master to the disciple.

Dasha Bhuja: ten-armed.

Datta: a short epithet for the Dattatreyá

Deha Shuddhi: body purification

Deodata: one pranic life forces.

Deva: 'shining one', a male deity, such as Shiva, Vishnu, or Brahma, either in the sense of the ultimate reality (Maha Deva) or a high angelic being.

Devaki: the mother of Lord Krishna

Devbhakta: devotee of God

Devdatta: granted by God

Deva Rishi: third in the hierarchical order of Rishis.

Devi: 'shining one', the feminine aspect of deva; a goddess or feminine angelic being such as Parvati, Lakshmi, or Saraswati.

Dhaba: a place of roadside fast-food in India.

Dham: place of rest, also meaning a sacred place of worship; home

Dhananjay: a victor over wealth and materialism, one of the five subpranas

Dharana: 'holding', concentration, the sixth limb (anga) of Patanjali's eight-limbed (ashtanga) system of Yoga.

Dharma: 'bearer', law or lawfulness, also correct action, conduct and righteousness and vitue.

Dhuni: a sacred fire lit by the nath yogis to demarcate their power centers of meditation (dhuna)

Digamber: the naked one; the one bereft of inhibitions; and the soul that has realized itself to be the cosmic consciousness regarding the sky to be his clothes

Dilip: King of the Solar Dynasty, 16th descendent from the sun. The son of King Ikshavaku.

Diptimana: the one who is shining and illuminated

Dhyana: meditation; the seventh limb (anga) of Patanjali's eight-limbed Yoga brought about naturally as a result of correct concentration (dharana); called cha'an by the Chinese and rendered later by the Japanese as zen.

Drishtanta: spiritual vision

Dronacharya: a Devarishi in the period of Mahabarata and the guru of kauravas and pandavars. Father of Ashvatama

Dronagiri: a sacred mountain which is in the Kumar range of the Himalayas

Durga: the white evolutionary energy; name for the goddess mother.

Dvaipayan: a sage who held the office of Veda Vyas at the time of the Mahabaratta (Krishna Dyvaipayan)

Dvapara Yuga: the second of the four yugas (Kali, Davapra, Tretta and Kritta/Satya)

Dwar: door/passage

Dvesh: repulsion

E

Elohim: a name of God in the Hebrew tradition; also the heavenly host of gods and angels in the Hebrew tradition.

El Morya: 400BC first emperor of India, who also incarnated as the legendary king, Vikramaditya, 57BC. Then as King Arthur in 600 CE and then the righteous king, Shiva-ji, then as Gyan Avatar Shri

Yukteshwar. It is this being who is destined to be the future Manu Savarni of our 6th root race.

F

Fire God: See Agni

Fire Mist: This is the mixture of fire and mist, which arose at the dawn of creation of our present world cycle. A certain class of pure Sages of the Fire Mist arose form the night of prehistory. These were the great founders and teachers of humanity who did guide and evolve our humanity to its present state. Also see Sages of the Fire Mist

Fukushima: The nuclear reactor on the East Coast of Japan, whose leakage could have triggered off a world catasrophy.

G

Gayatri: a Vedic mantra recited to enlighten the intellect and give liberation (moksha) chanted at the junctions of sunrise and sunset (sandhikal).

Gajar: elephant

Gajkanthar Nath: Lord Ganesh

Galava: ancient rishi after whom the city of Gwailor was named.

Gandharvas: heavenly songsters (Devas)

Gandiva: arrow given by Shiva to Lord Parashurama

Geheni Nath: disciple of Goraksha Nath and guru of Nivritti Nath

Ghagra-Chunari: a style of Rajasthani dress and Northern India including a tunic, top, and shawl.

Gorakh: see Gorakshanath

Gorakhnath: see Gorakshanath

Gorakhnathi: a devotee of Goraknath; also called a Kanphat Yogi or Gorakh Panthi.

Goraksha Shataka: first part of Goraksha Paddhati written by Shiva-Goraksha Babaji.

Gorakshanath: 'Lord Goraksha', Babaji; also called Shiva-Goraksha-Babaji, a renownly well documented avatar of Indian Yogic tradition, responsble for hastening the spiritual evolution of humanity. The personal aspect of Lord Shiva. see also Mahavtar.

Granthi: 'knot', any one of three common blockages in the central pathway (sushumna-nadi) preventing the full ascent of the serpent power (kundalinishakti); the three knots are known as Brahma granthi (at the muladhara chakra), the Vishnu granthi (at the heart), and the Rudra granthi (at the third-eye center).

Gudadal: rectal passage

Guna: 'quality', refers to any of the three primary 'qualities' or constituents of nature (prakriti): tamas (the principle of inertia), rajas (the dynamic principle), and sattva (the principle of lucidity)

Gupta Vidya: secret wisdom

Gurkha: a tribe in Nepal that follows Goraksha Nath

Guru: 'one with gravity', a teacher who cultivates the spiritual knowledge of a disciple.

Guru Darbar: conclave of spiritual monarchs.

Guru Granth Sahib: a sacred book of the Sikhs worshipping the Guru, Rama, Krishna and rightful living.

Guru Kripa: guru's grace

Gurutva Akarshan: gravitational attraction, also the magnetism of the master's knowledge

Gyan Bhaskar: the sun of knowledge; a title given to the rishi Yagnavalka and the great astronomer Asurya Meyar

Gyan Swaroop: embodiment of wisdom.

Gyana: see jnana.

Gyana Yoga: yoga of wisdom

Gyanavatar: divine incarnation of wisdom

Gyan Nath: an epithet of the Saint Janeshwar

H

Ha Ha and Hu Hu: the gandharva twins, the songsters of heaven

Hamsa: 'swan', the Soul, the individuated Consciousness (jiva); also refers to the life-breath (prana) as it moves within the body; the lateral ventricles in the human brain in the shape of a swan in flight, with its wings thrust toward the forehead and its posterior ventricle pointed to the back, like a swan flying back to the future, faster than light; see jivaatman.

Hamsa Yoga: 'swan yoga'; ancient text in the form of a conversation between Sanat Kumar (Shiv Goraksha Babaji), and his pupil Gautama; this is Kundalini Kriya Yoga, giving the levels of manifestions of the resonance of Omkar.

Haradwar: the entrance to the abode of Lord Shiva a place of pilgrimage at the foothills of the Himalayas

Hastajivhava: a subordinate prana

Hatha Yoga: 'Forceful Yoga', a major branch of Yoga, developed by Gorakshanath circa 1000CE, emphasizing the physical aspects of the transformative path, notably postures (asana) and cleansing techniques (shodhana), but chiefly breath control (pranayama).

Hatha Yoga Pradipika: 'light on the Sun/Moon Yoga' compiled by Svatmarama Yogi and dedicated to Shiv-Goraksha Babaji. This work comprises 389 couplets, and integrates the practices of Hatha and Raj Yoga.

Himalayas: snow mountains

Hinduanity: humanity living in peaceful coexisting. Also is a quin to Christianity and dwith deeper dimentions of existencial realism.

Hinduism: humanity living in peaceful coexisting

Hingalaaja: an ancient goddess shrine, now in Pakistan, dedicated to the goddess Durga.

Hiranyaloka: 'golden world', the highest astral heaven of luminosity to which some yogis ascend, to practice higher forms of Yoga under the guidance of Divine Teachers (Divya Gurus) such as Shri Yukteshwar.

Hridaya: the heart

I

Ida Nadi: 'pale conduit', the prana current or arc ascending on the left side of the central channel (sushumna-nadi) associated with the parasympathetic nervous system and having a cooling or calming effect on the mind when activated; cf. pingala-nadi.

Incernment: a word coined by Yogiraj Siddhanath; an inner discernment, which is a process of expansive withdrawal, resulting in the realization of oneself as divine consciousness and not the intellect. It is the great shift where one's Atma withdraws into its own, realizing that even its Buddhi is not itself.

Indra: the king of the Gods (Zeus)

Indrayani: the wife of Indra

Indu: the feminine energy of the moon

Isha Nath: another name for Jesus the initiate

Ishwar Pranidhana: 'the Lord as priority', total surrender to the Lord; in Patanjali's eight-limbed Yoga one of the practices of self-restraint (niyama).

Ishta Devata: your personal beloved deity

Ishwara: 'ruler', the Lord; an epithet or reference to God such as the Creator (Brahma) or, in Patanjali's Yoga-Darshana, to a special transcendental Self (purusha)

Is-ness of the Zero-not-Zero: Yogiraj has coined this term. The zero represents the Nothing of Creation. The naught-zero represents the Everything in Creation and the Is-ness pervades them and is beyond them both.

J

Jaal: the web of delusion; a net

Jagadamba: the mother of the world

Jageshwar: a holy pilgrimage of Ardhinareshwar in the Kumar regions Jaggan Nath: lord/father of the world

Jain: spiritual values followed by Mahavir which later became a religion Jainism

Jal: water

Jalandarbandh: the chin lock compression to hold the prana

Jalebi: a round and round and round sweet. Then stop. At the stop, the maximum syrup is attained. Shape of the coiled kundalini, lying in three-and-a-half coils.

Japa: 'recitation', the repeated recitation of mantras to focus and clarify one's mind for meditation.

Jati: a great Siddha yogi and greater

Jhilmilee Gufa: the name of one of Babaji's caves, tucked away in the Himalayas

Jhundi Yatra: A pilgrimage taken by yogis each year to Mangalore in honor of shiva goraksha wo is called Manju Nath, the Patra Devata. This is done for the washing away of the sins of the world after every kumba mela.

Jiva: 'individual self', the individuated consciousness, as opposed to the ultimate Self (param atman); also jivatman.

Jivanmukta: an adept who, while still embodied, has attained liberation (moksha) from his material condtion (samsara).

Jivatman: see Jiva

Jnana: 'knowledge' or 'wisdom', both worldly knowledge or worldtranscending wisdom, depending on the context; also gyan; see also vidya

Jnana Yoga: 'Yoga of wisdom', the path to liberation based on wisdom, or the direct intuition of the transcendental Self (atman) through the steady application of discernment between the real and the unreal, the Self and the not-self and renunciation of what has been identified as unreal or inconsequential to the achievement of liberation.

Judaism: the religion of the Jews/Yahudins, the father of whom is Abraham

Jyoti Mudra: also known as Yoni Mudra in tantric parlance called Shanmukh-Mudra; yogic practices of Shiva Goraksha Babaji

Jyoti Swaroop: form of the flame

Jyotsna: the moonbeam

K

Kaal Chakra: 'wheel of time'

Kaaba: the sacred place of worship for Islam

Kabir: a medieval saint of India who was given the spiritual Kriya Yoga by Babaji. He was also given the mantra of "Rama" by his guru called Ramananda.

Kacchha: avatara of Vishnu

Kacchya: tortoise (sea turtle)

Kadali Vana: the forest where Matsyenedra Nath went.

Kailash: the sacred mountain where the spirit of Lord Shiva is said to dwell

Kailasha Nath: Lord of Kailash (Shiva)

Kaivalya: 'isolation', the state of absolute freedom from conditioned existence, as explained in Ashtanga Yoga; in the non-dualistic (advaita) traditions of India, this is usually called moksha or mukti, 'release' from the fetters of ignorance (avidya).

Kaivalya Darshanam: a book written by Shri Yukteshwar

Kala: 'Time', the duration between one event and another.

Kali: a Goddess embodying the fierce (dissolving) aspect of the Divine

Kali Yuga: from kali 'the losing throw of a die', in the Hindu astralogical system, the dark age of spiritual and moral decline; the current age of the world in the universal cycle, not to be confused with the shorter equinoctial cycle expounded by Sri Yukteswar.

Kalki: the coming avatar of Lord Vishnu, 10th in order.

Kalki Purana: an ancient treatise about the coming of the Kalki Avatar/Maitreya who shall restore spirituality on this earth, and reinstate the Solar Dynasty.

Kalpa: the lifespan assigned to our planetary system.

Kalyuga: see Kali Yuga

Kama: 'desire', the appetite for sensual pleasure blocking one's path to liberation (moksha).

Kama Deh: the body of desire

Kamalasana: lotus posture, also known as padmasana

Kamandalu: a brass vessel to carry water/food

Kamrupa: a tantric pilgrimage of the goddess Sati

Kapila: the sage founder of the Samkhya tradition and composer of the Samkhya Sutra.

Kanda: bulb or root

Kanishka: a dynasty; one of its emperors was Harshavartan

Kanya: girl below the age of 12

Kapha: phlegm; one of the three humors

Karan Sharir: the causal body

Karma: 'action', activity of any kind, including ritual acts; the law of cause and effect, of balance and justice, binding one to material condition; destiny; the condition of an individual birth.

Karma Shrinkala: the chain of events which binds the soul to the cycle of reincarnation

Karma Yoga: 'Yoga of action', the liberating path of self-transcending action involving virtuous deeds (punya), holy ritual (puja), and astrologically prescribed methods.

Karna: eldest son of Queen Kunti born of immaculate conception by the inception of the Son God

Kartikeya: the son of Lord Shiva

Kaula Gyana: also Kaula-marga, The Kaul Tantra originated by Matsyendra Nath as disclosed in the Kaula-Jnana-Nirnaya involving the divinization of the body through stimulating the flow of 'the nectar of immortality' (amrit).

Kaurava: one of the opposing families of the pandavers

Kaya Kalpa: an ancient yogic/ayurvedic process form of rejuvenation

Kevali Samadhi: 'condition of aloneness', he who has 'become alone' and is established in seeing the Self.

Khappar: a bowl made from the human skull

Khechari: the sky walking mudra (technique)

Khechari Mudra: 'space-walking seal'; facilitates astral travel. The yogic practice of 'swallowing the tongue in order to seal the life energy (prana) to be given by a bonified Guru; the seal of the tongue beyond the ulvula, stimulating the pituitary gland to drink of amrit).

Korrak Nath: the south Indian mispronunciation of the original Goraksha Nath

Kosha: 'casing', any one of five 'envelopes' surrounding the transcendental Self (atman) and blocking its realization of its Divine nature: annamayakosha 'envelope made of food,' the physical body, pranamayakosha 'envelope made of life force,' manomaya-kosha 'envelope made of mind,' vijnanamaya-kosha 'envelope made of consciousness,' and anandamayakosha 'envelope made of bliss.'

Krikara: triple sound of creation, preservation and dissolution. A. U. M.

Krkara: a sub-prana

Krishna: an incarnation (avatar) of the God Vishnu, the Purna Avatar whose teachings can be found in the Bhagavad-Gita and the Bhagavata-Purana.

Kriya Yoga: 'Yoga of doing', the 'lightning path' which brings you to the path of non-doing (akarma); given by Babaji Gorakshanath for the dissolution of karma and acceleration of human evolution to Divinity.

Kuhus: a sub-prana

Kul Achara: carrying out the behaviors and traditions of the family

Kul Dharma: the behaviors and traditions of the family

Kula: dynasty

Kula Kundalini: the kundalini power that prevails through human existence for many ages, many generations and many dynastys.

Kulaugama: (kuloguma) the seed from which a dynasty sprouts

Kumaon: the foothill regions of the Himalayas.

Kumaras: a youthful man from the age of 16 to 21

Kumarika: a youthful woman from the age of 13 to 18

Kumbh: earthen pot, usually in a rounded shape to hold water or any form of liquid

Kumbhaka: 'potlike', in the science of Yoga, the retention of and constriction of the locks (bandas) to usher vital energy (prana) into the spinal cord (sushumna nadi) for the awakening of kundalini; see also puraka, recaka

Kunda: pond

Kundal: earring worn by men

Kundalini: 'coiled serpent of the fire-kundh', electro-magnetic pranic energy centralized in the spine; Kundalini is the lady of the cinders whom, when fanned by the alchemical fire of Shiva-Shakti pranayam, ignites and blazes up the chimney of the spine to unite with the immortal Lord Shiva in the crown chakra (sahasrara) to enlighten the yogi.

Kundalini Kriya Yoga: Kriya Yoga; when the Kriya Yoga pranayam is performed, the pranic life-force in one's spinal chord (sushumna) builds up to generate a great spiritual magnetism and voltage. By the ceaseless movement of the Shiva-Shakti Kriya, life-force (prana), breath, vital fluid, and mind become one to form the evolutionary life-force energy called Kundalini.

Kunti: the mother of the Pandavas

Kurma: turtle (the one on land)

Kushan Dynasty: also known as the Kushvahn Dynasty, which is the progeny of Lord Rama's second son Kusha

Kutumi: "that which I am"

L

Lakh: a hundred thousand

Lakshmi: Goddess of Prosperity and Light

Lakulish: 'the staff-holder', 'He who holds the lightning-staff of evolution', a representation of Lord Shiva or Babaji-Gorakhnath; also defined as the ancient founder of the Shiva Pashupat sect of yogis.

Lalita Vistara: the techings of Gautam the Buddha, which were formulated during the time of Jesus and King Shalivihan

Lifetron: a subatomic particle composed of pranic lifeforce energy

Lila: the play of the divine mother as Maya

Linga: 'mark', the pillar or penis as the creative principle; a symbol and popular icon of Lord Shiva; a symbol for the universe cf. yoni.

Linga Puran: one of the ancient texts of the episodes relating to Lord Shiva. The linga is an oval sphere, which represents Shiva. It symbolizes Him to be everywhere and nowhere at the same time. Shiva has his center everywhere and circumference nowhere. In tantric aspects it is also used as the symbol of rejeneration and procreation.

Lobha: greed

Lokeshwar: another name for Matsyendyra Nath c.f. Avalokiteshwar

M

Maan: pride

Macchendranath: see Matseyndranath.

Madh Maheswar: one of the five sacred shrines of Shiva representing his naval

Madhyama Vak: sound made a little over a whisper; mumbling

Maghayanti: one of the seven sisters of the Pleiades

Maha Yoga: Nirvana Moksha

Maha Yuga: one complete cycle of all of the four yugas, name sattya, dwapar, tretta, kali

Mahabharata: 'Great Bharata', one of two of India's ancient and famous epics during the time of Lord Krishna, telling of the great war between the Pandavas and the Kauravas and serving as a repository for many spiritual and moral teachings.

Mahabinishkaran: 'the Great Sacrifice', the author refers to Shiv-Goraksha Babaji, the highest Be-ness of Divinity, who explodes himself to enter the atoms of all sentient and non-sentient beings and evolve humanity and creation to Divinity. As the ceaseless sacrifice continues, this Divinity gives completely of itself and yet remains complete. This divine enigma is beyond the scope of our humanity and gods to understand.

Mahakaala: 'The Great Beyond Time', epithet of Lord Shiva in whose presence, causation/light, space and time stands still and subdued and this is the end of relativity and the beginning of supreme consciousness.

Mahamudra: the posture of the great liberation

Maharaja: Great (maha) King (raja)

Maharath Manjari: a sacred mystical treatise given by Shiva Goraksha

Maheshworananda: another name of Goraksha Nath "those who know about me call me Goraksha Nath; those who know about me, call me Maheshworananda"

Manas: 'mind', the lower mind, which is bound to the senses and yields information (vijnana) rather than wisdom (jnana, vidya); cf. buddhi

Manavantar: a reign of one manu

Mandakini: our nearest galaxy called Andromeda

Mangal: Mars (auspicious)

Manipur Chakra: the naval chakra with four petals

Manju Nath: a name given to Goraksha Nath in the city of Mangalore

Mano-Buddhi-Ahamkar: mind, intellect and ego

Manomayee Kosh: the body of emotions

Mantra: from the root man 'to think', a sacred sound or phrase, such as om, hum, or om namah shivaya, that has a transformative effect on the mind of the individual reciting it; to be ultimately effective, a mantra needs to be given in an initiation by a Master.

Mantra Yoga: the yogic path utilizing mantras as the primary means of liberation.

Manu: the primordial father of the human race.

Manu Savarni: El Morya Vikramaditya who is to succeed Spiritual King Vaivasvat Manu.

Manu Smriti: the memoirs of Lord Vaivaswat Manu

Manu Vivasvat: the victorious sun

Manu Vaivasvat: the father of our fifth root race

Marici: one of the rishis of the Supta Rishi (Great Bear Constellation)

Markandeya Purana: the Purana written by the rishi Markandeya

Matsar: a tingling jealousy

Matseyndranath: 'Fish Lord', an early Nath and Mahasiddha, who founded the Yogini-Kaula school of Tantra and who implored Shiva to give him a disciple more advanced than himself; the Guru of Gorakshanath on the earthly plane and his disciple in the celestial plane.

Matsya: a fish

Maya: 'measure', the deluding or illusive power of the world binding one to mortality; illusion by which the world is seen as separate from the Divine; ignorance, specifically in the form of duality.

Mayavi: of the nature of mayic illusion

Mayavi rupa: illusive form

Merkabah: the fire chariot throne upon which sits the our Sun, driven by seven splendid white horses, each representing an important planet of our solar system. The Sun rides this fire chariot-thron through the twelve signs of the zodiac, dispensing justice and propelling evolution to human and celestials alike. The four wheels represent the four gods Yama for earth-death, Varuna for water-regeneration, Kubera for fire-life and Indra for aerial-life force (prana).

Metatron: the collective Elohim Spirit of the Angelic Hierarchy. He is an important part of the incomprehensible Shiva Goraksha Babaji who rides upon His own fire chariot-throne (Merkabah) traversing the universe in His incomprehensible ways and work.

Moha: attachment to the objects of the senses

Mohan: the celestial charmer of all souls (Krishna)

Moksha: 'release', the condition of freedom from ignorance (avidya) and the binding effect of karma; also called mukti, kaivalya

Morchal: a fan made of peacock feathers used by the Guru for cleansing one's astral body and driving away negative forces.

Morya: Chandra Gupta Morya/El Morya; the first emperor of India destined to be the future World King of the inner government of the world, the Manu Saverni of the sixth root race

Mrityunjaya: the conqueror of death, epithet of Lord Shiva

Mukti: a step lower than moksha; a release from any lower condition state to a higher more unconditioned state of awareness

Mula Bandha: rectal lock

Muladhara Chakra: located at the base of the spine at the perineum

Mudra: 'seal', a hand gesture (such as chin mudra) or whole-body gesture (such as Mahamudra) performed for the flow of subtle energies.

N

Nabhi Kriya: see Nabho kriya

Nabho Kriya: a yogic technique to join pranapana at naval (manipur chakra) and get steadiness of mind

Nada: 'sound', the inner sound of Om, as it can be heard through the practice of Nada Yoga; see also Hamsa Yoga.

Nada Brahma: the unheard sound of the Omkar during the Omkar Kriya Nadi Shuddhi: the purification of the psychic nerves

Nada Yoga: Yoga of the inner sound; the Yogic practice or process of producing and intently listening to the inner sound as a means of concentration and ecstatic self-transcendence.

Nadi: 'conduit', one of 72,000 subtle-astral channels along or through which the life force (prana) circulates; the three most prominent being the ida nadi, pingala nadi, and sushumna nadi.

Nadi Shodhan: 'channel cleansing', the practice of purifying the conduits for higher evolutionary states of Yoga, especially by means of breath control (pranayama).

Naga: serpent beings who act as agents of weather phenomenon

Nagna Satya: the naked truth which remains after the whole of creation is dissolved and time, space and light are also non-existent (also called the Naked Singularity)

Nanak: a great medieval saint and master and founder of Sikh religion. He has sung the praises of Babaji Gorakshanath in the "japji gutka"

Nandi: the bull, a vehicle of Lord Shiva and a symbol of the sound of Om Narada: a Deva Rishi and devotee of Shiva who taught him divine music at Rudraprayag. He is the author of the Bhakti-Sutras as given by Lord Shiva.

Narada Bhakti Sutras: see Bhakti Sutra

Nath: 'Lord', appellation for the Masters of Yoga, the Lords of all forms of Yoga; adepts of the Kanphata 'split-ear,' school founded by Gorakshanath.

Nath Mandala: The electromagnetic spiritual field of the Nath Yogis.

Navnath: The primeval Nine Naths of the seventh degree of cosmic awareness and beyond.

Neelkanta: the blue throated epithet for Lord Shiva

Neophyte: a newly initiate pupil on the path; as he treads the path he is called a tenderfoot.

Nirakara: without form

Niranjana: a term used by Nath Yogis for the highest state of consciousness (samadhi).

Niranjana Nirvana: the final salvation; a state of God Realization

Nirbija Samadhi: consciousness without seed; the highest form of samadhi before the final dissolution of dharma megha samadhi.

Nirvana: cessation of all desire. synonymous with enlightenment; see also kaivalya.

Nirvana Moksha: see Brahma Nirvana

Nirvani: fully enlightened being

Niyama: self-restraint', the second limb of Patanjali's eightfold path, which consists of purity (shaucha), contentment (samtosha), austerity (tapas), study (svadhyaya), and surrender to the Lord (ishvara-pranidhana)

Non-Being Essentiality: a word coined by the Yogiraj Siddhanath; this word is a paradox because Para Brahma is so beyond mortal conception that He is a Non-Being as far as we are concerned; and yet He is the essentiality of the very fabric of our Soul-essence and Creation.

O

Ojas: 'vitality', the subtle energy produced through practice, especially the discipline of chastity (brahmacharya).

Om: the primordial sound and birthing hum of creation heard by the yogi in meditation and harnessed to evolve himself to evermore refined spheres of consciousness. Before creation began, Om was smaller than the nucleus of the atom, within which infinitely compressed the far limits of the mind and matter of the universe…

Omkar: At the beginning of time, the light-sound explosion of the instant Creation, reverberating throughout eternity as the birthing hum of existence. This fundamental vibration of creation contains in it the Sattva Raja Tama Gunas, it contains the limits of the mind and matter of the universe.

Omkar Kriya: This is a special technique in Kriya yoga with which all Kriya meditations begin. It consists of listening and experiencing the triple divine quality of light sound creation.

P

Padma Matrika: the cosmic womb; the universal lotus mother from which the later word, matrix evolved. Padma Matrika was also later called the transcendental matrix, which contains the farthermost limits of the mind and matter of the universe

Panch Kedar: five pilgrimages (Kedarnath, Tunganath, Rudranath, Kalpanath and Madmaheshwar) Pancha Klesha: five afflictions of delusion (avidya/ignorance, asmit/thinking oneself to be a body and not the divine soul, raga/attraction, dvesh/repulsion, abhinivesh/clinging on to bodily existence and its temptation)

Panchanan: a name for the five headed Shiva

Panchashika: one of the highest kumars; a Sage of the Fire Mist

Para Prakriti: superior subtle nature.

Paramhansa: 'supreme swan', the 4th level of initiation of a yogi; an honorific title given to great adepts, such as Ramakrishna and Yogananda

Paramartha: science of the study of the true self (Atma Vidya)

Paramatma: 'supreme self', the transcendental Self, which is singular, as opposed to the individuated self (jiva-atman) that exists in countless numbers in the form of living beings.

Parampara: tradition handed down

Paras-mani: 'mercury gem'; consolidated mercury

Parjanya: the watery element

Parkaya Pravesha: the entry of a yogi into another body whether alive or dead

Parmars: a Rajput clan descended from the fire gods, Agnivamshas.

Pashayanti Vak: the sound vibration which is mental (Chintan)

Patala: the Netherlands, one of the lower nether regions

Patanjali: the Master of Yoga who authored the Yoga-Sutras.

Pavaka: one of the names of the Sacred Fire

Pavamana: another sacred name for fire

Philosopher's Gem: consolidated mercury

Pingala Nadi: 'reddish conduit', the prana current ascending on the right side of the central channel (sushuma-nadi) and associated with the sympathetic nervous system and having an energizing effect on the mind when activated; see also ida nadi

Pitris: our lunar ancestors from whom humanity is thought to have descended and ascended until they evolved out of the lunar cycle.

Pitta: bile

Pralaya: partial or total delusion through cataclysms and/or holocausts

Prana: the upward flowing life-force energy in the spine; also the universal life enrgy animating the whole of creation, the breath of the Cosmic Purusha; in Kriya Yoga it is used for the evolution of human consciousness.

Prana Apana Anusandhana: name for Kriya Yoga, connecting inhaled with exhaled lifeforce

Prana Patishtha: to infuse lifeforce energy into a deity or a shivaling and make it responsive to your prayer and yogic necessities.

Pranamayee Kosh: the sheath or body composed of prana

Pranapat: a term coined by Yogiraj Siddhanath to denote the grace of a Sat-Guru, when he breathes through the breath of the disciple; see also shaktipat, shivapat.

Pranava: another name for the sound of Omkar

Prasava: breathing forth also known as faulty breathing.

Pranayama: 'life-breath extension', breath control and expansion, the fourth limb (anga) of Patanjali's eightfold path, consisting of conscious inhalation (puraka), retention (kumbhaka), and exhalation (rechaka); at an advanced state, breath retention occurs spontaneously and for prolonged periods of time.

Prasada: 'grace/clarity', divine grace, mental clarity; food consecrated by the Guru or a deity.

Prateyaka Rudras: High Rishis of the Fire Mist of the eigth degree

Pratiprasava: the inward withdrawal of the mind and matter of creation; the centripetal movement into the vortex of dissolution.

Pratishthaan: an ancient name for the present state of Maharastra in India

Pratyahara: 'withdrawal', sensory inhibition, the fifth limb (anga) of Patanjali's eightfold path.

Prayag: the confluence of two rivers

Prem: love

Prithvi: a name for the rotating earth

Puja: 'worship', prescribed rituals usually accompanied by the recitation of mantras or shlokas, an important aspect of many forms of Yoga, notably Karma and Bhakti Yoga

Pujari: The priest who performs the temple rituals and prayers.

Pulaha: one of the Seven Rishis of The Great Bear

Pulastya: another of the Seven Rishis of the The Great Bear

Puraka: 'filling in', inhalation, an aspect of breath control (pranayama)

Puran Bhagat: complete devotee; another name for Chorongee Nath

Purana: 'Ancient', often refering to the ancient spiritual literature of India dealing with royal genealogy, cosmology, philosophy, and ritual; there are eighteen major and many minor works of this nature.

Purandara: the name of the present Indra

Puranic: of the Puranas, an ancient text

Puranwala: a well in the name of Puran Bhagat

Purna Avatara: a full, enlightened avatar of the 8th degree

Purusharth: 'human purpose' the four efforts for which people are responsible to pursued. These are arth (material welfare), kama (physical comfort), dharma (moral way of life) and moksha, (liberation).

Q

Queen Archan: wife of King Shalivahan and mother of Chowrungee

Queen Bacchal: wife of King Jewar and mother of Guga Nath.

Queen Kausaleya: wife of King Desharath, mother of Raghu Nath (Lord Rama)

Queen Kunti: wife of King Pandu, mother of the Five Pandavas

Queen Lunan: the younger wife of King Shalivahan.

R

Raga: passion or attachment.

Raghu: Name of one of the Kings of the Solar Dynasty

Rahasayam: mystery

Raj Hansa: the king's swan

Raja: king

Raja Yoga: 'Royal Yoga', a late medieval designation of Patanjali's eightfold yoga-darshana, also known as Classical Yoga

Rajas: one of the three gunas: sattva (luminosity), tamas (inertia) and rajas (activity)

Rajput: a princely clan of Rajastan

Raksha: protection

Rama: an avatar of Vishnu preceding Krsna; the principal hero of the Ramayana.

Rechaka: 'expulsion' exhalation, an aspect of breath control (pranayama).

Regina Mundi: a Latin name meaning World Mother

Reincarnation: 'Punar Janma', the individual Soul rotating in the repeated cycle of birth, death (the kala chakra) owing to bondage creating karma.

Renuka: an aspect of Divine Mother

Ribu: one of the Seven Sages of the Fire Mist

Rishi: 'seer', the Lord of Irradiant Splendor the Lord of Irradiant Splendor; the Sages of Fire Mist; a category of Vedic sage; an honorific title of certain venerated masters and Cosmic Beings.

Romaka-Pura: a city in the western part of Shamballah where the great astronomer Asurya Maya lived

Roop: beautiful form

Rudra Granthi: situated pranic plexus situated in the third eye

Rudra Kumar: a name for the Sages of the Fire Mist

Rudraksha: the seed of a tree, sacred to Shiva (sacred bead)

S

Saakshatkara: seeing the spiritual being in a materialized body of rainbow-light.

Sabeeja Samadhi: an ectasy of expanded consciousness with seed/desire; as opposed to Nirbeeja Samadhi, without the seed of desire

Sada-Shiva: ever present Shiva

Sadhak: a spiritual practioner

Sadhna: 'accomplishing', spiritual discipline leading to 'perfection' or 'accomplishment' (siddhi).

Sadhu: a holy many who does sadhana

Sages of the Fire Mist: were born at the dawn of creation of our greater world cycle (the Kalp). The Sages were self-born essenceswho manifested through the fire mist and were the freat hierophants and celestial teachers of our humanity and are responsible for the evolution of our humanities and races to this present day. They are the Manu Swyambhu and Sanat Kumar, the lord of our world, to name a few.

Sahaja Samadhi: 'together-born', natural enlightenment; the fact that the transcendental reality and the empirical reality are not truly separate but coexist, or with the latter being an aspect or misperception of the former; often rendered as 'spontaneous' or 'spontaneity'; the sahaja state is the natural condition, that is, enlightenment or realization.

Sahasrara Chakra: thousand petaled lotus; crown chakra

Saivism: the religious path followed by worshippers of Lord Shiva

Sama: balanced

Samadhi: 'putting together', the ecstatic or unitive state in which the meditator becomes one with the object of meditation; the eighth and final limb (anga) of Patanjali's eightfold path; there are many types of samadhi, the most significant distinction being between samprajnata (superconscious) and asamprajnata (supra-conscious) ecstasy; only the latter leads to the dissolution of the karmic factors deep within the mind; beyond both types of ecstasy is enlightenment, which is also sometimes called sahaja-samâdhi or the condition of 'natural' or 'spontaneous' ecstasy, where there is perfect continuity of supra-conscious throughout waking, dreaming and sleeping.

Samana: a prana of a green hue connected with digestion

Samasara: the world of maya (illusion) driven by karma (the law of action and reaction), leading to punanjarma (rebirth) or moksha (liberation).

Samayama: a state of samadhi where the subject and the object become one

Sambalpur: often mispronounced Shamballah or Shangri-La; the place from where the Kalki Avatara is to emerge.

Sambandhar: a great south Indian avatar and worshipper of Lord

Glossary

Shiva

Samkhya: 'number', one of the main philosophies of Yoga, which is concerned with the classification of the principles (tattva) of existence and their proper discernment in order to distinguish between Spirit (Purusha) and the various aspects of nature (prakriti); this influential system grew out of the ancient (pre-Buddhist) Samkhya Yoga tradition and was codified in the Samkhya-Karika of Ishvara Krishna 3500 BCE.

Samsara: 'confluence', the finite world of change, as opposed to the ultimate reality (brahman or nirvana).

Samskara: 'activator', the subconscious impression left behind by each act of volition, which, in turn, leads to renewed psychomental activity; the countless samskaras hidden in the depth of the mind are ultimately eliminated only in asamprajnata-samadhi (see samadhi)

Samkhya Karika: the author of the book is Ishwar Krishna

Sanak: One of the Sages of the Fire Mist

Sanandana: Another of the Sages of the Fire Mist

Sanata Kumar: Chief of the Sages of the Fire Mist

Sanatana: the eternal

Sanatana Dharma: the eternal religion

Sanat-Sujata: Another of the Sages of the Fire Mist

Sanchit Karma: those karmas stored in the collective unconscious of the individual

Sangh: a collective body of like-minded people

Sanjeevan Samadhi: immortal state of samadhi

Sanjeevani Vidya: the yogic process of bringing others back to life, resurrecting their physical body, for specific spiritual work.

Santatii: offspring

Sapta-Sapti: one of the secret names of the coming Kalki Avatara

Saraswati: the goddess of learning; she is the informing spirit of the mystic word of learning called Vach; therefore, she is called Vach Saraswati Sanyasa: 'casting off', the state of renunciation, which is the fourth and final stage of life (see ashram) and consisting primarily in an inner turning away from what is understood to be finite and secondarily in an external letting go of finite things.

Sapta Rishi: the Seven Primordial Sages, corresponding to the seven stars of the Great Bear.

Sat: 'truth', the ultimate reality (Atman or Brahman)

Satanic: of the quality of satin; he slips you into devious ways without you knowing it

Sat-Nama: the true name, usually referred to as Omkar

Satguru: 'one with gravity', a Master who brings to light the Spiritual knowledge inherent in man; an enlightened aspect of the Divine

Sattvic Ahar: a diet which is pure and predominantly of sattva gunas

Saturn-Kronos: the planet connected with time

Savikalpa Samadhi: state of ecstasy with attributes of human perception

Seetali: form of yogic pranayama where you breathe through the tubular shape of the tongue

Shaastras: science

Shabda Yoga: mantra yoga

Shad Ripu: the six subtle sheaths connects with the physical spiritual being

Shad-chakra Bhedan: science of the penetration of the six chakras

Shakti: 'power', the kinetic aspect of the potential Shiva (God-realization), the power to transform and evolve aspirants to this enlightened state; see also kundalini shakti.

Shakti Chalan: making a vacuum of the stomach and moving it in and out

Shakti Pithas: power center

Shaktipat: 'descent of shakti', one of the three blessings (shivapat, shaktipat, and pranapat) SatGurunath bestows upon his disciples for their spiritual progress; the awakening of the dormant kundalini energy of a disciple.

Shalivahan: Was the ancient parmar king of the city of Sialkant of ancient northern India. The father of Chowrangee Nath

Shambala: see Shambalpur

Shambalpur: also known as Shambala, where Shiva-Goraksha-Babaji reigns as Spiritual King until the world cycle is over; its higher center is in the Aurora Borealis of the Northern Lights.

Shambhavey Mudra: outward gaze with inward attention

Shataka: a century or a hundred

Shiva: 'the Benevolent One', the Consciousness of the universe. The great destroyer of delusion and spiritual rejenerator of mankind. He is the divine potential aspect of his own kinetic shakti energy; also called Mahadeva 'Great God.'

Shiva Bhakti Sutras: originally given by Lord Shiva

Shivaji: the Medieval Marattha King who repelled the Mogul forces and restored India, saving it from total invasion and returning it to its Hindu glory

Shivanetra: the third-eye chakra; also the third eye of Shiva, the location of the Hamsa swan seen visually in meditation.

Shivapat: 'Shiva's grace', the Sat-Guru, as Consciousness, awares himself into the mind-disciple, transforming that mind into his own Consciousness to the degree of the disciple's receptivity to his Consciousness; see also pranapat, shaktipat.

Shravan Bhadrapad: the monsoon rainy season

Shringara Shataka: the romantic composition of love as opposed to the Vairagya Shataka, the hundred verses of renunciation; both works composed by the King Bhatari Nath

Shuddhi: 'purification/purity', the state of purity; see also shodhana.

Shukra: the planet Venus, symbolizes life and also the vital fluid

Shvetdeep: 'White Island', see Shambalpur.

Shweta Varaha Kalpa: 'World-Cyle of the White Boar.'

Shyama: the dark one; a name of the goddess

Siddha: 'accomplished', a perfected Master or adept; a mahasiddha or 'great adept' denoting one of the Nine Immortal Naths.

Siddhi: 'accomplishment/perfection', spiritual perfection, the attainment of flawless identity with the ultimate reality (atman or brahman); paranormal ability, of which the Yoga tradition knows many kinds.

Simhasta-Kumbha: the great Leo-Aquarius fair that occurs every twelve years in India, which over 40 million pilgrims attend, undoubtedly (the greatest show on earth).

Singaldweep: another name for Sri Lanka

Soma: the elixir which is God, from the practice of Khechari Mudra in yogic practices; it is also taken from plants and connected with the moon; anti-aging ambrosia may be extracted from moon plants

Soul-Star: the Kutastha Chaitanya seen in the third eye; one's individual star-gate, penetrating which, One enters from savikalpa samadhi to the nirvikalpa samadhi state

Sphurti Vada: inspired conversation

Sthul Deh: gross or coarse, the outer most aspect of something.

Suchi: a form of fire along with Pavaka and Pavamana

Sukhavati Heaven: of Lord Varuna as Amravati Heaven is of Lord Indra

Surya Nadi: the life-force flowing through the right nostril

Surya Putra: son of the sun; Lord Vaivaswat Manu is son of the Sun Lord Vivaswat Manu

Surya Yoga: a contemporary yoga developed by Yogiraj Siddhanath, the author

Sushmuna Nadi: 'very gracious channel', the central prana current in or along which the serpent power (kundalini shakti) must ascend toward the psycho-energetic center (chakra) at the crown of the head in order to attain liberation (moksha).

Svaha: the wife of Agni Abhimani, father of the three sub-fires (pavaka, pavamana, shuchi)

Svaroop Samadhi: also called samadhi with form and sanjeevan samadhi.

Svayambhu: self-born and eternal

Swadhishtan Chakra: the genital center chakra, located at the sacral tailbone

Swadhyaya: 'one's own going into', self-study, important to the yogic path, listed among the practices of self-restraint (niyama) in Patanjali's eightfold Yoga; the recitation of mantras; see also japa.

Swaha: going to the fire; also a name of the wife of the Fire God, Agni Abhimani

Swami: 'owner' or 'lord', title of respect for a spiritual personage.

Swaroop: (svaroop) embodiment of one's true Self; the essential nature of a thing.

Swayambhu: 'great unborn', the self-manifestation and personal aspect of Lord Shiva. The cosmic being Babaji-Gorakshanath will not incarnate from age to age, but is perpetually present until the world cycle (mahakalpa) is over. He broods over humanity, his children, from eternity to eternity and is thus known as "the Great acrifice". His work is far beyond the comprehension of mortals; see also aja.

T

Tabernacle: a tent and a portable dwelling place for the divine.

Takshaka Naga: one of the species of cobras

Tanmatras: 'fine matter', the subtle aspect of the material elements (bhuta) which may be seen in the form of light during yoni-mudra (also jyoti-mudra); the potentials of sound (shabda), form (rupa), touch (sparsha), taste (rasa), and smell (gandha).

Tantra: 'warp', the tradition of Tantrism and practice of tantric rights by which the laws of nature are manipulated and overcome; the esoteric and arcane practices of sadhus in India by which the sadhak may attain spiritual powers (siddhis) by means of tantric practice and tapa.

Tantra Aloka: Abhinav Gupta's magnum opus, which discusses in great depth the metaphysics and spiritual practice of Tantrism from the viewpoint of Kashmir Shaivism.

Tantra Yoga: a form of yoga, c.f. Raj Yoga, Hatha Yoga, Dyana Yoga, Bhakti Yoga..etc.

Tao Te Ching: a treatise written by Lao-Tzu, specifically to do with the taming of the bull of one's own passions and the practice of Indian yoga, such as the pranic Kriya Yoga

Tapa: 'glow' or 'heat', austerity or endurance of extremes, an element of all yogic approaches, since they all involve renunciation and transcendence; in yogic meditation, the act of stewing in one's own pranic energies thereby channelising and storing them.

Tara: a form of the goddess

Taraka Raj Yoga: system of yoga, founded by the Medieval chemist Aryasangh

Taranhara: the messiah or soul savior; also a name for avatar, the downward crossing

Tathastu: means "So Be It" just as we say "Amen"

Glossary

Tattva: 'thatness', a fact or reality; a particular category of existence such as the ahamkara, buddhi, manas; the ultimate reality; see also atman, Brahman.

Tejas: yogic brilliance along with ojas and prana

Thickosity: a term coined by Yogiraj Siddhanath that means with increased consistency

Tirthankar: the bridge builders in Jain religion

Trataka: one of the six kriyas of concentrating on a flame

Trilochana: one with the third-eye; an epithet of Lord Shiva

Trimuti: three faces of three faced sculpture of Trinity

Trishul: trident

Tushita Heaven: a heavenly sphere where the Kalki Avatara is preparing for his second advent; therefore, it is connected to Shamballah from where the Kalki is to appear.

U

Uccatan: a tantric technique to return the evil forces sent by another being

Udana: metabolic prana, concerned with the lymphatic and metabolic systems; one of the five main life forces namely Prana, Apana, Sapan, Udana and Vyena

Uddiyana Bandha: the abdominal lock

Ujjain: the city of the victorious one

Unmani Avasta: a clear-mind ecstasy of thoughtless awareness.

Utopia: a spiritual land, which we in India call Shambala, also called Shangri La in which an egalitarian and a happy society live in peaceful co-existance. Shambala, the land from where the Kalki avatar is expected to come as the second advent.

Uttar Pradesh: It is a province lying in the northern regions of

India

Uttara Khand: This is a province lying in the northern Himalayan regions of India

V

Vach: see Vak.

Vaidhatra: 'lightening holder', unborn manifestation of the Creator; Master of destiny; holder of the Cosmic Kundalini; a name of Shiva-Goraksha Babaji.

Vaikhari Vak: the grossest sound pattern emanating from Vak Saraswati

Vairagya: 'dispassion', the attitude of inner renunciation, the counterpole to abhyasa.

Vairagya Shataka: the treatise on renunciation by King Bhartari Nath

Vajra Nadi: the second of the psychic nerves. First is sushumna, second is vajra, third is chittra and fourth is Brahma

Vajrayana: the Lightning Path of which the Shiva-Shakti Kriya is the crest jewel

Vajroli: a tantric technique of the transformation of sexual into spiritual energy

Vak: also Vac 'speech', divine speech the power of manifestation; there are four vak, vaikhari (loud sound), madhyama (murmuring sound), pashyanti (mental sound), para (meditative unheard sound); a name of Sarasvati, Vak Sarasvati.

Vamana: the fifth dwarf avatar of a series of the ten avatars of Vishnu

Varaha: the third boar-faced avatar of a series the ten avatars of Vishnu

Varaha Mihir: one of the greatest astronomers and mathematicians who is said to be a direct incarnation of the even greater rishi Parashara, who is the Indian Hermes (Mercury)

Varkaris: a sect of Bhagvat devotees who worship Lord Krishna in the form of Lord Vitthal or Lord Pandhurang

Varuna: the deity presiding over the element of water and the oceans.

Varun Astra: a mantric hydro-missile used for elimination of negative forces

Varuna Rishi: see Varuna.

Vasikaran: conquest by mind power

Vastushpati: the planet Sirius; the hunter (Vyad) who slays the deer (Mrugnakshatra, the constellation Orion). From this originated the science of Vastu Gyan "geomancy."

Vayu: the Hindu deity presiding over the element of wind.

Veda: 'knowledge', the body of sacred wisdom found in the four Vedic hymnodes that form the source of Hinduism: Rig-Veda, Yajur-Veda, Sama-Veda, and Atharva-Veda; also the collective name for these hymnodies; see also Vedanta.

Vedanta: 'Veda's end', the teachings forming the doctrinal conclusion of the revealed literature (shruti) of Sanatana Dharma; see also Upanishad; cf. Aranyaka, Brahmana, Veda

Vidhata: a name for Brahma the creator, who holds the destinies of humanities, the nations and creation.

Vidhnaharta: the first born of Brahma, that is, the first Sage of the Fire Mist, Sanat Kumar, also known as Jaggan Nath, the Lord of the World

Vidmahe: may we know

Vidya: inner wisdom

Vidyut: electricity

Vijnanmayee Kosh: the mental sheath or the mental body of man

Viraj: the masculine aspect of light-sound, whose feminine aspect is Vak Saraswati

Viraj-Vach: 'light-sound', (Brahma-Sarasvati)

Vishaya Vasana: attachment to material desires

Vishnu: 'pervader', the preserver; worshipped by Vaishnavas and who has had nine incarnations, including Rama and Krsna, with the tenth incarnation (avatara) Kalki coming at the start of the Aquarian age.

Vishnu Granthi: the heart plexus chakra where this Vishnu knot is located, which has to be loosened and penetrated like the Brahma and Rudra Granthis

Vishnu Purana: ancient text according to the Vaishnava philosophy

Vishuddha Chakra: the lotus located in the spine, behind the throat

Vritti: 'whirl', in Patanjali's Yoga-Darshana, specifically the five types of mental activity: valid cognition (pramana), misconception (viparyaya), imagination (vikalpa), sleep (nidra), and memory (smriti)

Vyana: the breath driven prana; one of the five

Vyasa: 'arranger', the name of several great sages, but specifically referring to Veda Vyasa, who arranged the Vedic hymns in their current form and who also is attributed with the compilation of the Puranas, the Mahabharata, and other works, including the commentary on the Yoga-Sutras of Patanjali, the Yoga-Bhashya.

W

White Boar: The name of our present kalpa (In Sanskrit it is called the Shweta Varaha Kalpa) We are at present, halfway through this grand world cycle of the White Boar. The duration of the complete cycle is 4,320,000,000 years.

White Island: sveta (white) dvipa (island). In this island is the celestial city of Shamballa (Sambalpur) wherein reigns the King Sanat

Kumar. The Sages of the Fire Mist and the Kalki Avatara are also said to reside on this spiritual island.

Wings To Freedom: Yogiraj Siddhanath's previous book.

World Disciple: the collective consciousness of our humanity, which is striving to disengage itself from the trammels of the senses and the mire of materialism and ultimately find its inner light assisted by the great masters of Shamballa.

Y

Yajna: 'sacrifice', ritual fire sacrifice involving the chanting of mantras and shlokas. Yoga also knows of an inner sacrifice of kindling the internal flame of kundalini.

Yama: 'discipline', the first limb (anga) of Patanjali's eightfold path, comprising moral precepts that have universal validity (such as non-harming and truthfulness); the name of the gatekeeper of the netherworld, Yama 'The First Mortal.'

Yashasvini: one of the sub-pranas in the body

Yoga: 'union', the spiritual tradition and practice of uniting the individual soul (Jiva) with the Supreme Spirit (Shiva) origiinating in India; the unitive discipline by which inner freedom is sought; spiritual practice, as practiced in Hinduism, Buddhism, and Jainism, and transcending the entrapment of religious identification.

Yogacharya: an adept of Yoga capable of teaching others.

Yoga-Tirumantirum: a yogic treatise written by Raja Sundar Nath when he entered the body of Thiru Moolar

Yogi: a male practitioner of Yoga

Yogini: a female practitioner of Yoga

Yogiraj: 'King of Yogis', a title of exaltation and praise granted to a spiritual Master.

Yoni: the female genitalia; also a symbol for the the supreme Goddess and source of the universe, the primordial deep; see also linga

Yoni Mudra: also known as jyoti mudra and shan-mukhi-mudra, the blocking of one's ears, eyes, and nostrils with one's fingers where the inner sound, anahata-nada (omkar) is heard and the soul is seen as a spot of light at the third eye.

Yuga: 'age', a division of time; as expounded by Swami Shri Yukteshwar, the four ages of ascending and descending arcs (12,000 years in length), forming one Mahayuga of 24,000 years.

Z

Zero-Naught-Zero: an expression used by Yogiraj Siddhanath to express the everything and the nothing since the divine is beyond comprehension. Paradoxical words need to be used to paralyze the mind; only then can it see the clear light.

GLOSSARY

A

Aaryabhat 341
Aaryan Root Race 272
Abhimana Mada 310
Abhinav Gupta 165
Abhinivesh 311
Achalachambu Nath 60, 155
Adharas 250
Adi Nath 281, 283, 284
Adi Shankaracharya 84, 139, 140
Adi-Shesha 155
Aditi 329, 349
Aditya 318, 349, 354
Advaita 88, 118, 119, 120, 139, 202
Advaita Vedant 139
Advaita Vedanta 118
Agastya 21, 184, 212, 349, 357
Agni 87, 169, 213, 313, 327, 333, 339, 346
Agni Abhimanin 328
Agni Surya Yogi 208
Agni Vamsha 169
Ahirbudnya 8, 372, 374
Aja 25, 27, 110, 155, 206, 283
Aja Ek Pad 8
Ajapa Japa 256
Aja Purusha 179
Ajmer 171
Akarma 111

Akasha 301, 346, 372
Akashic Records 240
Akhadas 144, 145
Akula 165
Alakh 59, 75, 142, 155, 251, 282
Alakh Niranjan 1, 142, 225, 261
Alambusa 253
Alam Prabhu 61
Alkapuri 35, 36, 175, 186
Allah 141
Amarnath 156
Amaroli 291
Amba 8, 157, 159
Amla 307, 310
Amrita 173, 301
Amrita Anubhava 173
Anahata aj, 141, 227, 250, 252
Anahata Nada 141, 252
Anandamayi Ma 106, 124, 125
Ancient of Days i, 2, 11, 25, 70, 113, 129, 155, 160, 162, 177, 191, 219, 271, 281-283, 318
Angiras 188, 293, 357
Anuloma Viloma 313
Anumeena Pranayama 300
Anusandhan 255, 263, 312
Apana 220-222, 235, 254-56, 262, 265, 299
Aradhya Kalam 160
Archangel Gabriel 87
Archangel Michael 84, 87
Ardhnarishwar 1, 103
Arjuna 34, 35, 61, 88, 115, 172, 221, 282
Arundhati 31
Asamprajnata Samadhi 43, 45

439

Asana 96, 231
Ashram 18, 19, 63, 124, 130, 149, 282, 323
Ashvagandha 307
Ashvathama 115
Ashvin Kumars 282
Askesis 231
Asmita 311
Assam 71, 170
Asso Pat 163
Asta Bhuja 160
Astral Body 40, 114, 119, 121, 223, 297, 319
Astral Chakra 84, 206, 210
Asuramaya 349, 351, 357
Atma 117, 118, 196, 212, 277, 329, 339, 344, 370, 379-383
At-one-ment e, 4, 301
Atri 333, 334, 357
Aulia 119
Aum 305, 306, 354
Aunsh Avatara 113, 279
Aura 8, 9, 40, 47, 85, 88, 96, 116, 124, 188, 189, 201, 205, 316
Autobiography of a Yogi 11-13, 19, 22, 76, 130, 140, 145-53, 235, 247, 283
Avadhoot 76, 84, 109, 110, 116-124, 156, 186-190, 204, 207, 279
Avalokiteshwara 41, 164
Avasta 156, 165, 222, 302, 303
Avesh 170, 213
Avidya 202, 310, 311
Ayama 221, 300

B

Babaji Haidakhan I 17
Babaji Haidakhan II 18
Babaji Nagaraj 20-22
Badrinath 32-37, 156, 175, 186
Bali 88, 115

Bal Tripura Sundari 8
Bandh 170, 220, 257, 258, 262
Basti 310
Bela-Shailush 308
Bhadon 169
Bhagavad Gita 34, 110, 172, 197, 220-23, 226, 238, 241, 273
Bhairavi 157-160
Bhakti iv, 25, 31, 96, 122, 137, 172-74, 196, 205, 206, 263, 301, 306-309, 318
Bhakti Yoga iv, 25, 172, 205, 301, 307, 308, 318
Bharat 34, 70
Bharatvarsha vii
Bhartari Nath 162, 163, 283
Bhaskar 259, 349
Bhavani 157, 158
Bhavishya Purana 114, 181, 213
Bhima 61, 282
Bhisma 328
Bhrig 351
Bhrigu 293, 349, 357
bhrukuti 249
Bhur 263, 342
Bhut 310
Bhuta 166, 309
Bhuta Shuddhi 309, 310
Bikaner 170
Bindu 6, 260, 261, 264, 290, 293, 305
Bindu Rahasaya 290
Bodhidharma 366
Bodhisattva 84, 118, 164, 168, 199, 207
Bogar Nath 20, 132, 290
Brahma Astra 213
Brahmacharya 18, 290, 306, 308
Brahma Granthi 237
Brahma Nadi 237, 302
Brahmanaspati 214, 346
Brahmanda Purana 63
Brahma Nirvana 79, 118, 121, 160, 166, 202
Brahma Rishi 34, 340, 351

Buddha 41, 84-88, 106, 110-18, 125, 156, 160, 161, 168, 184, 186, 196, 199, 202, 206, 209, 212, 215, 278, 321, 338, 343
Buddhi 118, 192-196, 204, 205
Buddhism 41, 118, 186, 343, 366

C

Chalan 261, 306
Chanakya 136, 208
Chandeva 173
Chandi 157
Chandogya Upanishad 101, 114, 181
Chandra 261, 265, 292, 313
Chandrasoma 155
Charan Paduka 37
Chauhan 53, 169, 170
Chetannath 168
Chinna-masta 157
Chiranjeev 17, 88, 115
Chitra Nadi 237
Chitta 118, 260, 311
Chitta Shuddhi 311
Chola 18
Chowrangee Nath 59, 84, 130, 155, 166-168, 272, 283
Christ 37, 41, 61, 84-89, 115, 125, 197, 203-206, 272-74, 296, 351, 374
Christos 84, 197, 374
Chyvan Prash 307
Cittargiri 20-22
Cobra 7, 21, 22, 224, 283
Count St. Germain 88

D

Dabisthana 61
Daksha 158, 328, 329, 337

Dakshinmurti 129, 283
Damru 178, 328, 373, 376
Darshan 89, 104, 148, 149, 374
Darwinian theory of evolution 344
Dasha Bhuja 160
Dattatreya 60, 88, 115, 202
Deccan 71
Degree of Initiation 116, 186, 202
Devaki 76, 106
Devapi 115, 136, 198, 208-15, 241
Deva Rishi 17, 31, 96, 357
Devdatta 197, 254
Dhaba 123
Dham 262
Dhananjay 254, 299
Dharana 231, 237
Dhuni 60
Dhyana 61, 124, 231, 237, 254, 255, 366
Dilip 193, 272
Dronacharya 17, 88
Dronagiri 233
Durga 70, 157, 158, 160
Dvar 256
Dvesh 310, 311
Dwapara Yuga 110, 243
Dwarka 139

E

El Morya 115, 198, 210, 213, 215, 273
Elohim 78, 79, 113, 183, 191, 339
Everest 156

G

Gabriel 180, 331
Gajanan Maharaja 121
Gajar 310

Galava 333
Ganapati 41, 87, 330
Gandhari 252
Gandiva 61
Ganesha 60, 133, 155, 202, 271
Ganga 97, 99, 328
Garga Rishi 25, 130, 282
Garhwal 32, 103, 175, 291
Gauri 156-158
Gauri Shankar 156
Gautama Buddha 118, 156
Gayatri 188, 256, 283, 304
Gazni 171
Gopeshwar 175
Gopichand 68, 142
Gorakha 19, 70
Gorakh Narayana 19
Gorakhpur 13, 35, 71, 141, 150, 175
Goraksha Paddhati 272, 312
Goraksha Sahastranam 283
Goraksha Shataka 219, 223, 226, 227, 247, 267, 272
Granthi 237, 268
Gudadal 254
Guga Nath 53, 169, 170, 171, 284
Gujarat 171
Gunas 63, 76, 114, 120, 160, 178, 199, 214, 255, 278, 309, 377
Gupta Vidya 191
Gurkha 71
Guru Darbar 169, 170
Guru Kripa 308
Gurutva Akarshana 373
Gwalior 53, 54, 169, 333
Gyan 62, 73, 121, 166, 167, 172-174, 248, 250, 257
Gyan Swaroop 166, 167

H

Hanuman 61, 88, 115
Haradwar 162

Harischandra 193, 272
Hastajivhava 252
Hatha Yoga 47, 96, 187, 219, 222, 300, 302, 305-307
Himavat 158
Hinduanity 343
Hinduism 63, 186, 343
Hiranyaloka 88, 150, 274
Hridaya 254

I

Ida 43, 252-55, 312
Ikshavaku 193, 207, 212, 272
Indra 5, 61-64, 129, 180, 214, 282, 331, 332-36, 346
Indrayani 63
Ishanath 168
Ishvara Pranidhan 230, 232
Ishvar Krishna 123, 182

J

Jivatma 90, 231, 264
Jnaneshwari 172
Jnaneswar 121, 173, 174
Judaism 343
Jyoti Mudra 227, 229, 235, 236, 268, 306
Jyotirdhama 333
Jyotirmath 139
Jyoti Swaroop 25
Jyotsna 259

K

Kaaba 141
Kabir 61, 62, 70, 75, 76, 137, 140-

46, 208, 272
Kabul 171
Kacchha 112, 209, 338
Kadali-vana 72, 73
Kailash 141, 159, 212, 214
Kaivalya 149, 202, 284, 375
Kaivalya Darshanam 149
Kala Bhairavi 160
Kala Chakra 335
Kalagni Nath 129, 132-35, 160-62, 283, 366
Kaligarh Mountain 66
Kali Yuga 67, 110, 243, 352, 358
Kalki 27, 37, 41, 65, 88, 106, 112-16, 120, 125, 136, 181, 183, 195, 196-200, 203-15, 241-43, 272-74, 285, 338, 351, 372
Kalki Purana 114, 181, 197, 211, 213, 243
Kalpa 87, 110, 115, 179, 180-85, 192, 202, 203, 209, 277, 329-36, 354-58
Kalpanath 33
Kama 119, 163
Kamandalu 47, 163
Kama Sharir 119
Kamrupa 250
Kanda 249, 252, 256-58, 262
Kanishka 168
Kanthad Nath 60, 155, 193
Kanya 38
Kapha 297, 298, 309, 312
Kapil 87
Karan Sharir 311
Karma 3, 25, 29, 43, 45, 50, 79, 110-13, 116-24, 158, 164, 166, 172, 191, 205, 207, 212, 213, 225, 226, 238, 260, 261, 264, 273, 302, 306, 335, 336, 340, 367
Karma Shrinkala 302
Karma Yoga 172, 205, 212
Karna 88, 208, 282
Kartikeya 59, 87, 155, 193, 202, 271, 328, 330
Karur Siddha 20
Kashi 76, 96, 129, 140, 145, 147, 156, 163, 283, 366
Kashi Moni 76, 145
Kashmir 165, 168, 242
Kashyap 206, 209, 212, 349, 354
Kathiawar 70
Kathmandu 165
Kaula 59, 72, 73, 157, 165
Kaurava 17, 19
Kaya Kalpa 161, 185
Kebalananda 140
Kedarnath 33, 37, 156
Kerala 139
Kevali 220, 222, 238, 264, 265, 300
Kevali Kumbhak 222
Khechan 260
Khechari Mudra 226-28, 235, 238, 259, 260, 268, 300, 302, 309
Khwaja Khizra 171
King Amar 170
King Jewar 169, 170
King Pandu 282
Koothumi 213
Koti Surya 300
Krikara 299
Kripacharya 19, 88
Krishna 17, 25-7, 34, 35, 61, 64, 76, 84, 89, 101, 106, 110-13, 120-25, 129-31, 156, 165, 172, 182, 191, 196-99, 203-9, 212, 215, 221, 271-73, 281, 282, 338, 374
Kriya Shakti 111, 115, 118, 166, 181, 279, 285
Kriya Yoga 3, 4, 7, 11, 14, 20, 29, 43, 54-7, 62, 75, 79, 86, 97, 98, 112, 137, 141-52, 161-64, 184, 205, 214, 219-43, 247, 255, 256, 263-68, 271-74, 300-2, 306, 311, 317, 318, 366
Krkara 254
Kshatriya 65, 215
Kubera 129, 331, 336
Kuhus 253

Kula 115, 165, 250
Kul Achara 311
Kulagama 165
Kul Dharma 311
Kumaon 17, 18, 19, 103, 105, 233
Kumbh 67
Kunda 7
Kundalini 1, 4-9, 49, 62, 84, 87, 88, 105, 106, 119, 123, 125, 133, 161, 165, 174, 184, 188, 210, 220-5, 235, 236, 250-3, 256, 257, 271, 284, 295-8, 301-9, 366, 374
Kundalini Kriya Yoga 8, 18, 142, 236, 323, 365
Kunti 19, 106, 282
Kurma 254
Kushan Dynasty 168
Kuthastha Chaitanya 249
Kwaja Moin Uddin Chiste 171

L

Lakh 65, 204, 249
Lakshmi 73, 369, 372, 373
Lakulish 1, 3, 184, 206
Lalita Vistara 168
Lao Tzu 132, 133, 161, 366
Laya 178, 369, 376
Lifetrons 222
Lightless Light 1, 6, 40, 46, 69, 79, 99, 105, 142, 180, 191, 263, 271, 278, 279, 280, 283, 327, 373-6
Lila 34, 56, 65, 106, 179
Linga 191, 192, 224, 251-3, 305
Lipika 214, 347
Lobha 310
Lokeshwar 71, 72
Lomaharshana 332

M

Madhyama Vaak 304
Madhya Pradesh 169
Maghayanti 199, 240, 241
Mahabharata 17, 19, 34, 136, 172, 213, 315
Mahabinishkaran 56
Mahadeva 18, 64, 70, 282, 359, 360
Mahadyuti 63
Maha Guru 117, 121, 170, 208
Mahakalpa 6, 110, 182, 183
Maha Maya 155
Mahamudra 235, 236, 258, 259, 268, 306, 312
Mahamuni 12, 76
Mahandatta 160
Mahankal 271, 350, 371, 373, 375
Mahant 35, 170, 175
Maharaj 12, 53, 76, 121, 170, 208, 214, 347
Maharana Pratap 208
Maharashtra 71, 121, 137, 165, 174, 206
Mahasamadhi 18, 20, 122, 147, 150, 152, 174, 233, 234
Maha Shivaratri 323
Mahavir 186
Maha Yogi 76
Maha Yuga 331, 352, 354
Maheshwar 33, 62
Maheshworananda 64
Major Manu 354
Manas Sharir 311
Manavantar 202, 209, 241, 277, 332-34, 356
Manav Dharma Shastra v, 198, 273, 340, 354, 357, 384
Manda 258
Mandakini 31, 95, 96, 99
Mangalore 67
Manikarnika Ghat 186

Manjunath 199
Mano-Buddhi-Ahamkar 311
Mantra Yoga 141, 304, 311
Manu Savarni 88, 131, 132, 206, 208, 210, 213, 215, 243, 274, 337, 352
Manu Smriti 198, 272, 273, 339, 357
Manu Swayambhu 179, 210, 339
Marichi 188, 212
Markandeya Purana 123, 182
Marut Prana 301, 302, 303
Mary 61, 106
mast 121
Mataji 1, 3, 5, 39, 69, 87, 103-7, 271, 328
Matsar 310
Matsya 112, 209, 338
Matsyagandha 315
Matsyendra Nath 41, 59, 64, 68, 71, 72-4, 139, 140, 155-7, 164-6, 184, 206, 284, 286
Mayavi 76, 113, 114, 118, 191, 280
Mayavi Rupa 113, 191
Medhra Sthan 251
Meera 61
Mejda 13, 14
Merkabah 332
Messiah 114, 198
Metatron 198
Michael 180, 331
Mina Nath 157, 164
Minor Manu 339, 354, 355
Mitra 180, 212
Moha 310
Moksha 113, 117-9, 202, 204, 222, 226, 235, 256, 304, 331, 335, 336
Morchal 170
Moses 129-32, 208, 272-74, 283, 343
Mukti 202, 258, 262

N

Nabho Kriya 236
Nada 141, 227, 252, 263, 264, 300, 305, 372
Nada Brahma Yoga 300
Nadi Shodhana 312
Nadi Shuddhi 312
Naga 21, 69, 169, 170, 254, 283, 284
Nagaraj 20, 21, 22, 49, 283
Nagarjuna 22, 88, 207, 211, 272, 294
Nagna Satya 7, 375
Nakul 282
Nanak 62, 70, 143, 144, 343
Nara 34, 35
Narada 31, 96, 349, 351, 357
Narada Bhakti Sutras 96
Narsimha 112, 209, 338
Nasik 67
Navaratri 160
Nav-Nath 59, 65, 161, 173, 184
Neelakanteswar 37
Nilalohita Shiva 5, 122, 181
Niranjana Nirvana 110, 117
Nirbija Samadhi 85, 116
Nirvana 110, 113, 117-21, 123, 160, 166, 167, 180, 191, 202, 209, 257, 264, 298, 327, 330, 331, 335, 336
Nirvana Moksha 113, 117-9, 331
Nirvikalpa Samadhi 44-6, 50, 74, 83, 85, 98, 119, 121, 173, 235, 237, 274, 303
Nitya Nath 294

O

Ojas 290, 297-309, 312
Omkar 6, 62, 141, 144, 223, 227, 235-38, 253, 268, 298, 300, 311-14, 369, 372

Omkar Kriya 144, 223, 235-238, 268, 300, 312
Om purnamada purnamidam 2, 41

P

Padma Matri 5, 271
Padmasana 250, 257, 263, 268
Panchanan 327, 328
Panchashika 87
Panch Kashi 96
Panch Kedar 33, 96
Panch Klesha 310
Pandava 17, 19, 34, 106, 282
Panduranga 165, 203
Paramadham 380
Paramahansanath Yogi 110
Paramartha 100, 123
Paramatma 90, 255
Parameshwar 188
Paramguru 11
Paramhamsa 111
Paramhansa Yogananda 11, 14, 20, 75, 104, 140, 150-52, 223, 233, 234
Param-Mukta 117
Param Shiva 80, 375, 376
Para-Prakriti 221
Parashara 120, 129, 199, 211, 273, 293, 294, 314-316, 328, 340, 341, 351, 357, 372
Parashurama 65-7, 88, 106, 196, 197, 209, 215
Paras Mani 289, 323
Para Vaak 304, 373
Paravastha 235-39
Parkaya Pravesha 68, 140
Parmars 135
Parvati 34, 59, 60, 63, 71, 72, 96, 143, 155-59, 164, 193
Pashupat 1, 64
Pashyanti Vaak 304

Patala 69
Patanjali 6, 96, 115, 139, 220, 223, 226, 230, 231, 272, 290, 305, 307, 311, 315
Patanjali Process of hot fusion 290
Patra Devta 66-68
Pavaka 263, 328-9
Pavamana 263, 328-9
Philosopher's Gem 133, 289, 323
Pingala 43, 75, 135, 137, 162, 163, 227, 252, 253, 255, 312
Pitris 342
Pitta 297, 298, 303, 309, 312
Pradakshina 35
Prajapati Daksha 158
Prajapatis 329
Pralaya 330, 341
Prana 7, 43, 44, 62, 84, 97, 101, 187, 196, 220-8, 237, 240, 251-7, 262-6, 296, 299, 300-5, 309, 312, 320-2, 331, 377
Pranabananda 180
Pranapat 49
Pranava 253, 312, 354
Pranayama 7, 133, 220-4, 228, 231, 235, 237, 238, 241, 255, 268, 299, 300, 305, 310-3, 320, 366
Prasad 64, 130, 282
Pratiprasava 7, 371
Pratishthaan 71
Pratyahara 223, 228, 229, 249, 308, 309
Pratyeka Rudras 202
Prayag 31, 95, 96, 149
Prem 309
Princess Sharada 170
Pulaha 188
Pulastya 188, 357
Pune 35, 124, 169, 172, 323
Punjab 70, 71, 143, 167
Puraka 220, 222
Purana 25, 27, 63, 114, 123, 147, 168, 177-82, 191, 192, 197, 211, 213, 243, 279, 315, 329, 332, 334, 339, 341, 351, 384

Puran Bhagat 167
Purandara 333
Puranic 341, 350
Puranwala 167
Puri 131, 139, 150
Purna Avatara 112, 114, 120, 156, 181, 212, 213
Pusa 252

Q

Queen Archan 167
Queen Kunti 282
Queen Lunan 167

R

Radhika Nath 26
Raga 310, 311
Raghu 193, 272
Rahasaya 142, 290, 327
Raja 21, 35, 36, 47, 120, 135, 162, 169, 172, 175, 178, 185, 186, 187, 210, 211, 225, 237, 238, 268, 279, 300, 301, 306, 307, 318
Rajas 63, 114, 261
Raja Shitole Deshmuk 169
Raja Yoga 47, 172, 187, 210, 211, 225, 237, 238, 268, 300, 301, 307, 318
Rajput 135, 167, 169, 171, 210
Raksha 308
Rama 18, 62, 65, 112, 130, 137, 141-43, 155, 188, 207, 212, 272, 380
Ramananda 62, 140
Ramdas 208
Ramlinga Swami 20
Ranikhet 138, 145, 233, 234

Rasalu 167, 168
Ratan Nath 171
Ratna Maru 197
Ravana 143, 349
Ravi 261
Rechaka 220, 222, 265
Regina Mundi 106
Reincarnation 113, 136, 137, 143, 191, 302, 306, 320, 371
Renuka 106
Ribu 87
Rings-Pass-Not 42, 47, 89, 105, 332, 372, 374
Rishi Manjushri 215
Rishub Nath 157
Romaka-Pura 349
Root Manu 202, 330, 336, 337
Root Race 112, 115, 131-2, 177, 198, 200-3, 210, 272, 273, 318, 327, 328, 333, 336-38, 341, 342, 349, 352
Rudra 95, 115, 129, 180, 191, 202, 214, 281, 283, 327, 331, 337
Rudra Granthi 237
Rudraksha 35
Rudra Kumar 115, 180
Rudra Nath 33, 156, 191, 192
Rudraprayag 31, 95-7, 175
Rukmini 64

S

Sada-Shiva 64
Sadhak 71, 304
Sadhana 50, 98, 145, 247, 259, 268, 312
Sadhu 71, 96, 197
Sages of the Fire Mist 17, 60, 79, 87, 88, 112, 122, 129, 156, 157, 179, 180, 182, 190-3, 198, 201, 214, 240, 327, 328, 330, 331, 343

Index

Sahadeva 282
Sahaja Samadhi 6, 189, 226
Sahajoli 291
Sai Nath of Shirdi 121
Saint George 5
Saivism 141
Samadhi 6, 21, 31, 35, 43-7, 50, 60, 64, 66, 74, 83, 85, 89, 98, 105, 116, 119-25, 130, 133, 147, 150-2, 156, 159, 161, 172-5, 186, 189, 213, 220, 223, 226, 229-34, 237, 249, 251, 265, 274, 278, 281-4, 299-303, 366, 374
Samana 252, 254, 299, 309
Sambalpur 37, 201, 379
Sambandhar 20
Samkhini 253
Samkhya 101, 120, 123, 182
Samkhya Karika 101, 123, 182
Samprajnata 6
Samsara 109, 118, 186, 279
Samskara 43, 49, 124, 238, 295, 296
Sanak 87
Sanatana Dharma 54, 64, 139, 331, 383
Sanatana Rsi Naryana 113, 191
Sanat Kumar 87, 181, 201, 243, 271, 328, 330, 343, 350
Sanat-Sujata 87
Sanchit Karma 3
Sangh 186, 189, 190, 214, 323, 379
Sanjeevani Vidya 161
Sanjeevan Samadhi 35, 121, 122, 172, 173, 174
Santatii 329
Sanyasa 162
Sapta Rishi 34, 188, 190, 242, 335
Sapta-sapti 212
Sarfoji 20
Saroub Samadhi 122, 161, 174
Saswad 174
Satguru 8, 9, 47, 49, 53, 144, 224, 316, 374
Sat-nam 62

Sattva 63, 114, 120, 178, 279
Sattvic Ahar 309
Saturn-Kronos 328
Satya Nath 59, 155
Satyavati 328
Satya Yuga 110, 243, 356, 358
Savikalpa Samadhi 44, 46, 74, 121, 237, 303
Seed Manu 202, 330, 336, 337
Seetali 310
Self-Realization 26, 29, 33, 117, 125, 150, 157, 173, 186, 227, 230, 232, 239, 273, 298, 316, 370
Serampore 147
Serpent of the Fathomless Deep 8
Shabda (shabad) Yoga 141, 144
Shad Ripus 310
Shaegaon 121
Shakha Prakshalan 310
Shakti 1, 4, 7, 8, 18, 39, 49, 56, 79, 98, 99, 104-6, 111, 115, 118, 133, 157-60, 165-6, 181, 199, 222-5, 229, 230, 235, 250, 261, 268, 279, 285, 290, 296, 300-2, 306, 312, 315, 328, 366
Shakti Chalan 261
Shaktipat 49
Shakti Pithas 158
Shalivahan 130, 167, 168, 208, 283
Shamballah 37, 199, 201, 343, 349, 379-81
Shambhave Mudra 85, 99
Shambhu Chaitanya 27, 76, 131, 281
Shamz Tabrizi 208
Shani 293
Shanmukhi Mudra 227, 229, 305
Sharadvata 333
Sharir 119, 311
Shastanga Namaskara 40
Shataka 219, 223, 226, 227, 247, 248, 267, 272
Shatavari 308
Shel Nath 59, 155
Shipra River 75, 137
Shirdi 121

Shiva 1-5, 8, 12, 13, 18, 19, 25, 27,
   31-5, 39, 41, 48, 49, 59-65,
   70-2, 76-9, 87, 95, 96, 98, 104,
   110, 112, 115, 116, 122, 129,
   130-7, 141-5, 152, 155-66,
   169-212, 219, 222, 225, 229,
   230, 235, 249, 251, 256, 261,
   271, 273, 278-85, 293, 305,
   308
Shiva Baba 12, 59, 76
Shiva Bala Yogi 208
Shiva Bhakti Sutras 96
Shivaji 132, 208, 272
Shiva Kumars 112, 191, 192
Shivalinga 105, 165, 291, 294, 295,
   296, 323
Shivanetra 221
Shivangini 323
Shivapat 49, 239
Shiva Purana 63
Shivaratri 323
Shiva-Shakti 98, 105, 300-2, 306,
   312
Shiva Shakti Kriya 222, 229, 300,
   301, 302, 312
Shravan Bhadrapad 169
Shree Nath Tirthawali 64
Shrinagar Shatak 138
Shukra 292, 293
Shvetdeep 192, 381
Shweta Varaha Kalpa 87, 115, 179,
   183, 203, 209, 277
Shyama 145, 157, 158
Shyama Charan Lahiri 145
Sialkot 167
Siddhasana 227, 228, 249, 268, 313
Siddhi 68, 71, 135, 253, 304, 316-8
Sikandar Lodi 141
Sikhism 70, 343
Simhasta-kumbha 65
Sind 71, 171
Singaldweep 68
Sinhagad 35
Sisodia Gulablal Singh 213
Sita Mai 323

Sitkari 310
Skanda 63, 177, 258, 334
Skanda Purana 63, 177
Solar Archangels 344
Soma 169, 259, 260, 300, 308
Sonar Suli 35
Soul-Star 46
Sphurti Vada 137, 173
Sri Chandra 61, 144, 145, 208
Sringeri 139
Srishailya 71
Star-Gate 44-7, 120, 228, 229, 235,
   236
Sthavan 304
Sthiti 369, 376
Suchi 328, 329
Sukhavati Heaven 214
Sumitra 106
Sundar Nath 35, 36, 175, 186
Surya 64, 88, 129, 169, 193, 240-3,
   265, 282, 292, 293, 300, 318,
   319, 322, 327, 331, 332, 339
Surya Nadi 265
Surya Putra 282
Surya Yoga 240-3, 319, 322
Sushumna Nadi 43, 220, 222-5, 227,
   234-7, 252, 253, 257, 309, 312
Svaroop Samadhi 35, 161
Swadhyaya 230, 232
Swaha 263, 328, 329
Swami Rama 18
Swayambhu 110, 179, 185, 210, 224,
   248, 305, 332, 333, 337-9

T

Takshaka Naga 170
Tama 63, 114, 120, 178, 279
Tamil Nadu 20, 22
Tanmatras 166, 278
Tantra 59, 71-3, 88, 133, 159, 164,
   165, 316, 366

Tao Te Ching 161
Tapa 32, 68, 71, 124, 135, 136, 156, 162, 166, 175, 196, 207, 211, 230, 231, 284, 311, 342
Tara 105, 109, 371
Taraka Raja Yoga 268
Taranhara 256
Tathastu 42
Tejas 297-306, 309, 312
Thanjavur 20
Thokar Kriya 235-7, 268
Tilla 71
Tilotama 65, 73
Time-Reversed Phenomenon 3, 105, 350
Tirthankar 157, 189
Tirumular 20
Trailanga Swami 186
Trambak Baba 12, 76
Transcendental Matrix 5, 120, 271
Trataka 304
Treta Yuga 67, 110, 243, 352, 358
Trimurti 62, 63, 281, 293
Trishul 178, 328
Tryambakeshwar 67
Tunganath 33, 156
Tushita Heaven 199, 213-5

U

Udai Nath 59, 155, 157
Udana 254, 299
Uddiyan Bandh 258, 262
Uderolal 171
Udraka Ramputra 160
Ujjain 135, 137, 162
Uma Nath 87, 157
United Consciousness Conference 239
Unmani Avasta 302, 303, 311
Utpatti 369, 376
Uttar Pradesh 71

V

Vaak 20, 122, 181, 253, 304, 372, 373
Vaidhatra 5, 122
Vaikhari Vaak 304, 372
Vairagya Shatak 138
Vaishvanara 339
Vaivasvat Manu 202, 203, 212, 271, 318, 327, 328, 332, 338, 340, 341, 349, 351, 354, 357, 384
Vajra Nadi 237, 302
Vajroli 291, 307, 308
Vali 333
Varahamir 340, 349, 357
Varanasi 161, 186
Varkaris 122, 173, 174
Varuna 129, 199, 213, 214, 331, 336, 346
Varuna Astra 213
Vashishta 31, 34, 188, 199, 357
Vastushpati 240, 241
Vasudeva 69, 204, 235
Vasuki Naga 170
Vasumana 333
Vata 297, 298, 301, 309
Vayu 255, 261, 282, 332, 346
Veda 63, 118, 139, 149, 206, 297, 315, 321, 327, 329, 384
Vibhuti 53
Vidhata 5
Vidyut 5
Vikramaditya 61, 115, 130, 132, 135-8, 162, 198, 200, 206-15, 272, 283
Viraj-Vaak 122, 181, 372
Vishaya Vasna 231
Vishnu Granthi 237
Vishnu Purana 211, 329, 339
Vishuddha Chakra 250
Vishwakarma 340
Vishwamitra 34, 188, 349, 357

Vishwanath 129, 156
Visvodhara 299
Viswakarma 181
Vital Fluid 224, 290, 292, 296, 297, 300, 302, 307-9, 312
Vithoba 41, 165, 206
Vivasvat Agni 327, 332, 339
Vivasvat Manu 212, 240-1, 271, 314, 318, 338-9, 349, 352, 354, 357
Vritti 238, 371
Vyana 254, 299
Vyasa 315

W

White Boar 87, 115, 179, 183, 203, 209, 277
White Island 192, 201, 243, 343, 349, 379-81
Wings to Freedom 35, 75, 97, 157, 229, 238
World Disciple 65, 189, 240, 279

Y

Yama 129, 180, 214, 231, 282, 310, 331, 336
Yin Yang Yoga 133, 161
Yogacharya 157, 306
Yoga Shataka 272
Yoga Sutras 139, 226, 230, 272, 307
Yoga Tirumantiram 35
Yogini-Kaula 59, 165
Yogiraj Siddhanath 4, 30, 34, 41, 46, 49, 56, 62, 92, 132, 189, 200, 225, 226, 229-33, 239, 240, 243, 248, 281, 322, 324, 345
Yoni 229, 251, 252, 261, 262
Yoni Mudra 166, 227-9, 235, 238, 261, 268, 305

www.ingramcontent.com/pod-product-compliance
Lightning Source LLC
Chambersburg PA
CBHW061247230426
43663CB00021B/2929